OXFORD MEDIEVAL TEXTS

General Editors

V. H. GALBRAITH   R. A. B. MYNORS

C. N. L. BROOKE

THE LETTERS AND
POEMS OF
FULBERT OF CHARTRES

THE LETTERS AND
POEMS OF
FULBERT OF CHARTRES

EDITED AND TRANSLATED

BY

FREDERICK BEHRENDS

OXFORD
AT THE CLARENDON PRESS
1976

Oxford University Press, Ely House, London W. 1

GLASGOW   NEW YORK   TORONTO   MELBOURNE   WELLINGTON
CAPE TOWN   IBADAN   NAIROBI   DAR ES SALAAM   LUSAKA   ADDIS ABABA
DELHI   BOMBAY   CALCUTTA   MADRAS   KARACHI   DACCA
KUALA LUMPUR   SINGAPORE   HONG KONG   TOKYO

ISBN 0 19 822233 5

© *Oxford University Press 1976*

*Printed in Great Britain
at the University Press, Oxford
by Vivian Ridler
Printer to the University*

PREFACE

I FIRST began working on Fulbert at the suggestion of the late Professor L. C. MacKinney, who, with the characteristic generosity which he showed towards his students, handed over to me his translations and notes on Fulbert's letters and the books and other material he had collected. So little of the former remains as he left it, and the difference in our viewpoints will be so obvious to those who are familiar with his publications on Fulbert, that I also wish to say that he was no less generous in encouraging me to strike out on my own and in helping me to pursue my research.

My debt to the General Editors is of a different kind. Professor Brooke has supervised my work at every stage with wondrous patience and constant encouragement. There is hardly a page which has not benefited from the expert knowledge that he placed at my disposal, and to him and to Sir Roger Mynors I am especially indebted for such little as I know of the art of translation.

When my work was already well advanced, Dr. Margaret Gibson and Sir Richard Southern came forth with a theory concerning the underlying letter collection, which, after some hesitation, I accepted and which they have most graciously allowed me to make my own. I also wish to thank them and Dr. Harriet P. Lattin for several suggestions in the Introduction.

I received assistance in dating the manuscripts from the late Professor B. L. Ullman. For help with particular points I am indebted to Monsignor P. Collura, Professors W. Allen, F. L. Ganshof, R. B. C. Huygens, Berthe Marti, and S. Wenzel, and to Monsieur J. Monteil of the Library of the École de Médecine in Montpellier. I should like to express my appreciation to those in the Wilson Library of the University of North Carolina who have given me their aid. Most of all I wish to thank the staff of the Humanities Reference Division and especially Miss Louise Hall and Mrs. Kenneth McIntyre.

For allowing me to use manuscripts in their keeping and for providing me with photo-reproductions I am indebted to the following: his Grace the Archbishop of Canterbury for material in Lambeth Palace Library; the Deans and Chapters of Durham,

Hereford, and Lincoln; the Trustees of the British Museum; the Prefect of the Vatican Library; the director of the Archivio Storico della Curia Arcivescovile di Palermo; the authorities of the Bodleian Library in Oxford, the libraries of the University of Leiden and the École de Médecine in Montpellier, the Bibliothèque Nationale in Paris, the municipal libraries of Alençon, Rouen, Saint-Omer, and Valenciennes, the Deutsche Staatsbibliothek in Berlin, and the Bibliotheca Széchényiana of the Hungarian National Museum in Budapest.

My grateful thanks to the many libraries in the United States which have lent me material on inter-library loan, especially that of Duke University. A grant from the Research Council of the University of North Carolina in Chapel Hill helped to defray the expenses of a visit to Europe to inspect the principal manuscripts.

F. B.

January 1974

I wish to add my thanks to Dr. Diana E. Greenway for her generous help and encouragement in seeing the book through the press.

June 1975

CONTENTS

MANUSCRIPTS CITED BY INITIALS

B   Paris, Bibliothèque Nationale, latin 2872
C   Lincoln Cathedral, MS. 134
D   Durham Cathedral, MS. B. II. 11
F   London, British Museum, Royal 11. A. x
H   Budapest, Hungarian National Museum, Bibliotheca Széchényiana,
      latin 5
K   Hereford Cathedral, MS. P. ii. 15
L   Leiden, Vossianus latin Q. 12
M   Montpellier, École de Médecine, MS. 137
P   Paris, Bibliothèque Nationale, latin 14167
R   Vatican, Reginensis latin 278
V   Vatican, latin 1783

ABBREVIATED REFERENCES OF
PRINTED BOOKS AND ARTICLES

AASS
Acta Sanctorum, ed. J. Bollandus and others (Antwerp, etc., 1643–)

Adémar
Adémar de Chabannes, *Chronique*, ed. J. Chavanon (Paris, 1897)

BEC
Bibliothèque de l'École des chartes

Behrends
Behrends, F., 'Kingship and Feudalism according to Fulbert of Chartres', *Mediaeval Studies*, xxv (1963), 93–9

Benedictus Levita
Benedicti capitularia, ed. F. Knust, *MGH*, *Leges* in folio, ii, ii (1837), 17–158

Boussard
Boussard, J., 'Les évêques en neustrie avant la réforme grégorienne', *Journal des savants*, 1970, pp. 161–96

BPH
Bulletin philologique et historique du Comité des travaux historiques et scientifiques

Bresslau
Bresslau, H., *Jahrbücher des Deutschen Reichs unter Konrad II*, 2 vols. (Leipzig, 1879–84)

Cart. N.-D. Chartres
Cartulaire de Notre-Dame de Chartres, ed. E. de Lépinois and L. Merlet, 3 vols. (Chartres, 1862–5)

Cart. S.-Père
Cartulaire de l'abbaye de Saint-Père de Chartres, ed. B. Guérard, 2 vols. (Paris, 1840)

Cat. dépt.
Catalogue général des manuscrits des bibliothèques publiques de France. Départements (Paris, 1886–)

CCL
Corpus christianorum, series latina

Clerval
Clerval, A., *Les écoles de Chartres au moyen-âge* (Paris, 1895)

Coolidge
Coolidge, R., 'Adalbero, Bishop of Laon', *Studies in Medieval and Renaissance History*, ii (1965), 3–114

CSEL
Corpus scriptorum ecclesiasticorum latinorum

Depoin
Depoin, J., 'Essai sur la chronologie des évêques de Paris de 768 à 1138', *BPH*, 1906, pp. 216–40

DHGE
Dictionnaire d'histoire et de géographie ecclésiastiques, ed. A. Baudrillart and others (Paris, 1912–)

Du Cange
Du Cange, C., *Glossarium mediae et infimae latinitatis*, 10 vols. (rev. edn., Niort, 1883–7)

Duru	*Bibliothèque historique de l'Yonne*, ed. L. Duru, 2 vols. (Auxerre, 1850–63)
Fauroux	*Recueil des actes des ducs de Normandie de 911 à 1066*, ed. M. Fauroux (Mém. de la Soc. des Antiquaires de Normandie, xxxvi, Caen, 1961)
GC	*Gallia Christiana* (Paris, 1715–1865)
Gratian	*Decretum Magistri Gratiani*, ed. E. Friedberg in *Corpus iuris canonici*, i (Leipzig, 1879)
Guillot	Guillot, O., *Le comte d'Anjou et son entourage au XIe siècle*, 2 vols. (Paris, 1972)
Halphen	Halphen, L., *Le comté d'Anjou au XIe siècle* (Paris, 1906)
Helgaud	Helgaud de Fleury, *Vie de Robert le Pieux*, ed. R.-H. Bautier and G. Labory (Sources d'histoire médiévale, i, Paris, 1965)
Hinschius	*Decretales Pseudo-Isidorianae*, ed. P. Hinschius (Leipzig, 1863)
Hoffmann	Hoffmann, H., *Gottesfriede und Treuga Dei* (*MGH, Schriften*, xx, Stuttgart, 1964)
Lemarignier	Lemarignier, J.-F., *Le gouvernement royal aux premiers temps capétiens (987–1108)* (Paris, 1965)
Lex	Lex, L., 'Eudes, comte de Blois, de Tours, de Chartres, de Troyes et de Meaux (995–1037), et Thibaud, son frère (995–1004)', *Mém. de la Soc. académique de l'Aube*, lv (1891), 191–383
MA	*Le moyen âge*
MacKinney	MacKinney, L., *Bishop Fulbert and Education at the School of Chartres* (Notre Dame, Ind., 1957)
Manitius	Manitius, M., *Geschichte der lateinischen Literatur des Mittelalters*, 3 vols. (Munich, 1911–31)
Mansi	*Sacrorum conciliorum nova et amplissima collectio*, ed. J. Mansi and others (Florence, etc., 1759–98)
Merlet	Merlet, R., and Clerval, A., *Un manuscrit chartrain du XIe siècle* (Chartres, 1893)
MGH	*Monumenta Germaniae Historica*
AA	*Auctores Antiquissimi*
Ep.	*Epistolae*
SS	*Scriptores*
Munier	Munier, C., *Les Statuta Ecclesiae Antiqua* (Strasbourg, 1960)
Newman	Newman, W. M., *Catalogue des actes de Robert II, roi de France* (Paris, 1937)

Pabst	Pabst, H., 'Frankreich und Konrad der Zweite in den Jahren 1024 und 1025', *Forschungen zur deutschen Geschichte*, v (1865), 339–68
Pfister, *Fulbert*	Pfister, C., *De Fulberti Carnotensis episcopi vita et operibus* (Nancy, 1885)
Pfister, *Robert*	Pfister, C., *Études sur le règne de Robert le Pieux (996–1031)* (Paris, 1885)
PL	*Patrologiae cursus completus, series latina*, ed. J. P. Migne, 221 vols. (Paris, 1844–64)
Raoul Glaber	Raoul Glaber, *Les cinq livres de ses histoires (900–1044)*, ed. M. Prou (Paris, 1886)
RB	*Revue bénédictine*
RBPH	*Revue belge de philologie et d'histoire*
Rédet	*Documents pour l'histoire de l'église de St-Hilaire de Poitiers*, ed. L. Rédet, 2 vols. (Mém. de la Soc. des Antiquaires de l'Ouest, xiv–xv, 1847–52)
RHDFE	*Revue historique de droit français et étranger*
RHF	*Recueil des historiens des Gaules et de la France*, ed. M. Bouquet and others, 24 vols. (new edn., Paris, 1869–1904)
Richard	Richard, A., *Histoire des comtes de Poitou 778–1204*, 2 vols. (Paris, 1903)
RMAL	*Revue du moyen âge latin*
SB Wien	*Sitzungsberichte der Kaiserlichen [Österreichischen] Akademie der Wissenschaften, Philosophisch-historische Klasse*
Vita Burcardi	Eudes de Saint-Maur, *Vie de Bouchard le vénérable*, ed. C. Bourel de la Roncière (Paris, 1892)
Vita Gauzlini	André de Fleury, *Vie de Gauzlin, abbé de Fleury*, ed. R.-H. Bautier and G. Labory (Sources d'histoire médiévale, ii, Paris, 1969)
William of Malmesbury	William of Malmesbury, *De gestis regum Anglorum*, ed. W. Stubbs, 2 vols. (Rolls Series, London, 1887–9)
Zimmermann	*Papstregesten 911–1024*, ed. H. Zimmermann (Regesta Imperii, ed. J. F. Böhmer and others, ii, v, 1969)

INTRODUCTION

1. *Fulbert of Chartres and the Cathedral School*

By 987, when Hugh Capet came to the throne of France, the Carolingian Empire was little more than a memory, and in its western half the decline of royal authority and the attacks of the Northmen had combined to bring about certain fundamental changes in the political and social structure.[1] Given the conditions of the times, a strong central government was hardly possible, and actual power tended to aggregate on the local level. In earlier days the king had been represented here by counts and bishops whom he himself had chosen, but the ties which bound them to him had grown progressively weaker during the ninth and tenth centuries. The counts had become virtually independent and regarded their offices and rights as hereditary fiefs or outright possessions. Within their territories they had increased their authority at his expense. Their control of the local courts now served to remove the remaining freemen from direct dependence on the king and to subject them instead to an intermediate lord, and it was only with the greatest difficulty that the kings retained any of their rights over the church and appointment to church offices. The royal estates and revenues that had constituted the material resources of the monarchy were almost totally depleted by grant and usurpation, and little remained for the Capetians beyond their own dynastic rights and possessions.

The leaders of the great principalities which emerged during the later ninth and tenth centuries were technically the king's

---

[1] In the following I am especially indebted to Lemarignier. Cf. the reviews by F. L. Ganshof, *RHDFE*, Fourth Series, xlvi (1968), 263 ff., and C. Brühl, *Göttingische Gelehrte Anzeigen*, ccxxi (1969), 252 ff. M. Lemarignier's earlier (1957) sketch of his basic ideas is now translated in *Lordship and Community in Medieval Europe*, ed. F. L. Cheyette (New York, 1968), pp. 100 ff. For the history of the church during this period see his discussion in *Histoire des institutions françaises au moyen âge*, ed. F. Lot and R. Fawtier, iii (Paris, 1962), 3 ff., and E. Amann and A. Dumas, *L'église au pouvoir des laïques* (Histoire de l'église, ed. A. Fliche and V. Martin, vii (Paris, 1948)); and for the peace movement in its relation to church and state see Hoffmann. For Fulbert himself, in addition to the works cited below, see Manitius, ii. 682 ff.

fideles, but in practice this counted for little. The king was well-nigh excluded from their territories. Their conduct towards him was rather that of one equal towards another and was dictated by their own interests. Nor did they regard themselves as bound to the vassal services that were to be owed by their twelfth- and thirteenth-century descendants. The early Capetians had even less claim on their loyalty than the later Carolingians had had, weak though they may have been. The south of France went its own way. Even in the north the king's authority continued to decline, and all evidence indicates that the sphere of his activity and the occasions on which the great lords attended the royal court were steadily diminishing.

The fragmentation of public authority did not stop here, for the late tenth and early eleventh centuries saw the counts in turn threatened from below as, with the growth of multiple vassalage, vicomtes, castellans, and others of lesser standing began to build up their own power and to assert their independence. They acquired vassals of their own, and from the fortresses that they built they gradually extended their influence over the surrounding countryside and demanded new services and dues from those who lived around them. This in turn brought about a shift in the political geography as the territorial unity of the old Carolingian *pagus* gave way and public authority began to centre in new focal points.

The first Capetians, Hugh Capet (987–96) and his son and successor Robert II, the Pious (996–1031), were generally accepted as the lawful kings of France, and by virtue of their royal consecration they were regarded as God's anointed and as the fountain-head of peace and justice. But from the standpoint of actual power and the problems which they faced, they differed little from the other great princes. Their own domains stretched from the borders of Normandy down to the Loire, roughly describing an ellipse with the towns of Paris and Orleans as the two focuses. They also had control over certain outlying districts, of somewhat less than twenty 'royal' bishoprics, and of several near-by counties which were held as fiefs of the king, though he could not always enforce obedience. The kings too were troubled by the rise of lesser feudal lords, and much of their energy until well into the twelfth century was spent in trying to bring and to keep them under control. Royal government during this period was a simple affair, largely run by the king and a few officials in his household who were recruited from the lesser lords within the domain. On the local level, royal administration was in the hands of officials who are best regarded as manorial agents.

The economic life of the times was essentially agricultural, and its organization was in large part manorial; while the social structure consisted at the one end of a nobility whose position rested on a varying combination of wealth, birth, and privilege, and at the other of an unfree peasantry whose distinguishing feature was the tie that bound the serf to his master. Yet new forces were at work. The development and spread of new agricultural techniques were causing a virtual revolution in food-production, the population was again rising, and the towns were taking on new life and expanding beyond their narrow walls. As the attacks of the Northmen subsided, life in France became more settled, and the late tenth and early eleventh centuries saw the beginnings of the peace movement under the leadership of the local prelates and greater nobles. This improvement in the means and conditions of existence is reflected in another realm in the quickening of educational institutions and intellectual activity, which had also declined during the later ninth and tenth centuries. Here too a change was apparent, and it was now that the cathedral schools such as those at Rheims and Chartres first came into their own.

Nothing is known concerning the origin of the school at Chartres. Religious instruction had probably been given there since the early days of its Christian community, and some provision at least must have been made for the education of the clergy in late Roman and Frankish times. Yet the evidence for these early centuries is very meagre; and it is not until the tenth century that there is a definite reference to a schoolmaster, though even then he seems characteristically to have combined his duties in this capacity with those of chancellor.[2] Although there was at least one teacher of note there in the later tenth century, the cathedral school first became prominent about the turn of the millennium under the guidance of its master and later bishop, Fulbert. The school at Chartres was only one among many in the cathedral towns of northern Europe; but in Fulbert's day it reached a height which it was not to surpass, or even to equal, for nearly a century,

[2] Clerval, pp. 22 f. Cf. pp. xvii, xxxiv f.

if then.[3] Although Fulbert himself made no original contribution to knowledge, the breadth of his learning and his contact with the most recent developments in the learned world, his ability to present subjects in a meaningful way, and his own personal warmth and sympathy attracted students from far and near. In the following decades it was often said of a learned man that he had studied with Fulbert. Echoes of this continued until well into the twelfth century; and it was only then, as a result of new educational developments and changes in literary taste, that his letters and other writings gradually ceased to be copied.

Fulbert's Life and Pontificate

Little is known of Fulbert's life and career apart from the events described in his letters, and the lack of autobiographical details in these, though not unexpected, is disappointing. The years before he became bishop are almost totally unknown, despite two quasi-autobiographical poems (nos. 132 f.) in which he speaks of his youth. There is no sound evidence on which to establish the date and place of his birth. In no. 133 Fulbert says that he was still a young man (*iuuenis*) at the time he was consecrated. Yet he can hardly have been younger than his mid thirties, especially if he had studied with Gerbert, for this would probably have been in the later 980s. This would place his birth about 970 and make him close to sixty at the time of his death. Several attempts have been made to determine Fulbert's birthplace, but none has been altogether successful, though a strong case has been made for Picardy.[4]

---

[3] The connection of some of the major twelfth-century figures traditionally associated with the school of Chartres is now questioned. See R. W. Southern, *Medieval Humanism and Other Studies* (Oxford, 1970), pp. 61 ff.; but cf. P. Dronke, 'New Approaches to the School of Chartres', *Anuario de estudios medievales*, vi (1969), 117 ff.

[4] Namely by Pfister, *Fulbert*, p. 21. In his poem on Fulbert (see pp. xxxv f.), Adelman states that Fulbert and Hildegar were fellow townsmen; and Hildegar himself says that he had been under Fulbert's tutelage since childhood (no. 95). In no. 48 Hildegar addresses a certain E. as *senior*, apparently in the technical sense, and this would seem to be Ebalus of Roucy (Aisne, *arr.* Laon). Further support is perhaps offered by no. 15, for Fulbert refers to one of the addressee's clerks as his kinsman, and the only apparent candidate for addressee is in that area. This would also accord with Fulbert's having studied at Rheims. As for the other hypotheses which have been advanced, the only evidence that Fulbert was from Italy is an ambiguous statement in one of the *Fulbertus exiguus* letters (see pp. lxii f.); and his having two nephews at Chartres, one named Fulbert (*Cartulaire blésois de Marmoutier*, ed. C. Métais (Blois, 1889–91), p. 48) and

In any event, all the known details of his life point toward northern France.

In the two poems Fulbert says that he was of lowly origin and owed his episcopate neither to family nor to wealth. There is no evidence that he was a monk. In fact the opposite is indicated by his reference to monasticism towards the close of no. 1, by his attitude towards monastic exemption (nos. 7 f. and apparently 14), and by the closing exhortation in Odilo's letter to him (no. 50). When and where Fulbert received his formal education is not definitely known. He and King Robert are said to have been fellow students apparently under Gerbert, who taught for a time at Rheims.[5] But such statements connecting well-known figures in the intellectual world are so commonplace as to be suspect, though in this instance further support may perhaps be adduced from the educational developments discussed below. Even if this statement is correct, it need not mean that Fulbert did all his studies there. When he came to Chartres is likewise unknown. If he did in fact study with Gerbert, then it may have been after Charles of Lorraine captured Rheims in 989 or perhaps during the mid-990s, when Gerbert left France.[6] In any event he was firmly established at Chartres by 1004, the date of his earliest extant letter, for he refers to himself as deacon and describes an occasion on which he acted as an official witness there, and he was sufficiently well known for Abbo of Fleury to write, asking him to assist a student and to send him an account of a recent controversy. Fulbert was probably *scholasticus* or *magister scholae*, a position which at Chartres and elsewhere often included the duties and sometimes the title of chancellor.[7] It may also be presumed that he continued to hold this office during the pontificate of Bishop Ralph. When Ralph died in 1006, Fulbert was nominated to the

the other named Ralph (*Cart. S.-Père*, ii. 271), is not in itself sufficient evidence that he was from there.

[5] See the chronicles of Fontanelle (*RHF* x. 324) and Saint-Maixent (*Chroniques des églises d'Anjou*, ed. P. Marchegay and E. Mabille (Paris, 1869), p. 385). On the latter see L. Halphen, *BEC* lxix (1908), 405 ff., especially 408 n.

[6] Richer, who was also one of Gerbert's students, came to Chartres from Rheims in 991 to study medicine (see p. xxxiii). Although he does not mention Fulbert in his account of his studies at Chartres, this need not mean that Fulbert was not there.

[7] See Clerval, pp. 17, 22 f., 30 f., 47 ff.; G. Kurth, *Notger de Liège et la civilisation au Xe siècle* (Paris, 1905), i. 259 f. Hildegar later held this same position (see pp. xxxiv f.). Cf. p. xliii.

vacant see by King Robert and consecrated by Archbishop Leothericus of Sens (1000-32).[8]

As bishop of Chartres, Fulbert was one of the natural leaders in the French church and kingdom. In the ecclesiastical province of Sens he ranked next to the archbishop, thus taking precedence over his seemingly more important fellow suffragans of Orleans and Paris. At the same time, the bishopric of Chartres belonged to the royal domain. Its incumbent was virtually appointed by the king and was considered a royal vassal. The complications which might arise from such different loyalties were sometimes quite serious; and Fulbert's situation was further aggravated by Chartres's forming part of the principality of the powerful Count Odo II of Blois, Chartres, and Tours, whose efforts to secure control of first Burgundy and then Champagne—the latter successfully—brought him into open conflict with King Robert.[9]

The greater part of the letters which Fulbert wrote as bishop of Chartres are apparently lost: almost all of those which are extant come from the first years or the last decade of his pontificate. Yet the collection as a whole gives a broad picture of his various spiritual and secular activities and of the routine as well as the extraordinary problems which confronted churchmen during the feudal age. Most of all it tells of the difficulties which arose from the church's position in the feudal world, of the attempts of secular lords to control ecclesiastical offices and revenues, and of the continued, but often ineffective, efforts of the clergy to resist such secular domination and to enforce church law; of matters of

[8] Fulbert refers to his nomination by Robert in nos. 100 f. and to his consecration by Leothericus in no. 2. The profession of obedience which he made on this occasion was entered in a pontifical at Sens and has been printed by A. Staerk, *Les manuscrits latins du Ve au XIIIe siècle conservés à la Bibliothèque impériale de Saint-Pétersbourg*, i (St. Petersburg, 1910), 171 n., from MS. Q v. I, No. 35, f. 99, and earlier, though without any identification of the source, in G. Waitz's publication of some notes left by Arndt in *Neues Archiv*, iii (1878), 200. Fulbert became bishop about early October (Pfister, *Fulbert*, p. 48), the evidence for this being the date of his death, 10 April 1028 (see p. xxi), the statement in his epitaph that he ruled *Bis denos annos atque unum dimidiumque* (see Appendix A), and one of the legends in his obituary leaflet (see p. xliii): *Pavit oves domini pastor venerabilis annos / Quinque quater mensesque decem cum mensibus octo* (i.e. twenty-one years and six months). His predecessor, Bishop Ralph, died on a 15 July (Merlet, p. 36). For Leothericus' dates see Clarius of Saint-Pierre-le-Vif in Duru, ii. 498, 503, and *GC* xii. 34 ff.

[9] See Lex and the older literature cited there, which it does not altogether supersede, especially H. d'Arbois de Jubainville, *Histoire des ducs et des comtes de Champagne*, i (Paris, 1859), 189 ff.

church discipline and internal administration, of the age-old problems of simony and clerical immorality, of the new threat to episcopal authority posed by the increasing number of exempt monasteries; of the details of feudal law and government, of the rise of the castellans and lesser nobility and the constant growth of multiple vassalage and subinfeudation, and of the customary co-operation between the French clergy and monarch based on medieval notions of divine-right kingship and on their common interest in keeping the nobles from further encroachments.[10] Although a conscientious churchman, Fulbert hardly anticipates the Gregorian reformer. He was too much at home in the world of his day with all its confusion of things human and divine, ecclesiastical and secular; and we have the testimony of his clerks that he would silence their complaints by reminding them that the difficulties of this world were unavoidable and must be borne with patience (no. 65).

Yet Fulbert never seems to have become immersed in purely worldly matters or to have lost sight of his spiritual goals. In his own day he was highly respected for the holiness of his life, and he has retained his reputation for sanctity.[11] It is, moreover, as a shepherd of souls that Fulbert appears at his best. His exhortations to repentance and his concern for the souls of those who have erred are among the most moving passages in his letters, and perhaps the most touching of all is his plea for the fugitive monk who wishes to return to the paradise of his cloister (no. 11). In the history of spirituality Fulbert is usually accorded a distinguished place as regards the development of devotion to the Blessed Virgin and especially the feast of her nativity.[12] Such of his

---

[10] For Fulbert's ideas on kingship see Behrends. H. Mitteis, *Lehnrecht und Staatsgewalt* (Weimar, 1933), p. 274 n., has also called attention to Fulbert's use of ecclesiastical censure in support of the king. Cf. J. Leclercq, 'L'interdit et l'excommunication d'après les lettres de Fulbert de Chartres', *RHDFE*, Fourth Series, xxii (1944), 67 ff. As for the 'Clamor' sometimes associated with Fulbert, see R. Bauerreiss, 'Der "Clamor", eine verschollene mittelalterliche Gebetsform und das Salve Regina', *Studien und Mitteilungen zur Geschichte des Benediktiner-Ordens und seiner Zweige*, lxii (1950), 26 ff., and J. M. Canal, 'En torno a S. Fulberto de Chartres (†1028)', *Ephemerides liturgicae*, lxxx (1966), 211 ff.

[11] It was not until the mid-nineteenth century that Fulbert's cult was officially sanctioned, and then only for the dioceses of Chartres and Poitiers (see *GC* viii. 1117; *AASS*, April i, 847; Merlet, pp. 37 ff.).

[12] See P. Viard, 'Fulbert de Chartres', *Dictionnaire de spiritualité*, v (1964), 1605 ff.; Y. Delaporte, *Une prière de saint Fulbert à Notre-Dame* (Chartres,

teachings on the spiritual life as have come down in his letters and poems and a few passages elsewhere suggest that while he was familiar with the writings of the great Latin fathers and apparently fond of Prosper's *Sententiae* (which to be sure in no. 80 he ascribes to Augustine), he held the teachings of the desert fathers and Cassian's *Collations* in especial esteem.[13]

Our knowledge of Fulbert's pontificate before the 1020s is uneven, and there are virtually no connecting threads with which to weave a chronological narrative.[14] But it is possible to do so for the later years thanks to the fairly continuous series of his own letters and those of his closest disciple, Hildegar. On 7–8 September 1020 the cathedral of Chartres was completely destroyed by fire and the town itself was badly damaged. A new church was begun in the following years; but despite Fulbert's efforts, the crypts were not completed before late 1025, and the cathedral was still unfinished at the time of his death.[15] In late 1022 Fulbert

1928) and the addenda in *La vie spirituelle*, lxxxvi (1952), 467 ff.; H. Barré, *Prières anciennes de l'occident à la mère du Sauveur* (Paris, 1963), pp. 150 ff. and *passim*; J. M. Canal, 'Los sermones marianos de San Fulberto de Chartres', *Recherches de théologie ancienne et médiévale*, xxix (1962), 33 ff., 'Texto crítico de algunos sermones marianos de San Fulberto de Chartres o a él atribuibles', ibid. xxx (1963), 55 ff., 329 ff., and 'Los sermones marianos de san Fulberto de Chartres. Conclusión', ibid. xxxiii (1966), 139 ff., the last in reply to the criticisms of H. Barré, 'Pro Fulberto', ibid. xxxi (1964), 324 ff. The very fact that other writings in honour of the Blessed Virgin were later attributed to Fulbert is at least proof of his reputation in this regard, as is the miracle reported by William of Malmesbury (see p. xli). Moreover, in 1028–31 Hugh of Mondoubleau (Loir-et-Cher, *arr*. Vendôme) erected a church in honour of the Blessed Virgin *consilio uenerande memorie Fulberti, nostre Carnotene urbis episcopi* (*Cartulaire de l'abbaye de Saint-Vincent du Mans*, ed. R. Charles and M. d'Elbenne (Le Mans, 1886–1913), p. 110, no. 180).

[13] See nos. 71, 95, 131 (all three by Hildegar, but probably reflecting Fulbert's own taste, especially in view of what is said in no. 131 and of the following), 137–42, 153. Cassian's influence is also visible in the notes and charts in V. As for the short penitential ascribed to Fulbert, see F. W. H. Wasserschleben, *Die Bussordnungen der abendländischen Kirche* (Halle, 1851), pp. 90, 623 f., and H. J. Schmitz, *Die Bussbücher und die Bussdisciplin der Kirche*, i (Mainz, 1883), 766 f., 773 f.

[14] In lieu of this and for further details of the following see chapter III and Appendix C, though the latter is not as helpful as might be expected.

[15] See nos. 40 f., 51, 59, 107 f. The cathedral which burned in 1020 had been built after the fire of 962. Work on Fulbert's church continued under his successor, Bishop Thierry; but part of it was again destroyed by fire in September 1030, and it was not consecrated until October 1037. This structure lasted until the fire of 1194, after which the present cathedral was built. The architect of Fulbert's cathedral is unknown; however, it may have been a certain Berengar, who is described in the necrology as *hujus matris aecclesiae artifex*

made a pilgrimage to Rome, his only known journey of any great length. After he returned, he was appointed treasurer of Saint-Hilaire-le-Grand at Poitiers by Duke William V of Aquitaine (993–1030).[16] He delegated his duties there to Hildegar, who before this had been master of the school at Chartres; and though Fulbert often planned to go to Poitiers, he was never able to do so. The area of Chartres was disturbed by frequent warfare in the 1020s. In the struggle between King Robert and Count Odo, Fulbert's position seems to have been somewhat ambiguous: although he tried to protect the king's rights in the surrounding area, he apparently favoured Odo's claims. During these years Fulbert suffered from recurrent ill health. But as late as 1026 he was still sufficiently vigorous to take an active part in the controversy over the election of a successor to the throne. Yet his burdens were apparently too much for him; and when Hildegar returned for a visit in the summer of 1026, it was decided that he should stay at Chartres. Although Fulbert asked Duke William to appoint another treasurer, this was not done until after Fulbert's death. His last known official act was to witness a royal charter granted at Paris in early 1028 (Appendix C, no. 12). He died on Wednesday of Holy Week (10 April) and was buried the next day in the monastery church of Saint-Père, which was then outside the town walls.[17]

---

bonus (Merlet, pp. 127, 180). See M.-J. Bulteau, 'Saint Fulbert et sa cathédrale', *Mém. de la Soc. arch. d'Eure-et-Loir*, vii (1882), 288 ff.; Merlet, pp. 45 f., 55 ff.; H. H. Hilberry, 'The Cathedral at Chartres in 1030', *Speculum*, xxxiv (1959), 561 ff.

[16] See de Longuemar, *Essai historique sur l'église collégiale de Saint-Hilaire-le-Grand de Poitiers* (Mém. de la Soc. des Antiquaires de l'Ouest, xxiii (1856)) and R. Favreau, 'Les écoles et la culture à Saint-Hilaire-le-Grand de Poitiers des origines au début du XIIe siècle', *Cahiers de civilisation médiévale*, iii (1960), 473 ff.; and for Duke William see Richard, i. 139 ff.

[17] Although Fulbert's death is still frequently placed in 1029, the year 1028 was established by Pfister, *Fulbert*, p. 47, on the evidence of Fulbert's obituary (see Appendix A) and a detailed entry in the chronicle of Dol (*RHF* x. 323 f.). The date 10 April is also supported by the last lines of Fulbert's epitaph (Appendix A). See Merlet, p. 30 n., and A. J. Macdonald, *Berengar and the Reform of Sacramental Doctrine* (London, 1930), pp. 18 f. Fulbert's tomb is probably near the principal entrance to the choir of the present parish church of Saint-Père. See A. Lecocq, 'Dissertation historique et archéologique sur la question: où est l'emplacement du tombeau de Fulbert, évêque de Chartres, au XIe siècle?' *Mém. de la Soc. arch. d'Eure-et-Loir*, v (1872), 303 ff., and Merlet, pp. 49 f.

Fulbert's Writings and Learning

Fulbert's letters have come down as part of a larger collection which contains Hildegar's correspondence (including that in which he was engaged for the chapter of Chartres and Duke William)[18] and various non-epistolary works: sermons, poems, liturgical compositions, and notes which apparently Fulbert had taken from his reading and perhaps intended to work up later or to use in teaching.[19] There is still some question as to the authenticity of the various works which have been ascribed to him. The only writings in the collection which have any internal evidence of this are his letters, the two autobiographical poems, and the *Contra Iudeos*; and it is possible that some of the *opuscula* are not his, but rather copies that he had made of the works of others. In the absence of evidence to the contrary, however, their inclusion here is in favour of their being Fulbert's (or at least stemming from his school), especially if they possess some distinctive feature in common with one of his avouched works.[20] As for the writings which have come down outside the collection, somewhat more caution seems advisable, even though they are expressly attributed to him. It is not, of course, impossible that they are Fulbert's, but there is no certain example of this; and one of the more telling arguments against the authenticity of two such letters is that they

[18] The dukes of Aquitaine during this period often used scribes from Saint-Hilaire. See W. Kienast, *Der Herzogstitel in Frankreich und Deutschland* (Munich, 1968), pp. 251 ff.

[19] See pp. xxvii f. and the so-called sermons vii and viii in *PL* cxli. 331 ff., and compare the sources used in no. 80 with the end of sermon vii. Cf. no. 155. Sermon viii is a collection of excerpts on the Eucharist from the following: Augustine, *De doctrina christiana*, iii. 9, 13; 16, 24 (ed. J. Martin, *CCL* xxxii. 85 f., 92); Augustine, *In Iohannis evangelium tractatus*, xxvi. 15, 18; xxvii. 1 (ed. R. Willems, *CCL* xxxvi. 267 f., 270); Haimo, *In epistolam i ad Corinthios* (*PL* cxvii. 564); council of Ephesus (Mansi, v. 729; Hinschius, p. 279); *Vita Silvestri* (B. Mombritius, *Sanctuarium*, ed. Quentin-Brunet (Paris, 1910), ii. 521). The predominance of Augustine in these excerpts, which presumably (they are found only in L-class manuscripts, the sources being identified in C and space apparently left for them in L) stem from Fulbert or at least from his school, stands in marked contrast to the Eucharistic teaching in the *Fulbertus exiguus* letters (see pp. lxii f.). The inscription which is said by Berengar to have been on Fulbert's chalice also seems to derive from Augustine (*Briefsammlungen der Zeit Heinrichs IV*, ed. Erdmann-Fickermann (*MGH, Die Briefe der deutschen Kaiserzeit*, v), pp. 153 f.; R. B. C. Huygens, 'Textes latins du xie au xiiie siècle', *Studi medievali*, Third Series, viii (1967), 452 f.).

[20] e.g. the use of Boethius' *De differentiis topicis* in no. 152 and the *Contra Iudeos* (see pp. xxv ff.).

purport to have been written by him to Hildegar, but are not found in the collection which Hildegar himself helped to compile.[21]

Fulbert's contemporaries considered him one of the more learned men of their day, and modern scholars have usually upheld their judgement.[22] But it is quite difficult to assess the extent and depth of his knowledge. Almost all his extant writings were composed for a particular occasion. They were not intended to be learned treatises or to set forth an orderly exposition of his thought. Thus we must rely on isolated statements and on literary references and allusions. Yet a mere listing of the authors whom Fulbert cites is not a sure guide, for he may have been using an intermediate source. Nor does the lack of a reference to a particular author mean that Fulbert was unacquainted with him; for on several occasions Hildegar, who seems somewhat more ready to display his learning, cites standard authors who are not mentioned in Fulbert's own writings, but with whom we may confidently presume that he too was familiar.

By far the largest proportion of quotations and reminiscences in Fulbert's writings are first to the Scriptures and then to the Latin fathers and collections of ecclesiastical and secular law. This is quite in keeping with the nature of his works and especially his letters, for these were primarily concerned with religious matters and problems of ecclesiastical law and administration which were best solved by appeal to such authority. In this regard no. 125 is particularly instructive, since Fulbert states that he could cite appropriate passages from Livy, Valerius Maximus, and Orosius, but instead will use a writer whose trustworthiness is avouched by his standing as a Christian bishop, Gregory of Tours. The frequency with which Fulbert was consulted on such matters indicates that his knowledge of them was highly regarded, and it

---

[21] See pp. lxi f. The treatise *Misit Herodes* (*PL* cxli. 277 ff.) is now ascribed to Richard of St. Victor (J. Chatillon, 'Misit Herodes Rex Manus: Un opuscule de Richard de Saint-Victor égaré parmi les œuvres de Fulbert de Chartres', *RMAL* vi (1950), 287 ff., viii (1952), 256 n.; but cf. H. Silvestre, 'Un nouveau manuscrit du *Misit Herodes Rex Manus*', *Scriptorium*, xiii (1959), 259). Sermon ix (*PL* cxli. 336 ff.), which is also found among the spurious writings of Augustine (sermon cxciv in *PL* xxxix. 2104 ff.), is now attributed to Ambrose Autpert (*DHGE* ii. 1115). The *Vita Autperti* should apparently be ascribed to another Fulbert (see *Gesta Pontificum Cameracensium*, i. 78 (*MGH SS* vii. 430)).

[22] See Hilda Johnstone, 'Fulbert, Bishop of Chartres', *The Church Quarterly Review*, cii (April–July, 1926), 45 ff.; MacKinney, pp. 36 ff. ('The Fulbertian Legend'!).

was precisely these letters which retained their interest the longest. Here as elsewhere Fulbert, like his contemporaries, appears to have relied on a few standard works, but to have known these very well indeed, for such works were not systematically arranged or indexed. His favourite legal sources seem to have been a collection of Carolingian capitularies containing the works of Ansegisus of Fontanelle and Benedictus Levita and another of Pseudo-Isidorian decretals.[23] His quotations of the church councils are regularly from the Latin version associated with the latter. On one occasion, moreover, Fulbert accidentally reveals that he is citing a Carolingian regulation indirectly, namely from Benedictus Levita (no. 77). Fulbert also knew the Theodosian Code, for while he cites or alludes to several passages which might have been taken from the Breviary, the latter does not contain the law which he is apparently following in no. 13. For Fulbert's time this is an impressive number of sources to have at one's disposal, and for the most part it seems to have been adequate. But no less impressive is his ability to use these sources, to adapt the laws to the needs of his own day, to apply them to particular cases while carefully distinguishing the individual circumstances, and, when unable to consult the laws or to find an appropriate statement in them, to reason by analogy (e.g. nos. 38, 123).

As for quotations and allusions to the writers of classical antiquity, when Fulbert does use them, he can weave them in quite skilfully as in the allusion to Horace in no. 49 and apparently to Virgil in no. 61 or in the borrowing of an ironical phrase from Terence to set off the close of no. 25 asking for vengeance on a

---

[23] In his preface Benedictus states that he intended to supplement the work of Ansegisus, and the two collections were often combined (see F. L. Ganshof, *Recherches sur les capitulaires* (Paris, 1958), pp. 69 ff.). Fulbert also seems to have used a combined collection, for he cites Benedictus Levita ii. 91 as vi. 91 (no. 90). I have not been able to identify any manuscripts that Fulbert actually used (but cf. no. 34). The chapter library in the early eleventh century seems to have had at least three manuscripts containing legal collections: Chartres MSS. 26, 124, 376 (formerly 67 *bis*, 127, 140). The first and third are described in Hinschius, pp. xx and *passim*; the second in F. Schulte, 'Iter Gallicum', *SB Wien*, lix (1868), 458 ff., cf. *Cat. dépt.*, xi. 12, 67, 172. Chartres MS. 193 (formerly 172) from Saint-Père was a composite manuscript containing extracts from several legal works (Schulte, op. cit., pp. 460 ff.; *Cat. dépt.*, xi. 99 f.), the last of which dated from the later eleventh century (see P. Fournier and G. Le Bras, *Histoire des collections canoniques en occident depuis les fausses décrétales jusqu'au décret de Gratien*, i (Paris, 1931), 208 f., 220). All except MS. 376 were completely destroyed in the fire of 1944.

swindler. But perhaps the best indication of Fulbert's knowledge of literary Latin is his very ability to handle the language, an ability which is all the more noteworthy as many of his letters must have been written quickly and with little chance for revision (e.g. no. 13). Moreover, the corpus of metrical and rhythmic poetry (to be sure, mostly religious and devotional works and mnemonic verses) which has come down under his name shows a similar mastery of the language along with a certain inventiveness.[24] Fulbert's verse, unlike that of so many medieval writers, is never deliberately obscure; and his rendering—if indeed it is his —of the tale from the *Vitae patrum* of the monk who rashly thought that he could live alone in the desert and like the angels not be troubled by human needs, and his personification of Faith, Hope, and Charity, are all the more charming for their simplicity.[25]

On the whole Fulbert's learning would appear to be representative of the best that could be had in the schools of his day. Though not primarily a scholar, he undoubtedly engaged in some independent reading and study, and he seems to have kept up with the latest advances in the educational world. As we shall see later, the most important of these for the curriculum of the schools was the introduction of a virtually new programme for the teaching of dialectic based on the *Logica Vetus* and Boethius' commentaries and monographs. The impetus here probably came from Gerbert,

---

[24] The non-liturgical poems are edited here. For the liturgical poems and prose see Y. Delaporte, 'Fulbert de Chartres et l'école chartraine de chant liturgique au XIe siècle', *Études grégoriennes*, ii (1957), 51 ff.; J. Szövérffy, *Die Annalen der lateinischen Hymnendichtung*, i (Berlin, 1964), 353 ff. and *passim*. Almost every study of medieval Latin poetry has some discussion of Fulbert: e.g. F. J. E. Raby, *A History of Christian-Latin Poetry from the Beginnings to the Close of the Middle Ages* (2nd edn., Oxford, 1953), pp. 258 ff., and *A History of Secular Latin Poetry in the Middle Ages* (2nd edn., Oxford, 1957), i. 308 ff.

[25] Nos. 153, 150. The first is also included in the Cambridge Songs, as is the poem on the nightingale which is sometimes attributed to Fulbert (*Die Cambridger Lieder*, ed. K. Strecker (*MGH, Scriptores rerum Germanicarum*, xl), pp. 97 ff., 29 ff.). While the former is found in several of the principal manuscripts and so would seem to be his, the latter was apparently written before Fulbert's time and is found only in P, ff. 66[v]–67, omitting stanzas 8–11, 15–16. On the same line opposite the title is written *Lacuna. Require in finem*; but this may refer to the preceding glossary, which shows signs of having been recopied, though apparently from the original schedule and not from the rearranged glossary which was copied near the end of P and which is now bound in B (see M. McVaugh and F. Behrends, 'Fulbert of Chartres' Notes on Arabic Astronomy', *Manuscripta*, xv (1971), 175 f.).

and the effects of it are apparently reflected in two of Fulbert's works and in one of the school manuals from Chartres.[26]

The first is a mnemonic poem on the differences between dialectic and rhetoric (no. 152), which seems to be Fulbert's even though it is found in only one of the principal manuscripts of his writings. Dialectic and rhetoric are said to be 'faculties' of logic, but to differ as to their method, end, and matter. The matter of dialectic is the thesis, that of rhetoric is the hypothesis; dialectic proceeds by short questions and answers and perfect syllogisms, rhetoric by flowing speeches and enthymemes or imperfect syllogisms; the end of dialectic is to compel one's opponent to concede, that of rhetoric is to persuade. These are the same basic distinctions, in part in the same terms and similarly associating dialectic with the works of Aristotle and rhetoric with those of Cicero, which Boethius makes in a brief summary in *De differentiis topicis*, iv, one of the monographs which figured prominently in the new programme and which was to have a distinguished future as a textbook in the later eleventh and twelfth centuries.[27] This monograph and Fulbert's poem were both included in the school manual mentioned above, and thus it seems probable that they were actually used in teaching.

While there may be some question as to the attribution of the preceding work, there can be hardly any as regards the *Contra Iudeos*, for it is found in all the principal manuscripts containing non-epistolary works, and Fulbert refers to himself by name.[28] Its central theme is Genesis 49: 10: 'The sceptre shall not be taken away from Juda, nor a ruler from his thigh, till he come that is to be sent, and he shall be the expectation of nations.' Fulbert interprets this along the lines, traditional at least since

---

[26] See pp. xxxi f.

[27] *PL* lxiv. 1205 f., 1216. See R. McKeon, 'Rhetoric in the Middle Ages', *Speculum*, xvii (1942), 10 f., 16.

[28] It is printed in *PL* cxli. 305 ff. as a single treatise divided into three parts. P is the only manuscript of the Fulbert collection to have all three, and they are clearly separated there. V contains the first and apparently yet a fourth tract, while L-family manuscripts have only the third, which appears to be a more finished literary product. These would seem to be different redactions of the same tract or else separate works. See B. Blumenkranz, 'A propos du (ou des) *Tractatus Contra Iudaeos* de Fulbert de Chartres', *RMAL* viii (1952), 51 ff., with references to further manuscripts, and his *Les auteurs chrétiens latins du moyen âge sur les juifs et le judaïsme* (Paris, 1963), pp. 237 ff. For the event which may have prompted Fulbert see no. 27.

Augustine, that the Jewish kingdom came to an end during the time of Christ, and that since it no longer exists, the Messiah must have come.[29] He concentrates on the literal meaning and shows from the Scriptures and from history that its prophecy has been fulfilled.

In the course of his argument Fulbert discusses what makes a kingdom and specifically a Jewish kingdom. It must, he says, have a king, people, and land, and he compares these to the roof, walls, and foundations of a house. A kingdom, like a house, cannot exist unless all three parts are there, since a whole must have all its parts. A Jewish king would have to be anointed by Jewish priests; but there is no longer a true Jewish priesthood, and hence there cannot be a Jewish king, for there can be no effect without an efficient cause. The king himself must be Jewish. A foreign king who has Jews in his jurisdiction does not satisfy this requirement, for things which are defined differently have different essences. Fulbert's three logical formulas are almost certainly borrowed from the same monograph of Boethius, for they are found close together there, and Boethius uses the same example of the house and its parts to illustrate the first.[30]

It is tempting to pursue Fulbert's use of dialectic in expounding a scriptural passage; but too much emphasis should not be placed on it, for the *Contra Iudeos* is, after all, a polemic written for the express purpose of convincing the Jews by force of reason (*rationabiliter convincere*), and there was a long tradition of such works. Be that as it may, the source from which Fulbert got his dialectical armament is well-nigh certain, and his use of it would seem to be a reflection of what was to prove the most important development in the educational world during the eleventh century.

In another area Fulbert also shows some acquaintance with the latest advances, namely with the treatises on astronomy which had recently been translated from Arabic. Among his papers appear to have been an Arabic–Latin glossary of terms relating to the astrolabe based on the *Sententie astrolabii* and notes on a passage entitled *De stellis horarum* listing the zodiacal signs by their Latin names and for each giving the Arabic name of one of its bright

[29] Cf. Augustine, *De civitate Dei*, xviii. 45 f. (*CCL* xlviii. 643 ff.). For a brief list of other authors following the same interpretation see Behrends, p. 93 n.

[30] Fulbert: *PL* cxli. 308, 315 f.; Boethius: *PL* lxiv. 1178, 1188 f., 1199.

stars or else writing *nil* or leaving a space.[31] It was from this that he apparently worked up the mnemonic poem no. 148. Such knowledge was quite unusual in Fulbert's day and may again be an inheritance from Gerbert, though the latter's connection with the astrolabe is not altogether certain. Otherwise Fulbert's knowledge of scientific matters does not seem exceptional, nor does he appear to have shared Gerbert's experimental interests. But perhaps, as has been suggested,[32] this was part of his success; for while his learning surpassed that of most of his contemporaries, it was still within the traditional framework, and Fulbert himself was never beyond their reach.

The School of Chartres in Fulbert's Time

Our knowledge of the school at Chartres in Fulbert's day, apart from what we know of Fulbert himself, is quite sketchy. To some degree this is but a reflection of the very nature of the cathedral schools of the eleventh and twelfth centuries, for their reputation usually rested on the fame of an individual master who could attract the students as they wandered from place to place. The basic educational programme was much the same everywhere: the really successful teacher had to offer something special. We look for this in vain in the accounts of what was taught at Chartres. Proud as Fulbert's students may have been of having studied with him, they tell us next to nothing about the studies themselves. In fact it appears that what attracted them was Fulbert himself rather than the subjects which were studied. The warm personal devotion which he inspired is indicative of the man behind it, and no other master in Fulbert's day seems to have been quite so successful at this. Yet highly important as the bond between master and students may have been—and in the medieval schools it was indeed important—it none the less transcends the educational programme itself.

This educational programme and the system of the liberal arts on which it was based were an inheritance from antiquity, more

---

[31] See A. van de Vyver, 'Les premières traductions latines (x^e–xie s.) de traités arabes sur l'astrolabe', *Mémoires du 1er congrès international de géographie historique* (Brussels, 1931), pp. 287 f.; McVaugh and Behrends, op. cit.

[32] Namely by R. W. Southern, on whose sketch of Fulbert in *The Making of the Middle Ages* (London, 1953), pp. 197 ff., I have drawn heavily in the following pages.

directly from the Roman schools of grammar and rhetoric.[33] It had been developed to meet the needs of teaching oratory, and its goal was the well-rounded educated man who was capable of leading others to right action, in its classic formulation *vir bonus peritus dicendi*. The entire programme was directed towards this; and so within the system of the arts, rhetoric—the art of effective persuasion—held pride of place. Studies were both theoretical and practical. The student learned definitions, distinctions, and rules, and he learned to apply them in speaking and writing. At the same time he worked through a syllabus of standard authors who were set before him as models. Although oratory lost much of its importance under the Roman Empire and even more after its fall, the programme of predominantly literary studies to which it had given rise endured. It was transmitted to the Middle Ages through the living traditions of the schools and by such handbooks as the encyclopedias of Martianus Capella and Isidore of Seville and the syllabus of secular studies in Cassiodorus, *Institutes*, ii. The fathers often voiced their fear of the old education, based as it was on works which were permeated with paganism. But they developed nothing to take its place. Instruction in the teachings of Christianity was simply superimposed, and neither the syllabus of Christian studies in Augustine's *De doctrina christiana* nor that in Cassiodorus, *Institutes*, i, was an adequate substitute for it. Thus it continued, however diluted, to form the basis of the curriculum in the medieval schools.

Of all the schools of northern France about the turn of the millennium, the only one whose programme of studies is known in any detail is that of Rheims in the time of Gerbert. The historian Richer, who had studied with Gerbert and dedicated his work to him, gives a rather lengthy account of his teaching.[34] Although Richer is obviously more interested in Gerbert's scientific pursuits, he begins by describing how he taught dialectic and rhetoric and expressly states the order in which he expounded the

---

[33] In the following I am especially indebted to H. I. Marrou, *A History of Education in Antiquity*, tr. G. Lamb (London, 1956), pp. 274 ff.

[34] Richer, *Historia*, iii. 46 ff. (*Histoire de France*, ed. R. Latouche, ii (Paris, 1937), 54 ff.). In the following I am primarily relying on A. van de Vyver, 'Les étapes du développement philosophique du haut moyen-âge', *RBPH* viii (1929), 426 ff.; Harriet P. Lattin, 'The Eleventh Century MS. Munich 14436', *Isis*, xxxviii (1948), 205 ff., and *The Letters of Gerbert* (New York, 1961), pp. 5 f. and *passim*.

various texts. Gerbert began with the dialectical treatises: Porphyry's *Isagoge* in the two translations of Victorinus and Boethius, Aristotle's *Categories* and *Peri hermeneias*, and Cicero's *Topica*, with which he seems to have used Boethius' commentary. Next he expounded Boethius' monographs *De differentiis topicis*, *De categoricis syllogismis*, *De hypotheticis syllogismis*, *De definitionibus* (actually by Victorinus), and *De divisione*. Then, knowing that his students could not advance to the oratorical arts until they had mastered the kinds of speech, which are learned from the poets, he had them read the 'poets' Virgil, Statius, and Terence, the 'satirists' Juvenal, Persius, and Horace, and the 'historian' Lucan. After this they studied the art of rhetoric, and Gerbert brought in a 'sophist' with whom they engaged in practice disputation so that their speech might seem artless as becomes those who are masters of their art.

Richer obviously considers rhetoric the culminating art of the *trivium*. He does not speak of the art of grammar: it was apparently too elementary and ordinary to be noticed. Yet the poets were properly studied here, and that this should instead be regarded as preliminary to studying rhetoric reminds us that in practice the distinction between the arts was often blurred. As for dialectic, Richer, like Fulbert, subsumes it and rhetoric under logic; and to judge from the order of Gerbert's teaching, it was also regarded as a preliminary study. Richer stresses Gerbert's practical goal, namely to teach his students to speak effectively; and in one of his letters Gerbert himself says that the man in public life must be not only virtuous but eloquent.[35] It takes but little imagination to see behind this the ancient rhetorician's *vir bonus peritus dicendi*; and this same ideal, less explicitly stated, if with stronger Christian overtones, can likewise be seen in Fulbert's dictum that a bishop ought to be as skilled in speaking as he is prudent and forceful in his actions (no. 28). That rhetoric should have continued to occupy the same place in the educational programme that it did in antiquity is not surprising, for the programme itself was still essentially one of literary studies designed to teach the student to speak and to write well. Yet the study of rhetoric was not as narrow as might be thought, for among other matters it included what we should call legal reasoning

---

[35] Ep. 44 (*Die Briefsammlung Gerberts von Reims*, ed. F. Weigle (*MGH, Die Briefe der deutschen Kaiserzeit*, ii), p. 73).

—indeed, rhetorical theory had developed from judicial oratory. Thus Fulbert's knowledge of how to apply the law to individual cases was probably acquired from the rhetorical manuals; and his exposition of the feudal oath (no. 51), though couched in technical terms, is at least partly based on the specifications for *suasoria*, a kind of rhetorical argument which he seems to have associated with the feudal obligation of *consilium*.[36]

Although Richer's account may be somewhat idealized, it does accord with what is otherwise known of Gerbert and with the evidence of the school manuals of the period. Gerbert may have derived his idea for the basic syllabus from Cassiodorus,[37] but he seems to have been the first to teach the complete *Logica Vetus* and to have used Boethius' commentaries in teaching it and also the first to use the latter's monographs. This gave rise to a fairly standard corpus of such works that was used in the schools of the eleventh and earlier twelfth centuries as dialectic became increasingly important in the curriculum and in intellectual life in general.

Among the very first manuals in which this was found was Chartres MS. 100, which would seem to date from Fulbert's time.[38] It was not, to be sure, the first handbook of dialectic and rhetoric available at Chartres: among tenth-century manuscripts belonging to the chapter, Chartres MS. 71 contained Aristotle's *Peri hermeneias*, Cicero's *Topica*, and Boethius' commentaries on both, while several of Boethius' monographs and the Pseudo-Augustinian *Categoriae decem* were to be found in Chartres MS. 74.[39] But Chartres MS. 100 contained a much more comprehensive corpus: Porphyry's *Isagoge*, Aristotle's *Categories*, the *Categoriae decem*, Fulbert's *De distantia dialecticae et rhetoricae*, Victorinus' *De definitionibus*, Cicero's *Topica*, Aristotle's *Peri hermeneias* and that of Pseudo-Apuleius, Boethius' *De differentiis topicis*, the so-called *Antepredicamenta*, *De divisione*, Gerbert's *De ratione uti* (written in 997), and Boethius' monographs on the categorical and

---

[36] See Behrends, p. 96 n. A similar association of *suasoria* and *consilium* is found in Ratherius, *Praeloquia*, i. 27 (*PL* cxxxvi. 174).

[37] Cassiodorus, *Institutes*, ii, was available in its second interpolated version at both Rheims and Chartres (*Cassiodori Senatoris institutiones*, ed. R. A. B. Mynors (Oxford, 1937), pp. xxxii–xxxiii).

[38] See *Cat. dépt.*, xi. 52 f.; Lattin, 'Munich 14436', p. 223; van de Vyver, 'Étapes', pp. 446 ff. This and the following manuscripts were destroyed in 1944.

[39] See *Cat. dépt.*, xi. 37 ff. On the *Categoriae decem* see L. Minio-Paluello, 'Note sull'Aristotele latino medievale xv', *Rivista di filosofia neo-scolastica*, liv (1962), 137 ff.

hypothetical syllogisms. Although there are some differences in content and the order is not Gerbert's nor quite so consistent as his, the basic programme is essentially the same, and the connection with Gerbert would seem to be confirmed by the presence of one of his works, which must have been written only a few years earlier. Whether the manuscript was intended to be used in teaching cannot be determined. But as we saw above, the new programme of dialectical studies is apparently reflected in Fulbert's own writings; and when Hildegar went to Poitiers, among the books for which he sent back (no. 88) was Porphyry's *Isagoge*, the introductory treatise on dialectic.[40]

Almost no details are available as to what was actually taught at Chartres. Here as elsewhere the first rudiments were probably learned from such works as the psalter and the *Disticha Catonis* (cf. nos. 88, 115), and the basic rules of grammar and rhetoric from the manuals of Donatus and Priscian (cf. nos. 88, 82). The student would also read the standard authors; and to judge from the present collection, the favourites were Terence and Horace.

Instruction in the arts of the *quadrivium* was probably limited to basic definitions and the essentials of calculation such as are reflected in Fulbert's poems on weights and measures and the calendar (nos. 146 f.). In this regard too much emphasis has been placed on a letter from Ragimbold of Cologne to Ralph of Liège in which he says that he has discussed a point of geometry with Fulbert and that Fulbert defined the basic term involved, but did not further explain it. The very problem in question—what are the interior angles of a triangle?—suggests that such matters were not studied in depth; and in any case, it arose not from a mathematical work, but from a passage in Boethius' commentary on Aristotle's *Categories*.[41]

The art of music as studied in the *quadrivium* was essentially theoretical. Its practical side was an altogether different matter.

---

[40] This same programme is also reflected in a manuscript associated with another of Fulbert's students, Hartwic of St. Emmeram. See Lattin, 'Munich 14436'; B. Bischoff, 'Literarisches und künstlerisches Leben in St. Emmeram (Regensburg) während des frühen und hohen Mittelalters', *Studien und Mitteilungen zur Geschichte des Benediktiner-Ordens und seiner Zweige*, li (1933), 105 ff. (reprinted in his *Mittelalterliche Studien*, ii (Stuttgart, 1967), 80 ff.).

[41] P. Tannery and A. Clerval, 'Une correspondance d'écolâtres du XIe siècle', *Notices et extraits des manuscrits de la Bibliothèque Nationale et autres bibliothèques*, xxxvi, ii (1901), 487 ff., especially pp. 497 f. and 532 f. Cf. Manitius, ii. 778 ff.

Both were perhaps taught at Chartres. Hildegar is said to have devoted himself to the 'Pythagorean lyre', and another of Fulbert's students, Sigo, to have had no equal *organali . . . in musica* (i.e. organum?).[42] Moreover, the students at Chartres participated in the celebration of divine office (no. 105), and this meant that they had to have at least some instruction in chant, whether or not we are justified in speaking of a 'school' of liturgical composition there.[43]

There also appears to have been some tradition of medical study at Chartres. Richer went there for the express purpose of studying this with Heribrandus. He learned simple pharmacy and seems to have been especially interested in diagnosis and medical theory.[44] Fulbert himself appears to have given special attention to medical matters before he became bishop (no. 24). Both he and Hildegar were familiar with the usual handbooks of remedies and knew how to administer medicine (nos. 47 f.), and Fulbert shows some knowledge of the underlying theory (no. 49).

As for instruction in religious matters, there is almost nothing that can be said with assurance. We are told, though the statement seems little more than a commonplace, that Fulbert taught sacred as well as secular subjects.[45] Fulbert himself says of one student that he came to Chartres *causa discendae honestatis* and of another that he was learning there how to vanquish the armies of vice (nos. 76, 127); and in the sole description that we have of him and his students, we see him exhorting them to the pursuit of Christian

[42] Thus Adelman (see pp. xxxv f.). Cf. no. 115. The theoretical side was also studied at Rheims (Richer, *Historia*, iii. 49 (ed. Latouche [p. xxix n. 34], ii. 58)).

[43] Cf. Y. Delaporte, *Études grégoriennes*, ii (1957), 51 ff. One of Fulbert's students, Arnulf, precentor of Chartres, is said to have composed an office for the feast of St. Évroul (*The Ecclesiastical History of Orderic Vitalis*, ed. M. Chibnall, ii (Oxford, 1969), 108).

[44] Richer, *Historia*, iv. 50 (ed. Latouche, ii. 224 ff.). Cf. L. C. MacKinney, 'Tenth-Century Medicine as seen in the Historia of Richer of Rheims', *Bulletin of the Institute of the History of Medicine*, ii (1934), 347 ff., and *Early Medieval Medicine with special Reference to France and Chartres* (Baltimore, 1937); L. Dubreuil-Chambardel, *Les médecins dans l'ouest de la France aux XIᵉ et XIIᵉ siècles* (Paris, 1914), pp. 6 ff. and *passim*.

[45] Namely by Adelman (see pp. xxxv f.); *Explicabat altioris archana scientiae. . . . Tu divina, tu humana excolebas dogmata.* The discussions of Fulbert in this regard are primarily based on the *Fulbertus exiguus* letters (see pp. lxii f.): e.g. M. Grabmann, *Die Geschichte der scholastischen Methode*, i (Freiburg-i-B., 1909), 215 f.; J. A. Endres, 'Fulbert von Chartres als Freund der freien Künste', *Forschungen zur Geschichte der frühmittelalterlichen Philosophie* (Beiträge zur Geschichte der Philosophie des Mittelalters, xvii, ii–iii (Münster, 1915)), pp. 21 ff.; O. Capitani, *Studi su Berengario di Tours* (Lecce, 1966), pp. 37 ff. and *passim*.

wisdom.[46] Yet specific details are lacking, and there is nothing to indicate that such matters were studied in a systematic way.

There is almost no evidence as to the methods of instruction used at this time. A great part of the student's education consisted in memorization. This was best done by oral repetition, such as is reflected in the dialogue form, which was so popular with medieval writers and of which the closest modern equivalent would be the questions and answers of the catechism. Mnemonic devices also had their place. Some of Fulbert's poems were apparently written for this purpose,[47] and his expositions of the feudal oath and of the requirements for the episcopacy, though in prose, have a similar ring (nos. 51, 28, 56). The teaching in more advanced classes probably included the reading and glossing of standard authors. There may also have been something along the lines of the later 'question', centring around a particular problem and comparing different opinions, such as those treating of Solomon's salvation which Fulbert sent to Hildegar (no. 92). There was certainly some individual instruction and perhaps what we should call directed readings.[48] Almost everyone who works with the texts used in the medieval schools is appalled at the dryness of the material and the sheer quantity of what had to be memorized. This also appears to have been somewhat dismaying even then, for Hildegar was once reproved for his levity and warned that it was unbecoming for a teacher to introduce anything into the construing of Donatus which was so unseemly as to cause laughter (no. 88).

The teaching staff at Chartres was small. The everyday running of the school was apparently entrusted to the *scholasticus* or *magister scholae*, who, as we have seen, also performed the duties of chancellor. He had an assistant; but the latter's teaching duties were probably limited, and one of the older students might be used in this capacity (no. 92). Fulbert can hardly have continued the everyday teaching after he became bishop, and he probably appointed a new schoolmaster then, though direct evidence is lacking. Hildegar held this position in the early 1020s, and it is likely that he had been doing so for some time. After he went to

[46] See p. xxxvi.

[47] Nos. 146–8, 152. In the manuscripts the various symbols used for weights and measures are sometimes found in the margins or between the lines of no. 146, and no. 147 is usually accompanied by tables of regulars and concurrents.

[48] Cf. Richer's account of his studies with Heribrandus (see p. xxxiii).

Poitiers, it was given apparently to Sigo and then to Ebrardus; but the latter resigned, and Fulbert himself took charge until Hildegar returned (nos. 92, 106, 108). Yet even when there was a schoolmaster, Fulbert apparently did some teaching, for most of his known students studied there while he was bishop, and it is expressly stated (for whatever it is worth) that they did so with him. Thus it would seem that while the schoolmaster saw to the running of the school and probably the elementary instruction, Fulbert himself continued to teach at least the more advanced subjects and remained in close contact with the students.

The most important immediate influence which Fulbert exercised was in fact through his students and not his writings. The number of those who are said to have studied with him at one time or another is surprisingly large, and this was still considered worth mentioning in the time of Orderic Vitalis.[49] Among them were Angelramnus, *scholasticus* and later abbot of Saint-Riquier, Humbert of Montmajour, who studied at Chartres for nine years, Olbertus, abbot of Gembloux, Bernard, *scholasticus* of Angers, Adelman, *scholasticus* of Liège and later bishop of Brescia, and the celebrated Berengar of Tours, of whose destiny Fulbert was later said to have had a premonition while on his death-bed.[50]

To Adelman we owe the only contemporary account of Fulbert and his students. In the early 1030s he composed a poem in memory of his former master and those of his students who were already dead.[51] It is a sort of poetic catalogue in a form which was

---

[49] See Clerval, pp. 58 ff., and MacKinney, pp. 12 ff. As for Orderic, see p. xxxiii n. and edn. cit. iii (1972), 120.

[50] Angelramnus: see the preface to his *Vita Richarii*, which is dedicated to Fulbert (*PL* cxli. 1423 f.); *AASS*, April iii, 445 ff.; Hariulf, *Chronicon Centulense*, iv. 1, 8 (*Chronique de l'abbaye de Saint-Riquier*, ed. F. Lot (Paris, 1894), pp. 180, 195). Humbert: see Le Comte de Lasteyrie, 'Restitution d'une inscription du xie siècle', *Centenaire 1804–1904: recueil de mémoires de la Soc. nat. des Antiquaires de France* (Paris, n.d.), pp. 239 ff. (Only half of this inscription was previously known, having been printed in J. Mabillon, *Annales ordinis sancti Benedicti*, iv (Paris, 1707), 641; and on the basis of this, Clerval, p. 62 and *passim*, and MacKinney, p. 16 and *passim*, spoke of a student of Fulbert's named 'Domnus'. The restored inscription reveals that 'Domnus' was actually Humbert.) Olbertus: see Sigebert of Gembloux, *Gesta abbatum Gemblacensium*, c. xxvi (*MGH SS* viii. 536); Manitius, ii. 59 f., 457 ff. Bernard: see his *Liber miraculorum sancte Fidis*, preface and c. xxxiv (ed. A. Bouillet (Paris, 1897), pp. 1 ff., 85). Fulbert's premonition concerning Berengar: see William of Malmesbury, iii. 285 (ed. Stubbs, ii. 341).

[51] Ed. J. Havet, 'Poème rythmique d'Adelman de Liège', *Notices et documents publiés pour la Soc. de l'hist. de France à l'occasion du cinquantième*

popular throughout the Middle Ages from Augustine to Chaucer and which is sometimes called 'alphabetic' or 'ABC' as the stanzas begin with successive letters of the alphabet. But despite this artificiality and a certain clumsiness, Adelman's warmth and affection come through. He begins with Fulbert himself; and even as 'words flee, the heart melts, and fresh tears well forth', he sings of the golden fount of his honeyed mouth, the gravity of his teaching, and the sweetness of his words. The first of Fulbert's students to be mentioned is, not surprisingly, Hildegar, who was known as *pupilla* because of his small statue, but who excelled in medicine, philosophy, and music. Then come Ralph of Orleans, more distinguished for his love of learning than for his learning itself; Lambert of Paris and Engelbert of Orleans, both professional teachers; the grammarian Reginald of Tours; Gerard, who died while returning from the Holy Land; Walter of Burgundy, who toured Europe in search of learning; Ragimbold of Cologne, whom we have already met; and three of Adelman's fellow clerks from Liège.

About 1050 Adelman wrote to Berengar in an effort to persuade him to abandon his teaching on the Eucharist.[52] It was apparently now that he revised his poem, making several changes and replacing Ralph of Orleans with Sigo, who had died in the meantime. Adelman appealed to the sweet comradeship of their student days at Chartres. He reminded Berengar of Fulbert's holy life and sound teaching, of how he used to talk with them in the chapel garden at vesper-time, urging them to follow in the footsteps of the fathers and not to stray down new and deceiving side-paths, and of how in the midst of speaking he sometimes burst forth into tears from the fire of his ardour. This is Fulbert as his students remembered him in later years, and it is this more than anything else that explains their devotion to his memory.

Fulbert's Letters and the Letter Collection

So far as modern scholarship is concerned, the principal monument to Fulbert and his school is, of course, the present letter

anniversaire de sa fondation (Paris, 1884), pp. 71 ff. Cf. H. Silvestre, 'Notice sur Adelman de Liège, évêque de Brescia (†1061)', *Revue d'histoire ecclésiastique*, lvi (1961), 855 ff.

[52] Ed. R. B. C. Huygens, *Studi medievali*, Third Series, viii (1967), 459 ff. The passage cited here is on pp. 476 ff.

collection. The letters themselves are of great importance not only for what they tell about Fulbert and his students, but also as sources for the history of France in the early eleventh century and for the many glimpses which they give of the concrete realities of everyday life. As a letter collection it has still other claims on our attention. It is one of the first collections since Carolingian times and one of the earliest to emanate from a cathedral school, and its importance is enhanced by the unusually clear picture which it gives as to how it was put together and for what purposes it was copied.

The literary composition which we call a letter is not easy to describe. This is as true for the Middle Ages as for the modern world. We speak, for example, of 'personal', 'business', or 'official' letters; we call some letters 'friendly', others 'open', and yet others 'Letters to the Editor'. The letter can run from a few lines to a full-length treatise, and the variety of its subject-matter is well-nigh limitless. On the other hand, the letter is a means of communication. As such we expect not only that it will be comprehensible to the person or persons for whom it is intended, but also that it will reflect some of the polite conventions which we commonly observe in our relations with each other. The determining factors here are usually the respective standing of the writer and the addressee and the nature of the subject-matter. How this is carried out in practice depends on the literary tastes of the age. While the literary standards have varied over the centuries, the excellence of the letter-writer has always depended on his ability to conform to the conventions of his day and yet somehow to transcend them and within a brief framework to produce a composition which would be an artistic whole and convey something of the writer's individuality.

The basic form of the medieval letter—salutation, exordium, narration, request, conclusion—was again an inheritance from the schools of the Roman rhetorician.[53] The form itself was eminently logical and could easily be adapted to the subject-matter at hand. Of the various literary conventions, the most striking to the modern reader is the style of address. The order in which the names of the addressee and the writer were placed in the salutation

[53] As regards medieval letters and letter-collections, see *The Letters of Peter the Venerable*, ed. G. Constable (Cambridge, Mass., 1967), ii, 1 ff., and the bibliography cited there.

was so carefully observed that any deviation from the usual practice immediately suggests some change in their relationship.
Within the body of the letter the writer similarly referred to
himself in what are called 'formulas of humility', while he addressed
the receiver in such abstract terms as 'your paternity' or 'your
benevolence', thus emphasizing the latter's position or qualities
which the writer wished to stress. He was also expected to adorn
his composition with appropriate rhetorical figures and common-
places and with quotations and allusions, but without losing sight
of the traditional ideal of epistolary brevity. Moreover, the
medieval letter was meant to be read aloud. Hence careful attention
was paid to the sound of the words, and it was from this that
developed the use of rhyme and metrical patterns to set off the
end of clauses and sentences. To write a letter was thus an
arduous task, and one which was well written was regarded as a
fine gift to send to a friend. Even personal letters might be widely
circulated. The writer who was conscious of his literary reputation
kept copies of his letters, and he himself revised and arranged
them and saw to their publication.

Although Fulbert did keep copies of his writings,[54] there is
nothing to indicate that he undertook to revise them or selected
and arranged them with a view to publication. The compiling and
editing of his works appear instead to have been done by his two
closest disciples, Hildegar and Sigo, both of whom may have
served him—the latter certainly did so—as secretary.[55]Fulbert's

---

[54] To be sure, the only evidence for this is their very existence and the
chronologically arranged letter-groups (see pp. li–liii). The references to
cancellarii tabulas (no. 108) and *armaria* (no. 89) are too vague to permit any
conclusion. On the one occasion when Fulbert expressly cites an earlier letter
he does so by quoting the last line (no. 33). In nos. 27, 45, and 57 he includes
copies of other letters, but these were probably written at the same time. In
any event it seems clear that these were all by way of personal papers, and there
is no evidence of any official calendar or archives which would include this
kind of material.

[55] Direct evidence for Hildegar is lacking, but cf. no. 48. As for Sigo,
Hildegar seems to be presuming at the close of no. 114 that he will be handling
Fulbert's mail, and in his obituary he is described as *levita . . . cantor . . .
ammirandi presulis Fulberti, dum terris exularet, fidus a secretis, post, ut datur
cerni, tumulator liberalis* (Merlet, p. 169). The Sigo who became abbot of
Saumur has his own place in the necrology (ibid., p. 166). A charter granted in
favour of the monastery of Pontlevoy, 11 July 1034, was witnessed by two
Sigos, one as precentor and the other as canon (Lex, pp. 339 ff.). The identity
of the Sigo *magister scolarum* who witnessed a charter granted to the monastery
of La Trinité of Vendôme 31 May 1040 (*Cartulaire de l'abbaye cardinale de la

literary remains seem to have consisted of small gatherings and individual leaves of varying size containing, as we have seen, letters, sermons, poems, and other *opuscula*. Most of these were probably in fair copy, if not altogether without corrections, though for nos. 132 and 135 and perhaps for the *Contra Iudeos* we have more than one version. Since Hildegar's letters were added to it, the corpus would seem at one time to have been in his possession; and from him—perhaps after his death *c.* 1030—it apparently passed to Sigo, who added the draft of the obituary leaflet which he had composed in Fulbert's honour.[56] The format of the corpus was that of collected papers only loosely kept together. It could be, and was, rearranged. Several copies were made of it in the following years. Some were apparently taken from the material as it came to hand, others show an effort toward systematic rearrangement according to the rank of the addressee, which, as we have also seen, was one of the determining factors as regards style. Not long after 1037,[57] an edited version was produced in which the corpus was tidied up: the underlying quires and schedules containing the letters were arranged in a particular way, duplication of material (including variant versions) was avoided, some of the *opuscula* and notes were omitted, and the letters in particular were emended with a view to style. Though it is not certain that this was done by Sigo—there is no trace of his obituary leaflet, and the over-all chronology of the letters has been disturbed—or even at Chartres, it would seem to be the version which was intended for publication. It was in fact the most widely diffused and before the end of the century was to go through a second revised edition.

Thus it is that from one point of view the collection, and even more the published version, is as much the product of Fulbert's school as of Fulbert himself, and the interests and tastes of his

Trinité de Vendôme, ed. C. Métais, i (Paris, 1893), 85 ff.) and of the archdeacon Sigo who attended a hearing 1048–61 in which the cathedral necrology was cited in support of a land-grant (*Cartulaire de Marmoutier pour le Dunois*, ed. E. Mabille (Paris, 1874), pp. 102 ff.) is not certain, though the first is probably and the second almost surely not the Sigo associated with Fulbert. The subdean Hildegar who witnessed these charters is not our Hildegar, as he was dead when Adelman first wrote his poem and is commemorated in the necrology as *subdecanus et magister scolae hujus ecclesiae* (Merlet, p. 178).

[56] See p. xliii.

[57] Or so it would appear from the date of the interpolated document in Appendix B, no. 1, and from the early date of L. Appendix B, nos. 2 f., were apparently added at the same time as the former.

disciples and their successors are reflected in its later history. The letters form the largest part of the collection. These cover a wide variety of topics which would interest the medieval reader; and the diffusion of the manuscripts as well as the care with which they were copied show that he was indeed interested. Moreover, Fulbert's letters concerning problems of church law and similar matters offered the reader not only Fulbert's opinions, but also pertinent passages from the fathers and the lawbooks, sources which were not easy to use.[58] Yet the copyists' interests were not confined to the letters. They retained Fulbert's sermons and other *opuscula* as an integral part of the collection. Some of these continued to be included in the later abridgements and also circulated separately.

The diffusion of Fulbert's writings as they have come down to us is primarily northern French and English, almost, if not quite, Anglo-Norman, though this is all but true of the published version. They had their greatest success in the eleventh and earlier twelfth centuries, and it may be more than accidental that they are sometimes found with the letters of Lanfranc and Ivo, collections of a similarly practical bent. After that their popularity declined, perhaps partly because of the changed conditions of life, but more as a result of changes in the educational world and in the fashions of letter-writing which in large part rendered their contents obsolete and their style antiquated. Later copyists, in marked contrast to their predecessors, either abridged the collection or copied only select letters, or even excerpts, treating of legal matters and the like. In this regard Fulbert was still held in sufficient esteem for someone toward the mid twelfth century in north-eastern France or Belgium to include two of his own letters in just such a short collection and to put them forth as Fulbert's and for these to be copied as late as *c.* 1200.[59] Except for this, Fulbert's reputation seems to have endured longest in England, but here too his writings soon gave way to the more advanced theological and legal compilations of the schools and the more stylized *ars dictaminis*. A few select works continued to be copied sporadically, but otherwise Fulbert was chiefly remembered as

---

[58] Thus in nos. 71 and 128 Hildegar is probably using nos. 22 and 26. I have not, however, found any direct borrowings in later letter collections. Is Hildegar referring to some of Fulbert's writings in no. 131?

[59] See pp. lxi f.

the author of the classic exposition of the feudal oath or as a writer of sermons on the Blessed Virgin, who had once cured him of an illness with milk from her breast.[60]

In working with Fulbert's letters it is well to remember how little is actually known of the circumstances surrounding their composition and how much of what the writer put into them may accordingly have lost its meaning, for in some respects the letter-form seems particularly suited to Fulbert's literary talents. His style is characterized by brevity and a feeling for the precise word, especially the right connective, hence its clarity and speed. Although Fulbert obviously shares his contemporaries' love of personification and the metaphorical phrase, he is on the whole rather sparing with his use of rhetorical devices. Yet both he and Hildegar use rhymed prose—Fulbert to a lesser degree and most noticeably, perhaps, at the end of a letter—as well as the gnomic greetings in the salutation which later became so popular.

Most of Fulbert's letters are of an official or semi-official nature for which there were more or less set forms of correspondence.

---

[60] For the diffusion and influence of Fulbert's letter on the feudal oath (no. 51) see p. lxi n.; Behrends, pp. 97 f. (the two references in note 19 there lack sufficient foundation); E. H. Kantorowicz, *The King's Two Bodies* (Princeton, 1957), p. 349, who notes that it contributed to the new episcopal oath which was formulated in the later eleventh century; G. Giordanengo, 'Epistola Philiberti', *Mélanges d'arch. et d'hist. de l'École française de Rome*, lxxxii (1970), 809 ff., who traces its influence on feudal law, primarily in the Dauphiné. Peter Damian also quotes at length from no. 4 (J. Ryan, *Saint Peter Damiani and his canonical Sources* (Toronto, 1956), p. 70). For Fulbert's cure by the Blessed Virgin see William of Malmesbury, iii. 285 (ed. Stubbs, ii. 341), and *De miraculis sanctae Mariae*, c. xlvii (xxxi) (ed. J. M. Canal, *Recherches de théologie ancienne et médiévale*, xxix (1962), 50 f., xxx (1963), 86 f.). Also see the entries for Fulbert in the Melk Anonymous, *De scriptoribus ecclesiasticis* (E. Ettlinger, *Der sog. Anonymus Mellicensis de scriptoribus ecclesiasticis* (Karlsruhe, 1896), p. 85), the continuation (*c.* 1270–3) of Sigebert of Gembloux's *De viris illustribus* (N. Häring, 'Der Literaturkatalog von Affligem', *RB* lxxx (1970), 76), and J. Trithemius, *De scriptoribus ecclesiasticis* (Basel, 1494 (=*PL* cxli. 187)); and the late epitaph and fourteenth-century chronicle in *Cart. N.-D. Chartres*, i, pp. xxxiv, 14. In the modern period, Fulbert is cited several times by the sixteenth-century polemicist Matteo Zampini in his attack on Gallicanism (L.-P. Raybaud, 'La royauté d'après les œuvres de Matteo Zampini', *Le prince dans la France des XVIe et XVIIe siècles*, by C. Bontems and others (Paris, 1965), p. 191 n.), and the title of the 1608 edition mentions the value of Fulbert's writings for the history of France and for refuting heresy (see p. lxiv). There are two eleventh-century 'portraits' of Fulbert (Chartres, nouv. acq. ms. 4, f. 32; Munich, Bayerische Staatsbibliothek, Clm. 14272, f. 1ᵛ) and a twelfth-century mural of him at Saint-Hilaire (MacKinney, plates I–III; the first is also reproduced in Merlet, frontispiece, and between pp. 46 and 47).

Despite some personal touches these usually remain to the point, and in his letters of advice to Hildegar he jumps from one topic to the next. In his letters of friendship, however, he sometimes gives vent to those flights of imaginative metaphor and literary fancy which were so highly prized in his day, and he is quite ready to play Isaac to Hildegar's Jacob (nos. 117 f.). Yet in Fulbert's hands all this seems rather restrained, and only in nos. 118 f. and some of the poems do we catch sight of a lighter side to his character, and even then but a glimpse.

11. *The Letter Collection: Manuscripts, Formation, Editions*

The Principal Manuscripts

P: Paris, Bibliothèque Nationale, latin 14167.[1] The present volume contains 88 leaves (195 × 140 mm), eleven gatherings of eight leaves each except the seventh which is of ten and the tenth which is of six, varying from 20 to 27 lines to the page, in a seventeenth-century vellum binding. The manuscript breaks off toward the end of *Contra Iudeos* iii, but the former ff. 89–90 and 95–6 are now bound in B as ff. 25–8.[2] The major part of the manuscript is written in a rather bold mid eleventh-century hand, though ff. 1–3, 9–10^v, and 15–16^v may be in another hand; and two more contemporary hands seem responsible for ff. 76^v ff. The following title is written in the top margin of f. 1 in a fourteenth-century hand: *Epistole salutatorie domini Fulberti episcopi Carnotensis et quedam dictamina atque uersus*; and P is probably the manuscript of this title in the fourteenth-century catalogue of the library of Saint-Père.[3] Moreover, an almost imperceptible library inscription in the upper right margin of f. 1 reads *de libraria sancti Petri Car[notensis]*. According to a seventeenth-century history of Saint-Père, the manuscript was borrowed by a religious who refused to return it; and in preparing his edition of 1608, Charles de Villiers used it

---

[1] See M.-Th. Vernet, 'Notes de Dom André Wilmart† sur quelques manuscrits latins anciens de la Bibliothèque nationale de Paris', *Bulletin d'information de l'Institut de recherche et d'histoire des textes*, vi (1957), 22 ff.; Pfister, *Fulbert*, pp. 2 ff.

[2] P's original foliation is still partly visible, and the conclusion of the poem at the bottom of f. 26^v and the beginning of that at the top of f. 27^r are missing.

[3] *Cat. dépt.*, xi, p. xxxii.

at the College of Navarre.[4] It later passed to Achille de Harlay, the abbey of Saint-Germain-des-Prés, and the Bibliothèque Nationale.[5]

The first items in P are several verses, which may be grouped as follows, and Fulbert's obituary and epitaph (Appendix A):

> *Vltimus in clero Fulberti nomine Sigo*
> *Andreae manibus haec pinxit Miciacensis;*
> *Det quibus unica spes mundi requiem paradysi.*

> *Actibus his studuit*
> *Instruxit iuuenis nonnullos discipulorum*
> *Artibus haec [!] septem multum studiosus earum.*

> *Pauit oues domini pastor uenerabilis annos*
> *Quinque quater mensesque decem cum mensibus octo.*

> *Infirmos, nudos, sicientes, esurientes,*
> *Visere, uestire studuit, potare, cibare.*

The first three lines and the second couplet as well as the obituary itself are also found in two detached leaves from Fulbert's obituary leaflet (or *tumulus*) which were inserted in the cathedral martyrology.[6] There the couplet is a legend accompanying a picture of Fulbert, and the complete leaflet probably contained two more pictures for which the other two couplets were intended. It appears from the first three lines, which in the *tumulus* are a colophon, that the leaflet was composed by Sigo and executed by André of Saint-Mesmin de Micy (near Orleans). The arrangement of this material in P and the way in which Fulbert's death is dated at the beginning of the obituary notice suggest that they were not copied directly from the leaflet, but rather that both derive from a common source, namely Sigo's draft. Two other variants in P's text (*sancti templi suae diocesis* and *illum locum* for

---

[4] Merlet, p. 51 n.

[5] See L. Delisle, *Le cabinet des manuscrits de la Bibliothèque nationale* (Paris, 1868–81), ii. 47 ff., 100 ff.

[6] See Merlet, pp. 47 ff., and the preceding facsimile. In 1946 the manuscript (then Saint-Étienne MS. 104) was returned to Chartres, where it is now marked nouv. acq. ms. 4. A fragment bound in Bibliothèque Nationale, latin 17177, ff. 68ᵛ and 69ᵛ, contains the epitaphs of Fulbert and his successor Thierry (d. 1048/9) and Abbots Gisbertus (d. c. 1004), Arnulf (c. 1013–33), and Landri (1033–69) of Saint-Père (cf. Merlet, p. 80). Fulbert's actual tomb was destroyed in the fire of 1134; and when the church was rebuilt, the original epitaph was replaced by another (ibid., p. 50 n.).

huius sancti templi and *hunc locum*) indicate that it was not copied at the cathedral, but may have been at Saint-Père, which was not taken within the city walls until much later.[7] Yet P is not mentioned in the eleventh-century catalogue of the library of Saint-Père, which, though not necessarily complete, does include a set of gospels bequeathed by Sigo and an unidentified *Pastoralis episcopi Fulberti pro nostro* marked as already lost in the fifteenth century.[8] Sigo himself is probably not responsible for P, for it is not well copied—the scribes were apparently not professionals—and in 92 his name is rendered as *sed*, though this may be in another hand.

P's contents are as follows (numbers from 132 on are poems):
5 29 30 31 32 33 99 100 101 21 94 41 28 53 59 61 2 3 4 6 18 36 77 80 42 43 82 26 64 35 63 7 9 11 12 17 19 20 22 23 38 40 39 72 73 74 76 75 84 85 86 87 132 88 89 90 91 92 93 34 44 47 45 49 51 52 54 55 46 56 57 58 60 25 24 146 148. A new incipit is found on f. 39[v]: *Expistolae domni Fulberti Carnotensis episcopi et alia quedam opuscula eiusdem.* This is followed by 1, five short private prayers,[9] 65 66 67 68 48 79 69 70 71 95 81 83 96 102 103 104 105 106 110 109 111 112 113 114 116 117 119 121 128 129 130 131, and the following poems scattered among the miscellaneous items: 140 141 142 137 138 139 146 135 132 143 144 136 133 145 134 148 147. A new series of letters begins on f. 69[v]: 126 127 124 98 118 123 78 97 125 107 122 120 27 108 81. This is followed by sermons and other miscellany and *Contra Iudeos* i, ii, iii. The leaves bound in B include the conclusion of *Contra Iudeos* iii and 149 155 150 151 152 153 (incomplete) 147 (incomplete) 148 154.

B: Paris, Bibliothèque Nationale, latin 2872.[10] A late sixteenth-century volume containing three incomplete manuscripts of Fulbert's writings probably made by Nicolas Le Fèvre, from whom it passed to de Thou, Colbert, and finally the Bibliothèque Nationale. The first and most important manuscript (ff. 1–24[v])

---

[7] Merlet, p. 52 n. Cf. *Cart. S.-Père*, i, p. ccxlv.

[8] See L. Merlet, 'Catalogue des livres de l'abbaye de Saint-Père de Chartres, au XIe siècle', *BEC*, Third Series, v (1853–4), 263 ff. But cf. the reference to Fulbert's writings in *Cart. S.-Père*, i. 12.

[9] Printed in H. Barré, *Prières anciennes de l'occident à la mère du Sauveur* (Paris, 1963), p. 153.

[10] See *Bibliothèque Nationale, Catalogue général des manuscrits latins*, iii (1952), 179 ff.; Vernet, op. cit., pp. 20 ff.; Delisle, op. cit., i. 470 ff.

is written in a small, but very clear, hand of the second half of the
eleventh century, three gatherings of eight leaves each, 33 lines
to the page (185 × 125 mm), the incipit reading: *Epistolae domni
Fulberti Carnotensis episcopi et alia quaedam opuscula eiusdem.* It
contains the following letters: 1 5 2 3 4 6 18 26 30 42 43 55 77 80
15 38 35 56 74 75 7 44 45 46 73 12 29 47 57 89 32 33 84 93 20 58
76 87 126 127 39 91 124 36 22 40 54 90 60 64 63 49 85 98 11 14 8
16 19 23 31 34 88 92 118 123 17 21 62 41 28 53 59 61 78 94 97 125
86 37 52 72 13 51 107 122 119 100 (incomplete). The second
manuscript (ff. 25–8ᵛ) has already been identified as part of the
missing final quire of P. The third manuscript (ff. 29–130ᵛ) is an
incomplete copy of R written on paper in a later sixteenth-century
hand with notes by Le Fèvre and Papire Masson.

V: Vatican, latin 1783.[11] A small volume composed of several
unrelated works in various hands. Fulbert's writings are copied in
a very small eleventh-century hand, 25 lines to the page (155 × 92
mm), and are in two parts: ff. 97–128ᵛ and f. 137ʳ⁻ᵛ (incorrectly
bound in the present volume) contain his letters and two tracts
Contra Iudeos;[12] ff. 153–62ʳ, sermons and *opuscula*. Since the
second part begins on the last leaf of a quire containing other
works, the two parts have not been separated accidentally. The
first part consists of four quires of eight leaves each. As the letters
which begin on ff. 120ᵛ and 104ᵛ continue on ff. 97 and 121 respectively, the quires should be rearranged as follows: ff. 105–20,
97–104, 121–8. The first part contains the following without an
incipit: 72 73 74 76 77 78 80 75 84 85 86 87 132 88 89 90 91 92
93 94 98 97 118 123 124 122 125 126 127 42 41 34 28 44 47 45
49 51 43 2 3 5 4 10 13 14 8 15 16 6 7 9 11 12 17 18 19 20 21 22 23
38 36 40 39, an interpolated letter (=Appendix B, no. 4), 52 54 55
53 46 56 57. The last letter is incomplete, but the *Contra Iudeos*
follows immediately. Among the *opuscula* in the second part are
155 149 150 151 135 137 138 139 132 140 141.

M: Montpellier, École de Médecine, MS. 137.[13] This is composed
of two manuscripts from the library of Pierre Pithou which

[11] See B. Nogara, *Codices Vaticani latini*, iii (1912), 238 ff. The marginalia
on ff. 113ᵛ–14 is from Eusebius 'Gallicanus', *Hom.* li. 3, 5 (ed. Glorie, *CCL*
ciᵃ. 595 f.).   [12] See p. xxvi n.
[13] See P. Fournier, 'Notice sur le manuscrit H. 137 de l'École de Médecine
de Montpellier', *Annales de l'Université de Grenoble*, ix (1897), 357 ff.

passed to the Oratory at Troyes, where they were bound together. The second is an eleventh-century collection mainly of canons and capitularies which begins with Fulbert's penitential (f. 167), includes letter 4 (f. 314), and ends with the following series without an incipit (ff. 316ᵛ–20ᵛ): 42 41 34 28 44 47 45 49 51 43 2 3 5 4 (incomplete) 10 13 14 8 15 16 6 7 9 11.

H: Budapest, Hungarian National Museum, Bibliotheca Széchényiana, latin 5.[14] This contains the following letters without an incipit copied in an eleventh-century hand (ff. 10–13ʳ): 12 17 18 19 20 21 22 23 38 36 40 39 52 54 55 53 46 56 57 (incomplete). Although the hands of M and H show strong similarities, I cannot be certain from photo-reproductions alone that they are the same; but apart from the omission of the interpolated letter, the two together constitute a parallel to the latter portion of V.

L: Leiden, Vossianus latin Q. 12. The present volume, which came to Leiden by way of Paul Petau and Isaac Voss, contains several unrelated manuscripts and includes a collection of episcopal and abbatial professions made to the archbishops of Sens between 1190 and 1221 (ff. 65ᵛ–68ʳ).[15] The Fulbert collection, entitled *Epistole Fulberti*, is found on ff. 1–58ᵛ, seven gatherings of eight leaves each except the fourth which is of ten, marked P Q R S T V X, the first four leaves in each gathering being also numbered, written in a hand of the first half of the eleventh century, 31 lines to the page (265/70 × 190 mm). There are no clues to provenance except a sixteenth-century library inscription on f. 58ᵛ: *Liber sancti Martini Sagien[sis]* (Saint-Martin of Sées (Orne, *arr.* Alençon)).[16] Since this comes at the end of the Fulbert collection, the rest was apparently added later. Until recently the first six leaves were partly pasted over with strips of paper; and despite efforts to restore them, some are partly illegible. L's

[14] See E. Bartoniek, *Codices latini medii aevi*, i (Budapest, 1940), 9 f.; G. Morin, 'Lettres inédites des papes Alexandre II et saint Grégoire VII', *RB* xlviii (1936), 117 ff.

[15] See E. Chartraire, 'Une nouvelle liste de professions épiscopales et abbatiales faites à l'église métropolitaine de Sens', *Bulletin de la Soc. arch. de Sens*, xxiii (1908), 122 ff. Cf. p. xviii n.

[16] Cf. K. A. De Meyier, *Paul en Alexandre Petau en de Geschiedenis van hun Handschriften* (Leiden, 1947), pp. 123 ff., who lists other manuscripts from Saint-Martin, which was plundered by the Calvinists. This same ex-libris is found in Vatican, Reginensis latin 285, f. 32.

contents are as follows: 2 3 5 4 10 13 14 8 15 16 6 7 9 11 12 17 18 19 20 21 22 23 38 36 98 97 118 123 124 122 125 126 127 147 40 39 72 73 74 76 77 78 80 75 84 85 86 87 132 88 89 90 91 92 93 94 119 99 100 101 26 64 146 24 29 30 35 62 63 31 37 32 33 148 25 79 81 82 83 42 41 34 28 44 47 45 49 51 43 52 54 55 53 46 56 57 58 59 60 61 154 *Contra Iudeos* iii, an interpolated notice announcing the election of Abbot Bernard of Montier-la-Celle (Appendix B, no. 1), 50 120 27 65 67 66 68 48 69 70 71 95 96 102 103 104 105 106 110 109 111 112 113 114 116 117 121 128 129 130 131 115. The last letter seems to be partly written in another hand. These are followed by various *opuscula* including 155 144 134 153 135 137 138 139 140 141 142 149, Appendix B, nos. 2 f., and a *Vita Sancti Pantaleonis*,[17] which comes at the end of the collection, is not found in the other manuscripts even of the same family, and so is probably not by Fulbert.[18]

D: Durham Cathedral, MS. B. II. 11.[19] This may have been copied for William of St. Carilef, bishop of Durham 1081–96, who left it to the library. It contains a characteristic collection of largely spurious *opuscula* ascribed to St. Jerome which had a distinguished Anglo-Norman circulation (one of the surviving copies coming from Sées), the present collection entitled *Epistolae Fulberti Carnotensis episcopi* (ff. 109–37ʳ) and written in double columns of 37 lines to the page (325 × 238 mm), and miscellaneous items. The arrangement is the same as L's.

R: Vatican, Reginensis latin 278.[20] A volume of 73 leaves written in a twelfth-century hand, 36 lines to the page (257 × 165 mm), containing the Fulbert collection (ff. 1–42ʳ), the letters of Hildebert of Lavardin (ff. 42ᵛ–72ʳ), and a report of the council of Rheims of 1148 (ff. 72–3ʳ).[21] It came to the Vatican from Queen Christina; and she had acquired it from the heirs of Paul Petau,

[17] *PL* cxli. 339 ff., where it is printed as a hymn or sequence.

[18] The addendum on f. 58ᵛ is from John the Deacon, *Vita Gregorii Magni*, ii. 44 (*PL* lxxv. 105 f.).

[19] See R. A. B. Mynors, *Durham Cathedral Manuscripts to the End of the Twelfth Century* (Oxford, 1939), p. 38; and for the Jerome collection, H. Schenkl, *SB Wien*, cxxxix (1898), part ix, pp. 78 f.

[20] See A. Wilmart, *Codices Reginenses latini*, ii (1945), 80 ff.

[21] See M. Colker, 'The Trial of Gilbert of Poitiers', *Mediaeval Studies*, xxvii (1965), 152 ff.; N. Häring, 'Das sogenannte Glaubensbekenntnis des Reimser Konsistoriums von 1148', *Scholastik*, xl (1965), 55 ff.

whose signature appears in the lower margins of ff. 1 and 42ᵛ. The incipit reads: *Incipiunt epistole Fulberti Carnotensis episcopi pro diuersis negotiis ad diuersos misse.* This is probably the manuscript mentioned in a twelfth-century catalogue of Bec or a twin: *in alio epistole Laufranci. in eodem epistole Fulberti Carnotensis et Hildeberti Cenomanensis episcopi. in eodem liber Ernulfi de incestis coniugiis. item IIII questiones diuine solute ab eo.*²² The missing collection of Lanfranc's letters is now bound in a collection of fragments marked Vatican, Reginensis latin 285.²³ The Fulbert collection is arranged as in L except that the poems scattered among the letters have been placed with the *opuscula* at the end.

C: Lincoln Cathedral, MS. 134.²⁴ A composite volume containing several works in various hands. The Fulbert collection (ff. 33–84ᵛ) is written in a plain twelfth-century hand, seven gatherings of eight leaves each except the last which is of four, usually 28 lines to the page (approximately 220 × 135 mm), the lower half of f. 83ᵛ and all of f. 84ʳ⁻ᵛ being blank. The incipit reads: *Incipit scriptum uenerabilis episcopi Carnotensis F.W. duci aquitanorum de forma fidelitatis.* Then come 51, *Contra Iudeos* iii, the notice from Montier-la-Celle (Appendix B, no. 1), 78, and an exchange of letters between Berengar of Tours and Ascelin of Chartres not otherwise included in this collection.²⁵ The main body of the collection begins on f. 40ᵛ: 2 3 5 4 23 13 14 8 15 16 7 11 18 19 20

---

²² G. Becker, *Catalogi bibliothecarum antiqui* (Bonn, 1885), p. 262. The other items are Ernulf of Rochester (d. 1124), *De incestis coniugiis* (*PL* clxiii. 1457 ff.), and apparently his letter to Lambert (ed. L. d'Achery, *Spicilegium*, iii (2nd edn., Paris, 1723), 470 ff.).

²³ See Wilmart, op. cit., pp. 94 ff. It is written in the same hand, 36 lines to the page, and an almost identical script-area (190 × 115 mm, as compared to R's 190/3 × 112/15 mm), and is composed of two quaternions plus two leaves (ff. 17 f.), the last letter being complete and f. 18ᵛ blank. The incipit reads: *Incipiunt epistole lanf[ranci] archiepiscopi pro diuersis negotiis ad diuersos misse.*

²⁴ See R. M. Woolley, *Catalogue of the Manuscripts of Lincoln Cathedral Chapter Library* (Oxford, 1927), p. 96.

²⁵ Edited by R. B. C. Huygens, 'Les lettres de Bérenger de Tours et d'Ascelin de Chartres', *Essays presented to G. I. Lieftinck*, ii (Amsterdam, 1972), 16 ff. The two letters, 71, and 51, are also found in a twelfth-century fragment bound in Bibliothèque Nationale, latin 9376, ff. 34–8ᵛ, from which they were earlier printed by d'Achery in his introduction to Lanfranc's works (reprinted in *PL* cl. 66 ff.). This was also apparently d'Achery's source for the letter from Pope John XIX to Odilo of Cluny, the manuscript of which has not hitherto been identified (cf. L. Santifaller and others, 'Chronologisches Verzeichnis der Urkunden Papst Johanns XIX.', *Römische historische Mitteilungen*, i (1956–7), 68, no. 67).

21 22 46 98 97 118 123 125 126 127 72 73 74 76 77 78 80 75 88
89 24 132 38 36 90 91 92 93 94 119 99 100 26 31 37 32 33 81 34
28 44 47 43 52 54 56 58 59 61 154 50 120 67 66 48 69 70 71 95
96 111 112 113 117 128 129 130 131 115, select *opuscula* including
155 144 153 137 138 139 140 141 142, and Appendix B, nos.
2 f. This is apparently an abridgement of the collection found
in L, the material standing in the same relative order except for
the position of 23 46 24 132 38 36.

K: Hereford Cathedral, MS. P. ii. 15.[26] A twelfth-century manuscript from Cirencester containing the letters of Ivo of Chartres
arranged in eleven *distinctiones*, Fulbert's letters (ff. 147–61ʳ)
without an incipit though the first initial is florid, and five letters
by Lanfranc and Anselm. K contains the following: 74 (incomplete) 77 80 84 92 93 123 125 4 14 8 12 22 51 57 5 7 11 9 17 19 20
21 38 98 118 126 127 40 72 88 31 79 81 82 83 41 28 44 45 43 52
54 55 53 46 56 58 60 61 13 15 16 6 23 36 97 124 122. The first
fifteen letters have marginal rubrics (as do Ivo's), and these
indicate that the letters were chosen because they treat primarily
of legal matters.

F: London, British Museum, Royal 11. A. x.[27] A twelfth-century
manuscript which once contained the same collection of Ivo's
letters and the first fifteen of Fulbert's found in K, but which
now breaks off near the beginning of 22, the last two of Fulbert's
letters being lost (ff. 167–72ᵛ). In contrast to K there are no
marginal rubrics, but there is an incipit, *Exceptiones de epistolis
Fulberti Carnot[ensis] episcopi*, which suggests that the scribe of
F or its exemplar was working from a larger Fulbert collection.
A fourteenth-century catalogue of the library of Lanthony by
Gloucester lists as MS. 201 *Epistole Yvonis, mediocre volumen*, and
as MS. 202 *Epistole Fulberti episcopi et Laufridi Cantuariensis,
mediocre volumine*.[28] Though their contents might suggest that the
two constituted a twin of K, that they are given in the catalogue
as two separate volumes would seem to eliminate the possibility

---

[26] See A. T. Bannister, *A Descriptive Catalogue of the Manuscripts in the
Hereford Cathedral Library* (Hereford, 1927), p. 126.

[27] See G. F. Warner and J. Gilson, *British Museum, Catalogue of Western
Manuscripts in the Old Royal and King's Collections*, i (London, 1921), 339 f.

[28] H. Omont, 'Anciens catalogues de bibliothèques anglaises', *Centralblatt
für Bibliothekswesen*, ix (1892), 214.

of the former's being F, unless, perhaps, some of Fulbert's letters were concealed at the end of the Ivo collection.

The Relationship between the Principal Manuscripts

None of the extant manuscripts contains the complete corpus of letters and miscellaneous writings: the only ones which even approach completeness are P and, to a lesser degree, LDR. The evidence which they offer as to their relationship to each other and to the underlying collection (= ω) consists in the different ways in which the letters are arranged within them and their variant readings. Despite some reservations, primarily as to L and its kindred, the main lines of this relationship may be expressed as follows:

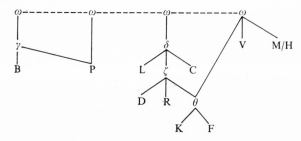

A general survey of the letter collection reveals that it is composed of two related, but distinct, collections, the one containing Fulbert's, the other Hildegar's correspondence. The latter includes letters which Hildegar wrote for the chapter of Chartres and others and the correspondence in which he engaged for Duke William at Poitiers. That he was actually the author of these letters is indicated not only by stylistic similarities and borrowings from Fulbert's letters—these could also be true of writings by Fulbert's other students—but also by the presence of letters which Hildegar wrote in his own name and by the over-all chronological arrangement. Moreover, Duke William's correspondence can hardly have found a place here unless it were somehow connected with Hildegar; and as regards the letters written for the chapter, Hildegar was apparently in Chartres and probably acting as chancellor at the time, and his name is found superscribed above the dean's in the salutation to 65 in P. The underlying Hildegar collection (= HC) can be reconstructed by comparing the order in P and L, omitting the four of Fulbert's letters which were interpolated in the former:

65 66 67 [67 66 in L] 68 48 69 70 71 95 96 102 103 104 105 106
110 109 111 112 113 114 116 117 121 128 129 130 131 115

The last letter is found only in L and its relatives. It is out of chronological order and was apparently added at the end.

The nature of the underlying collection of Fulbert's own letters was first worked out as follows in an unpublished memorandum by Dr. Margaret Gibson and Sir Richard Southern. A comparison of the arrangement of letters in PLV reveals that they can be divided into a number of groups in which the letters remain in the same order, and the differences in the over-all arrangement of the three manuscripts can be explained as resulting from a mechanical rearrangement of these groups. Hence the underlying collection was not a bound codex, but consisted of small gatherings and separate leaves which could be rearranged.[29] Moreover, the letters within the individual groups possibly stand in chronological order.

These letter-groups are as follows and in the following discussion will be cited by Roman numeral, while Arabic numerals will be used for the letters.

    I. 2 3 5 4
    II. 10 13 14 8 15 16
    III. 6 7 9 11 12 17 18 19 20 21 22 23 38 36
    IV. 98 97 118 123 124 122 125 126 127 147
    V. 40 39
    VI. 72 73 74 76 77 78 80 75 84 85 86 87 132 88 89 90 91 92
        93 94
    VII. 119
    VIII. 99 100 101
    IX. 26 64
    X. 146 24
    XI. 29 30

---

[29] A similar mechanical rearrangement also seems to lie behind the different arrangements of letters in the manuscripts of the correspondence concerning Becket's murder and of the stories about St. Francis compiled by Brother Leo and others. In both cases the over-all arrangement of the manuscripts is different, but they contain groups of letters or stories which are found in the same order. This again suggests that the underlying collections consisted of just such groups which were kept together in some sort of loose-leaf fashion, perhaps like a pile of file-folders. Cf. *Scripta Leonis, Rufini, et Angeli, sociorum S. Francisci*, ed. R. B. Brooke (Oxford, 1970), pp. 47 ff.

As we shall see in the following chapter, the arrangement of the letters within the individual groups is essentially chronological. There are to be sure some exceptions, but most of them can be explained on the basis of the way in which the collection was put together. For example, all the letters in XVI appear to be in chronological order except 34 and 28; and these are not only earlier than any of the others, but 28 was written before 34. Since they were written earlier, they cannot have been added in the margin. Thus they were probably on a separate leaf which was inserted in the letter-group. Given the length of the two letters, this need have been only a scrap of writing material; and if one letter were on each side, it would be simple enough for their order to be reversed.

The chronological unity within a letter-group is most clearly apparent where several letters relate to the same event: e.g. XIII, where all the letters except one concern the same case and are obviously in chronological order, or, to use one of the larger letter-groups, 73 74 75 in VI. On the other hand, II seems to have been on a leaf or bifolium which was somehow displaced from its proper position within III, and the same is true of XV, which appears to have fallen out of VI. Examining the collection as a whole, we find that I II III come from the first years of Fulbert's pontificate; XI XIII from c. 1018–19; V XVI XVII from c. 1021; VI XV from 1023–4. IV covers an unusually long period (c. 1025–7) for the relatively few letters; but VII, VIII, one letter in XVIII, one found only in PB, and another found only in P also belong here. This suggests that several leaves—again they need have been little more than scraps of writing material—have been detached from IV or else that Fulbert's correspondence in his last years was not kept in quite such orderly fashion as before. Thus the majority of Fulbert's letters come from only a few years of his pontificate, but these years are well represented; and the chronological

arrangement within the letter-groups indicates that they were
copies (or perhaps drafts), possibly only of certain letters, made
by the sender when they were written.

The arrangement of letters in L and V is essentially a matter of
the letter-groups as given above. Since L's order is being used as
the basis of comparison, the letter-groups run numerically I–XVII.
These are followed by 154, *Contra Iudeos* iii, the interpolated
announcement from Montier-la-Celle, and Odilo's letter to Fulbert
(50), which obviously derives from the receiver's copy. Then
come XVIII, HC, and miscellaneous works. The arrangement of
letter-groups in V is VI IV (without poem 147 at the end) XVI I II
III V XVII (incomplete) with the interpolated letter inserted between
the last two. VI IV and the interpolated letter are lacking in V's
twofold twin M/H. K is of interest here as showing almost the
same two patterns in juxtaposition. As we have seen, the first
fifteen letters in K are provided with rubrics, while the others are
not. The former were excerpted from VI IV I II III XVI XVII; the
latter, from I III IV V VI XIII XV XVI XVII II III IV. These two different
patterns of the same underlying letter-groups and the presence of
rubrics for only the first suggest that this was a collection of select
letters which was supplemented by later additions, and that the
former came from an exemplar whose arrangement was close to
V's and the latter from one arranged like L. The letters at the
end probably represent a further addition from the latter exemplar.

The arrangement of letters in P and B involves more than a
reshuffling of the letter-groups, for in both an effort was made
toward a systematic arrangement according to the rank of the
addressee. This was consistently carried through only in B. The
letters to churchmen are placed before those to laymen, and
within each category they are further arranged according to rank
and addressee, the principal exception being the first letter, to
Abbo of Fleury. The scribe was not totally successful. He was
sometimes mistaken as to the addressee (who is frequently identified only by initial), and on other occasions he seems to have
added a letter which he had accidentally overlooked earlier.
Because of this, the relatively few letters to most addressees, and
the fact that he sometimes seems to have been working backwards
through his exemplar, any reconstruction of the underlying collection as B used it is tenuous; however, if one compares the order
of letter-groups from which letters to some addressees were

abstracted, a certain pattern does emerge. Fulbert's letters to Archbishop Leothericus (2–80, the last being written not to Leothericus, but for Leothericus and himself) were taken from I III IX XI XVI XVII VI; those to King Robert (17–125) from III XII XVI XVII VI IV, the next letter (86) from Count Odo to Robert being again from VI; those to (or in one case mentioning) Odilo of Cluny (64–98) from IX XII XVI VI IV; and those to Hildegar (88–118) from VI IV. If these are superimposed, the arrangement of letter-groups which lies behind B appears to have been I III IX XI XII XVI XVII VI IV. The position of the other groups is less certain, and X XIV XV XVIII are not represented at all, though presumably some of their letters should be there if B was using the full collection. On the other hand, the order 11 14 8 16 19 23 suggests that II may have stood in the middle of III, and this appears to have been its original position.

P's copyist also seems to have begun with the idea of grouping by addressee. He first copied Fulbert's obituary material and then his only letter to a pope. He followed this with the letters from XI and XIII concerning the case of Bishop Ralph of Senlis, whom he apparently confused with the Count Ralph who is the subject of the letter to Pope John. The next letters (99–61) are to King Robert and were excerpted from VIII III VI XVI XVII; and these are followed by letters to Archbishop Leothericus (2–43, including 80 as noted above), which were taken from I III VI XVI. After thus gathering Fulbert's letters concerning the pope, the king, and his archbishop, the scribe abandoned his systematic scheme and seems to have copied only what he regarded as the more important letters from the letter-groups at hand: XV IX XII III V VI XVI XVII XIV X. Comparing these three arrangements, we find that I III V VI XVI XVII appear to have stood in the same order as in L and that this includes all the larger letter-groups which were used, II and IV—and of the smaller groups, VII and XVIII—being totally absent. The remaining groups used here (XI XIII VIII XV IX XII XIV X) are all quite short, such as might be found on a scrap of writing material, and one wonders whether these may not have been scattered at random among the longer letter-groups, which would have consisted of bifolia and small gatherings. In this regard, it seems noteworthy that almost all the shorter letter-groups (VII–XV) are found together in L; and of the three exceptions (I V XVIII), I contains Fulbert's earliest letters as bishop and seems to have stood with II and III at the beginning of the underlying collection, while XVIII apparently came at the end. This suggests that VII–XV were collected and inserted as a group in L. Moreover, it is precisely these groups of Fulbert's letters which are missing in V; and if they were once there, they must have preceded the extant portion and thus again would have stood together, if not necessarily in the same order as in L.

The next item in P is Fulbert's earliest extant letter, and this is introduced by an incipit which is all the more striking as it occurs on the verso of a leaf. This is the same incipit and letter with which B begins. However, it appears from the different ways in which P and B copied the list of names in the letter that they derive separately from the original.[30] This suggests that the letter may once have been the first item in the collection and may then have been displaced in favour of the draft of Sigo's *tumulus*. This might also explain why the letter is not found in the other collections; for P comes from Saint-Père, and it was not much later that the letter was copied in the cartulary there and may have been removed from the Fulbert collection for this purpose.

After this come a group of prayers, which are not found in the other manuscripts, and HC. The three letters in XV which were not copied earlier (79 81 83) and the sole letter in VII (119) are interpolated in the latter. The reason why they are placed here is not clear; but from the standpoint of chronology, their position is not unsuitable, and the last is correctly placed as regards both subject-matter and date.[31] This would appear to indicate either that they originally stood here and were later taken out, which seems highly improbable, or else that they were inserted by someone who was sufficiently close to Fulbert to have the necessary detailed knowledge. Yet P's rather slovenly execution and

---

[30] This is also true of the Arabic–Latin astronomical glossary which P copied among the miscellaneous writings after HC and again at the end of the manuscript: their different arrangements point to a separate derivation from the original (see pp. xxvii f.).

[31] If this is the correct chronological order, then HC, VI, and XV (see pp. lxxxi ff.) should be integrated: ... 68 72 73 74 76 77 78 79 69 70 71 95 81 82 83 80 etc. The letters before 71 should then be dated prior to 10 June (instead of 27 July) 1023. Similarly, because of the position of 81, 95 and thus the beginning of Hildegar's vicariate would date from before 27 July. Before 10 June, however, seems early for 74, and the other evidence points to somewhat later in 1023 as the earliest date for Fulbert's acceptance of the treasurership of Saint-Hilaire.

such errors as confusing the two Ralphs or garbling Sigo's name would seem to eliminate the latter possibility, though parenthetically it might be remarked that Hildegar himself was apparently not a professional copyist (cf. 105). All things considered, it seems more likely that the scribe found xv in HC and inserted its letters largely at random, just as he apparently inserted the smaller letter-groups earlier.

HC is followed by the main body of Fulbert's non-epistolary writings and another series of letters. The order in which the latter is arranged does not correspond to any pattern of the letter-groups, but rather to the position of the letters in B. The first eleven letters stand in the same relative order as they do there, where they have been displaced from their original position in the letter-groups as a result of B's systematic rearrangement. Nine of them are from IV (hitherto unrepresented in P), 78 was previously omitted from VI, and 107 is otherwise found only in B. Then follow 120 and 27 (= XVIII); 108, which is found only in P; and 81, which had already been copied from xv in HC. These last four letters and HC are not found in the extant portion of B. Yet it appears that this final series of letters and probably the miscellaneous writings which follow were copied from an exemplar arranged like B, for B itself is apparently of later date and has errors which would preclude its being P's parent. If this is true, then XVIII may have come toward the end of Fulbert's letters in B, as it does in L, and xv might also have been placed here.

A general survey of the variant readings reveals that the usual divergences are between PBV on the one hand and L and its kindred on the other. The latter descend from an exemplar which was emended with a view to style. Both L and C derive separately from it;[32] for though C is marred by many unique variants and errors, it sometimes has the original reading where L does not. DR also derive from the same emended exemplar by way of a common parent whose text was emended still further. Since they sometimes preserve the true reading where L does not, they cannot come from L itself; and though these and similar passages are often indicated in the outer margin of L by a horizontal slash which is apparently in contemporary ink and seems to be a corrector's mark, L's text frequently remains unchanged. The relationship

---

[32] As does 71 in Bibliothèque Nationale, latin 9376, which sides now with L, now with C (see p. xlviii n.).

between these four manuscripts is most clearly seen in Appendix B, no. 2, where the text can be controlled by that in the *Vita Gauzlini*, and where the original readings are preserved now by LC, now by DR, neither pair having a monopoly of the truth. As for the two stages of emendation, though numerous examples may be found in the notes to the present edition, the following may serve by way of illustration.

In 57 *auaritiae* is marked for deletion in L and is omitted in DR. L's original reading in 117 was *eius*, but the last two letters were erased, and DR have *ei*. In 88 L changed the preposition in *cum psalterio* to *et*, but did not at first make the necessary change in the case-ending of the noun. The accusative ending was later superscribed, and it alone is found in DR. In 87 *precursorem antichristi* is rendered *precursorem Christi* in L, *persecutorem Christi* in DR. The omission of the prefix *anti-* distorted the meaning of the sentence, and the second emendator tried to correct it. This same type of emendation is also found in 36, where in place of *extra ciuitatem* LC have *contra ciuitatem* and DR *non contra ciuilitatem*. Further examples may be cited to illustrate the place of C. In 26 C has *respicere* instead of *resipiscere*, as did L before the additional letters were superscribed; and in 132 C has *ambiguis* for *ambiguus*, as again did L before it was corrected. The true reading in 8 is probably *ratiocinationis inuenire possum qui uos ab iugo subiectionis huius absoluat*. Several words seem to have been omitted in the text of LC's exemplar, and the omission was only partly made good. Thus C reads *rationis huius absoluat*; L has *racionacionis huius absoluat* with *qui uos* superscribed after *huius* and *inuenio* added in the margin after *absoluat*; while DR have *ratiocinationis huius qui uos absoluat inuenio*. A similar explanation probably lies behind the variants involving *opus* in 43.

As might be expected from the double pattern of letter-groups in K, the first series of letters belongs to the unemended, the second to the emended, tradition. However, in 123 and 125 K (and F) have some variants belonging to the latter, and in 57 *auaritiae* is marked for deletion as in L. In the second series, K has most, but not all, of DR's variants.

The variant readings are of little help so far as determining the relationship between the different collections, and common variants might always point to the presence of alternative readings on the schedules of the underlying collection which the scribe could choose between, possibly on the basis of the different hands involved. Each of the major collections has its own eccentricities, and none can have been copied from another. But this is precisely what one would expect if, as the different arrangements indicate, each derives independently from the underlying collection. Whether they were copied directly from the latter or from an intermediate parent is hard to say. Although the last series of letters in P was copied from an intermediate manuscript which was also B's parent, the earlier part of P was probably taken from the schedules. Both V and M/H have numerous variants in common; but each has its own eccentricities, and V has some unique errors and lacunae not found in M/H. This might suggest that they derive from a common intermediate parent; yet the position of the interpolated letter in V and perhaps the fullness and nature of its non-epistolary material would argue against it, and their common variants may be due to changes made on the schedules. Similarly, while V, M/H, and the first group of letters in K have some distinctive readings in common with B, these may have been alternative readings on the schedules which were rejected by P and L-family manuscripts. As for LC and DR, if V and M/H represent a later rearrangement, only L can have been copied directly from the underlying collection, and C and DR must descend from intermediate parents. There seem to be three ways in which these might be related:

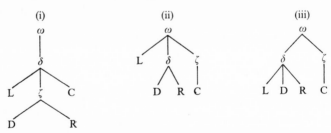

In (i) the first set of emendations would have been made on δ; in (ii) all, in (iii) some of them would have been made directly on the schedules. If they were made on the schedules, it might explain the handful of variants peculiar to C and V and the apparent contamination in KF mentioned above. On the other hand, DR's having the original reading where LC do not is more easily explained in (i) or (ii), for in (iii) it would be necessary to presume that the same alternative readings were found on both ω and δ. Yet the numerous variants found in LDR as opposed to C and the process of emendation as illustrated above are perhaps best explained by (iii), where the second set of emendations would have been made on δ after L had been copied from it. I see no way to decide which is right, and I placed (i) in the stemma earlier merely because it made it easier to grasp their basic relationship.

Although it seems certain that the different collections derive separately from the underlying letter-groups, the order in which they were copied is not clear; and any effort to determine this is hampered by the incompleteness of B and perhaps V and by the uncertainty as to the order of the letter-groups when B and P undertook their systematic rearrangements. Within limitations, it does, however, seem possible to get something of a general picture.

Although the very position of the last series of letters in P and the duplication of material here suggest that it is a later addition, B's identically arranged parent was clearly in existence before this; and in fact, the earliest form of the collection would seem to be represented by the arrangement of letter-groups which apparently lies behind it. The collection began with the letter to Abbo, prefaced by an incipit, and the letter-groups were for the most part arranged in chronological order. This is true of I, III, at least the first letter in IX, XI, again the first letter in XII, XVI, XVII, VI, and IV. II may still have belonged to III, though XV had apparently slipped out of VI. It would appear from the last series of letters in P that the missing part of B may have included XVIII; and if it also had HC, then P likewise suggests that XV may have been placed here. This would mean that only X and XIV, each containing one letter, were apparently missing, but the copyist did not transcribe all the letters even in the groups which he used. The copying of P did not begin until the letter to Abbo had been displaced from its initial position in favour of Sigo's *tumulus*, II had apparently fallen out of III, and the over-all chronology had otherwise been disturbed, primarily by the displacement of VI and presumably IV. L appears to have been copied still later; for it contains neither the letter to Abbo nor the *tumulus*, yet nothing of the Fulbert collection seems to have been lost from the beginning, even though it may have formed the last part of a composite manuscript. As for V and M/H, while their text is perhaps closest to B's, and V's coupling of vi and iv is likewise reminiscent of B, the position of i and iii (with or without ii) at the beginning of BPL and their joining of xvi and xvii make it difficult to see how V and M/H (where i ii iii come in the middle and between xvi and xvii) could have been copied between them. But in any event, the basic collections appear to have been copied within a relatively brief period, and their different transmission vouches for the accuracy of their common text.

Other Manuscripts

The remaining manuscripts contribute virtually nothing toward establishing the text, and most of them contain only select letters chosen for their subject-matter (cf. KF). Nos. 2 3 5 were added in a twelfth-century hand at the end of Bibliothèque Nationale, latin 2281, f. 198ᵛ (from Moissac); but the last letter breaks off in the middle of a line, and the following pages, though ruled, are blank. British Museum, Additional MS. 19835, twelfth-century and containing several works, has the following letters (the last in excerpt) copied in the same hand as the rest of the volume and entitled *Epistolae Fulberti episcopi*: 89 90 91 93 94 2 5 4 10 13 14 8 125 92 (ff. 20ᵛ–26ʳ).[33] British Museum, Royal 5. A. xiii, ff. 180–97ᵛ, twelfth-century, from Worcester Priory, contains 155 4 14 8, Appendix B, nos. 2 f., 125 50 49 80 17 and some of the miscellaneous items, including among them and without identifying it Hildebert, ep. i. 22[34] Hildebert's letter is also found in Lambeth Palace MS. 363, of the late twelfth or early thirteenth century, possibly from Lanthony, containing *Contra Iudeos* iii, one of the *Fulbertus exiguus* letters discussed below, and the following, mostly in excerpt and each introduced by a rubric: 4 7 20 38 123 77 90 88 51 (ff. 101ᵛ–110ᵛ). The penitential ascribed to Fulbert and 123 29 4 14 8 7 11 (incomplete) are found near the end (ff. 148, 157ᵛ–159ᵛ) of a miscellaneous, but distinctive collection of canons and patristic excerpts in Palermo, Archivio Storico della Curia Arcivescovile, MS. 14 (late eleventh or twelfth century).[35] Fulbert's exposition of the feudal oath (51) was often

---

[33] See Dorothy M. Schullian, 'The Excerpts of Heiric "Ex Libris Valerii Maximi Memorabilium Dictorum vel Factorum" ', *Memoirs of the American Academy in Rome*, xii (1935), 156 f. The excerpt beginning on f. 26 (*Paradisus est locus . . .*) is from Isidore, *Etymologiae*, xiv. 3. 2 ff. (= Rabanus, *De universo*, xii. 3 (*PL* cxi. 334)).   [34] *PL* clxxi. 197 ff.

[35] See E. Besta, 'Di una collezione canonistica Palermitana', *Il circolo*

copied separately, and to a lesser degree so was his explanation of
what is portended by a rain of blood (125).[36]

Among the letters usually attributed to Fulbert, *PL* cxli, nos.
112 f., are later compositions which were deliberately ascribed to
him. They are virtually short tracts loaded with scriptural and
patristic quotations, the one against bishops who participate in
warfare, the other against the misuse of the church's treasury and
especially the altar vessels. These letters exist in both a longer
and a shorter version. The longer is found in two manuscripts of
almost identical contents from the later twelfth and early thirteenth
centuries respectively: Valenciennes MS. 482 (from Saint-Amand)
and Saint-Omer MS. 253 (from Saint-Bertin), the second probably copied from the first. Here the two letters are found in a
select group of Fulbert's letters treating of similar matters: 38 88
92 51 125 80. The shorter version is found only in a twelfth-
century fragment bound in Bibliothèque Nationale, nouv. acq.
latin 2243, ff. 50–3ᵛ; however, the first printed editions of the two
letters appear to have been based on another manuscript containing the shorter version.[37] I have dealt elsewhere with these
letters and, on the basis of their composition and manuscript
tradition, the use of terms and ideas associated with the reformed
canonical life which began about the mid eleventh century, and
several interpolations in 92 in the first two manuscripts which
seem to have been taken from an unknown source also used by

---

giuridico, xl (1909), 8 ff.; J. Rambaud-Buhot, 'Un corpus inédit de droit
canonique', *Humanisme actif: Mélanges . . . offerts à Julien Cain*, ii (Paris, 1968),
271 ff., who discusses its relation to M.

[36] The following list of manuscripts containing 51 is mostly based on library
catalogues: Douai MSS. 318, 319, 320; Troyes MS. 964; Bibliothèque Nationale,
latin 2892ᵃ, 3004, 8625, 12315, 16216; Florence, Biblioteca Medicea Laurenz-
iana, Plut. 16. 15; Milan, Biblioteca Ambrosiana, Q. 54. sup., apparently along
with 90 (see A. Paredi, *La biblioteca del Pizolpasso* (Milan, 1961), pp. 133 f.).
It is also cited by the correctors of Gratian (c. 18 C. XXII q. 5) from a manuscript of Beauvais (*Corpus Iuris Canonici*, ed. E. Friedberg (Leipzig, 1879–81),
i. 887 n.). 125 is found separately in Bibliothèque Nationale, latin 4998, and
Avranches MS. 163. London, Congregational Library, MS. I. b. 14, contains
4 (N. R. Ker, *Medieval Manuscripts in British Libraries*, i (Oxford, 1969), 15);
and Cambridge, Corpus Christi College, MS. 299, includes 19 in a collection
of Anselm's letters (see A. Wilmart, *RB* xliii (1931), 53; F. S. Schmitt, ibid.
228). Cf. p. xlviii n.

[37] Respectively, E. Martène and U. Durand, *Thesaurus novus anecdotorum*,
i (Paris, 1717), 130 ff.; L. d'Achery, *Spicilegium*, ii (Paris, 1657), 827 (= 2nd
edn., iii (Paris, 1723), 386 f.).

Philip of Harveng, tried to show that they are probably polemics written in the earlier twelfth century in the general area of north-eastern France (including Belgium) by someone who had a vested interest in the new style of canonical life.[38]

The authenticity of *PL* cxli, nos. 3 and 5, is also quite doubtful. The manuscripts in which they are found may be divided into two classes. The first is represented only by Rouen MS. 1385 (eleventh-century, from Jumièges); the second by a volume of which the remains are now Vatican, Reginensis latin 435, ff. 33–40^v, and 285, f. 31$^{r–v}$ (late eleventh- or early twelfth-century, from Sées, containing only fragments of the letters), Alençon MS. 14 (early twelfth-century, from St. Évroul, in part copied by Orderic Vitalis), British Museum, Royal 6. A. xii (twelfth-century, from Rochester), Lambeth Palace MS. 145 (twelfth-century, from Croyland), British Museum, Royal 5. E. v (twelfth-century, of undetermined provenance), and Lambeth Palace MS. 363, which was discussed earlier and contains an abridged version of the second letter only. Bibliothèque Nationale, latin 2663 (thirteenth-century, from Saint-Sauveur-le-Vicomte in the diocese of Coutances) also apparently belongs to the second class, though the part presumably containing the letters is lost. There was also a lost or unidentified manuscript of the second class at Bury which later passed to Pembroke College, Cambridge, and another at Westminster Abbey.[39] Whether the early printed text was based on Rouen MS. 1385 with corrections from one of the other manuscripts or on another, now lost, manuscript of the first class cannot be determined.

If these two letters are Fulbert's, it is quite surprising that they are not found in any of the major manuscripts of his works, especially when one considers that it was precisely in northern France and England in the later eleventh and twelfth centuries that his writings enjoyed their greatest popularity. Moreover,

[38] 'Two Spurious Letters in the Fulbert Collection', *RB* lxxx (1970), 253 ff. The interpolated version of 92 is also found in Bibliothèque Nationale, latin 2145, ff. 160–1^v, in a later addition to a thirteenth-century manuscript from Saint-Martin of Tournai.

[39] M. R. James, *On the Abbey of S. Edmund at Bury* (Cambridge Antiquarian Society, Octavo Publications, xxviii (1895)), p. 27; id., *A Descriptive Catalogue of the Manuscripts in the Library of Pembroke College, Cambridge* (Cambridge, 1905), pp. xxi–xxii; J. A. Robinson and M. R. James, *The Manuscripts of Westminster Abbey* (Cambridge, 1909), pp. 33, 43, 55.

although Durand of Troarn quotes (*c.* 1053–4) from the second letter and expressly ascribes it to Fulbert of Chartres,[40] in the salutations to the two the author refers to himself only as *Fulbertus exiguus*, a style which is not used in any of Fulbert's authentic letters. The only manuscript in which they are found which has any of Fulbert's own works or otherwise connects the letters with him is Lambeth Palace MS. 363; but in the manuscripts of the second class they are usually accompanied by a dialogue telling of a recent miracle performed by St. Martin of Tours.[41] The dialogue was written sometime after 1022 by Hugh, archdeacon of Tours, and dedicated to his friend Fulbert. Hugh and Fulbert are the speakers, and Hugh addresses him as an equal and even chides him for his reputed lack of confidence in St. Martin. This could hardly be Fulbert of Chartres, who was a well-known bishop; and if the letters and the dialogue belong together, then the Fulbert of the dialogue may be *Fulbertus exiguus*. In any event, the two letters do not form part of the present collection, and I intend to return to them later.

Several medieval library catalogues mention manuscripts containing Fulbert's letters.[42] The only ones which can be identified are those of Chartres (P), Durham (D), Lincoln (C), and probably Bec (R). The others are as follows: Saint-Aubin d'Angers MS. 74 (twelfth-century), *Epistole Fulberti, i vol.*; Cluny MS. 290 (twelfth-century), *Volumen in quo continentur epistole domni Fulberti, et aliud ipsius de versibus, rhytmis, hymnis, prosa et cantu;* Rolduc MS. 74 (late twelfth- or early thirteenth-century), *Epistole Fulberti episcopi*; Glastonbury (1247–8), *Epistolae Fulberti episcopi, & quorundam aliorum. bon.*; Bayeux MS. 65 (1436), . . . *epistolas Fulberti episcopi . . .* ; St. Augustine's, Canterbury, MS. 945 (late fifteenth-century), *Epistole Fulberti . . .* ; and the Lanthony volume

---

[40] *Liber de corpore et sanguine Christi*, c. xx (*PL* cxlix. 1405 f.). For the date see R. Heurtevent, *Durand de Troarn et les origines de l'hérésie bérengarienne* (Paris, 1912), p. 103. A similar reference was once seen in Peter Damian, sermon lxix (*PL* cxliv. 900, 903); but it has since been shown that this is to Ivo of Chartres, sermon iv (*PL* clxii. 527 ff.), and that Damian's sermon actually belongs to Nicholas of Clairvaux (see J. Leclercq, *Recueil d'études sur saint Bernard et ses écrits*, i (Rome, 1962), 64 n.).

[41] Printed in J. Mabillon, *Vetera analecta* (2nd edn., Paris, 1723), 213 ff. Cf. *Hist. litt. de la France*, vii (1746), 231 f.

[42] The present list is based on M. Manitius, 'Geschichtliches aus mittel-alterlichen Bibliothekskatalogen', *Neues Archiv*, xxxii (1907), 695, which I have verified and supplemented.

discussed earlier.[43] William of Malmesbury also refers to a volume of Fulbert's letters.[44] Some of them may be hidden among the extant manuscripts, but further identification has not been possible.

Editions

The first edition of Fulbert's letters was prepared by Papire Masson and published in Paris in 1585 by Denis Du Pré.[45] It was Masson's first editorial venture, and for the most part he merely transcribed B. But unless B was more complete than it is now, he must also have used another manuscript; for he printed all of 100, which is incomplete in B, and included 109 and 115, which are not found there at all. He may have taken them from the sixteenth-century copy of R, which has notes in Masson's hand and which may have been more complete before it was bound with B. He did not, however, otherwise use this second manuscript.

A new edition was produced by Charles de Villiers and published in Paris by Thomas Baluze in 1608. It included 124 letters (with the two of *Fulbertus exiguus*), the *Contra Iudeos*, sermons, and *opuscula*, and was based on PLB.[46] It was reprinted in the *Magna Bibliotheca Patrum*, xi (Cologne, 1618), and iii (Paris, 1654), and in the *Maxima Bibliotheca Patrum*, xviii (Lyons, 1677).

André Du Chesne published another, but less complete, edition of Fulbert's letters based on L or R in his *Historiae Francorum*

---

[43] Saint-Aubin: L. W. Jones, 'The Library of St. Aubin's at Angers in the Twelfth Century', *Classical and Mediaeval Studies in Honor of Edward Kennard Rand* (New York, 1938), p. 152. Cluny: Delisle, op. cit. ii. 469. Rolduc: P. J. M. van Gils, 'Eenige opmerkingen over de middeleeuwsche boekenlijst der Abdij Rolduc', *Handelingen van het vijfde Nederlandsche Philologencongres* (1907), p. 151. Glastonbury: T. W. Williams, *Somerset Mediaeval Libraries* (Bristol, 1897), p. 67. A memorandum by John Leland, who visited Glastonbury shortly before it was dissolved, also mentions a *Liber epistolarum Fulberti* which is coupled with *Epistolae Lanfranci* (ibid., p. 83). Bayeux: *Cat. dépt.*, x. 278. Canterbury: M. R. James, *The Ancient Libraries of Canterbury and Dover* (Cambridge, 1903), p. 298. Lanthony: see p. xlix.

[44] William of Malmesbury, ii. 186 (ed. Stubbs, i. 226).

[45] *Fulberti Carnutum Episcopi liber epistolarum* . . . The following discussion is based on Pfister, *Fulbert*, pp. 16 ff., which I have verified where possible. Cf. P. Ronzy, *Un humaniste italianisant: Papire Masson (1544–1611)* (Paris, 1924), pp. 326 ff.

[46] D. *Fulberti Carnotensis episcopi antiquissimi opera varia. Ex M.S. cod. biblioth. reg. colleg. Navarrae et clarissim. virorum D. Petavii Senat. Reg. et N. Fabri, quae tam ad refutandas hereses hujus temporis quam ad Gallorum Hist. pertinent* . . . Since it includes the life of St. Pantaleon, the Petau manuscript was apparently L rather than R.

Scriptores, iv (1641). A new edition using P appeared in *RHF* x (1760, repr. 1874); however, it included only some of Fulbert's letters (partly in excerpt) and none of his other works. Hence the text in current use is that in *PL* cxli, which is primarily based on the edition of 1608, but includes material from other printed sources. As usual, the principal virtues of the *PL* edition are its completeness and accessibility. At one time Alexandre Clerval apparently considered preparing a new edition, but did not actually do so.[47] All previous editions have thus been based on PBL and possibly R, though Cardinal Baronius made some use of V in his *Annales Ecclesiastici*.[48]

The Present Edition

For the present edition I have personally collated all known manuscripts of the collection and most of the excerpts from it in other manuscripts, though in establishing the text I have limited myself to the manuscripts listed on p. ix. My collations were essentially made from photocopies, but I have examined most of the principal manuscripts and checked some details. Although the oldest manuscripts were copied within a few decades after Fulbert's death, none of them has any special authority, and the choice of a basic manuscript is limited. The collection is relatively complete only in P and LDR. But P was rather carelessly copied, and the number of its variants and obvious errors is unusually large. Hence I have turned to L as the oldest representative of its family, even though its text has been emended, and its first pages are to a large degree illegible. L is a beautifully written manuscript and was copied and corrected with care. Where possible, I have used it as the basic manuscript and departed from its text only where it was obviously erroneous or appeared to have been emended for stylistic or other reasons. (It should be noted that where P is the only manuscript not belonging to the L-family it is sometimes difficult to determine which has the original reading.) As for the pages which are illegible, I have continued to use L as the base where only a few words were involved and there seemed little chance of error. Otherwise, I have turned to D, not only

---

[47] See L. Duchesne's letter in P. Bizeau and E. Jeauneau, 'Bibliographie du Chanoine Alexandre Clerval (1859–1918)', *Bulletin de la Soc. arch. d'Eure-et-Loir: Documents*, iv (1964), appendix i.

[48] Ed. A. Theiner, xvi (Bar-le-Duc, 1869), 422 ff. and *passim*.

because it represents the same family and its text is the closest to L's, but also because some of these letters are not found in P. Even here L has been used as one of the supporting manuscripts where it was possible to verify most of the text and all cited variants, for otherwise it would not be clear which readings were peculiar to DR. Where it was not possible to do even this, L's symbol and such evidence as it offers concerning the variants have been placed in parentheses. For letters which are found only in P and B, P has been used as the basic manuscript.

The manuscripts used for each letter and poem are listed at the head of the apparatus: the basic manuscript is cited first, and the others are arranged by family. The number of variants is often rather large, and a full apparatus would be somewhat impractical, if not confusing. Hence only such variants have been noted as seem significant for establishing the text and the relationship of the manuscripts, though I have tried to include all that might offer any real information. Those which appear in a single manuscript have been noted only for the basic manuscript, a manuscript which is the only representative of an entire class (especially P, and sometimes C as opposed to LDR), or where the text is otherwise questionable, but even here I have omitted those that seemed without significance. Scribal corrections in the same hand, even for the basic manuscript, have not been noted unless there was a particular reason to do so, and a fair number of scribal eccentricities have been tacitly suppressed in both text and apparatus. Minor variants in word order have only been noted where they involve the basic manuscript, and orthographical variants (including *dominus/domnus*) have not been noted at all. As for *uale/ualete*, I have followed the style of address used in the body of the letter and again noted variants only where the basic manuscript was in question.

I have followed the spelling of the basic manuscript except where it was misleading or an obvious scribal slip. Abbreviations, including highly abbreviated scriptural quotations, have been tacitly expanded in accordance with the scribe's usual spelling; and *ę* has been rendered *ae* or occasionally *oe* where the word or a cognate was so spelt elsewhere in the manuscript. The spelling of each variant is that found in the first manuscript cited after it; but where such readings have been taken up into the text, their spelling has been brought into line with that of the basic manuscript. Of the various words which are sometimes joined in the manuscripts and sometimes not, I have retained only *siquis* and similar compounds, where the manuscripts are consistent. For the most part the orthography of the manuscripts is quite in keeping with medieval practice, but L in particular has some peculiarities. It normally spells out *mihi* and *nihil*. Dissimilation is frequent in words composed of a prefix added to a base (e.g. *adquiesco, inprouiso, comuentus*) and is on occasion carried to the point of such analogical re-formations as *cumformis*. L sometimes simplifies a double consonant (e.g. *miti* for *mitti*) and less frequently doubles a single one (e.g. *comittor, deffuit*). Most of these, especially where they might cause confusion, have again been tacitly suppressed, including proper names (e.g. *Guillemus*, though I have retained *Leuthericus* in the Latin as being an attested variant of the more common *Leothericus*).

As regards punctuation, I have tried to follow the consensus of the manuscripts, though I have used modern punctuation marks. On the whole the manuscripts are fairly consistent, at least as regards the more important stops. In comparison with the others, however, L and V tend to punctuate too much, and P to punctuate too little, though the last may be another reflection of scribal inattention. I have departed from the manuscript punctuation only after careful consideration in each case, but I have regularly done so to set off vocatives and parenthetical expressions, and I have ignored stops which might confuse the reader by breaking up a sentence or a clause or separating phrases which logically belong together. It should be noted that it is not always clear whether a mark is intended as a stop or not, especially where an abbreviation is involved, and punctuation marks are not infrequently omitted at the end of a line.

So far as possible I have tried to identify the quotations and allusions, but I cannot hope to have found all, and it is sometimes hard to tell whether the writer is making an allusion or not, especially where the Scriptures and certain standard authors are concerned. Biblical references are to the Vulgate, and the translations are from the Douai Bible with a few small changes. References to conciliar decrees are to the Latin version associated with Pseudo-Isidore. It has not always been possible to identify the persons and places which are mentioned with any assurance, but I have tried to choose the most likely in each case. Biographical details are usually given on the first occasion a person is mentioned and are not repeated thereafter. To discuss all points where there is disagreement among scholars would lengthen the notes unduly, and for the most part I have set forth what I regard as the correct argument and referred the reader elsewhere for further discussion. The arrangement of the letters is discussed in the following chapter, and the poems are arranged as follows: personal (132–6), moral instruction (137–45), elements of the *quadrivium* (146–8), the peace movement (149), and *rithmi* (150–5).

III. *Arrangement and Dating of the Letters*

The letters in the Fulbert collection, as in most medieval letter collections, are not dated. In determining when they were written we must rely on references to persons and events known from other sources and on such internal evidence as will allow related letters to be arranged as nearly as possible in chronological order. Yet the evidence which has survived from early eleventh-century France is not especially helpful in this regard. Though we sometimes have a few dates for the career of an important noble or churchman, there are others of as much or only slightly less importance for whom we have almost none; and even for the former all we can sometimes establish is that they were in office by a particular date when a reference is made to them or their name appears in a charter and that after a later date they are no longer found or their successor has appeared. Nor are the necrologies of much help here, for though they specify the days on which the deceased were to be commemorated, it is not always possible to identify the names with certainty, and the year is almost never given. If we further consider that even when the year is stated in a source the way in which it was reckoned varied from place to place, that even an apparently authentic document may (especially in cartularies) contain interpolations, and that entries in chronicles may have been added sometime after the event, not to mention possible literary borrowings, then precise dating seems almost hopeless.

Fortunately some help is offered as regards the present collection by the underlying letter-groups, at least where they can be shown to have some chronological unity; and for the letters from 1022 on, there is also the Hildegar collection. But at best there remains a fair margin of error; and the dating of a letter or group of letters will often be found to rest not on any explicit evidence, but on a number of inferences which appear quite tenuous if taken separately, but which point in the same direction.

In arranging the letters I have followed a few basic principles. I have in general attempted to place them in chronological order, but I have sometimes departed from this in order to bring together those concerning the same event. In practice this will be found to have resulted in relatively minor displacements, but it does explain what might otherwise seem to be a discrepancy between the number assigned to a letter and the date given it. I have also tried to keep the letters in a letter-group as close together as possible; but where there was a conflict between the position of a letter there and the other evidence as to its date, I have given preference to the latter. In the absence of other criteria, I have arranged and dated the letters by their position in a given group; and where even this was wanting, I have inserted them where they seemed to fit best by reason of their subject-matter or general tone, and where they would cause as little disturbance as possible in the over-all arrangement. I have indicated for each letter the date which seems to me the most probable or else the outside limits.

In the following discussion I should like to set forth the criteria on which I arranged and dated the letters and, at the same time, to examine the composition of the letter-groups. As before, references to the letters are in Arabic, to the letter-groups in Roman numerals; and the Hildegar collection is cited as HC. Where no reference is given to the source for a statement concerning a letter, see the letter itself or, where several letters are involved, the first of them.

The only letter to survive from the years before Fulbert became bishop is 1. Abbot Gisbertus' death is commemorated in the cathedral necrology on 15 January,[1] and Fulbert states that Magenardus was installed as abbot on 2 February. The year of Gisbertus' death is unknown: his last act is dated in the fifth year of King Robert's reign.[2] If this was calculated from the death of Hugh Capet, it would begin on 24 October 1000, but it may have been reckoned more generally from the beginning of the year.[3] Fulbert refers to Count Thibault as bishop-designate, i.e. he had

[1] Merlet, p. 152.   [2] *Cart. S.-Père*, i. 91.   [3] See Newman, p. xxix.

been nominated by King Robert, but not yet consecrated; and he is probably to be identified with the Thibault who is commemorated as *clericus, comes Carnotensium* on 11 July in the necrology of Saint-Père.[4] His predecessor, Bishop Odo, died on 25 August, presumably in the preceding year.[5] According to *Cart. S.-Père*, i. 103 f., Count Thibault died before the affair was settled while returning from a pilgrimage to Rome; King Robert then had the dean Ralph (also mentioned in Fulbert's letter) made bishop, and Ralph removed Magenardus from office and forced him to live in his own household until he was satisfied that he would make a suitable abbot.[6] Thibault was presumably alive in April 1004, when Pope John XVIII confirmed a charter in which he is mentioned,[7] and this may have been on the occasion of his pilgrimage to Rome. The addressee of Fulbert's letter, Abbo of Fleury, was killed on 13 November 1004.[8] Hence it would seem that Thibault's death can be dated 11 July and Fulbert's letter between 2 February and 11 July 1004.

The first years of Fulbert's pontificate are represented by three letter-groups:

   I. 2 3 5 4
   II. 10 13 14 8 15 16
   III. 6 7 9 11 12 17 18 19 20 21 22 23 38 36

I is a compact group. In 3 Fulbert informs Leothericus of the results of a message mentioned in 2, and 4 was apparently written in answer to a further question concerning the simoniac priest of 2. The opening statement in 2 suggests a date not long after Fulbert's consecration. I would seem to be earlier than II–III and can probably be dated late 1006–early 1008 (cf. the reference to February in 12 in III).

The relationship between 10 and 8 in II and 7 and 9 in III and the fact that 22 in III is later than 13 in II (since Thierry's predecessor, Fulk, witnessed the charter at Chelles) indicate that II

---

[4] See R. Merlet, *Procès-Verbaux de la Soc. arch. d'Eure-et-Loir*, ix (1898), 87 ff.; A. Longnon, *Obituaires de la province de Sens*, ii (ed. A. Molinier, Paris, 1906), pp. viii, 192.   [5] Merlet, p. 174.

[6] Magenardus died 30 March (Merlet, p. 158). The year is not known, but it was probably *c.* 1012 (cf. Pfister, *Fulbert*, pp. 71 f., though the year when his successor, Arnulf, died is not as certain as he would make it (cf. p. xliii n.)).

[7] Zimmermann, no. 991.

[8] E. Sackur, *Die Cluniacenser*, i (Halle, 1892), 297.

may have formed part of III. This is apparently confirmed by the arrangement of B (see p. liv), which suggests that II once stood somewhere between II and 19. In 12, which is the next letter after 11 in III, Fulbert refers to the coming 17 February, and the letter must have been written sometime earlier.[9] Since this would accord with the date of 9 discussed below, I have inserted II immediately after it. But if II should precede it, then the reference to Christmas in 16 would mean that 12 should be dated in the following year and 6 7 9 11 should be dated before Easter (28 March) instead of before 17 February 1008.

The crucial letter for the over-all dating is 13, where Fulbert refers to what appears to have been a council held at Pentecost and attended by the king, clergy, and nobles. The only known council to which this could refer was held at Chelles (Seine-et-Marne, *arr.* Meaux) at Pentecost, 16 May 1008. The only extant record of this council is a royal charter dated 17 May (Appendix C, no. 1). The year is not specified, but would seem to be 1008.[10]

9 and 10 apparently go together, and 9 would seem to be the earlier. Since they were written after Fulbert became bishop, the approaching Easter in 10 can only be that of 1007 or 1008, probably the latter (28 March) in view of the apparent date of 13 and the protracted negotiations which would presumably have preceded Fulbert's threatening his subvassals with excommunication.

Several difficulties are offered by 7 and 8, which form a similar pair, the one referring to an approaching episcopal synod, the other to an excommunication apparently pronounced there. The controversy with which they are concerned arose as a result of Bishop Fulk of Orleans's attempt to assert his episcopal jurisdiction over the monastery of Fleury. In 996–7 Abbot Abbo of Fleury had obtained a grant of exemption from Pope Gregory V which prohibited any archbishop, bishop, or clerk from entering the monastery or exercising his priestly office there without the abbot's permission.[11] Shortly before the feast of St. Benedict, Fulk came to Fleury, but was driven away. The matter was

---

[9] Although Pfister, *Fulbert*, p. 79, identified the addressee of 12 as Azelinus of Paris, its position here is against this, and the meeting-place which Fulbert proposes is in the opposite direction. If Avesgaudus is the correct addressee, the identity of Haimo seems almost certain.

[10] See Newman, pp. 39 n.–40 n., in part resting on Fulbert's letter, though additional support is furnished by the date of the consecration of Beaulieu discussed below. [11] Zimmermann, no. 777.

brought to the attention of a council (apparently that mentioned by Fulbert) attended among others by King Robert, Archbishop Leothericus, and the papal legate, Peter of Piperno; and when Abbo's successor, Abbot Gauzlin (1005–8 March 1030),[12] produced the papal charter, his opponents threatened to burn it. The legate returned to Rome and reported to Pope John XVIII, who called on Robert to uphold the papal privilege and summoned Leothericus, Fulk, and Gauzlin to appear at Rome the following Easter.[13] The outcome of the case is not known.

T. Schieffer[14] and following him Zimmermann, nos. 1026–30, would make the feast that of 11 July 1007 (Schieffer notes that this would accord with Fulbert's giving Gauzlin until 1 October to submit) and have the papal summons issued for Easter 1008. The papal legate was apparently in France in 1007; for he is said to have consecrated Count Fulk of Anjou's church at Beaulieu (Indre-et-Loire, *arr.* Loches) in May, and this can hardly have been May 1008, when Fulk was threatened with excommunication for the murder of Hugh of Beauvais (13).[15] However, the date of the legate's return is not known; and *sollemnitas* could apparently be used for any of the feasts of St. Benedict: 21 March, 11 July, or 4 December.[16] If the position of the letters in II is correct (cf. the reference in 10 to Easter, 13 to Pentecost, 8 to 1 October, and 16 to Christmas), 8 is later than 13 and was written after 16 May 1008; and if III's chronology is also correct and if 9 was at least written about the same time as 10 (i.e. before Easter, and from 9's position in III probably before 17 February), the same date should hold for 7. This would mean that the case was left over

---

[12] See Newman, p. 99 n.

[13] *Vita Gauzlini*, c. xviii (ed. Bautier–Labory, pp. 50 ff.). Although in c. xix (pp. 58 ff.) Gauzlin's journey to Rome is connected with this incident, it was obviously later, for he is said to have received the pallium from Benedict VIII (21 May 1012–9 April 1024 (Zimmermann, nos. 1075, 1276)) at that time, and it is otherwise known that his election to the archbishopric of Bourges followed that of Fulk's successor, Thierry (see 26 and *Vita Gauzlini*, pp. 22 f.). As regards the importance of this controversy in the development of monastic exemption, see J.-F. Lemarignier, 'L'exemption monastique et les origines de la réforme grégorienne', *A Cluny, congrès scientifique* (Dijon, 1950), pp. 311, 323 f.

[14] *Die päpstlichen Legaten in Frankreich* (Berlin, 1935), pp. 46 f.

[15] Cf. Halphen, p. 85.

[16] See E. Pellegrin, 'Notes sur quelques recueils de vies de saints utilisés pour la liturgie à Fleury-sur-Loire au XIe siècle', *Bulletin d'information de l'Institut de recherche et d'histoire des textes*, xii (1963), 24 ff.; A. Vidier, *L'historiographie à Saint-Benoît-sur-Loire* (Paris, 1965), pp. 175 n., 254.

from the preceding year; for the only possible feast in 1008 would be that of 21 March, and this must be ruled out, since it would not allow sufficient time for 7 to have been written before Easter (28 March), even if the feast of St. Benedict had been moved because 21 March was Palm Sunday. Thus it would seem that 7 9 10 date from at least before Easter and 13 and 8 after Pentecost 1008. This would mean that the papal summonses (if the letters in the *Vita Gauzlini* are authentic) were for Easter 1009, the last possible year as Pope John died about the end of June (see 5).

The remaining letters in II–III have been dated by their position there, which would suggest that 6 was written before 17 February and 14 between 16 May and 1 October. 15 and 16 can only be dated as after 8, though the period hitherto covered by II suggests that the approaching Christmas in 16 is that of 1008. The only reason for assuming, as Pfister does,[17] that 21 concerns Franco's consecration is the reference to Paris; but its position here would mean that it could not be Franco or his predecessor, Azelinus. Moreover, it is not clear from Fulbert's letter that an episcopal consecration did take place; and he was possibly summoned to discuss the bishopric of Orleans, though it appears from 22 that Thierry was consecrated in his own cathedral.

Precisely when Thierry became bishop of Orleans is not known. His predecessor, Bishop Fulk, was still alive 16 May 1008, when he attended the council at Chelles (see p. lxxi) and, if the dating of his controversy with Fleury is correct, even later. On the other hand, Thierry's consecration preceded Gauzlin's in 1012–13 (see 26). The position of 22 and 23 would indicate that they were written toward late 1008 at the earliest, but given the relatively brief period covered so far by II–III, they were probably not much later. Yet 36, the last letter in III, is demonstrably later. It may have been added by itself or perhaps have been on a separate leaf with 38 on the other side (they are almost the same length); but it would also be possible for any of the last letters in III to be later additions.

24 and 25 have no clues as to date, though the opening statement in 24 suggests that it was written in the first years Fulbert was bishop; and if so, it may have been to Fulk of Orleans. The addressee of 25, despite his title, has not been identified, but he might be the Hugh who was later archdeacon of Tours and author

---

[17] *Fulbert*, p. 80.

of the dialogue associated with the *Fulbertus exiguus* letters (see p. lxiii). These are the only letters in X and XIV respectively, and so the latter cannot help date them.

Only three letters can definitely be assigned to the decade between 1008–9 and 1018–19, but their dates are relatively certain: 26 (from IX), 1012–14; 27 (from XVIII), about April 1015; and 28 (from XVI), 9 June 1017–12 May 1018. The letter-groups are again of no help. IX and XVIII contain only one other letter (64 and 120 respectively); and the first is probably, and the second certainly much later than the letters here. 28 was apparently on a leaf with 34 which was inserted into XVI (see p. lii).

29–36 concern the murder of Evrardus, subdean of Chartres, by Bishop Ralph of Senlis and his family. Evrardus' death is entered in the necrology on 21 February.[18] Both Fulbert and Ralph witnessed Appendix C, no. 6, on 9 June 1017, and Pfister argues from this that the crime must have been committed later.[19] Tenuous as this is, it does accord with the other evidence, which points to 1018–19 and probably the latter, though the case may have continued into a second year. It appears from 34 that the murder had been committed and that Ralph was still alive and had not cleared himself at the time Deodatus was chosen to succeed Bishop Fulk of Soissons (d. 6 August 1019). It also seems from Fulbert's reference in 35 to the necessity of settling a matter left over from Ralph's pontificate, from the absence of any reference to him as alive in 36, and from an entry for him in an apparently contemporary list of bishops in a sacramentary from Senlis (*Rodulphus, cui Deus misereatur*),[20] that the case was still pending when Ralph died. In 36 Fulbert states that he waited six months after summoning Ralph's brother Guido before he excommunicated him, and the letter was probably written soon after this; and in 35 to Ralph's successor, also named Guido, though there is no reason to identify him with Ralph's brother, he expresses concern over his consecration and refers to the approaching 18 November. 35 can be dated after 6 August 1019, when Ralph was still alive, and, if the entry cited in note 20 is

[18] Merlet, p. 155.   [19] *Fulbert*, p. 85 n.

[20] L. Delisle, 'Mémoire sur d'anciens sacramentaires', *Mémoires de l'Académie des inscriptions et belles-lettres*, xxii (1886), 145, 371, from Bibliothèque Sainte-Geneviève, BB 20 (=111). *GC* x. 1390 f. also mentions this entry and one for Ralph in a necrology under 5 September. There is some question about the latter, but the date is not inconsistent with the other evidence.

correct, after 5 September, and before 5 March–9 June 1021, when Guido witnessed a charter as bishop of Senlis.[21] The reference to 18 November would further narrow it to 1019–20. As for the letter-groups, XI (29 30) and XIII (31 37 32 33) appear to be in chronological order. As was seen earlier, 34 was apparently on an interpolated leaf in XVI, and 36 seems to have been attached to the end of III. 35 is the first letter in XII, the others (62 f.) are apparently later (see pp. lxxvi f.). I do not see why Cnut is entitled only king of Denmark in 37, for by the earliest possible date he was also king of England (1016–35). The Anglo-Saxon Chronicle, however, reports that he spent the winter of 1019–20 in Denmark; and if 37 were written then, the arrangement of XIII would indicate that Ralph was still alive and that his death and Guido's election should be dated 1020. 37 and 38 are dated on the basis of their position in XIII and III respectively (see p. lxxiii).

The letters concerning Abbot Odilo of Cluny in the later part of the collection present several problems. With the exception of Odilo's letter to Fulbert (50), which probably derives from the receiver's copy, his name is found in full only in the address to 63 and the body of 43 and 64, neither of which was written to him. The addressee of 49 85 98 is indicated only by his initial. The style of address compares as follows:

49 *Prudenter humili et preclare magnifico patri O. F. suus, ut ait.*

63 *Venerabili patri suo Odiloni F. sacerdos . . .*

85 *Sanctissimo atque dilectissimo patri O. F. humilis sacerdos . . .*

98 *F. indignus episcopus ineffabiliter caro patri et domino suo O. cum cherubin et seraphin odas loqui.*

In the first three the arrangement of addressee and sender is parallel. Though Fulbert otherwise uses *pater* in his letters, it seems noteworthy that it appears in all four addresses here and that in 43 he refers to Odilo as *patrem nostrum*. Moreover, the gnomic greeting in 98 might be compared to 64's *illo sancto monachorum archangelo Odilone* and *nostrum archangelum*.

In 49 Fulbert thanks O. for a warm reception and for the concern he has shown over his health. In 64 Fulbert assures the monk O. that he is in good health (hence he had apparently been ill), ays that he had not written earlier as he had intended to visit

[21] Newman, no. 55.

him, and asks him to convey his greetings to Odilo. In 85 he
states that he has had to change his plans to visit the addressee,
and in 98 (where MS. V has *O.* expanded to *Odiloni* in the salutation) he says that he would like to visit him, but is held back by
local disturbances. In 63, where Odilo is expressly named, Fulbert
says that he has wanted to visit him for a long time and that he
still does, but that he is prevented from doing so by difficulties
in the area; however, he hopes that some day he can visit him and
ask his advice as regards his salvation. The last may be compared
with 49, where Fulbert tells O. that he has resolved to follow his
counsel in all matters. Fulbert is unusually effusive in these letters
and in the references to Odilo, and the absence of this in 85 might
be explained by its brevity and the haste with which it was probably written and dispatched. Except for the letters discussed here,
Fulbert's only correspondent whose name begins with O is
Odolricus of Orleans; and the style of address and the general
tone of his letters to him are quite different. This is all the
evidence; but on the whole it seems sufficient to identify the
addressee of 49, 98, and probably 85 as the abbot of Cluny.

The dating of these letters is also uncertain. 49 and 85 can
be approximately dated from their position within XVI and VI
respectively, and 98 (from IV) by its relation to 99 ff. The letter-
groups are less helpful for dating 63 and 64. 64 is the second of two
letters in IX, the other (26) having been written 1012–14. 63 is
the third of three letters in XII, the first of which (35) has already
been dated *c.* 1019–20. In the second letter in XII (62), Fulbert
informs King Robert that he has received the message which he
sent by Ralph, *economus* of Sainte-Croix of Orleans,[22] and that he
is again postponing his journey. He would like to confer with
Robert, but he cannot come himself, since it is not safe for him
to travel unarmed, and he is prohibited from bearing arms by his
office and the sacred season (probably Lent). It would seem that
62 and 63 were written about the same time, that Fulbert had
planned to visit both Robert and Odilo, and that he was held back
by local disturbances. If IX and XII are compact chronological
letter-groups, 64 should be dated *c.* 1012–14 and 63, *c.* 1019–20.

---

[22] Ralph otherwise figures in the collection *c.* 1026–7 (123). His dates as
economus are unknown. He is possibly the Ralph who helped Odolricus earlier
and for whom Fulbert apparently felt some concern (23). If so, he may have
been appointed by Odolricus himself after he became bishop in 1021 (cf. 42).

However, the salutation and opening statement in 49 and Fulbert's closing plea for Odilo's support suggest that this was the beginning of their correspondence, and so the three letters would be later than the others in their letter-groups (cf. XVIII and 34 and 28 in XVI). Although in his later letters Fulbert on several occasions mentions unrest in the area and his own ill health (cf. 81 99 ff. 124), and although he was still hoping to visit Odilo as late as *c.* early 1025 (98), his assuring O. in 64 that he has recovered from his illness and his praise for what Odilo has done for him are reminiscent of 49. As for hostilities in the area, cf. 55 59 60 (1021–2) and 85 93 (1023–4). In the absence of more precise details, I have dated the three letters 1021 or later and inserted them in the break between XVII and HC. As for Odilo's letter to Fulbert (50), it does not appear to have been his reply to Fulbert's first letter as Fulbert expressly states that Odilo had called him *suus*, but it may have been that to 49; and so I have placed it after the latter and dated it 1021 or later.

The year *c.* 1021 is represented by three letter-groups:

V. 40 39
XVI. 42 41 34 28 44 47 45 49 51 43
XVII. 52 54 55 53 46 56 57 58 59 60 61

That these belong together may be seen by comparing 40 and 41, where Fulbert explains to the bishop of Orleans and then to the king why his clerks cannot make a procession; 44 45 46, concerning Galeran and apparently in chronological order; 47 56 58, in which Ebalus of Rheims figures before, at the time when, and after he became archbishop; 45 53, which refer to mid-Lent and 29 June respectively; and 42 43 56, which can be dated in the first half of 1021. In 40 51 59 Fulbert mentions the recent fire at Chartres (7–8 September 1020) and alludes to it in 41. That there is an over-all chronological unity would seem to be indicated for XVI by 42 and 43 concerning Odolricus' ordination and consecration respectively and by 44 and 45 concerning Galeran, and for XVII by 56 and 58 involving Ebalus of Rheims and by 52 53 61, which have to do with the bishopric of Meaux. The only certain chronological irregularity concerns 34 and 28 in XVI (see pp. lii, lxxiv).

In 40 Fulbert writes to Bishop Thierry of Orleans that it will not be possible to make the usual procession because of the recent fire and in 41 he again explains this to King Robert. In 42, which stands between these two letters, Fulbert justifies his action in ordaining Odolricus, bishop-elect of Orleans, to the priesthood, and he later participated in his episcopal consecration (43). Fulbert was obviously one of Odolricus' chief supporters as he had been earlier (cf. 22), and it hardly seems possible that Robert's intervention was prompted by him. It may be that 42 and 41 are reversed or that Robert had intervened at Thierry's request and that Odolricus had in the meantime been chosen bishop. But though XVI and XVII belong together and the chronological unity of XVII seems assured, the only possible addressee for 54 in the latter appears to be Thierry. His last known act is from January 1021, and he died on 27 January, while Odolricus first appears as bishop 5 March–9 June 1021; and so Thierry's death has been placed in 1021.[23] According to the life of Thierry in *AASS*, Jan. iii. 404 f., after he became bishop, he and Odolricus were reconciled, and he placed Odolricus next to himself in authority so that he might become his successor.[24] It further says that Thierry frequented the monastery of Saint-Pierre-le-Vif at Sens and died on a pilgrimage to Rome. A slightly different version is found in another life of Thierry and in the chronicle of Clarius.[25] As sources they are not altogether satisfactory, and they are apparently related. They state that after the heretics were condemned at Orleans (December 1022), Thierry left his bishopric and withdrew to Saint-Pierre and died on a pilgrimage to Rome. Odolricus was definitely bishop of Orleans before this, and his name is again found among the witnesses to a charter issued shortly after the heretics were tried.[26] Yet these accounts seem to preserve an authentic tradition as regards Thierry's arranging for Odolricus to succeed him and retiring from his bishopric, and this would accord with the way the letters are arranged in the groups here.

39 was presumably occasioned by Bishop Roger of Lisieux's first attempt since the grant of 1014 to collect the dues owed at a

---

[23] Newman, no. 55 and pp. 69 n., 79 n. Cf. Coolidge, p. 85.

[24] An *Udulricus in re honorabilis sacerdos, in spe episcopus venerabilis* is mentioned in the acts of a council held at Verdun-sur-le-Doubs (C. J. Hefele, *Histoire des conciles*, ed. H. Leclercq, iv, ii (Paris, 1911), 1410; Hoffmann, p. 51). If this is Odolricus of Orleans, the council can be dated early 1021. Odolricus died after November 1035 (*GC* viii. 1437).

[25] The former is printed in J. Mabillon, *Acta Sanctorum ordinis sancti Benedicti*, vi, i (Paris, 1701), 196; the latter in Duru, ii. 502.

[26] Newman, no. 58.

diocesan synod, though there seems to be no other evidence for a synod at this time. As was seen earlier, where a group contains only two letters, it is possible for their order to be reversed, and this may be the case here. Hence the outside dates can only be given as 1014–22 (cf. 66).

XVI and XVII are so interrelated that they must be considered together. According to the charter evidence (which is the same for both), Odolricus was bishop of Orleans by, and Ebalus became archbishop of Rheims between, 5 March and 9 June 1021 (see p. lxxviii); however, the position of 43 in XVI and 56 in XVII indicates that Odolricus' consecration preceded Ebalus'. In 45 Fulbert writes to Bishop Franco of Paris that he has given Galeran until mid-Lent (=12 March, Easter being 2 April) to make amends and Franco should excommunicate him if he does not do so; and in 53 Fulbert advises King Robert to have a letter written calling on Lisiardus to submit before 29 June. Both letters must have been written somewhat earlier than the dates they name. This would mean that the letters up to 45 were written by *c.* early March, and those not only up to 53, but also 56, by *c.* early June. Two letters have been inserted here from elsewhere in the collection. In 47 Fulbert says that he is sending some doses of *hiera* to Ebalus of Roucy (apparently the future archbishop of Rheims) and in 48 Hildegar sends E. directions on how to take this. The two letters thus appear to belong together, and so 48 has been added from HC. As for 50, see p. lxxvii.

Though all the letters in XVII may have been written by early 1022, the later ones seem to cover a slightly longer period; for in 58 Fulbert tells Ebalus, who recently (cf. the end of the letter) became archbishop of Rheims, that he has persuaded Count Odo to make amends, while in 61 he informs King Robert that he has not seen Odo for nearly six months. In 55 and 60 Fulbert refers to local disturbances, and in 58 Odo is in control of Rheims. There is hostility towards King Robert in the vicinity of Chartres (59), and there is a dispute between Robert and Odo over the bishopric of Meaux (61) which apparently began in the time of Count Stephen of Meaux and Troyes (52 f.). Hence this would seem to be the beginning of the conflict between Odo and Robert over Stephen's inheritance, namely Champagne.[27]

[27] See Pfister, *Robert*, pp. 239 ff.; Lex, pp. 220 ff., 276 ff.; F. Lot, *Études sur le règne de Hugues Capet* (Paris, 1903), pp. 397 ff.; L. Halphen, 'La lettre

On Stephen's death his lands passed to his cousin, Count Odo, perhaps with King Robert's consent (cf. 61, 86). Odo took possession of Rheims, where he minted coins in his own name as count of Troyes. He also entered into alliance with anti-imperial nobles and built fortresses in Lorraine. But Robert was also, though more distantly, related to Stephen, and he apparently decided to claim Stephen's inheritance for himself. His natural ally against Odo was Count Fulk of Anjou, and he seems to have instructed Bishop Hubert of Angers to join Fulk in attacking Odo. They appear to have ravaged lands near Tours, whereupon Archbishop Hugh of Tours excommunicated them (cf. 71 f.). The matter may have been discussed at a royal council held at Compiègne on 1 May 1023 and attended among others by Duke Richard of Normandy, who later attempted to bring Robert and Odo to terms (cf. 86), and by legates of the Emperor Henry II.[28] On 10–11 August 1023 Robert and Henry held a conference (cf. 81); and on 8 September Henry met Odo at Verdun to discuss the latter's activities in Lorraine and may have tried to mediate between him and Robert.[29] However, the struggle continued throughout 1024, and it was not until *c.* early 1025 that Robert and Odo made at least a temporary peace, perhaps in order to ally against the new emperor, Conrad II.[30]

d'Eudes II de Blois au roi Robert', *Revue historique*, xcvii (1908), 287 ff. (reprinted in his *A travers l'histoire du moyen âge* (Paris, 1950), pp. 241 ff.). As regards the comital powers of the archbishop of Rheims, see F. Vercauteren, 'Note sur les comtes de Reims aux xe et xie siècles', *MA* xl (1930), 83 ff.

[28] The only evidence for this assembly is a charter supposedly issued on this occasion by Bishop Garin of Beauvais (Newman, no. 132). The charter itself is a forgery probably dating from the late eleventh century; however, it seems to have been based on an authentic document, and the historical circumstances appear to be accurate. See M. Prou, 'Une charte de Garin, évêque de Beauvais: l'assemblée de Compiègne de 1023 ou 1024', *Centenaire 1804–1904: recueil de mémoires de la Soc. nat. des Antiquaires de France* (Paris, n.d.), pp. 383 ff.

[29] *Gesta Pontificum Cameracensium*, iii. 37 f. (*MGH SS* vii. 480 f.). Cf. Pfister, *Robert*, pp. 369 ff.; S. Hirsch and others, *Jahrbücher des Deutschen Reiches unter Heinrich II.*, iii (Leipzig, 1875), 257 ff.

[30] According to the identical entries in the *Annales Vindocinenses* and *Annales qui dicuntur Rainaldi* (*Recueil d'annales angevines et vendômoises*, ed. L. Halphen (Paris, 1903), pp. 60 f., 86), Robert and Odo did not come to terms until 1026. But Conrad was already in control of Lorraine and Lombardy before then (see p. lxxxv), and Robert and Odo seem to have reached an agreement even earlier (see p. lxxxvii and nos. 98 ff., which must have been written before the death of King Hugh, 17 September 1025). Yet the entries in the annals apparently concern the present incident, for they state that Robert and Queen Constance made peace with Odo and left Fulk fighting against him, and in

To return to the beginning of the controversy, almost nothing is known of the bishops of Meaux during this period. Pfister places Lisiardus' attempt to gain the bishopric (52 f.) after the death of Bishop Gilbert (*c.* 1009).[31] His only evidence for this, however, is that it occurred during Count Stephen's lifetime, and such a date would seem quite unlikely if this is the same Lisiardus who is mentioned in a charter granted by Gilbert's successor, Macarius, in the second year of his pontificate.[32] The integrity of XVII also argues against this date. The new bishop in 61 was probably Bernerius, though there is no evidence for him until 1028. The dispute over Meaux seems to have lasted the better part of a year; and though Count Stephen's death is placed anywhere between 1019 and 1023, it would seem to be *c.* mid 1021 that he died and Odo succeeded him. Whether Odo's expedition against Fulk (46), who was later allied with Robert against him (71 f.), was connected with it is not known; but it would seem from 61 that at first Robert accepted Odo's claims. How far these letters extend into 1022 cannot be determined. There seem to be no more of Fulbert's letters until *c.* mid 1023, but this can be partly explained by his pilgrimage to Rome.

The dating of the letters from 1022 on is in large part a matter of fitting together HC, the relevant letter-groups, and some other letters by Fulbert.

HC. 65 66 67 [67 66 in L-family manuscripts] 68 48 69 70 71 95 96 102 103 104 105 106 110 109 111 112 113 114 116 117 121 128 129 130 131 115

VI. 72 73 74 76 77 78 80 75 84 85 86 87 88 89 90 91 92 93 94

XV. 79 81 82 83

99 ff. Fulbert assumes that Constance and Odo might be with Robert. Hence either the date 1026 is erroneous (and in fact there is some question as to the date of the entry in the *Annales Vindocinenses*: cf. Halphen's note), or else they may have made a truce in 1025 (cf. 97) and only reached a final agreement in 1026 (cf. 116, though the agreement there apparently concerns which of Robert's sons should succeed him). On the other hand, if 98 ff. were written earlier, it would have to have been before mid 1023, for Robert and Odo were openly hostile by then (cf. 71); and if my identification of Geoffrey as the nephew of Archbishop Hugh of Tours is correct (98), it would seem to exclude not only a date *c.* late 1022 (when Fulbert was in any event on a journey to Rome), but also probably an earlier one (cf. the canons' attitude toward Geoffrey in 65).

[31] *Fulbert*, pp. 65 f.; Newman, p. 39 n.

[32] *Cartulaire de l'église Notre-Dame de Paris*, ed. B. Guérard (Paris, 1850), i. 321. In the index, however, Lisiardus is identified with the archdeacon of Paris who figures here in 79 f.

IV. 98 97 118 123 124 122 125 126 127
VIII. 99 100 101
VII. 119

The other letters are 120 (from XVIII), 107 (found only in PB), and 108 (found only in P).

The letters in HC fall into several fairly distinct groups. 65–71 seem to have been written before Hildegar went to Poitiers; 95–6 have no clues as to date, though Hildegar was apparently in Poitiers when they were written; 102–13 probably date from 1025; 114, from late 1025 to early 1026; 115 and 116–21, from 1026–7; and 128–31, after Fulbert's death. HC appears to be in chronological order except in three places: 48, 110–109 (which are clearly reversed), and 115. The last is found only in L-family manuscripts and was apparently attached out of place; it probably belongs before 116. As was seen on p. lxxix, 48 seems to go with 47, and so it would be earlier than 65–6. This raises the question as to whether the two pairs 67 f. and 69 f., which have no clues as to date, might not also be earlier; for they are private letters, and 65 f. may have been placed first because they were written for the chapter. Be that as it may, only 48 has any evidence of an earlier date; and in the absence of this for the others, it seems best to leave them where they are. Moreover, the interlocking arrangement of 65–8 in L-class manuscripts may be the original order; and if so, it suggests that 67 f. were either contemporary with 65 f. or later additions. As for 69 f., if Hildegar's correspondent was Duke William, they might be connected with the treasurership of Saint-Hilaire. There is also the possibility that 67 f. and especially 69 f. may have been epistolary exercises, though there seems to be no other example of this in the collection except perhaps the interpolated letter in V (Appendix B, no. 4).

VI also appears to be in chronological order: 72 was written before 10 June, 89 after 25 November 1023; 73 74 75, which concern the same case, are correctly arranged; reference is made to harvest-time and a synod to be held on 15 October in 74, to Lent and the approaching Easter in 88, to gathering the first-fruits in 92, and to a council to be held at Christmas in 94. This also indicates that VI extends into 1024.

The reference to Lisiardus in 79 in XV suggests that it was written before 80 in VI. In 81 in XV Fulbert states that he should have been notified sooner of a meeting between King Robert and the Emperor Henry II scheduled for 27 July. The only known meeting between them during this period took place on 10–11 August 1023, and this would accord with the apparent date of 81. Thus xv would also date from 1023 and so would either be earlier than vi or else have been on a leaf which was displaced from it. The decisive point is the respective dates of 72 and 81. Even presuming that Hugh excommunicated Fulk only shortly before his own death on 10 June and that 72 might have been written a few days later, it would still leave about six weeks before the meeting in 81, and this is hardly such short notice as Fulbert claims. Hence xv would seem to have been dislodged from somewhere between 72 and 80 in vi, and I have inserted it before the latter. Moreover, in 83 Fulbert speaks of an attempt to force his men to use a mill, and this possibly points toward harvest-time (cf. 74) or a little later.

The letters in this period can be dated as follows. In 65 f. Fulbert is said to be on a journey to Rome. The only time he is known to have gone there was in late 1022. According to *Cart. S.-Père*, i. 110, Fulbert was on a pilgrimage to Rome when heretics were discovered at Orleans, and his name is not found on a charter issued shortly after the trial and witnessed by several royal bishops.[33] This date seems to be confirmed by the two addressees; for Archbishop Hugh died on 10 June 1023, and 66 suggests that this was Herbert's first attempt to collect visitation dues from his diocese (cf. 39) and thus that his elevation to the bishopric of Lisieux was fairly recent.

The next letter that can be dated in HC is 71, which seems to go with 72 in vi. The occasion was an attack on Tours by Count Fulk of Anjou and Bishop Hubert of Angers as supporters of King Robert in his struggle with Count Odo. The outside date for 71 is Archbishop Hugh's death, 10 June 1023, and Hugh himself indicates that he excommunicated Hubert almost immediately after the attack. Hildegar seems to have written Hugh's letter and so had probably not yet gone to Poitiers; for if he had, he would hardly have referred to Fulk as he did, since Fulk was one of Duke William's vassals and relations between them were quite good (cf. 104, 109). 72 is apparently the first letter that Fulbert wrote after he returned from Rome.

[33] Newman, no. 58.

The following letters date from mid 1023 to early 1024. More precise indications are lacking except for 81, which was discussed above. There appears to have been some trouble in the vicinity (85), and this probably arose from the struggle between Odo and Robert. Fulbert seems to have supported Odo's claims. There are only two letters from Fulbert to the king (78, 81), and in both he appears to be avoiding a possible confrontation. Robert had apparently taken Tours from Odo, and this may explain why Fulbert refused to meet him there (78).[34] Moreover, Fulbert seems to have written Odo's letter to Robert (86), and the occasion for this may have arisen from the meeting between the Emperor Henry and Robert in August or Henry and Odo in September (see p. lxxx).

The dating of the next letters depends on when Fulbert accepted the treasurership of Saint-Hilaire. It appears from 116 that he actually went to Poitiers,[35] and it was probably on this occasion that he witnessed Appendix C, no. 9. In 114, from late 1025 to early 1026, Hildegar reminds Fulbert that he has not been there for more than two years; and in 119, which dates from mid 1026 at the earliest and is probably later, Fulbert says that it has been almost three years since he accepted the office. Thus he seems to have accepted it in late 1023 to early 1024, his predecessor, Bishop Gerald of Limoges, having died 11 November 1022/3 (see 92). It appears from the instructions which Fulbert sent to Hildegar in 88 that the latter had not been in Poitiers very long; and Hildegar's question about the psalms and Fulbert's reference to Easter (5 April 1024) suggest a date in Lent, apparently the first Lent that Hildegar was there. This would also accord with 89, where Fulbert advises Arnulf, archbishop of Tours on 25 November 1023, not to resign merely because he has not yet received the pallium.

92 was apparently written in the summer (cf. the reference to the first-fruits) of 1024. This would place the beginning of the controversy over Jordan of Limoges in this year, for Fulbert indicates that it had not yet acquired its later notoriety. This would also accord with the apparent date of Gerald's death and Fulbert's being named treasurer and, if the interpolation in Adémar is correct, with the royal council held at Pentecost (24

---

[34] Odo recovered Tours before 97 was written.
[35] Cf. Adémar, iii. 41 (ed. Chavanon, p. 164).

May). In 94 Fulbert advises Robert against holding a council at Orleans at Christmas, and there is clearly enough time for Robert to move it elsewhere. The only known council at Orleans at Christmas during this period was that of 1022 (see p. lxxxiii). Fulbert states here that he will attend the council; but he did not attend the one in 1022 as he was on a pilgrimage to Rome, and this was not undertaken on the spur of the moment (cf. 65). Moreover, Fulbert says that there has been a recent fire at Orleans, that sacrilege has been committed, and that the city is under interdict, and it also appears that relations between King Robert and the bishop of Orleans were strained. Nothing else is known about any of these matters, but it seems noteworthy that none of them are mentioned in the reports of the council of 1022.[36] The remaining letters in VI have been dated solely by their position. 95 f. in HC can only be dated after Hildegar's arrival in Poitiers and before 102 (i.e. late 1023–mid 1025).

The nature of French intervention in imperial politics between the death of the Emperor Henry II (13 July 1024) and the time Conrad II secured general recognition in Germany and Italy (late 1025–6) is not altogether clear.[37] Even before Henry's death, Count Odo had attempted to extend his influence into Lorraine, but had been forced to withdraw (see p. lxxx). He also appears to have pressed his claims in Burgundy as nephew of the childless King Rudolf III. After Henry died, some of the north Italian nobles decided to free themselves from German control. They offered the Italian crown to King Robert[38] and, when he refused, to Duke William of Aquitaine. A meeting was arranged between the Italian legates, William, and Odo, and Odo asked Robert to agree to a truce and to send a representative to attend the negotiations (97). It was apparently after this that Fulk of Anjou wrote to Robert, telling him that William had provisionally accepted the crown for his son and asking him to try to prevent the Lotharingians from coming to terms with Conrad and instead to support

---

[36] See C. J. Hefele, *Histoire des conciles*, ed. H. Leclercq, iv, ii (Paris, 1911), 924 ff.

[37] See Pabst; Bresslau, i. 65 ff., 106 ff.; *Die Regesten des Kaiserreiches unter Konrad II.*, ed. N. von Bischoff and H. Appelt (Regesta Imperii, ed. J. F. Böhmer and others, iii. 1 (2nd edn., 1951)), nos. q, r, 8^{d-e}, 22^b, 40^b; Pfister, *Robert*, pp. 371 ff.

[38] Raoul Glaber, iii. 9 (ed. Prou, pp. 82 f.), reports that they asked for Robert's son, King Hugh, and this would accord with William's accepting the crown for his son. But cf. 104.

William (104). Somewhere during this period Robert and Odo made peace and seem to have undertaken a joint, but apparently unsuccessful, expedition at some distance from north-central France, perhaps in Lorraine. William himself went to Italy to investigate the situation. Finding it unsatisfactory, he returned and abandoned the venture (111–13).

The dating of these events and of the relevant letters is somewhat uncertain. The first letter in HC is 102, where Bishop Isembertus of Poitiers informs Bishop Hubert of Angers that the Italians have met William and that William has instructed him to take care of some urgent matters which make it impossible for him to attend the consecration of the cathedral of Angers, 16 August 1025. In 103 William tells Bishop Leo of Vercelli of his plans and asks for his aid, and in 104 Fulk informs Robert of what has happened and asks for his help in Lorraine. The next letters in HC (105 f.) are two private letters by Hildegar, which were probably sent together. In the first he tells Fulbert that he cannot return to Chartres before vintage-time, and in the second he sends his greetings to Ebrardus, who has recently been made *scholasticus*. 110 and 109 appear to be reversed. In 109 Hildegar tells Fulbert that William is going to leave for Italy on the following Thursday, and so Fulbert must decide whether to carry out his plans to visit Poitiers. In 110 Bishop Isembertus of Poitiers thanks Archbishop Arnulf of Tours for accepting the invitation to attend the dedication of the cathedral, which is set for 17 October, and mentions that Duke William will not return from an expedition until the day before. 111 was apparently and 112 f. were certainly written after William's return about late October 1025.[39]

Fulbert's letters for the same period are scattered (see p. lii). Although IV seems to be in chronological order or almost so, only the first two letters appear to belong here. In 98 Fulbert tells Abbot Odilo of the injuries inflicted on him by Geoffrey of Châteaudun; he intends to ask Count Odo for help and, if he refuses, King Robert or Duke Richard of Normandy. In 97 Fulbert conveys Odo's message to Robert concerning the meeting with the Italians and his request for a truce.

The three letters in VIII (99 100 101, apparently in chronological order) also concern Geoffrey, and this suggests that VIII

[39] Pabst, p. 364.

may have been on a leaf which was detached from between 97 and 118 in IV. In 99 Fulbert tells Robert that before Christmas Geoffrey rebuilt a fortress which Robert had earlier destroyed and shortly after Epiphany began to build another; he himself has sent messages to King Hugh and Count Odo, but has not received a reply. It appears that Robert was engaged in some distant undertaking and that Fulbert thought Odo might be with him. In 100 Fulbert repeats his complaint and asks Robert to put pressure on Odo to destroy the fortresses, and he reiterates this in 101, where he also tells of the difficulties experienced by King Hugh. In 107 Fulbert declines William's invitation to attend the dedication of the cathedral of Poitiers and tells him that he is going to meet King Robert in the autumn to try to settle the case of Jordan of Limoges. In 108 he writes to Hildegar that his journey to Poitiers has been delayed by the restoration of the cathedral, business for the king, robbers in the area, the harvests, and Jordan's case; the monk Ebrardus (presumably the Ebrardus in 106) has left, and he himself is running the school.

It does not seem possible to date these letters with any assurance. There is no way to tell whether 97 was written before or after 98. But it is clear from the relations between Robert and Odo that 97 is earlier than 99, and the latter was probably written not long after Epiphany. Whether Robert and perhaps Odo were on an expedition to Lorraine (or possibly Burgundy) is uncertain; and even if they were, it does not mean that these letters would have to follow 104. Moreover, if the dating of 107 is correct, Robert seems to have returned before autumn, and so his expedition would not coincide with William's journey to Italy.

If the letters in HC are arranged chronologically, the ones here should date from 1025. That this is the correct year for the consecration of the cathedral of Angers seems to be confirmed by the reference to William's negotiations with the Italians, which could not have taken place so early in 1024, even though 16 August was a Sunday (the usual day for the consecration of a church) in 1024, but not in 1025. As for the consecration of the cathedral of Poitiers, though the year has been given as either 1024 or 1025,[40] the latter seems to be correct, since it would accord with the position of the letters here and 17 October was a Sunday. This would help to identify William's expedition in 110 as that

[40] Richard, i. 176 f.

to Italy, and it would suit the notoriety of Jordan's case (cf. 92, 107 f.).

Precisely when Fulbert wrote 107 to William is puzzling. It was presumably during the summer and before William set out for Italy; but in 109 Hildegar was clearly expecting Fulbert as late as the week before William's departure. Moreover, 108, which by its reference to Ebrardus is apparently later than 106, also seems to belong here. In both 107 and 108 Fulbert refers to the rebuilding of the cathedral and to Jordan's case, both were apparently written during the summer, and in both the closing greeting is virtually identical. This might indicate that they were sent at the same time; but it does not solve their relation to 109 unless Fulbert changed his mind or the letters crossed. Moreover, Hildegar seems to have planned to visit Chartres about the same time (105). The absence of any reference to William's expedition and the general tone of the letter might suggest that it was written in 1024 and with it perhaps 106 and thus 108. Yet the arrangement of HC is against this, and the master of the schools in mid 1024 was apparently Sigo and not Ebrardus (92). An earlier date would also not suit the status of the controversy over Jordan of Limoges. In the absence of additional evidence it again seems best to leave the letters where they stand and to date them simply mid 1025.

As was seen on p. lxxxvi, 111–13 appear to have been written after William's return c. late October. In the following letter (114) Hildegar says that it has been more than two years since Fulbert was in Poitiers, and he refers to Jordan's case as having been settled sometime earlier. From this and its position in HC it would seem to have been written in late 1025 or more probably early 1026.

King Robert's eldest son Hugh, who had been crowned in 1017 (see Appendix C, no. 6), died on 17 September 1025, and Robert then proposed to have the next eldest, Henry, crowned in his place.[41] He was opposed, however, by Queen Constance and some

---

[41] See Pfister, *Robert*, pp. 75 ff.; J. Dhondt, 'Élection et hérédité sous les Carolingiens et les premiers Capétiens', *RBPH* xviii (1939), 938 ff.; P. E. Schramm, *Der König von Frankreich* (2nd edn., Weimar, 1960), i. 98 f. Guillot, i. 34 n., would date 116 and thus Henry's election to 1027. However, Duke William presumes that Fulbert will be able to come to Poitiers, whereas his ill health in 1027 prevented him from attending Henry's consecration (124). Moreover, 116 does not take it for granted that Odo will be at the king's council. Instead it appears that Odo and Robert were at odds.

of the nobles, who favoured a younger son, Robert. The king called a council to meet at Pentecost, 29 May 1026, and the conflict between the two seems to have been generally known before this (cf. 115 f.). Whether a formal election took place at this time is not certain, but it appears from 124 that Fulbert thought there could still be considerable opposition at the time of Henry's consecration, 14 May 1027. In 115 Hildegar informs Fulbert that he has incurred the queen's displeasure by supporting the king in this matter and suggests that it would be safer for him to take the same line as his fellow bishops. This would seem to indicate that the letter was written before the council at Pentecost, but it is not impossible that it was written afterwards and that Hildegar was reporting the results of Fulbert's action on that occasion. If so, 115 should follow 118.

116 was written after the Rogation days preceding the feast of the Ascension (19 May 1026) and, to judge from the invitation to Fulbert to come to Poitiers during the octave of Pentecost, before the latter feast (29 May). The reference to a letter of William's at the beginning of 117 suggests that it accompanied 116; but at the end Hildegar tells Fulbert that he will set out for Chartres on Monday after the octave of Pentecost (6 June) to see if he is coming to Poitiers for the feast of St. John (24 June). Thus it would seem that when 116 f. were written Hildegar had reason to believe Fulbert would not come to Poitiers during the week after Pentecost or else that 117 is somewhat later than 116 and Fulbert had in the meantime sent word that he could not come earlier. In 118 Fulbert reproaches Hildegar for not coming to Chartres when he had said he would, and the scriptural allusion connects it with 117. Thus it can probably be dated after 6 June.

Hildegar had apparently been back at Chartres for some time, but still intended to return to Poitiers when 119 was written, and Fulbert states that it has been almost three years since he accepted the office at Saint-Hilaire. Thus it is earlier than the following letters and should probably be ascribed to the latter part of 1026. In 120 Fulbert offers to resign, and in 121 Hildegar states that he himself will not be able to return to Poitiers and asks the addressee to convey a message to Count William from Fulbert, requesting him to appoint a new treasurer. The last would seem to indicate that the two letters were not sent at the same time, and 121 would appear to be the later. The last of the letters concerning this matter is 122, and its position in IV would date it May–June 1027. Hence the meeting with the king mentioned there does not seem to have been that when Appendix C, no. 12, was issued.

124 was probably written shortly before Henry's consecration, 14 May 1027. As for 125, from Robert's letter to Abbot Gauzlin (Appendix B, no. 2) it appears that the rain of blood was supposed to have fallen on 21/2 June, and according to the *Vita Gauzlini* it occurred in 1027. This date accords with 125's position in IV. It would seem from Fulbert's statement that Robert had asked for a quick reply and from Robert's asking this of Gauzlin and saying that he was detaining Count William's messenger until he heard from him that 125 was written *c.* late June. If the occasion for the writing of 126 has been correctly identified, it can probably be dated not long after the death of Richard III of Normandy, 5/6 August 1027. 123 and 127 in IV are dated by their position.

The controversy over Thierry's election (128–30) occurred after Fulbert's death, 10 April 1028. According to the later *Translatio S. Aniani*, the cathedral was burned on 11 September 1030 in the second year of Thierry's pontificate.[42] Hence Thierry became bishop of Chartres in 1028 or 1029, and he was present at the consecration of Saint-Aignan of Orleans in 1029.[43] The way in which Fulbert is mentioned in 131 suggests that he has been dead for some time, and the position of the letter in HC and the reference to gathering the first-fruits point to late spring or early summer 1028 at the earliest. Hildegar himself died before Adelman wrote his poem in the early 1030s (see pp. xxxv f.).

[42] Edited by A. Clerval, *Analecta Bollandiana*, vii (1888), 331.
[43] Helgaud, c. xxii (ed. Bautier–Labory, p. 110); and the apparently related account of the translation of Saint Euspicius (*RHF* x. 370), which adds the date 16 June. Thierry died 16 April 1048/9 (Merlet, pp. 78 ff., 160; cf. *Cart. N.-D Chartres*, i. 89 ff., no. xiv).

CONCORDANCE WITH EARLIER EDITIONS OF THE LETTERS

Concordance of *PL* cxli with this Edition

PL	This Edn.	*PL*	This Edn.	*PL*	This Edn.
1	82	37	30	73	119
2	1	38	29	74	42
3	*	39	32	75	43
4	47	40	33	76	55
5	*	41	84	77	77
6	9	42	93	78	App. B, 2
7	87	43	20	79	App. B, 3
8	25	44	58	80	125
9	24	45	76	81	81
10	10	46	126	82	89
11	2	47	127	83	104
12	3	48	39	84	5
13	4	49	91	85	97
14	6	50	36	86	44
15	18	51	40	87	45
16	8	52	54	88	46
17	7	53	90	89	73
18	16	54	21	90	12
19	19	55	41	91	14
20	23	56	28	92	78
21	31	57	59	93	86
22	34	58	51	94	72
23	83	59	120	95	13
24	27	60	108	96	79
25	95	61	35	97	80
26	22	62	56	98	15
27	94	63	88	99	38
28	26	64	92	100	53
29	75	65	92	101	61
30	100	66	118	102	124
31	101	67	123	103	60
32	98	68	17	104	64
33	11	69	37	105	63
34	99	70	52	106	49
35	57	71	107	107	85
36	74	72	122	108	62

* See pp. lxii f.

PL	This Edn.	PL	This Edn.	PL	This Edn.
109	115	120	70	131	113
110	App. B, 1	121	71	132	114
111	50	122	96	133	116
112	†	123	102	134	117
113	†	124	103	135	121
114	65	125	105	136	128
115	66	126	106	137	129
116	67	127	110	138	130
117	68	128	109	139	131
118	48	129	111		
119	69	130	112		

† See pp. lxi f.

Concordance of *RHF* x with this Edition

Fulbert's Letters

RHF	This Edn.	RHF	This Edn.	RHF	This Edn.
1	82	28	101	55	125
2	1	29	93	56	42
3	*	30	21	57	87
4	47	31	28	58	81
5	9	32	57	59	89
6	10	33	29	60	58
7	7	34	32	61	5
8	8	35	36	62	97
9	25	36	30	63	78
10	24	37	123	64	14
11	2	38	51	65	34
12	3	39	59	66	45
13	4	40	41	67	44
14	18	41	40	68	46
15	55	42	54	69	13
16	77	43	92	70	79
17	83	44	37	71	80
18	27	45	35	72	53
19	39	46	88	73	61
20	22	47	17	74	†
21	94	48	120	75	91
22	26	49	108	76	62
23	43	50	107	77	60
24	74	51	122	78	124
25	98	52	56	79	72
26	99	53	52		
27	100	54	119		

* = *PL* no. 3 (see pp. lxii f.).

† = *PL* no. 112, no. 113 being in *RHF* xi. 495 ff. (see pp. lxi f.).

Duke William's Letters

RHF	This Edn.	RHF	This Edn.
1	96	4	111
2	70	5	113
3	103	6	116

Hildegar's Letters

RHF	This Edn.	RHF	This Edn.
1	48	6	106
2	95	7	109
3	69	8	114
4	105	9	121
5	117	10	131

Miscellaneous Letters

RHF	This Edn.	RHF	This Edn.
10	App. B, 2	18	104
11	App. B, 3	19	112
12	65	20	86
13	66	23	115
15	71	27	128
16	102	28	129
17	110	29	130

THE LETTERS OF
FULBERT OF CHARTRES

1

Fulbert to Abbot Abbo of Fleury:[1] thanking him for his letter and recounting the forced election of Abbot Magenardus of Saint-Père of Chartres   2 February–11 July 1004

Pleno uirtutis et gratia circumfuso patri Alboni Fulbertus diaconus.

Quanam te resalutatione digner, o sacer abba et o magne phylosophe, quid rependam muneris sanctae amicitiae quam promiserunt signa gemmatae facundie, uix estimare sufficio. Nam cum illa que dicuntur esse uictor animo teneas, cum illa quae non esse forsitan uilipendas, quid ego conferre possim, quod tu aut non habeas, aut non habere contemnas? Sed quoniam phylosophicis essentiis magnum quiddam superest, atque ex his quae non esse dicuntur quaedam perpetua fiunt ideoque sapientibus aliquando grata sunt, recipe quaeso quod ab utroque tibi lectum offero. Denique ut participando superessentiam deitatis deus fias,[2] sic te resaluto, ac perennem fidelitatis habitum amicitiae tuae rependo, hac scilicet differentia tuam beniuolentiam meamque distinguens, ut illa pro maiestate persone gratia uocetur ut domini, ista fidelitas ut alumni. Preceptis itaque tuis modestissime deseruire cupiens, Mediolano[3] discipulo quod praecatus es facio. Queque tibi scribenda petisti, en omnia fere iuxta fidem exarta transmitto.

Abbate sancti Petri[4] grauiter egrotante, sed adhuc mentis et sermonis compote, Magenardus monachus, ante michi non

---

1 PB It is also found, except for the first paragraph, in *Cart. S.-Père*, i. 101 ff.; but this has not been used here.

---

1. ¹ 988–13 November 1004 (see P. Cousin, *Abbon de Fleury-sur-Loire* (Paris, 1954), pp. 92, 181 ff.; above, p. lxx).
   ² As Clerval, pp. 118 f., and following him M. Cappuyns, *Jean Scot Érigène* (Louvain, 1933), p. 241, have pointed out, this passage seems to reflect some knowledge of the works of John Scotus Eriugena, the ninth-century philosopher and translator of Pseudo-Dionysius. Although Fulbert does not seem to be drawing on any particular passage, his thought here can be illustrated from Eriugena's *Periphyseon* or *De divisione naturae*, i (ed. I. P. Sheldon-Williams,

Fulbert to Abbot Abbo of Fleury[1]
2 February–11 July 1004

To Abbot Abbo, who is filled with virtue and suffused with grace, from the deacon Fulbert.

How I can suitably return your greeting, O holy abbot and great philosopher, what I can give you in return for the gift of holy friendship which you promised me in tokens of sparkling eloquence is almost more than I can judge. For since you have mastered and grasp those things which are said to exist, and since you may not value those which are said not to exist, what might I offer that you do not have or would not disdain to have? But since there is something above and beyond philosophical essences, and since some of those things which are said not to exist become eternal and so are pleasing to the wise, I beg you to accept what I have chosen from both to offer you. In short, I am returning your greeting with the wish that you may become divine by participating in God's transcendental nature,[2] and I am repaying you for your friendship by offering you my eternal fidelity, though I distinguish thus between your kindness toward me and mine toward you: that in accordance with the majesty of your person, yours may be called grace and favour as being that of a master, while mine may be called fidelity as being that of a pupil. Since I want to obey your commands so far as in me lies, I am doing what you requested for the student from *Mediolanum*.[3] As for what you asked me to write and tell you, I am enclosing an accurate account of almost everything.

While the abbot of Saint-Père[4] was seriously ill, but still in sound mind and able to speak, the monk Magenardus, who was

Scriptores Latini Hiberniae, vii (Dublin, 1968)). Eriugena begins by dividing *natura* into those things which exist and those which do not exist: the former can be grasped by the human mind, while the latter are beyond it (pp. 36 ff.). God is said to be 'superessential' in that he is above all essence (pp. 76 ff.); and Eriugena uses *deificatio* to denote man's return to God, his participation in God's nature (pp. 48 ff.).

[3] A fairly common place-name which cannot be identified with certainty (see Graesse–Benedict–Plechl, *Orbis Latinus*, ii (Braunschweig, 1972), 536).

[4] Gisbertus (see p. lxix).

mediocriter carus, noctu sese de claustro surripuit, et ad Tel-
baldum comitem,[5] qui Blesis tunc morabatur, abbatiae petendae
gratia properauit. Comes illum post tridie remisit ad nos cum
legatis, qui denuntiarent recipiendum magnifice sicut abbatem
monachis et canonicis. At uero nobis fere omnibus ea res aeque
noua et horribilis fuit. Respondimus itaque longe nobis aliter
uideri; nec aenim legitime fieri abbatem nec debere recipi, qui
abbatiam alterius ipso uiuente per ambitionem petit,[a] qui a
fratribus non eligitur, et super illos nititur dominari, postremo
qui noster neque monachus sit neque clericus, et plures habeat
testes curialiter agitandi quam monastice uiuendi. Haec ille non
gratanter accipiens ad comitem redequitat, iramque iuuenis
aduersum nos uehementer inflammat. Sed die quinto postquam
suum ambitum publicauit, praedictus abbas aegritudinem suam
morte limitat. Conueniunt ad capitulum monachi nostri et quidam
canonici quos ratio postulabat admitti. Interrogamus an aliqui
fratrum incepto Magenardi faueant. Negant singuli, negant omnes.
Decreuimus ergo quosdam eorum esse mittendos ad comitem
(nobis uidelicet designatum episcopum),[6] ut patris obitum nun-
tiarent, et alterius eligendi regularem praecarentur licentiam.
Quibus missis, ecce alii duo (Viuianus scilicet et Durandus, alter
illitteratus, alter litterarum malesanus interpres, ambo praepositi),
simulantes causa communis commodi ad obedientias suas se uelle
exire, ac ne aliorsum pergerent sibi interdicente decano monasterii, Magenardum tamen secuti sunt, cui ceptam praesumptionem
occulte persuaserant, et[b] Blesis in praesentia domni Telbaldi ipsum
Magenardum a fratribus peti et eligi perfide[c] mentiti sunt. Horum
suffragio laetus comes statim eum[d] baculo pastorali publice donat.
Quo audito fratres qui in claustro remanserant, contra hanc
fraudulentiam zelo diuine legis accincti, libellum reprobationis
fecerunt atque subscripserunt huiusmodi:

Sciat omnis ecclesia quia Magenardum monachum nostrum abbatem
fieri non eligimus, non laudamus, non uolumus, non consentimus; sed

---

a quaerit B   *b* et] ut B   *c* perfidem B   *d* eum] cum B

---

[5] 995–1004 (see Lex, pp. 204, 208 ff.).   [6] See pp. lxix f.

very dear to me before this, stole from the cloister by night and hurried to Count Thibault,[5] who was then at Blois, to ask for the office of abbot. The count sent him back to us three days later with messengers who were instructed to announce that the monks and canons should receive Magenardus as abbot with due solemnity. But to almost all of us this was as unprecedented as it was shocking. So we replied that we favoured an altogether different course, for no one may lawfully be made or received as abbot who solicits the office of an abbot while he is alive, who has not been elected by the brothers and yet strives to rule over them, and finally who is not one of our monks or clerks and who has more witnesses of his courtly behaviour than of his monastic life. Magenardus heard this with displeasure, rode back to the count, and vehemently inflamed that young man's anger against us. On the fifth day after Magenardus had made his canvassing public, the abbot's illness ended with his death. Our monks assembled in chapter along with those of the canons whose presence was required by the nature of the case. We asked whether any of the brothers approved of what Magenardus had done. They denied it one and all. So we decided that some of them should be sent to notify the count (namely our bishop-designate)[6] of the abbot's death and to ask for permission to elect another in accordance with the Rule. After these had been sent, two others (namely Vivian and Durand, the one illiterate, the other of unsound learning, both being provosts) pretended that for the good of the community they wished to go to their obediences. Though the dean of the monastery forbade them to go anywhere else, they followed Magenardus, whom they had secretly persuaded to embark on his rash venture, and in Count Thibault's presence at Blois they treacherously lied that Magenardus had been chosen and elected by the brothers. The count was delighted with their support and thereupon publicly presented Magenardus with the pastoral staff. When the brothers who had remained in the monastery heard this, they girded themselves with zeal for divine law against this deception and wrote and signed the following notice of their disapproval:

May the whole church know that we do not elect, approve, wish, nor consent to the monk Magenardus' being made our abbot; but we

reprobamus, refutamus, et omnino contradicimus, nos uidelicet*e* de cenobio sancti Petri, quorum nomina subscripta sunt:

Durandus decanus	Gauldricus
Genesius	Rotbertus
Isembertus	Marcuinus
Alueus	Guarnerius
Richerius	Guarinus
Herbertus	Eurardus
Benedictus	Galterius
Arnulfus	Durandus
Walterius	Beringerius
Herbertus	Bernardus*f*

Isti itaque omnes sua nomina aut subscripserunt aut subscribi fecerunt me uidente. Die proxima comes Telbaldus redit, se in monasterium recipi cum processione praemandat. Monachi respondent se libenter hoc agere, si praesumptorem illum non adduxerit secum. Ille denuo iratus, ipso tamen die sustinuit, sed insequenti cum strepitu*g* comminantium in sancti Petri monasterium suum Magenardum obtrusit. Ad cuius uiolentum ingressum sancti fratres contaminari ipsius communicatione timentes, sanctuario domini salutato cum lacrimis exierunt, atque refugium aliud nescientes, ad limina principalis ecclesiae confugerunt. Ibi quoque non inuento pastore, utrinque desertae*h* oues mestis sese uocibus consolantur. Sed recipit sancta mater Domini solita pietate, recipit Rodulfus tuus[7] dulci benignitate. Inde transierunt ad caenobium sancti patris Herberti,[8] cuius diues caritas de paupere censu quaeque potest illis necessaria sumministrat. Caeterum ille, cuius fratres importunitate depulsi sunt, ab Heruiso quodam (ut aiunt) Britannice regionis*i* episcopo[9] iiii nonas Februarii abbas simulatus est in suburbio Carnotensi absente clero, indignante populo, legato archipraesulis[10] palam contradicente ne

---

e uero B   *f* *In both MSS. the names are written serially. Their different arrangements, however, indicate that they originally stood in two columns as printed here. In copying them P went down each column vertically, while B alternated between the two, omitting* Arnulfus, Durandus, Walterius.   *g* strepitum P
h disertae B   *i* religionis B

---

[7] Dean of the cathedral and bishop 1004–6 (see pp. xvii f.).
[8] Of Lagny (Seine-et-Marne, *arr.* Meaux), *c.* 1000–33 (Clerval, pp. 25 f.).

condemn, refute, and utterly oppose it—we of the monastery of Saint-Père whose names are written below:

Durand, the dean	Gauldricus
Genesius	Robert
Isembertus	Marcuinus
Alveus	Guarnerius
Richer	Guarinus
Herbert	Evrardus
Benedict	Walter
Arnulf	Durand
Walter	Berengar
Herbert	Bernard

All these wrote their names or had them written in my presence. On the next day Count Thibault returned and sent ahead word that he was to be received in the monastery with a procession. The monks replied that they would gladly do so if he did not bring that usurper with him. Though he again became enraged, he controlled himself on that day; but on the next, with thundering threats he thrust his Magenardus into the monastery of Saint-Père. On his forcing his way in the holy brothers, from fear of being contaminated by communicating with him, took their leave of the church and went forth in tears; and knowing no other place of refuge, they fled to the threshold of the cathedral. When they found no shepherd there either, the sheep, abandoned on both sides, comforted each other with words of sorrow. But the Lord's holy mother received them with her wonted affection; and your servant Ralph,[7] with sweet kindness. From there they passed to the monastery of Abbot Herbert,[8] who rich in charity, though straitened in resources, provided so far as he could for their needs. Meanwhile, he whose importunity had driven the brothers away went through the motions of having himself made abbot on 2 February in the suburbs of Chartres by someone named Hervé, who is said to be a bishop from Brittany,[9] though the clergy were absent, the people were outraged, a messenger from the archbishop[10] publicly forbade it, and some monks who had remained

---

[9] Bishop Hervé or Hervi of Nantes (991/2–after 1004), who seems to have spent his last years at the court of the count of Chartres and to have died at Blois (see F. Lot, 'Hervi évêque de Nantes', *Annales de Bretagne*, xiii (1897–8), 45 ff.).

[10] Leothericus of Sens.

id fieret, reclamantibus etiam quibusdam monachis qui in loco remanserant uero uultu, uiua uoce, atque regulari auctoritate.[k] Sed quid inter furentes ratio? Sed et nunc ille primas in abbatiae suggestu, saeculari potentia fretus, de peracta uictoria gloriosus, factores eius, abbates, episcopos, atque ipsum papam ambiendo, ne quid grauius statuatur in illum modis omnibus elaborat.[l] Iacet interim uicta confusaque fratrum expulsorum humilitas; nec est praesul in Galliis cuius uiscera tangat affectio pietatis, aut zelus sacre legis imflammet, ut consurgat ad frangendos impetus errorum, ad releuandas[m] spes dolore tabescentium. Defuncta etenim est Dionisii fortitudo, non comparet[n] pietas Martini. Tu quoque dereliquisti nos, sancte pater Hilari, qui olim unitatem aecclesie spiritus sancti gladio tuebaris.[11] O derelicta, o mesta, o desolata Galliarum aecclesia! Quae iam erit spes salutis ulterior? Vbi amplius afflicta Christiani anima respirabit? Hoc nempe solum uel maxime nos confortare uidebatur, quod si contingeret ruinas maenium tuorum resarciri non posse, liceret saltem ad firmum adhuc capitolium monasticae uitae confugere. Quod aetiam si furibus irreptare aut impune quibuslibet ambitiosis inuadere licet, pro dolor! funditus cecidisti. Vnde iam ad te reuertens, uenerande pater, quem ego credo et uideo adiutorem[o] a Domino nobis esse prouisum, cum domino meo tuoque fideli Rodulfo deprecor et obtestor per ea que tibi data sunt sapientiae sanctae carismata, per dulcedinem fraternae caritatis, siquid potes impugna hostes Domini, fratres allisos refoue, nec perire sinas inopia solatii tui pro quibus credis esse fusum sanguinem Christi. Vale.

---

[k] auctoritate *om.* P   [l] elaborant PB   [m] reuelandas P   [n] comparet *corr. to* compararet P   [o] adiutorem] ad nitorem B

---

[11] i.e. the bishops of Fulbert's day are not living up to the standards of their heroic predecessors, Saints Denis of Paris, Martin of Tours, and Hilary of Poitiers. Cf. Eph. 6: 17.

there with bold face voiced their protests based on the Rule. But what reason is there among madmen? So now his eminence installed on the abbot's throne, relying on secular power and glorying in the victory he has won, is canvassing his supporters, abbots, bishops, and the pope himself, and striving in every way to prevent more serious action from being taken against him. Meanwhile, the expelled brothers lie humbly prostrate, conquered and thrown into confusion, nor is there a bishop in all Gaul whose heart is so touched with fatherly affection or who is so inflamed with zeal for holy law as to rise up to crush the attacks of evil-doers and to restore the hopes of those languishing with grief. Indeed, the courage which was Denis's is dead, and the piety which was Martin's is nowhere to be seen. You have also deserted us, O holy father Hilary, who once protected the unity of the church with the sword of the Holy Spirit.[11] O church of Gaul, abandoned, sorrowful, desolate! Is there any hope left for your safety after this? Where can a Christian's afflicted soul still recover its breath? This alone once seemed our greatest comfort: that if your outer walls were ruined and could not be mended, we might at least take refuge in the citadel of monastic life, which was as yet secure. But if thieves are allowed to steal in and anyone who wants an office to seize it without being punished—alas, you have utterly fallen! So now I am turning to you, reverend father, whom I believe and see to be the helper the Lord has provided for us; and with Ralph, my lord and your faithful servant, I beg and entreat you by those gifts of holy wisdom which have been given to you and by the sweetness of fraternal charity to do all that you can to fight the enemies of the Lord and to revive the stricken brothers and not to allow those for whom you believe Christ's blood was poured forth to perish for want of your consolation. Farewell.

2

Fulbert to Archbishop Leothericus of Sens: thanking him for consecrating him and congratulating him on finding relics; his action as regards a complaint and advice as to a simoniac priest   *late 1006–early 1008*

Dilectissimo patri et archiepiscopo suo L(eutherico) F(ulbertus) Dei gratia Carnotensium episcopus orationis suffragium.

Multum amoris atque fidelitatis tibi, pater, me debere censeo, per cuius manum a Deo benedictionem et sacram unctionem accepi. Vnde et animus meus ita pendet ex tuo,[1] ut quicquid te iusta ratione aut contristat aut hilarat, idem me si resciscam*a* simili modo afficiat. Congratulor itaque tibi super inuentis sacris,[2] et Deo qui ea tempore tuo reuelari maluit pronus gratias ago. Deinde uero quod Arnulfum casatum aecclesiae nostrae[3] tibi tuisque scripsisti iniurium, egre contra illum et accepi et fero. Vnde mox ad uillam Alogiam ubi tunc esse dicebatur misi legatum meum, sed in alias partes abierat. Vxor tamen eius michi remandauit, quod ubi redierit statim ad me ueniet. Quod si ueniens tibi satisfacere uoluerit, per meas litteras scies. Alioquin ultra terminum qui a te praefixus est in nostra communione non erit. Simoniacum uero praesbiterum de quo michi mandasti in diocesim ordinatoris sui repelli suadeo, aut si in tua manserit, ab officio suspendi, ne aecclesiae tuae*b* candor immundae heresis contagione sordescat.[4] Vale, pater optime, filii tui memor.

2 DRCPBVM (L)   *a* si resciscam *om.* VM   *b* tuae *om.* VM

---

2. [1] Cf. Gen. 44: 30.

[2] Probably the relics of Saints Savinian and others, which had been missing since the Norse invasions and were discovered at Sens by Leothericus and Abbot Rainardus of Saint-Pierre-le-Vif. See the account apparently deriving from Odorannus and that of Clarius in Duru, ii. 367, 499; Helgaud, c. xv (ed. Bautier–Labory, p. 88); and Raoul Glaber, iii. 6 (ed. Prou, p. 68), who appears to be referring to this discovery and dates it 1008.

[3] Arnulf of Yèvre-le-Châtel (Loiret, *arr.* Pithiviers), nephew of Bishop Arnulf of Orleans, advocate of the monastery of Fleury, and vassal of the

Fulbert to Archbishop Leothericus of Sens
late 1006–early 1008

To his very dear father and archbishop, L(eothericus), from F(ulbert), by grace of God bishop of Chartres, with the support of his prayers.

I believe that I have a great obligation to love and to be faithful to you, father, for from your hand I received God's blessing and the holy anointing. Hence my state of mind is so dependent on yours[1] that whatever rightly makes you sad or happy, if I should learn of it, makes me sad or happy too. So I congratulate you on discovering holy relics,[2] and on my knees I thank God for having chosen to reveal them in your day. But as for the injury which you wrote that Arnulf, a vassal of our church,[3] had committed against you and yours, I was grieved to hear it, and I hold it grievously against him. I immediately sent my messenger to the village of Alluyes, where he was said to be at that time, but he had gone somewhere else. His wife, however, sent me word that he will come to me as soon as he returns. If he is willing to make satisfaction to you when he comes, I shall write and tell you. Otherwise he shall not remain in communion with us beyond the date that you set. As to your question about the simoniac priest, I advise you to make him return to the diocese of the bishop who ordained him or, if he should remain in yours, to suspend him from office so that your church in its purity may not become soiled and contaminated by a foul heresy.[4] Farewell, dear father, and remember your son.

church of Chartres apparently for holdings at Alluyes (Eure-et-Loir, *arr.* Châteaudun). In 993/4 Arnulf had renounced certain dues that he was exacting from Fleury's dependants at Yèvre in return for an annual payment from the monastery during the lifetime of Bishop Arnulf (Newman, no. 6). As for the present incident, see no. 3. Abbot Gauzlin of Fleury eventually succeeded in having the fortress at Yèvre destroyed, though it was later rebuilt (see *Vita Gauzlini*, c. xlii (ed. Bautier–Labory, pp. 78 ff.); Newman, no. 80).

[4] See no. 4. On the notion of simony as a heresy see J. Leclercq, 'Simoniaca Heresis', *Studi Gregoriani*, i (1947), 523 ff.

3

Fulbert to Archbishop Leothericus of Sens: notifying him that Arnulf of Yèvre-le-Châtel has agreed to plead his case
late 1006–early 1008

Dilectissimo patri et archiepiscopo suo L(eutherico) F(ulbertus) Dei gratia Carnotensium episcopus suffragium orationis et obsequium fidelitatis.

Arnulfum fidelem meum arguendo conueni de his iniuriis unde michi quaerimoniam scripsistis.[1] Sed ille respondit se non diffugere iudicium, sponte uenire ad placitum.[a] Vnde per consilium et suasum eius totam hanc causam in uestram dispositionem mittimus, ut constituatis diem quo uos et nos et alii quorum interest conuenire possimus iuxta castellum Ebrae, uidelicet super ipsam terram sancti Benedicti de qua contentio est. Arnulfus enim in expeditionem cum Odone comite[2] proficisci constituit. Vnde uos talem diem praescribere oportet, ut et ille de expeditione possit esse reuersus, et ego meis negotiis exoccupatus possim uobis occurrere.[b]

4

Fulbert to Archbishop Leothericus of Sens: advising him as to the penance for a simoniac priest
late 1006–early 1008

Sancto ac uenerabili[a] primati suo L(eutherico) F(ulbertus) episcoporum humillimus fidelitatis affectum et obsequium.

De praesbitero uestro ab alio episcopo per pecuniam ordinato,[1] ex auctoritate sanctorum canonum tale uobis consilium dono. Primum degradetur. Deinde ab aecclesia separatus, duobus annis seuera poenitentia multetur,[b] ut honoris gradus, quos precio taxauerat, lacrimis conquirere et reparare contendat. Postea si digne poenituerit, restauretur. Haec uero quae diximus cum in aliis locis, tum satis expresse inuenietis in canone Toletano undecimo, capitulo nono.[2] Caeterum rebaptizationes et reordina-

---

3 DRCPBVM (L)   *a* palatium VM   *b* Valete *add.* P   Vale *add.* B

4 DRCPBVMKF (L) It is copied twice in M (see p. xlvi), the second time breaking off after *ordinato*, though a partly cut-off note in the margin (*Requi-*)

Fulbert to Archbishop Leothericus of Sens
late 1006–early 1008

To his very dear father and archbishop, L(eothericus), from F(ulbert), by grace of God bishop of Chartres, with the support of his prayers and the service of his fidelity.

I summoned my vassal Arnulf and charged him with those injuries of which you wrote to me in your complaint.[1] He replied that he was not fleeing from judgement, but would willingly stand trial. By his counsel and advice we are placing this entire case in your hands for you to fix a day when you, we, and the others who are involved can meet near Yèvre-le-Châtel, that is, on the very land of Saint Benedict's which is in dispute. Since Arnulf has made plans to go on a campaign with Count Odo,[2] you should set a day when it will be possible for him to be back from the campaign and for me to be free from my own affairs to meet with you.

Fulbert to Archbishop Leothericus of Sens
late 1006–early 1008

To his holy and venerable primate, L(eothericus), from F(ulbert), most humble bishop, with the good will and service of his fidelity.

As regards your priest who paid another bishop to ordain him,[1] on the authority of the holy canons I advise you to do as follows. First let him be degraded. After he has been separated from the church, let two years of heavy penance be imposed on him so that he may strive to seek and to recover by tears the standing of his orders, which he thought he could buy. Then, if he has done suitable penance, let him be restored. While you can find what we have said in several places, it is explicitly stated in the canons of the eleventh council of Toledo, chapter nine.[2] Since the canons

may refer to the earlier copying. It is here collated from f. 314.   [a] Sancto ... uenerabili *om.* BM, *but found in* M, *f.* 319   [b] multatur KF

3. [1] See no. 2.   [2] Of Chartres.

4. [1] See no. 2.   [2] Mansi, xi. 142 f.; Hinschius, p. 410.

tiones fieri canones uetant.[3] Propterea depositum non reordina-
bitis, sed reddetis ei suos gradus per instrumenta et per uestimenta
quae ad ipsos gradus pertinent ita dicendo: 'Reddo tibi gradum
hostiarii (et caetera) in nomine Dei[c] Patris et Filii et Spiritus
sancti.' Nouissime autem benedictione laetificabis[d] eum sic con-
cludendo:[e] 'Benedictio Dei Patris[f] et Filii[g] et Spiritus sancti super
te descendat, ut sis confirmatus in ordine sacerdotali, et offeras
placabiles hostias pro peccatis atque offensionibus populi omnipotenti Deo, cui est honor et gloria[h] in saecula saeculorum. Amen.'

5

Fulbert to Pope John XVIII:[1] *lodging a complaint against
a local count who has gone to Rome for absolution*
                                                late 1006–early 1008

Domino sancto[a] et uniuersali papae Io(hanni) F(ulbertus) Carnotensium humilis episcopus orationum fidelia.

Gratias agimus omnipotenti Deo qui more benignitatis suae
tuam, pater, humilitatem respexit,[2] et summo (ut decebat) dignitatis apice sublimauit. Proinde totus mundus ad te conuertit
oculos, teque unum omnes beatissimum praedicant. Contem-
plantur altitudinem tuam sancti uiri et gaudent quod eis simi-
litudine omnium uirtutum alludis. Respiciunt[b] persecutores
aecclesiae districtionis tuae baculum formidantes. Suspiciunt hi
qui flagellantur ab impiis et respirant sperantes adhuc restare sibi
consolationis remedium. De quorum numero sum ego magne ac[c]
praeclarae aecclesiae pusillus episcopus, qui tibi, pater, de angu-
stiis meis quaerimoniam scribens auxilium tuae pietatis imploro.
Est enim comes quidam malefactor nomine Rodulfus,[3] nimium
uicinus nobis, qui res aecclesiae nostrae per iniustam occasionem
inuasit, unum de clericis nostris suis manibus interfecit, duos
alios captos sacramentis illigauit;[d] et de his omnibus appellatus in

---

    c Dei *om.* CB   *d* laetificabitis BVKF laetificabimus M   *e* dicendo
DRC didendo V   *f* omnipotentis *add.* DKF (*marked for deletion* D)   *g* et
Filii *om.* KF   *h* gloria *om.* KF

5 DRKCPBVM (L)   *a* suo CV   *b* Resipiscunt DRK (Respici . . . L)
c et BVM   *d* alligauit CM

---

   [3] As regards reordinations, see E. Amann, *Dictionnaire de théologie catholique*,
xiii, ii (Paris, 1937), 2385 ff., especially the discussion of Fulbert's letter, 2412 f.
Although he states that there is no known source for the ceremony which

forbid rebaptisms and reordinations,[3] you should not reordain
one who has been deposed, but restore his orders to him using the
instruments and vestments which pertain to those orders and
saying: 'I restore to you the order of doorkeeper (and so forth) in
the name of God the Father, Son, and Holy Spirit.' At the close,
you should gladden his heart by giving him your blessing and
ending: 'May the blessing of God the Father, Son, and Holy
Spirit descend upon you so that you may be confirmed in the
priestly office and offer acceptable sacrifices for the sins and
offences of the people to almighty God, to whom is honour and
glory for ever and ever. Amen.'

Fulbert to Pope John XVIII[1]   *late 1006–early 1008*

To the holy and universal pope, John, from F(ulbert), humble
bishop of Chartres, with his faithful prayers.

We give thanks to almighty God, who in his wonted kindness
had regard for your humility,[2] father, and raised you, as was
fitting, to the highest height of honour. The whole world turns
its eyes toward you, and all proclaim you alone most blessed. Holy
men contemplate your highness and rejoice to see in you the image
of all their virtues. Those who persecute the church are mindful
of you, fearing the punishment of your staff. Those who are
scourged by the wicked look up to you and are revived in the hope
that there still remains for them your help and consolation. I am
one of them, a lowly bishop of a great and famous church; and I
am writing to you, father, to complain of my distress and to
implore your fatherly aid. There is a count, an evil-doer by the
name of Ralph,[3] who lives very close to us and who, on an unjust
pretext, seized possessions of our church, killed one of our clerks
with his own hands, and captured two others and bound them to

---

Fulbert proposes (but cf. Toledo IV, c. 28 (Mansi, x. 627) = c. 27 (Hinschius,
pp. 368 f.)), it seems to be merely a reversal of that for degrading a clerk: cf.
the proceedings at the councils of Saint-Basle in 991, c. lv (*MGH SS* iii. 686),
Orleans in 1022 (*Cart. S.-Père*, i. 114), Limoges II in 1031 (Mansi, xix. 540).
The final blessing is adapted from the rite of ordination in the pontifical.

5. [1] 25 December 1003–late June 1009 (Zimmermann, nos. 980, 1035).

   [2] Cf. Luke 1: 48.

   [3] Identity unknown, but cf. no. 62.

curia regis, et coram plena aecclesia sepe uocatus, nec propter hominem nec propter Deum ad iusticiam uenire dignatus, a nobis tandem excommunicatus est. Nunc uero ad limina sancti Petri contendit, tanquam ibi possit accipere de peccatis absolutionem, unde uenire non uult ad emendationem. Vnde rogamus te, dilectissime pater, cui totius aecclesiae cura commissa est, ut eum de sanguine atque iniuria filiorum tuorum ita arguere et castigare memineris, sicut meritum esse tua prudentia*e* nouit. Nec tua sanctitas iniuste in communionem recipiat, quem diuina auctoritas sicut ethnicum alienat. Vale, bone pastor, et uigila super nos, ne per incuriam tuam grex Domini detrimentum sustineat.

6

Fulbert to Archbishop Leothericus of Sens: thanking him for excommunicating an enemy   *before 17 February 1008*

Plurima sciencia et sanctitate pollenti patri et archiepiscopo L(eutherico) F(ulbertus) utinam Dei paruulus oracionis suffragium.

Quod aduersarium nostrum Gozonem[1] excommunicastis, a Deo mercedem et a nobis fideles gratias habeatis. Hoc enim faciendo et Deo prebuistis obsequium, et uestro discipulo dilectionis indiculum.*a* Quapropter si me uestra dignacio de hac aut de alia causa rogauerit, benignam se uobis et obsequentem nostra humilitas exibebit. Valete.

7

Fulbert to Bishop Fulk of Orleans:[1] advising him as regards Abbot Gauzlin of Fleury's claim of exemption
before 17 February 1008

Fratri et coepiscopo suo F(ulconi) F(ulbertus).

Quod ad praesens uestrum placitum non adeo, de malicia huius temporis ortae difficultates obsistunt, uobis exponendae per ocium.

e prouidentia DRKB (prudencia L)

6 LDRKPBVM   *a* indicium LDRK
7 DRKCPBVM (L)

himself by oaths. On all these charges he was summoned to the king's court and repeatedly cited before a full church council; and when he did not deign to come to trial out of respect for either God or man, we finally excommunicated him. Now he is hastening to the threshold of St. Peter's, as if there he could be absolved from sins for which he is unwilling to make amends. So we beg you, dearest father, to whom the care of the entire church has been entrusted, to be sure to charge and to chastise him for the blood and injuries of your children as you in your wisdom know he deserves. May your holiness not receive into communion, contrary to all justice, one whom divine authority casts out as a heathen. Farewell, good shepherd, and watch over us so that the Lord's flock may not suffer harm because you neglected it.

Fulbert to Archbishop Leothericus of Sens
before 17 February 1008

To his father and archbishop, L(eothericus), who has the strength of great knowledge and holiness, from F(ulbert), a mere child (and would that he were God's!), with the support of his prayers.

Because you have excommunicated our enemy Gozo[1] may you have God's reward and our faithful thanks, for in doing this you have done your duty to God and shown your love for your disciple. So if your grace should ask anything of us in this or in any other matter, we shall humbly show ourselves well-disposed and obedient to you. Farewell.

Fulbert to Bishop Fulk of Orleans[1]
before 17 February 1008

To his brother and fellow bishop, F(ulk), from F(ulbert).

I am not attending your court on the present occasion as I am held back by difficulties arising from the evils of the times which I shall have to explain to you at leisure. But what I would say if

6. [1] Identity unknown.

7. [1] After December 1003–after 17 May 1008 (Newman, p. 42 n.; above, p. lxxiii). For the circumstances see pp. lxxi–lxxiii.

Sed quod praesens dicerem, per hos apices significare curaui.
Defensores legum paucos, impugnatores uero plures esse uidetis.
Quin etiam dominus noster rex, cui summum iusticiae caput
incumbit, perfidia malorum sic circunuentus est, ut ad praesens
neque se uindicare, neque nos ut oportet adiuuare praeualeat.[2]
Non haec iccirco dixerim, ut fortitudinem animi uestri frangere
uelim, sed ut sana discretione causam uestram tractare memineritis. Igitur si abbas sancti Benedicti[3] de uestro contemptu[a] culpam
suam recognouerit, et illam deinceps subiectionem promiserit
quae uobis canonice debetur, hortor et suadeo ut recipiatis.
Sacramenta uero et caetera quae ad mundanam legem pertinent
propter amorem domini regis missa faciatis, ut religionem magis
quam secularem ambitionem uos sectari cognoscat. At si abbas in
tantam superbiam intumuerit ut ipsam quoque subiectionem
canonicam uobis derogare contendat, superbiae cui non parcit
Deus Dei seruus quomodo parcat nescio.[b] Valete.

8

*Fulbert to Abbot Gauzlin of Fleury: admonishing him to be
obedient to his bishop*   *16 May–1 October 1008*

F(ulbertus) Dei gratia Carnotensium episcopus G(auzlino) abbati
regulariter agere.

Presul Aurelianorum,[1] qui uos excommunicauit, coepiscopos
suos idem facere poscit. At ego, correpcionis[a] uestrae non expes,[b]
in kalendas[c] Octobris ei respectum dedi. Vnde nunc fraterne[d]
commoneo, ut gradus humilitatis interim uel usque ad tercium
relegendo,[2] episcopo uestro subiciamini sicut decet; aut si uobis
non ita faciendum esse uidetur, cur fieri non debeat, racionem
nobis intimare ne pigeat. Ego enim neque legem neque modum
raciocinationis[e] inuenire possum, qui uos ab iugo subiectionis
huius absoluat.[f] At[g] siquis alius preter uos se inuenisse fateatur,

---

    [a] contemptu uestro DRK (uestro contemptu L)   [b] parcat? Nescio.
DRK (L)

8 LDRCBVMKF   [a] correctionis RVKF   [b] expers BM, *post corr.* D
    [c] kalendis VM   [d] frater CB   [e] racionacionis LVF   rationis C
    [f] inuenire . . . absoluat] huius qui uos absoluat inuenio LDR (qui uos *supra*,
inuenio *in mar.* L)   huius absoluat C   *cf. p.* lvii   [g] Aut KF

I were present I have tried to let you know in these lines. That there are few who support the law, but many who violate it should be obvious to you. Indeed, even our lord the king, whose position makes him the fountain-head of justice, is so beset by the treachery of the wicked that at present he is unable to avenge himself or to aid us as he should.[2] I have not said this in order to break the firmness of your resolve, but rather to remind you to handle your case with prudence and discretion. So if the abbot of St. Benedict's[3] acknowledges his guilt in disobeying you and promises from now on the obedience that he owes you in accordance with the canons, I urge and advise you to accept it. As for the oaths and other matters which pertain to secular law, put them aside out of love for the king so that he may know that you are pursuing religious rather than worldly goals. But if the abbot is so swollen with pride that he attempts to withhold even canonical obedience from you, how God's servant can forgive that pride which God himself does not pardon, I do not know. Farewell.

Fulbert to Abbot Gauzlin of Fleury
16 May–1 October 1008

F(ulbert), by grace of God bishop of Chartres, to Abbot G(auzlin), with his admonition to live in accordance with the Rule.

The bishop of Orleans,[1] who has excommunicated you, is asking his fellow bishops to do this too. But since I still have hope that you can be corrected, I have given you until 1 October. Now I admonish you as your brother to read again in the meantime the degrees of humility as far as the third[2] and to be obedient to your bishop as you should. If you do not think that you are obliged to do so, please let us know the reason why, for I cannot find a law or any manner of reasoning that might release you from the yoke of this obedience. If anyone except you should claim to have found it, I would think him a reincarnation of that famous

[2] Perhaps a reference to the murder of Count Hugh of Beauvais (see no. 13).
[3] Abbot Gauzlin of Fleury (see no. 8).
8. [1] Fulk (see no. 7).
[2] St. Benedict, *Regula*, c. vii, the third degree of humility being obedience to one's superior.

nouum illum rethorem de caelo magis cecidisse quam descendisse crediderim.[3] Videte ne quis uos seducat inanibus uerbis.[4] Valete.

9

Fulbert to Bishop Reginald of Paris:[1] *stating his terms for accepting him as a vassal   before 17 February 1008*

Noto notus, R(egenaldo) F(ulbertus).

Haec a uobis exigo: securitatem de mea uita[a] et membris et[b] terra quam habeo uel per uestrum consilium adquiram, de auxilio uestro contra omnes homines salua fidelitate Roberti, de receptu[c] Vindocini castri ad meum usum et meorum fidelium qui uobis assecurabunt illud; commendationem uestrorum militum qui de nostro casamento beneficium tenent salua fidelitate uestra; iusticiam de quaerimonia Sanctionis et Huberti, et de quaerimoniis canonicorum aecclesiae nostrae,[2] et de legibus atriorum nostrorum. Si haec facere uultis, paratus sum conuentionem quam uobiscum inii obseruare. Si non uultis, nolite me itinere fatigare. Valete.

10

Fulbert to the vassals of Bishop Reginald of Paris at Vendôme: calling on them to fulfil their obligations as his own subvassals[1]   *before 28 March 1008*

Fulbertus Dei gratia Carnotensium episcopus Gundacro,[a] Huberto uicecomiti, Rogerio, Burcardo, Hugoni filio Hugonis, Otredo,

9 DRKPVM (L)	[a] uita mea DRK (L)	[b] et] de DRK (et L)
[c] recepto VM		
10 DRVM (L)	[a] Gundracco DR	

---

[3] Apparently—and so I have translated it—a reference to the fall of Lucifer (cf. Isa. 14: 12 ff.; Apoc. 12: 9 f.) used here to mean that only someone who had fallen from divine favour would attempt to justify Gauzlin's claims.

[4] Cf. Eph. 5: 6.

9. [1] April 991–12 September 1016 (Depoin, pp. 232 ff.). In 1006 he entered into his inheritance from his father, Burchard, which included Vendôme

orator who did not descend, but rather fell from heaven.[3] See to it that no one lead you astray with empty words.[4] Farewell.

Fulbert to Bishop Reginald of Paris[1]
before 17 February 1008

To one friend from another, to R(eginald) from F(ulbert).

This is what I require of you: assurance as to my life and limbs and the land which I have or shall acquire with your advice, as to your aid against all men saving the fidelity you owe to Robert, and as to the handing over of Vendôme castle for me and my vassals to use, for which they will give you surety; the commendation of your knights who hold a benefice from the land with which we enfeoffed you saving the fidelity they owe to you; justice as regards the complaint of Sanctio and Hubert, the complaints of the canons of our church,[2] and the laws of our courts. If you accept these terms, I am prepared to keep the agreement which I made with you. If you do not, please do not put me to the trouble of making the journey. Farewell.

Fulbert to the vassals of Bishop Reginald of Paris at Vendôme[1]
before 28 March 1008

Fulbert, by grace of God bishop of Chartres, to Gundacrus, Hubert the vicomte, Roger, Burchard, Hugh the son of Hugh,

---

(Loir-et-Cher), a fief held of the bishop of Chartres (see *Vita Burcardi*, p. xviii). Nos. 9 f. have been much discussed from the standpoint of feudal law, especially as regards the development of subvassalage and the *salva fidelitate* clause by which a vassal reserved the fidelity he owed to a lord with whom he had earlier entered into a feudal contract (here King Robert). See W. Kienast, *Untertaneneid und Treuvorbehalt in Frankreich und England* (Weimar, 1952), pp. 28 ff.; F. L. Ganshof, 'Les relations féodo-vassaliques aux temps post-carolingiens', *Settimane di studio del centro italiano di studi sull'alto medioevo* ii (1955), 87 f., 106, 112; Guillot, i. 28 ff.

   [2] The nature of these complaints is unknown. Hubert is perhaps the vicomte mentioned in no. 10; Sanctio, the brother of Fulbert's predecessor, Bishop Ralph (Merlet, p. 155).

10. [1] See no. 9.

Hamelino, Hugoni filio Herbrandi, et uxori Guismandi,[2] et omnibus illis qui tenent casamentum sanctae Mariae Carnotensis aecclesiae per donum Regenaldi episcopi.

Voco uos et admoneo ex parte Dei et sanctae Mariae et nostra,[b] ut infra proximum pascha ueniatis ad nos, aut nostrum seruicium facere, aut de uestris casamentis legitimam rationem reddere.[3] Quod si non feceritis, excommunicabo uos propter contumaciam[c] uestram; et interdicam ut non audiatis diuinum officium, nec uiui recipiatis communionem, neque mortui sepulturam. Quin etiam castellum Vindocinum et territorium eius anathematizabo, ut in eis diuinum officium non caelebretur, neque mortuus sepeliatur. Postea uero ipsa casamenta quae tenetis aut uni aut pluribus dabo, nec ultra iam uobiscum de illis concordabo. Deus uos conuertat, filii mei.

11

Fulbert to Abbot William:[1] *asking him to take back a fugitive monk*   *before 17 February 1008*

Quem iugiter in sinu memoriae fouet domno abbati Guill(elmo) F(ulbertus) Carnotensium sacerdos abundanciam caritatis.

Peregrinus quidam frater nomine Hermengaudus nos consolacionem petiturus adiit, uultu, sermone, et habitu penitentis. Sentus enim et squalidus,[2] pallentique macie deformatus, sua culpa de uestri caenobii paradyso se conquerebatur[a] expulsum, in

---

[b] nostrae VM	[c] contumeliam DR
11 LDRKCPBVM	[a] conquirebatur VM

---

[2] In view of the frequent occurrence of these names in eleventh-century documents relating to Vendôme, and the widespread practice of naming a child after a parent or grandparent, it is hardly possible to identify the persons named here with any certainty. A Walter, son of Hamelin, is mentioned in Fulbert's grant to Marmoutier (Appendix C, no. 3) and among the vassals of Vendôme in *De consuetudinibus Burcardi comitis in Vindocino* (printed as an appendix in *Vita Burcardi* and dated (p. ix) *c.* 1032 (cf. Guillot, i. 49 f.)), p. 35. Whether these are to be identified with Hamelin of Langeais (Indre-et-Loire, *arr.* Chinon) and his son Walter, who appear rather frequently in the charters of Marmoutier and La Trinité de Vendôme, is not certain, though it would seem from the various charters which mention them that there may have been two

Otredus, Hamelin, Hugh the son of Herbrandus, Guismandus's wife,[2] and all who hold a benefice of the church of St. Mary of Chartres by grant from Bishop Reginald.

I summon and admonish you on behalf of God, St. Mary, and ourselves, to come to us before next Easter to do service to us or to render a due account of your benefices.[3] If you do not do so, I shall excommunicate you for being contumacious and prohibit you from attending divine service and receiving communion while you are alive and burial when you are dead. I shall also lay an interdict on Vendôme and its surroundings so that divine service may not be celebrated there and the dead may not be buried. Then I shall give the benefices that you hold to one or more persons, and after that I shall not come to terms with you concerning them. May God convert you, my children.

Fulbert to Abbot William[1]   *before 17 February 1008*

To Abbot William, whom he ever cherishes in the memory of his heart, from F(ulbert), bishop of Chartres, with his wish that he may abound in charity.

A wandering brother named Hermengaudus came to us seeking comfort, his face, speech, and dress those of a penitent. Unkempt and dirty,[2] marred by pallor and emaciation, he complained that it was his own fault that he had been driven from the paradise

---

Hamelins, the second being Walter's son (see Halphen, p. 159, and his 'Étude sur l'authenticité du fragment de chronique attribué à Foulques le Réchin', *Bibliothèque de la Faculté des lettres de l'Université de Paris*, xiii (1901), 23 ff.; Guillot, i. 292 f.). An Otradus, father of Solomon, is also found in the customary, and Solomon figures in the *Cartulaire de Marmoutier pour le Vendômois*, ed. C. A. de Trémault (Paris, 1893), pp. 38 ff., in connection with a dispute concerning the mill of La Chappe, once held by Guismandus and then sold by him with the consent of his wife Emelina, daughter of Hugh Doubleau (pp. 46 ff.; cf. above, p. xx n.) and possibly the wife addressed by Fulbert. Among others mentioned in the customary are Hubert, vicomte of Vendôme and father of Bishop Hubert of Angers (cf. Halphen, pp. 114 f.), and Gundacrius, a name which occurs several times in mid eleventh-century charters for Marmoutier.

[3] Comparison with no. 9 would seem to indicate that Fulbert is using *seruicium facere* as equivalent to *commendatio*; however, Guillot, i. 29 n., takes it to mean that Fulbert was calling on them to perform services which they owed as a result of having commended themselves earlier.

11. [1] Identity unknown.   [2] Cf. Terence, *Eun.* 236.

corpore fesso morientem animam circumferre. Quod uerbum interius admittentes,[b] compassione[c] carere, uosque pro illo non rogare nequiuimus. Precamur itaque si ius, si fas est,[3] in nomine eius[d] Domini, qui iuxta est his qui tribulato sunt corde,[4] ut paterna pietate recipiatis hunc[e] filium, iam tandem sero postliminio reuertentem, quo de conuerso peccatore non tantum angeli Dei, uerum etiam sancti fratres quorum propius interest gratulentur.[5] Valete[f] memores nostri, uestri non inmemorum.

12

Fulbert to Bishop A(vesgaudus of Le Mans?):[1] *setting a date for a meeting   before 17 February 1008*

In Domino fratri et coepiscopo suo A(uisgaudo) F(ulbertus) omnium expetendorum summam.

Gaudeo signis officii uestri curam uos habere monentibus: quod me alloqui uultis, quod querimoniae nostrae finem facere, quod incesta conubia castigare. Sunt enim haec studiosi, iusti, atque casti animi indicia. Et quia me his gerendis diem locumque statuere uoluistis, sit dies iiix[a] kalendas Marcii, locus uilla Masingiaci.[2] Quo si occurritis, Haimonem[3] adducere mementote. Alioquin, resignate mihi tempestiue, ne frustra uiam tanti laboris ingrediar.[b]

[b] admittens LC	[c] compassionem L	[d] eius *om.* LDRKC
[e] uestrum *add.* DRK	[f] Vale L?, CVM	
12 LDRPBVHKF	[a] in x B xii K^{mo} x^{o} F	[b] Valete *add.* PB

[3] A commonplace, perhaps from Terence, *Hec.* 387.

[4] Cf. Ps. 33: 19.

[5] Cf. Luke 15: 10.

12. [1] 997/1004–1028/38 (R. Latouche, *Histoire du comté du Maine pendant le Xe et XIe siècle* (Paris, 1910), pp. 132 ff.).

of your monastery and that he was carrying about a dying soul in an exhausted body. Having taken his story to heart, we could not but feel pity or fail to intercede with you in his behalf. So we beg you, if it is just and right,[3] in the name of that Lord who is near to those who are troubled of heart,[4] to receive with a father's kindness this son who at this late hour is at last returning home, that not only the angels of God, but also the holy brothers, to whom it is of closer concern, may rejoice over the converted sinner.[5] Farewell, and remember us, as we remember you.

Fulbert to Bishop A(vesgaudus of Le Mans?)[1]
before 17 February 1008

To his brother in the Lord and fellow bishop, A(vesgaudus), from F(ulbert), with his wish for every excellence.

I am delighted by the indications of your concern with your duties: that you wish to confer with me, to put an end to our complaint, and to punish incestuous marriage. These show that your intention is zealous, just, and pure. Since you want me to set a day and a place for attending to these matters, let the day be 17 February and the place, the village of *Masingiacum*.[2] If you are going there, remember to bring Haimo.[3] Otherwise let me know in time to keep me from setting out on such a difficult journey for nothing.

[2] Possibly Mazangé (Loir-et-Cher, *arr.* Vendôme), where the church of Chartres later had holdings. As for the way Fulbert numbered the days of February in leap year, see no. 147.

[3] Probably the Haimo who is the earliest known lord of Château-du-Loir (Sarthe, *arr.* Le Mans) and who married Avesgaudus's sister (see Latouche, op. cit., p. 62 n.; J. Boussard, 'La seigneurie de Bellême aux xe et xie siècles', *Mélanges d'histoire du moyen âge dédiés à la mémoire de Louis Halphen* (Paris, 1951), pp. 45 ff.).

13

Fulbert to Count Fulk Nerra of Anjou:[1] *calling on him to clear himself as regards his part in the murder of Count Hugh of Beauvais*   *16 May 1008 or soon after*

Fulbertus Dei gratia Carnotensium[a] episcopus comiti Fulconi commonitorium salutis.

Tam horrendo facinore praesentiam domni regis tui dedecora-uere satellites, ut mundani iudices asserant capitale, te quoque reum maiestatis, qui eis postea patrocinium tuum et receptacula praebuisti.[2] Proinde rogabatur[b] a multis, ut die sacro pentecostes et te et illos excommunicaremus.[3] Sed nos[c] tuae prouidentes saluti, trium ebdomadarum ab ipso die petiuimus inducias, ut litteris te conuenire possemus. Talem etiam a rege conditionem impetrauimus si ueneris in iudicium, ut non super uitas aut super membra reorum, sed super facultates[d] ultio reflectatur. Vnde te commonemus, ut ante praescriptum terminum auctores tanti sceleris aut in iudicium adducas, aut propter honorem regis tui repudies, temetipsum deinde sicut per abbatem sancti Albini[4] promisisti expurges, et humili satisfactione regis animum places. Quod si reos ipsos nec ad iusticiam ducere, nec propter seniorem tuum repudiare uolueris, Christianam communionem nobiscum ulterius non habebis. Vigila ergo sicut propter temetipsum,[e] et quid habeas animi[f] cito michi remanda. Optimam partem consilii det tibi Deus eligere.

---

13 DRKCBVM (L)   *a* Carnotensis DK; C. R   *b* rogabamur DRK
(. . . batur L)   *c* nos *om*. VM   *d* eorum *add*. DRK (*om*. L)
e pro temetipso B   pro temetipsum M   *f* animi habeas DRKC (L?)

---

13. [1] 987–1040.
    [2] After King Robert was forced by the church to separate from his second wife, Bertha of Troyes, he married Constance, a relative of Count Fulk of Anjou. Relations between Robert and Constance were strained; and one of Bertha's supporters, Count Hugh of Beauvais, attempted to sow further discord between them. Fulk sent some of his followers to murder Hugh, and the crime was committed during a hunt in the presence of the king himself. Fulk may

Fulbert to Count Fulk Nerra of Anjou[1]
16 May 1008 or soon after

Fulbert, by grace of God bishop of Chartres, to Count Fulk, with a warning as regards his salvation.

Your followers have disgraced the king's presence by committing such a dreadful crime that secular judges say it is a capital offence and that you too are guilty of treason for having afterward given them your protection and a place of refuge.[2] Numerous persons asked us to excommunicate all of you on the feast of Pentecost;[3] but since we were concerned for your salvation, we asked for this to be postponed for three weeks so that we could write and admonish you. We also got the king to agree that if you will stand trial, vengeance will not be taken on the life and limbs of the guilty, but rather on their possessions. So we warn you to bring the perpetrators of this monstrous crime to trial before the prescribed date or to repudiate them out of honour for your king, and then, as you promised through the abbot of Saint-Aubin,[4] to clear yourself and to appease the king's mind by humbly proving your innocence. But if you are not willing to bring those who committed the crime to trial or to repudiate them for the sake of your lord, you will not remain in Christian communion with us after that date. So be on your guard as though for yourself, and quickly let me know what you intend to do. God grant that you choose the best course.

---

have made a pilgrimage to the Holy Land in expiation. See Raoul Glaber, iii. 2 (ed. Prou, pp. 57 f.); Pfister, *Robert*, pp. 41 ff.; Halphen, pp. 32 f., 213 ff. Fulbert's reference to secular law and his definition of the crime and the penalties prescribed for it point both in substance and verbally to *Cod. Theod.* ix. 14. 3 (see J.-F. Lemarignier, 'A propos de deux textes sur l'histoire du droit romain au moyen âge (1008 et 1038)', *BEC* ci (1940), 157 ff.).

[3] Apparently a reference to the council of Chelles, 16 May 1008 (see p. lxxi).

[4] Hubert of Saint-Aubin d'Angers, 1001–27 (see Halphen, p. 92 n. and *passim*; Guillot, ii. 31). Here, as in no. 36, Fulbert is apparently referring to the practice by which a defendant cleared himself by swearing that he was innocent; but it is also possible that he is simply speaking of Fulk's making proper satisfaction (i.e. 'to cleanse yourself and to appease the king's mind by humbly making satisfaction').

14

Fulbert to Abbot Richard of Saint-Médard of Soissons:[1]
admonishing him to be obedient to his bishop

16 May–1 October 1008

F(ulbertus) Dei gratia Carnotensium episcopus R(icardo) abbati et omnibus sancti Medardi monachis orationis[a] suffragium.

Quandiu de uobis quae de bonis[b] et sapientibus uiris audiuimus, gaudentes Deo gratias agebamus. At nunc sinistro rumore lesi uestrum periculum formidamus. Dicuntur enim uestri domestici atrium et aecclesiam beati Medardi cruenta caede uiolasse. Dicitur de uobis quod in eadem uiolata basilica sine episcopali reconciliatione Deo sacrificare praesumitis. Quod si uerum est, profecto praesumptio ista et noua est et nimia, et bonis omnibus acriter insectanda. Quid enim mali est quod in sancta aecclesia machinari incipitis? Vultis dare partes episcoporum praesbiteris, praesbiterorum laicis? Vbi uobis conceditur aecclesiam aut nouam dedicare aut prophanatam reconciliare? Sed nec oratorii quidem domum uobis edificare nisi per episcopum licet; positi nanque estis omnino sub potestate ipsius, qui, ut ait Ieronimus, potestatem habet peccantem monachum tradere sathanae in interitum carnis.[2] Sed ne parua auctoritate fretus haec dicere uidear, testem michi allego[c] magnam synodum Calcedonensem sescentorum triginta episcoporum sub papa Leone, sub Martiano[d] principe congregatorum, in qua Eutices abbas Constantino-politanus condemnatus est, in qua etiam de supradictis causis ita sancitum est: 'Placuit neminem aut edificare aut constituere monasteria aut oratorii domum sine conscientia ipsius ciuitatis episcopi. Eos uero qui per singulas ciuitates seu possessiones in monasteriis sunt subiectos esse debere episcopo, et quieti operam dare, atque obseruare ieiunia et orationes in locis in quibus semel Deo se deuouerunt permanentes. Et neque communicare aeccle-siasticas[e] neque seculares aliquas attrectare actiones, relinquentes

---

14 DRCBVMKF (L)   [a] orationis *om.* C (L)   [b] quae . . . bonis] ut de magnis DR (*post corr.* L)   [c] alligo CVM (L) *ante corr.* F   [d] Marco DR (L)   Matono C   Matriano V   Maraone KF   [e] aecclesiasticas] aecclesiasticis negotiis DRK

Fulbert to Abbot Richard of Saint-Médard of Soissons[1]
16 May–1 October 1008

F(ulbert), by grace of God bishop of Chartres, to Abbot R(ichard) and all the monks of Saint-Médard, with the support of his prayers.

As long as we heard that you were conducting yourselves as good and wise men, we rejoiced and gave thanks to God. But now we are troubled by evil report and fear you are in danger. Your servants are said to have violated the forecourt and church of Saint-Médard by bloodshed and slaughter, and it is said that you are venturing to offer sacrifice to God in that same basilica which has been violated without first having had it reconciled by the bishop. If this is true, such presumption is indeed new and beyond measure and must be sharply censured by all good men. What schemes are you contriving against holy church? Do you wish to give the functions of bishops to priests, of priests to laymen? Where are you given the right to dedicate a new church or to reconcile a desecrated one? Indeed, you are not even allowed to build an oratory without the bishop's consent; for you have been totally placed under his authority, and he, as Jerome says, has the power to give an erring monk over to Satan to the ruin of his flesh.[2] So that my claims may not seem unsupported by competent authority, I cite as my witness the great synod of Chalcedon, where six hundred and thirty bishops gathered under Pope Leo and the Emperor Marcian, where Abbot Eutyches of Constantinople was condemned, and where the following was decreed concerning such cases: 'Be it resolved that no one is to build or to establish a monastery or oratory without the knowledge of the bishop of that city. Those who live in monasteries in the cities or on private estates should be subject to their bishop, lead a secluded life, fast, and pray, remaining in the houses where they vowed themselves to God for ever; nor should they leave their monasteries to take part in church affairs or to handle any secular business

---

14. [1] Before 1005–after 1037 (*GC* ix. 413). The cause of his dispute with his diocesan bishop, Fulk of Soissons (before 25 August 1005–6 August 1019 (Newman, p. 8 n.; *DHGE* viii. 878)), is not known, but may have been the burning issue of exemption (cf. nos. 7 f.).
   [2] Ep. xiv. 8 (ed. Hilberg, *CSEL* liv. 55). Cf. 1 Cor. 5: 5.

propria monasteria, nisi forte iubeantur propter urgentes necessitates ab ipsius ciuitatis episcopo.'³ Item in eadem: 'In ptociis, monasteriis, aut martyriis constituti sub potestate sint eius qui in ea est ciuitate episcopus secundum traditionem sanctorum patrum, nec per praesumptionem recedant a suo episcopo. Eos uero qui ausi fuerint rescindere huiusmodi institutionem*f* quocunque modo, uel si noluerint subiacere proprio episcopo, siquidem fuerint clerici, personarum ordinatione*g* subiaceant condemnationibus canonum; si uero laici uel monachi fuerint, communione priuentur.'⁴ Poteram alia multa de legibus diuinis huic rationi firmamenta subnectere, sed breuem me*h* scribere memini; et, ut ait Ysidorus, 'sicut militi illa arma sufficiunt quae ferre ad tempus congruenter potest, sic nobis de multis sententiis paucae prout tempus exegerit.'⁵ Nunc uobis caritatiue suadere uolo, ut sano consilio praebeatis assensum,*i* ad subiectionem episcopi uestri suppliciter redeatis, de praeterita culpa requiratis ueniam, de futura assumatis cautelam, ut et uobis fiat quies de oboedientia, et nobis de uestra quiete laeticia. Alioquin, pro certo sciatis, quia si (quod absit) in contumacia contra illum manseritis, in proximo conuentu episcoporum graue dispendium incurretis.

15

*Fulbert to Bishop Guido (of Châlons-sur-Marne?):*¹ *sending his greetings and commending the bearer*

16 May–25 December 1008

Dilecto patri et coepiscopo suo Guidoni F(ulbertus) uiuere et ualere.

Vester clericus et propinquus noster F.*a2* ad nos ueniens eo se gratiorem exhibuit, quod de uobis bene per omnia nunciauit. Vnde nunc illum salutationis gerulum facientes, et claritati*b* uestrae comparati munusculi, exorare uolumus si non est inportunum, ut eam gratiam sibi sentiat prodesse, quam apud uos iamdudum nos credimus habuisse. Valete.

f instaurationem VM   *g* personarum ordinatione *om.* RVM   *h* me *om.* DR (L)   *i* et *add.* DRC (*add. in mar.* L)

15 DRKCBVM (L) *a* F.] E. DRC (L)   *b* caritati DRKC

³ The fourth ecumenical council held at Chalcedon in 451 under Pope Leo I (440–61) and the Emperor Marcian (450–7), c. 4 (Mansi, vii. 385; Hinschius, p. 285).

unless it should happen that they are ordered to do so by the
bishop of that city because of pressing necessity.'[3] Also in the
same council: 'Let those who reside in poorhouses, monasteries,
or at the shrines of saints be under the authority of the bishop of
that city in accordance with the teachings of the holy fathers, and
let them not venture to cut themselves off from their bishop. As
for those who dare to violate this ordinance in any way or who are
unwilling to be subject to their bishop, if they are clerks, by reason
of their calling let them be condemned in accordance with the
canons, but if they are laymen or monks, let them be severed from
communion.'[4] I could add much more from divine law to support
this argument, but I have it in mind to write briefly; and as
Isidore says, 'just as a soldier is content with the arms which he
can conveniently carry at the time, so we are content with citing
only a few of many pronouncements in accordance with the
dictates of time.'[5] Now in all charity I wish to persuade you to give
your assent to sound advice and humbly to return to obedience
to your bishop, to seek forgiveness for your past sins, and to take
care for the future so that your conscience may be at rest as to
your obedience and that we may rejoice because of this. Otherwise
you may rest assured that if (God forbid) you continue to be
contumacious toward your bishop, you will be severely condemned
in the next episcopal council.

Fulbert to Bishop Guido (of Châlons-sur-Marne?)[1]
16 May–25 December 1008

To his dear father and fellow bishop, Guido, from F(ulbert), with
his wishes for long life and good health.

When your clerk, our kinsman F.,[2] arrived, he made us all the
happier to see him by telling us that all was well with you. So now
in making him the bearer of our greetings and of a small present
which we have prepared for your eminence, we wish to ask, if it is
not unsuitable, that he may have the advantage of enjoying the same
favour that we believe has long been ours with you. Farewell.

[4] Ibid., c. 8 (Mansi, vii. 386; Hinschius, p. 286).
[5] Pseudo-Isidore, *Decretales*, preface, vi (Hinschius, p. 19).

15. [1] 1002–9 (M.-J. Gut, 'Liste critique des évêques de Châlons-sur-Marne
aux xie et xiie siècles', *BPH*, 1958, p. 118).
[2] Perhaps Fulbert's nephew, Fulbert (see p. xvi n.).

16

Fulbert to his clerk G.: summoning him to come for judgement *before 25 December 1008*

F(ulbertus) Dei gratia Carnotensium episcopus G. suo clerico.

Quicquid boni de te sperare praesumpseram totum fere in contrarium cedit. Non solum enim nullum ex te consilium uel auxilium capio, uerum insuper odium pro dilectione reddis, et iniuriis me afficis immerentem. De quibus iam apud te per uerba legati bis quaerimoniam feci, per scripta mea nunc tercio queror. Doleo nanque quod temetipsum aecclesiae nostrae ministerio fraudas, prophanae uitae et armatae miliciae mancipatum, quod decimas et oblationes nostras ausu sacrilego detines, quod monachorum nostrorum ecclesias inuasisti, quod tui domestici canonicorum uillas praeda et incendio uastant. Haec denique omnia ut dictum est indigne michi abs te fieri quaeror, cui nichil unquam incommodi uel opera mea uel instinctu memini contigisse. Quod siquid esset unde me suspectum haberes, pro incerta causa certas offensiones non oporteret inferre.[1] At siquid in te manifeste peccassem, et tu scripturarum consiliis adquiescere uelles,[2] tuum tamen praesulem cum patientia sustineres. Sed dum in te discrecionis oculum ira turbat,[3] cupiditas caecat, nec causam satis diligenter attendis, nec opem consilii salutaris admittis. Vnde iam[a] tibi satis expectato praenuntio, quod nisi ante natale Domini resipiscens ad correptionem[b] ueneris, senties me diuinas leges acriter exequentem, quem modo neglegis suauiter admonentem. Vale.[c]

17

Fulbert to King Robert: notifying him that he has followed his instructions and postponed his journey *mid 1008 or later*

Benignissimo atque dilectissimo domino suo R(otberto) F(ulbertus) Dei gratia Carnotensium sacerdos.

Cognita benigna uoluntate uestra, consilioque prudenciae uestrae comperto, quia sanum est ut solet, uoluntati obsequor,

---

16 DRKCBVM (L)   [a] etiam DRK (L)   [b] correctionem K, *post corr.* RV   ad correptionem *om.* C   [c] Valete V (L)   *om.* M   interim *add.* BV
17 LDRKPBVH

Fulbert to his clerk G.   *before 25 December 1008*

F(ulbert), by grace of God bishop of Chartres, to his clerk G.

Whatever good I had ventured to expect of you turns out almost totally to the contrary; for not only do you fail to give me counsel or aid, but you return hatred for love and injure me unjustly. In this regard I have already made two complaints to you by messenger; now I am sending a third in writing. I am grieved that you are defaulting in your service to our church and have given yourself up to an ungodly life and armed warfare, that with sacrilegious rashness you are keeping back tithes and offerings that are ours, that you have attacked churches which belong to our monks, and that your servants are destroying farms which belong to our canons, plundering and burning them. Finally I charge you with having done all these injuries to me without reason, for I do not remember that any harm has ever come to you by my actions or at my instigation. But even if you should suspect me of having done you some harm, it is not right to inflict undoubted injuries for a doubtful cause.[1] Even though I had obviously sinned against you, if you were willing to accept the counsel of the Scriptures,[2] you would bear patiently with your bishop. While wrath clouds and cupidity blinds the eye of your discernment,[3] you will neither pay the careful attention to the matter that you should nor admit the aid of salutary advice. I have waited for you long enough, and I warn you that if you do not recover your senses and come for correction before Christmas, you will find me, whose gentle admonitions you still refuse to heed, strictly following divine law. Farewell.

Fulbert to King Robert   *mid 1008 or later*

To his most kind and very dear lord, R(obert), from F(ulbert), by grace of God bishop of Chartres.

I have received your good wishes and learned what you in your wisdom advise; and since it is, as usual, the only sensible course,

16. [1] Cf. Pseudo-Zepherinus, ep. i. 4 (Hinschius, p. 131).
    [2] Cf. ibid., c. 8 (Hinschius, p. 132); Heb. 13: 17; Ecclus. 3: 9.
    [3] Cf. Ps. 6: 8 (Roman Psalter); 30: 10.

consilio adquiesco; et iter institutum ad presens omittens, in tempus a uobis constitutum differo peragendum, si annuerit Deus. Si ergo de iustitia, de pace, de statu regni, de honore ecclesiae uultis agere, ecce habetis me paruum satellitem pro uiribus opitulari paratum. Valete.[a]

18

Fulbert to Archbishop Leothericus of Sens: cautioning him against duplicity[1]   mid *1008* or later

Karissimo patri et archiepiscopo suo L(eutherico) F(ulbertus) episcopus.

Proreta nauis regiae cautus et circumspectus esto. Terreni spiritus insolenter assibilant, fluctus huius seculi intumescunt, promunctoria mundanae potestatis pericula minantur et mortes, more pyratarum insidiantur ypocritae. Inter haec omnia tendendum est ad portum caelestis patriae.[a] Noli ergo tute ipse tibi bythalassum dubietatis ac duplicitatis in corde tuo miscere. Simplex enim est uia Domini; et qui ambulat simpliciter, ambulat confidenter.[2] Si de uia legis diuinae qualibet occasione seductus aberraueris, in tartaream Carybdim naufragus demergeris. Regat te ualida manus omnipotentis Domini.

19

*Fulbert to a former clerk or student: explaining his apparent coolness and asking him to get in touch   mid *1008* or later*

Caro suo D. F(ulbertus) sacerdos.

Ne turberis, fili mi, nec decidat cor tuum ab amore et fiducia nostri, non enim dereliquit te anima mea; sed quia minus credere sibi et inoboediens esse uidebaris, paululum dissimulato uultu

---

[a] Vale LRBVH

18 LDRCPBVH   [a] Inter . . . patriae *om.* LDR

19 DRKCPBVH (L)

I am complying with your wishes and accepting your advice. So I am abandoning for the present the journey that I had planned and postponing it until the time that you set, when (God willing) I hope to make it. If you wish to treat of justice, peace, the welfare of the kingdom, and the honour of the church, you have in me a little follower who is prepared to do all that he can to help you. Farewell.

Fulbert to Archbishop Leothericus of Sens[1]
mid 1008 or later

To his very dear father and archbishop, L(eothericus), from Bishop F(ulbert).

As watchman on the king's ship you must be cautious and circumspect. Gales of earthliness are whistling violently, waves of this world are surging up, headlands of secular power threaten danger and death, and hypocrites lie in ambush like pirates. Amidst all these you must hold your course for the harbour of the heavenly homeland. So do not let the twin seas of doubt and duplicity mingle their waters in your heart; for the way of the Lord is simple, and he who walks in simplicity walks in confidence.[2] If on any occasion you are lured from the way of divine law and go astray, you will be shipwrecked and sink into the infernal Charybdis. May the strong hand of the almighty Lord guide you.

Fulbert to a former clerk or student
mid 1008 or later

To his dear D. from Bishop F(ulbert).

Do not be troubled, my son, or let your heart fall away from its love and trust in us; for my soul did not abandon you, but since you seemed to have less confidence in it and to disobey it,

18. [1] The body of this letter is an adaptation of Pseudo-Clement, ep. i. 14 (Hinschius, pp. 34 f.), in which the state of the church is compared to a ship with Christ at the helm and the bishops at the prow.
[2] Cf. Prov. 10: 9.

ad exemplum Domini ire se longius finxit.[1] At nunc ad hospitali-
tatem amici pectoris[a] dulciter reuocata, et oblato pane diuinarum
scripturarum oblectata, in ipsius panis fractione omnem uultus
ambiguitatem deponit, et antiqua specie tibi renitens hilarescit.
Praecor itaque si copia uehiculorum suppetit, ut nos corporaliter
uisites. Si non, a nobis tibi mitti iure debitum[b] mandes.[c] Vale.[d]

20

*Fulbert to a priest: advising him against celebrating mass by
himself and explaining the lawfulness of mass stipends*
mid *1008 or later*

Caro suo R. F(ulbertus) episcopus.

Occupatus erga plurima, paucis tibi respondere compellor.
Ecclesiae nomen, extra quam ueri sacrificii non est locus,[1] inter-
pretacione sua pluralitatem innuit. Sacerdotalis quoque salutatio
qua[a] 'Dominus uobiscum' dicitur, non ad unum solum sed ad
plures dirigitur. Sed et ille uersiculus de quo mihi questionem
fecisti, plane sibi circumstantes requirit.[2] Pro his ergo atque aliis
huiusmodi, non ex auctoritate quidem canonum quos mihi modo
retractare non licuit, sed meo interim arbitratu, tutius esse suadeo
te a missarum celebratione suspendere, quam eas sine duorum
saltem aut trium fidelium attestacione celebrare. Scrupulus autem
ille de offerentibus ita solui potest: quod dum sacrificamus, illi pro
quibus agitur per manus nostras offerunt Deo sacrificium laudis.
Haec ad praesens me respondisse contentus, aueto. Quod si noua
legendo uel retractando uetera de his quippiam magis ratum
inuenero, tibi caritatiue rescribam. At[b] si tute prior aliquid tale
reppereris, eandem nobis exibe caritatem.[c]

---

[a] peccatoris D   [b] debito DRK (L) debitam BC   debitam *corr. to* -um? P
[c] tibi . . . mandes] tibi mitti postules V   mitti postules H   [d] Vale *om.* VH
20 LDRKCPBVH   [a] quia L   [b] Aut CP   [c] Valete *add.* B Vale *add.* H

it followed the Lord's example in disguising its face for a little while and making as if it would have gone further.[1] But now that it has been sweetly recalled to the hospitality of a friendly breast and gladdened by the offering of the bread of divine scriptures, while breaking that bread it lays aside all that would conceal its face and happily beams on you, smiling as of old. So I beg you, if you have a way to travel, to visit us in person; but if not, to let us know what we ought in justice to send to you. Farewell.

Fulbert to a priest   *mid 1008 or later*

To his dear R. from Bishop F(ulbert).

I am extremely busy and forced to send you a brief reply. The very word 'church'—and it is the only place where the true sacrifice can be offered[1]—signifies more than one; and the priest's greeting where he says 'The Lord be with you' is addressed not to just one, but to several persons. Moreover, the versicle about which you asked me obviously presupposes the presence of bystanders.[2] Basing my judgement for the time being on these and similar reasons and not on the authority of the canons, which I have not been able to consult at present, I think it is safer for you to stop celebrating mass rather than to celebrate it without at least two or three of the faithful present. Your anxiety concerning those who are making the offerings can be solved like this: while we are the ones who are sacrificing, those for whom we are doing it are offering the sacrifice of praise to God through our hands. Let this reply suffice for the present, and farewell. If in reading new works or re-reading old ones I should find anything more definite about this, out of charity I shall write and let you know. But if you yourself should come across something first, please show the same charity to us.

19. [1] Cf. Luke 24: 15 ff., especially 28.
20. [1] Prosper, *Liber sententiarum*, c. xv (ed. Gastaldo, *CCL* lxviii[a]. 260).
    [2] Perhaps (along with 'sacrificium laudis' below) a reference to the canon of the mass ('omnium circum(ad)stantium').

21

*Fulbert to King Robert: explaining his failure to meet him
and asking forgiveness*[1]   *mid 1008 or later*

Inperpetuum diligendo domino suo regique R(otberto) F(ulbertus) sacerdos.

Queso, domine mi,[a] ne indignanter accipias quod tibi proxima
dominica Parisius non occurri. Scias enim[b] pro certo quod nuncii
fefellerunt me, dicentes te illuc[c] ipso die non adfore, sed propter
ordinacionem cuiusdam episcopi me uocari, quem omnino non
noueram, nec sacram tuam nec epistolam archipresulis mei de
ordinacione ipsius acceperam. Vnde siquid delicti penes me est
seductum aliena fallacia, facilis tamen debet esse remissio apud
regiam pietatem, cum aetiam apud forenses iudices status sit
huiusmodi uenialis. 'In toto corde meo diligo te; ne repellas me a
mandatis tuis.'[2]

22

Fulbert to Bishop Thierry of Orleans:[1] *explaining why he
refused to consecrate him and describing the crisis which
followed*   c. *late 1008–1012/13*

Fratri Theoderico Fulbertus sacerdos.[a]

Quod te pridem ordinare noluimus,[b] mirantur tecum (ut aiunt)
amici tui, insuper et dominus noster rex;[c] et cur omissum sit
causam ignorantes, omnes fere id iniuste ac contumeliose factum
clamant.[2] Nos uero qui non iniuste nec contumeliose factum esse
scimus, non unam tantum sed plures ueras et autenticas inde
reddimus rationes, quae tibi et illis finem recti persuadeant, et a
praua suspicione remoueant.

21 LDRKCPBVH   [a] mi *only in* PB   [b] autem LDRKC   [c] illic
DRK

22 DRCPBVHK (L). F *breaks off near the beginning and has not been used
here.*   [a] *written as a cryptogram* DRP (L): Fratri Thfpdfrkcp (-rkchp P(L))
Fxlbfrtxs sbcfrdps. *The solution is written above the cryptogram in* R. *The cipher
has been erased in* V, *and the solution placed in the margin. The solution alone is*

Fulbert to King Robert[1]   *mid 1008 or later*

To his ever beloved lord and king, R(obert), from Bishop F(ulbert).

I beg you, my lord, not to take offence at my failure to meet you at Paris last Sunday. You may know for a truth that the messengers deceived me, saying that you would not be there on that day and that I was summoned to consecrate a bishop of whom I knew nothing at all, nor had I received a letter from your highness or from my archbishop concerning his consecration. So if I committed an offence as a result of being treacherously misled by another, it should be easy to obtain forgiveness at the hands of a pious king, since even civil-law judges are ready to pardon a transgression of this kind. 'I love thee with my whole heart; let me not stray from thy commandments.'[2]

Fulbert to Bishop Thierry of Orleans[1]
c. *late 1008–1012/13*

To his brother Thierry from Bishop Fulbert.

Our refusal to consecrate you amazes not only you, but your friends, so they say, as well as the king; and since they do not know why your consecration should have been stopped, almost all declare that it was done unjustly and insultingly.[2] But we who know that it was done neither unjustly nor insultingly hereby offer not one, but several good reasons for it based on competent authority in the hope of convincing all of you of the honesty of our intention and of freeing us from the suspicion of evil.

given in CBHK. *As regards such cryptic writing, see W. Levison, England and the Continent in the Eighth Century (Oxford, 1946), pp. 290 ff.*   [b] uoluimus BV   [c] *Insuper . . . rex*, DCP (L)

---

21. [1] See p. lxxiii.   [2] Ps. 118: 10.

22. [1] See pp. lxxiii, lxxviii. The life of Thierry in *AASS*, Jan. iii. 405, mentions the controversy over his election, but not its irregularity. It appears, however, that Thierry gained the bishopric over his rival Odolricus as a result of King Robert's and Archbishop Leothericus' (cf. no. 26) support. See Boussard, pp. 179 f.   [2] Cf. Terence, *Ad.* 91 f.

Vna igitur causarum haec fuit: quia die illo quo sacrandus esse uidebaris, conprouincialium episcoporum qui aberant nec litteras nec legatos habuimus. Quod solum tantum ualet, ut si nullo amplius adminiculo indigeres, tamen sine isto regulariter ordinari non posses. Talem enim ordinationem irritam esse testantur*d* Niceni concilii capitulum quartum et Antiocheni nonum decimum.[3] Haec tamen causa datis induciis*e* corrigi potuisset.

Altera fuit quod sub ipso deliberatae ordinationis articulo, propter crimen homicidii quod audierat, missum a domno papa uidimus interdictum. Quod si ille non mitteret, esset tamen obseruanda sententia apostoli dicentis, oportere non solum episcopum sed praesbiterum quoque et diaconum sine crimine esse.[4] Nec spernendum illud quod apertissime scriptum est in Regiensi concilio his uerbis: 'Qui deinceps non proueantur ad sacerdotium ex regulis canonum, necessario credidimus*f* inserendum, id est qui in aliquo crimine detecti sunt', et caetera usque 'subiacebit'.[5] At siquis obiciat aliquem de patribus post peractam poenitentiam et longam anachoresin propter religionem suam raptum fuisse ad episcopatum, respondetur quod legi communi et uniuersali singulares persone uel causae non praeiudicant,[6] deinde certe quod nichil ualet exemplorum inductio, ubi neque personarum neque negotiorum similitudo consequitur. Nunc caetera uideamus.

Terciam nobis causam tua confessio dedit, quae nos maxime a tua ordinatione deterruit. Nam pro captu nostrae simplicitatis caeteras quidem graues, sed terciam hanc magis periculosam esse rati sumus. Proprium capitulum huius causae noluimus*g* ascribere, sed commune, hoc est Niceni concilii capitulum nonum: 'Siqui*h* sine examinatione promoti praesbiteri sunt, et postea examinati confessi sunt peccata sua, et cum*i* confessi non fuissent, contra regulam uenientes homines manus eis temere imposuerunt, hos aecclesiasticus ordo non recipit. In omnibus enim quod irreprehensibile est defendit aecclesia.'[7]

---

d testatur esse DR (esse testatur L)   *e* indiciis PH   *f* credimus CBVH   *g* noluimus *om.* R   nolumus VK   uolumus H   *h* Si DRC (-qui *apparently erased* L)   Sed qui VH   *i* cum *om.* PV   *add. supra* B (L) (*altera manu* B?)

---

[3] Mansi, ii. 686 f., 1333 f.; Hinschius, pp. 258, 272.
[4] 1 Tim. 3: 2 ff.; Titus 1: 5 ff.

The first reason was this: that on the day you were to be consecrated we had neither letters nor messengers from the bishops of the province who were absent. This alone is so important that even if nothing else were wanting in your favour, the lack of it would prevent your being lawfully consecrated, for the fact that it is necessary for a valid consecration is attested by chapter four of the council of Nicaea and chapter nineteen of the council of Antioch.[3] But this could have been corrected by postponing it.

A second reason was that at the very moment set for your consecration we saw a letter which the pope had sent prohibiting it because he had heard that you were charged with homicide. Even if he had not sent it, we were obliged to follow the teaching of the apostle, who said that not only bishops, but also priests and deacons should be free from crime.[4] Nor should we reject what was quite plainly prescribed by the council of Riez as follows: 'Let those who in the future are not raised to the priesthood in accordance with the canons—we think it necessary to add, that is, those detected in any crime', and so forth as far as 'he will be subject'.[5] But if anyone should object that one of the fathers who had done penance and lived for a long time as a hermit was forced into the episcopate because of his sanctity, let him be told that individual persons and cases do not prejudice common and universal law,[6] and that it is not valid to argue from precedents where there is similarity neither of persons nor of circumstances. Now let us look at the rest.

Your own confession provided us with a third reason which especially deterred us from consecrating you; for though to our limited intelligence the others seemed quite serious, the third seemed even more dangerous. We do not want to cite the specific chapter for this case, but the general one, namely chapter nine of the council of Nicaea: 'If any have been promoted to the priesthood without being examined, but being examined afterwards have confessed their sins, if prior to their confession they were ordained rashly and in violation of the law, they are denied admittance into the clergy; for in all matters the church defends that which is irreproachable.'[7]

---

[5] The attribution to the council of Riez is erroneous. Actually Toledo IV, c. 19 (Mansi, x. 624 f.) = c. 18 (Hinschius, pp. 367 f.).

[6] Cf. *Cod. Theod.* i. 1. 4 (= *Brev.* i. 1. 4), *Inter.*

[7] Mansi, ii. 689; Hinschius, p. 259.

Quartam[k] uero mouit[l] proscriptio refragantium clericorum et extorta[m] timore electio. Verum non electio. Nam cum sit electio unius de pluribus maxime complaciti secundum liberam arbitrii uoluntatem acceptio, quomodo electio recte dici possit, ubi sic a principe unus obtruditur, ut nec clero nec populo nec ipsis summis sacerdotibus ad alium deflectere concedatur? De uiolentia huius-modi Constantinus A(ugustus) talem contra se et contra alios principes sententiam dedit: 'Quecunque',[n] inquit, 'contra leges fuerint a principibus obtenta non ualeant.'[8] Et Regiense concilium: 'Sed nec ille', inquit, 'deinceps episcopus erit, quem nec clerus nec populus propriae ciuitatis elegerit.'[9] Ecce tibi promissas rationes exoluimus. Quae si iustae sunt, displicere non debent. Adiecimus etiam pauca propter breuitatem capitula diuinae legis. Quam[o] primo quidem condere, magni consilii; postea uiolare,[p] summae reuerentiae; seruare hactenus gloriae tantae fuit, ut quisquis secundum illam uixerit, procul dubio inter beatos com-putatus sit. Propter has itaque rationes non audentes tibi manus imponere, utpote deinceps ordinandi potentia carituri, quia praeuaricatores legis esse noluimus,[10] o sacrilegam impietatem![q] in ipso sinu sanctae matris aecclesiae a fautoribus tuis pene perempti sumus; et quidem ita nobis carum fuit euasisse uiuos,[r] ut subsecutae praedae leuis esse iactura uideatur. Sed quia haec scandala propter te nobis fiunt, iam ut desistant te apud eos obtinere oportet, apud quos hanc persequendi sacerdotes gratiam inuenisti. Nosti enim quid portendatur homini per quem scanda-lum uenit.[11] De caetero autem, frater, est quod te celare non debemus, uideris enim nobis uehementer errare, qui sine respectu Dei praesulatum uiolentus[s] inuadis. Nam si sola damnatur ambitio, quid de uiolentiae importunitate censebitur? Verum non solum hoc, sed[t] in ipsa uiolata nec postea reconciliata aecclesia missarum sollemnia caelebrare praesumis. Vtrum tamen impru-denter an consulto haec facias habemus incertum.[12] Sed si im-prudenter, instruenda simplicitas; si uero consulto, presumptio

---

[k] Quarta DR (L)   Quartum C   [l] mouit] nos mouit DR (nos *supra* L)
promouit P   monuit B   [m] exorta CK   [n] Quicumque VH   [o] Quae
VH   [p] uilare VH   [q] pietatem DR (L)   [r] uiuos *om.* VH
[s] uiolenter DR (L)   uiolentiis PV   [t] et *add.* DR (*om.* L)

---

[8] *Cod. Theod.* i. 2. 2 (=*Brev.* i. 2. 1), *Inter.*   [9] As in n. 5.
[10] Cf. Leo I, ep. xii. 9 (*PL* liv. 654; Hinschius, p. 624).
[11] Cf. Matt. 18: 6 f.; Luke 17: 1 f.   [12] Cf. Terence, *Phorm.* 659 f.

The fourth reason which moved us was the condemnation of the clerks who opposed you and the securing of your election by intimidation. Indeed, it was no 'election'; for since an election is the free and voluntary choice of the candidate who is the most generally acceptable, how can it rightly be called an election when one person is thrust forward by a prince so forcibly that neither the clergy, the people, nor even the bishops are permitted to turn to another? As regards force of this kind, the Emperor Constantine rendered the following judgement against himself and other princes: 'Let whatever is done by princes contrary to law be null and void.'[8] The council of Riez declared: 'No one in the future shall be bishop who is not elected by the clergy and people of his city.'[9]

Now we have fulfilled our promise and set forth our reasons. If they are just, they should meet with your approval. We have also added a few chapters—and only a few so as to keep the letter short—of divine law. To lay this down for the first time was the part of great wisdom; to violate it thereafter has been of the utmost dread; and to observe it thus far has brought such glory that whoever lives in accordance with it is doubtless to be reckoned among the blessed. When for these reasons we did not dare to place our hands on you as we should thereby be unable to ordain since we would not be transgressors of the law,[10] O sacrilegious impiety! in the very heart of holy mother church we were nearly killed by your partisans; and indeed, we were so glad to have escaped alive that our loss during the plundering which followed seems insignificant. But since these outrages are committed against us on your behalf, you should see to it that they are abandoned by those who have done you the kindness of persecuting bishops, for you know what is foretold for one who leads others astray.[11] As for the rest, brother, there is a matter which we should not conceal from you, for you seem to us to be committing a grievous sin in usurping a bishopric by force and without respect for God. If mere office-seeking is condemned, what will be judged as regards demands backed up by force? But this is not all, for in that same church which was violated and has not been reconciled you are venturing to celebrate mass. Whether you are committing these sins out of ignorance or by design we cannot tell.[12] If out of ignorance, your simplicity must be instructed; but if by design, your presumption must be punished.

est punienda. Nam si te canones scire constat, et tamen inpudenter[u] obsordescere et contraire contendis, non modo praesulatum fugientem non assequeris, sed nec quod apprehendisse debueras presbiterium[x] tenuisti.

23

Fulbert to Herfridus:[1] *advising him to accept the terms offered by Bishop Thierry of Orleans* c. *late 1008–1012/13*

F(ulbertus) Dei gratia Carnotensium[a] episcopus caro suo Her(frido).

Auctor signatae scedulae quam michi mittere uoluisti, seu fideliter siue impure id agat, consulit tamen iusta, leniterque[b] blanditur. Iustum est enim[c] aecclesiam te in qua sis ordinatus, quoad in ea tuto degere possis, non deserere, ouesque tibi commissas studiose curare. Blandum etiam est appellari filium, desiderium significare uidendi,[d] corollarium gratiae polliceri. Vnde si haec fideliter oblata probaueris, fideliter autem dico sine circunuentione animae tuae, per noxia iuramenta non suadeo refutare. Nam quod in ordinatione ipsius erratum est neque tu corrigere potes, nec amodo sic tua refert, ut ob aliorum[e] culpam tuum debeas officium deuitare. Tamen quicquid huius egeris cum Rogero episcopo[2] te ante pertractare moneo, et cum domno Rodulfo cui tecum una causa est et par poena exilii. Vale non dubius amiciciae meae.

24

Fulbert to Bishop F.:[1] *sending him some ointment* 1006–28

Patri et consacerdoti suo F. F(ulbertus).

Crede, pater, nullam me composicionem unguenti laborasse, postquam ad ordinem episcopalem accessi. Quod tamen pauxillum

---

[u] imprudenter PBH   [x] presbiteratum DR (presbiterium L)   presbiterum V, *ante corr.* P   CH *are too abbreviated to determine*

23 DRKCPBVH (L)   [a] Carnotis PH   Carnot̄ CV   [b] leuiterque CV
[c] enim est DRKCH   [d] uiuendi DRKB (L)   [e] illorum VH

24 LDRCP

23. [1] Herfridus and Ralph, who is mentioned later in the letter, appear to have been clerks of Orleans who supported Odolricus and opposed Thierry's election

If it turns out that you know the canons and yet are shamelessly striving to turn a deaf ear and to disobey them, not only will you fail to overtake the bishopric which is fleeing from you, but you will also lose the priesthood which you should have retained.

Fulbert to Herfridus[1]   c. *late 1008–1012/13*

F(ulbert), by grace of God bishop of Chartres, to his dear Her(fridus).

Whether the writer of the page with the affixed seal that you sent me is doing so with sincerity or duplicity, still he is giving you good advice and speaking graciously. It is good advice that as long as you can live there safely you should not desert the church for which you were ordained and should diligently care for the flock which was entrusted to you, and it is gracious for him to call you 'son', to say that he wishes to see you, and to promise you the gift of his favour. So if you are satisfied that the offer is sincere (and I emphasize sincere—that no attempt is being made to bring your soul into jeopardy), I advise you not to reject it because of the unlawful oaths; for the irregularity which was involved in his consecration is not something that you can correct, nor is it of such importance to you for the future that you should neglect your own duties because of the sins of others. But whatever you do in this matter I recommend that you work out in advance with Bishop Roger[2] and with Ralph, who has a common cause with you and who is also under penalty of exile. Farewell, and rest assured as to my friendship.

Fulbert to Bishop F.[1]   *1006–28*

To his father and fellow bishop, F., from F(ulbert).

Believe me, father, I have not prepared any ointments since I was raised to the bishopric. But the little that is left of what

---

(see nos. 22, 42). They may be Herfridus, the precentor, and Ralph, the dean of Sainte-Croix, who witnessed Appendix C, no. 12. Ralph is possibly the *economus* discussed on p. lxxvi.

[2] Of Beauvais (*c.* 998–24 June 1016 (Newman, p. 51 n.)), an uncle of Odolricus.

24. [1] See p. lxxiii.

ex dono cuiusdam medici² supererat mihi fraudans tibi largior,ᵃ
rogato sospitatis auctore Christo, ut tibi illud faciat salutare. Vale.

25

*Fulbert to H., subdean of Tours:*¹ *asking him to bring a
swindler to trial*   *1006–28*

F(ulbertus) Dei gratia Carnotensium episcopus domno H. Turonensium subdecano sibi dilectissimo gratiam et benedictionem
Dei.

Cum uestram caritatem nouerim plurimis in obsequiis libenter
mihi paruisse, adhuc etiam parereᵃ cupientem uix sacietati cedere,
mando uobis obnixe precans, ut accingamini ad causam quam
expono. Apud nosᵇ morabatur olim quidam bonorum extortor,
legum contortor² Girardus nomine, qui susceptum unum caballum
a famulo nostro Deodato debuit comparareᶜ xxx duobus solidis,
pro arrabone datis duodecim nummis. Cumque reliquos speraret
Deodatus ad prefixum terminum se recepturum, fefellit eum ille
subdolus, a nobis Turonim profugiens, nec equum postea nec
precium remittens, quamuis eum sepe Deodatus utrumlibet agere
per legatos postulauerit. Hac de causa mitto ad uos unum ex
nostris hominibus qui ipsum G(irardum) notum uobis faciat, in
audientiaque uestra uice Deodati hanc ipsi querelam intendat,
qualibet lege censueritis reuicturus eum,³ si forte (ut est impurus)
dissimulauerit se rem istam scire, aut si ita esse negauerit. Deinceps
uos talem in eum qualem ius poscit date, queso, sentenciam, ut
uel Deodato rem suam legaliter soluat, uel debitas penas luens,
ornetur ex suis uirtutibus.⁴ Vigeat semper alacritas uestra.

ᵃ largio P

25 LDRP   ᵃ patere L   ᵇ uos P   ᶜ comparere L

---

² The term *medicus* may indicate that the doctor was a layman (see F.
Vercauteren, 'Les médecins dans les principautés de la Belgique et du nord de
la France, du viiiᵉ au xiiiᵉ siècle', *MA* lvii (1951), 61 ff.).

25. ¹ See pp. lxxiii f.
² Cf. Terence, *Phorm.* 374.

a doctor² gave to me I am sending as a gift from me to you with the prayer that Christ, the author of good health, may make it help you. Farewell.

*Fulbert to H., subdean of Tours*¹   *1006–28*

F(ulbert), by grace of God bishop of Chartres, to his very dear H., subdean of Tours, with the grace and blessing of God.

Since I know that you in your charity have gladly performed many services for me and that you are still willing to do so and are not inclined to feel that you have done too much, I earnestly beg and enjoin you to gird yourself for the case that I am setting forth. There once stayed with us an extorter of goods and distorter of laws² named Gerard, who agreed to pay thirty-two shillings for a horse that he bought from our servant Deodatus and gave him twelve pennies as a deposit. Deodatus expected to receive the rest on the day that they had set, but that scoundrel tricked him and fled from here to Tours. Since then he has not sent back the horse or the money, though Deodatus has often sent messengers to demand that he do one or the other. So I am sending one of our men to put you wise to G(erard) and as Deodatus' proxy to bring this as a charge against him in your court with every intention of refuting him and proving it in whatever way you think best³ if it should happen that Gerard, shameless as he is, pretends to know nothing about it or denies that the charge is true. Then I beg you to render the judgement against him that justice demands: either to discharge his debt to Deodatus in accordance with the law, or to be rewarded as befits his merits by suffering the penalty that he deserves.⁴ May long life and vigorous health be always yours.

---

³ This apparently refers not to any particular law, but rather to the means of proof, which was decided by the person who presided over the court. See L. Halphen, 'Les institutions judiciaires en France au xie siècle. Région Angevine', *Revue historique*, lxxvii (1901), 279 ff. (reprinted in his *A travers l'histoire du moyen âge* (Paris, 1950), pp. 175 ff.).

⁴ Cf. Terence, *Ad.* 176.

26

Fulbert to Archbishop Leothericus of Sens: reproving him for consecrating Abbot Gauzlin of Fleury as archbishop of Bourges[1]   *1012–14*

L(eutherico) Senonensium presidi[a] F(ulbertus) Carnotanus sacerdos.

Quod me, pater, amicum appellas gratanter annuerem, si te quoque exhiberes amicum. Sed cum sine meo consilio episcopos ordinando dignitatem suam ecclesiae Carnotensi derogas, cumque in eodem negocio legem canonicam multimode soluis, non solum me ledis, sed omnes pariter qui iustitiam colunt. Ego quidem meam adhuc multe[b] pacior; sed lex ipsa diuina suam iniuriam bene ex parte uindicat, quae dum a te soluitur, tua opera cassat. Hoc pridem in T(heoderico) factum[2] in G(auzlino) nuper iterasti, qui sic a te pastor est constitutus, ut nec gregem sibi commissum nouerit, nec grex ipsum recipere uelit. Reprobatus itaque et a finibus episcopatus extorris,[3] cum palam intrare per hostium non potest ut legitimus pastor, nec aliunde furtiuus ascendere,[4] per uiolenciam regis irrumpere nititur ut tyrannus. Nec miror adeo si iuuenis ille tali patuit[c] ambicione temptari, cui uel aetas ipsa uel quae eius aetatis pedisequa solet esse inprudencia locum forsitan obtineat excusandi. Sed tu, pater, non solum mirandus, uerum insuper exhorrendus es, quem nec inprudencia fallit, nec casus turbat, nec urget ulla necessitas, sed scienter et quasi cum deliberacione quadam ultro te atque alios perdis. Nec illud sane tibi tacere debeo, quod ad tuas ordinaciones domnum F(rotmundum) Trecacensem episcopum[5] periculose tibi socium addis, quem certam ob causam esse non dubitas imparatum.[d] In qua re dupliciter te delinquere constat, cum eum ad tantam presumpcionem animando, de poenitencia prioris culpae facis esse securum. De

---

26 LDRCPB   [a] praesuli DRB   [b] *corr. to* multam L   multam DR
[c] potuit DRB   [d] imperatum L, *perhaps* C   impurum DR

---

26. [1] On the death of Archbishop Dagbertus of Bourges (18 January or 15 (16) February 1012/13), King Robert nominated Abbot Gauzlin of Fleury. Though Gauzlin was then consecrated, he was prevented from entering Bourges until 1 December 1014 by the hostility of the vicomte, Geoffrey, and the people of Bourges. See Adémar, iii. 39, 49 (ed. Chavanon, pp. 161 f., 172); *Vita Gauzlini*, cc. xvii, xix–xxi (ed. Bautier–Labory, pp. 50, 58 ff.). For the problems involved

Fulbert to Archbishop Leothericus of Sens[1]   1012–14

To Archbishop L(eothericus) of Sens from Bishop F(ulbert) of Chartres.

For you to address me as your friend, father, would make me quite happy, if you would also show yourself my friend. But when you detract from the honour of the church of Chartres by consecrating bishops without consulting me, and when in this same affair you violate canon law in many ways, you injure not only me, but all who are devoted to justice. I indeed am bearing with the great wrong that has been done to me; but divine law takes due vengeance for that done to it, for when you violate it, it brings your efforts to naught. What you earlier did in the case of T(hierry)[2] you recently repeated with regard to G(auzlin), when you made him a shepherd though he did not know the flock entrusted to him and the flock was not willing to have him. Now, rejected and banished from his diocese,[3] since he cannot enter openly through the door like a true shepherd nor climb in through another way like a thief,[4] he is striving with the help of royal power to force his way in like a tyrant. I am not especially surprised that that young man lay open to the temptation of such ambition, for perhaps his age or the imprudence which usually accompanies it can provide grounds for excusing him. But as for you, father, one must be both surprised and horrified, for you are not deceived by imprudence, disturbed by misfortune, nor pressed by any necessity, but knowingly and, so it seems, with some deliberation you willingly destroy yourself and others. Nor indeed should I fail to tell you that in having Bishop F(rotmundus) of Troyes[5] as one of your co-consecrators you are acquiring a dangerous associate, for you know full well that there is a definite reason why he cannot lawfully do this. In this matter it is clear that you are committing a twofold sin, for by inciting him to such great presumption, you make him feel it unnecessary to do penance for his former sin.

---

in the dating cf. A. Gandilhon, *Catalogue des actes des archevêques de Bourges antérieurs à l'an 1200* (Bourges, 1927), pp. xix ff.; *Vita Gauzlini*, pp. 20 f.

[2] See no. 22.

[3] Cf. Virgil, *Aen.* iv. 616.   [4] Cf. John 10: 1 f.

[5] After 991–*c.* 1034 (*GC* xii. 494 f., the charter cited for the date 998 being a forgery (= Newman, no. 120)). Why he was ineligible to assist at Gauzlin's consecration is not known.

his ergo et huiusmodi te resipiscere*e* iam et peniteri*f* oportet, si cum apostolo 'horrendum' credis 'incidere in manus Dei uiuentis.'[6] Sed ego fortassis aspere loqui uidear, aput te tamen (ut credo) non male mereri, si sis de quo dicitur: 'Argue sapientem, et diliget te.'[7] Ceterum in fine huius scedulae exoratum te uolo, ne amodo (sicut soles) scripta mea*g* publicando, mihi inimicos adquiras. Vnde si morem tuum inmutare nolis, ego tamen idcirco uera uel dicere uel scribere non desistam. Vale.

27

Fulbert to his vassals: explaining his position in the struggle against Count Raginardus of Sens[1]   c. *April 1015*

F(ulbertus) Dei gratia Carnotensium episcopus comiti Gualeranno et comiti Gualterio[2] ceterisque filiis fidelibusque suis salutem et benedictionem.

Sciatis, fratres, quia rex R(otbertus) benefacit cum Christianos adiuuat et hereticos dampnat, et ad*a* hoc debent eum comfortare et adiuuare mecum omnes sui fideles, quia hoc est*b* ministerium eius per quod saluus esse debet. Sciatis iterum quod archiepiscopus Senonensis requisiuit a me consilium quid deberet facere de Raginardo heretico qui persequebatur aecclesiam Dei, et ego dedi ei tale consilium quale ad suum ordinem pertinebat. Et ecce mitto uobis utrumque scriptum, et conplanctum suum et consilium meum quod dedi ei secundum ordinem suum. Siquis autem falsarius dicat, quod ego ei alterum*c* consilium deinceps uel scripserim uel dixerim uel mandauerim, rogo ut me sicut patrem uestrum spiritualem defendatis, quia fiducialiter hoc facere potestis. Valete.*d*

---

e respicere C, *ante corr.* L   *f* *corr. to* penitere L   poenitere DRC
g scriptam meam C   meam *ante corr.* L

27 LDRP   *a* et *om.* P   ad *om.* L   *b* est *om.* P   *c* alterum ei P
d Vale L

---

[6] Heb. 10: 31.   [7] Prov. 9: 8.

27. [1] There was constant difficulty between Count Raginardus, who was suspected of Jewish leanings and heresy, and Archbishop Leothericus of Sens. In April 1015 Raginardus was driven from Sens by a royal army, but continued

With regard to this and similar offences it is time that you came to your senses and did penance if you believe with the apostle that 'it is a fearful thing to fall into the hands of the living God.'[6] Perhaps I seem to be speaking harshly, but I do not think that I deserve badly of you if you are he of whom it is said: 'Rebuke a wise man, and he will love thee.'[7] As for the rest, at the end of this letter I want to urge you for the future not to make enemies for me as you usually do by circulating what I have written. But even if you are unwilling to mend your ways, I shall not cease to speak and to write the truth. Farewell.

Fulbert to his vassals[1]   c. *April 1015*

F(ulbert), by grace of God bishop of Chartres, to Count Galeran, Count Gautier,[2] and his other sons and vassals, with his greetings and blessing.

May you know, brothers, that King R(obert) acts rightly when he aids Christians and harms heretics; and all his vassals, myself included, should strengthen and aid him in doing this, for it is his office, and through it he must work out his salvation. May you also know that the archbishop of Sens has asked my advice as to what he should do with regard to the heretic Raginardus, who has been persecuting God's church, and that I have advised him as to the proper action for him as archbishop to take. I am enclosing both of our letters, his complaint and the advice I gave him as to his duty. If anyone should later lie and say that I advised him differently either by letter, word of mouth, or messenger, I ask you to defend me as your spiritual father, for you can do so with confidence. Farewell.

---

to ravage the surrounding area. A compromise was eventually arranged by which Raginardus recovered Sens, but on his death it was to be divided between the king and the archbishop, the latter also receiving comital powers. See Raoul Glaber, iii. 6 (ed. Prou, pp. 69 ff.); the chronicle of Clarius (Duru, ii. 500 f.); E. Houth, 'La campagne, en Bourgogne, de Galeran, comte de Meulan, en 1015', *BPH*, 1959, pp. 155 ff.

[2] Galeran I of Meulan, by 1015–68 (*Cartulaire de l'abbaye de Saint-Martin de Pontoise*, ed. J. Depoin (Pontoise, 1895–1909), pp. 307 ff.; P. Grierson, *MA* xlix (1939), 107 n.); Gautier II le Blanc, count of Valois, Amiens, and Pontoise (Depoin, op. cit., pp. 245, 307, 331 f.; P. Feuchère, *MA* lx (1954), 35 f.), who died after 9 June 1017, when he witnessed Appendix C, no. 6.

28

Fulbert to King Robert: approving his nomination of Franco to the bishopric of Paris[1]   *9 June 1017–12 May 1018*

Benignissimo domino suo regique R(otberto) F(ulbertus) humilis sacerdos siqua potest oracionis suffragia.

Ex parte celsitudinis uestrae dictum est nobis quod domnum Franconem Parisiacensi ecclesiae dare uultis episcopum, et ad hoc peragendum nostrae humilitatis habere fauorem. Nobis autem uidetur quia si episcopatus de quo agitur apertus est, clericus est obtime litteratus et ad sermonem faciendum agilis (in qua re omnes episcopos decet esse non minus quam in operatione potentes atque discretos), unde si hoc fieri posse canonice domni archiepiscopi Senonensis[2] et coepiscoporum nostrorum probauit sagacitas, nostrum etiam, qui de hac discussione appellati non fuimus, habeatis assensum. In nullo enim quod bonum sit coram Deo uestrae uoluntati nitimur contraire.

29

Fulbert to Bishop Adalbero of Laon:[1] *recounting the murder of Evrardus, subdean of Chartres, and asking for his aid*
21 Feb. 1018/19–5 Sept. 1019/20

A(dalberoni) claro Laudunensium presuli F(ulbertus) Carnotensium sacerdos.

De grandi iniuria nobis facta conquerimur apud te, magne[a] pater, quem ex debito caritatis et officii talia curare oportet. Causa uero huiusmodi est. Quodam ecclesiae nostrae subdecano defuncto petiit a nobis R(odulfus) Silnectensis episcopus[2] dari

28 LDRKCPBVM

29 LDRPB   [a] magne *om.* DR

28. [1] On the death of Bishop Reginald of Paris, 12 September 1016 (see p. 20 n.), King Robert chose Azelinus of Tronchiennes (Dronghene, near Ghent), an illegitimate son of Count Baldwin III of Flanders and twice an unsuccessful candidate for the bishopric of Cambrai (see *Gesta Pontificum Cameracensium*,

Fulbert to King Robert[1]   *9 June 1017–12 May 1018*

To his very kind lord and king, R(obert), from F(ulbert), humble bishop, with, for whatever it may avail, the support of his prayers.

We have been told in your highness's behalf that you wish to make Franco bishop of Paris and in doing so to have the support of our humble selves. It seems to us that if the bishopric in question is vacant, if the clerk is well-educated and can speak with ease (for bishops ought to be skilled in speaking as well as forceful and prudent in action), and if in their wisdom the archbishop of Sens[2] and our fellow bishops are satisfied that this can be done in accordance with the canons, then you may also have our consent, though we were not invited to discuss this matter; for we are not trying to oppose your wishes as regards anything that may be good in God's sight.

Fulbert to Bishop Adalbero of Laon[1]
                  21 Feb. 1018/19–5 Sept. 1019/20

To the illustrious bishop of Laon, A(dalbero), from F(ulbert), bishop of Chartres.

We are laying our complaint before you, eminent father, who are obliged by the duties of charity and your office to attend to such matters, of a monstrous wrong done to us. The case is as follows. On the death of the subdean of our church, Bishop R(alph) of Senlis[2] asked us to give his office to him or to his brother. We

i. 110, 122 (*MGH SS* vii. 448, 454)). Azelinus, however, soon withdrew and returned to Flanders (see no. 57; F. Kieckens, 'Adalbert [*sic*] de Tronchiennes', *Messager des sciences historiques*, 1882, pp. 186 ff.). Robert then chose the royal chancellor, Franco, who became bishop between 9 June 1017, when he subscribed a charter only as chancellor, and 12 May 1018, when he signed as bishop of Paris (Appendix C, nos. 6, 7). See *Vita Burcardi*, c. vi (ed. Bourel de la Roncière, p. 18); Depoin, p. 235.   ² Leothericus.

29. ¹ 1 April 977–27 January 1030/1 or later (Coolidge, pp. 17, 92 f.). Coolidge, p. 83, suggests that Fulbert was appealing to Adalbero as Archbishop Arnulf of Rheims was unable to attend to his duties (cf. no. 34). See pp. lxxiv f.

² After October 1008–5 September 1019/20 (see E. Dhomme and A. Vattier, 'Recherches chronologiques sur les évêques de Senlis', *Comptes rendus et mémoires du Comité arch. de Senlis*, 1865, pp. 65 f.; above, pp. lxxiv f.).

sibi aut fratri suo ministerium eius. Nos autem respondimus non conuenire sibi eo quod episcopus esset, neque fratri suo aetate adhuc et moribus inmaturo. Tunc elegimus de numero sacerdotum nostrorum ad illud officium Eurardum quendam scientem ac religiosum uirum. Quod factum predictus R(odulfus) materque et frater ipsius adeo inuiderunt, ut sancto uiro coram pluribus (qui testes inde sunt) terribilia minarentur; et dictum facto non caruit. Venerunt enim de ciuitate Silnectis ad nostram quidam ex domesticis eorum sic necessarii, ut absenciam illorum nec per unum diem ignorare potuerint.^{b} Qui interdiu quidem^c latuerunt, sed profunda nocte egressi sanctum illum presbiterum more solito uenientem ad aecclesiam quasi lupum rabidum^d lanceis falcastris et gladiis in ipso atrio principalis ecclesiae trucidarunt. Clerici autem eius, qui expeditum dominum tarde secuti sunt, inuenerunt eum adhuc extrema uerba protomartyris Stephani proferentem.^{e}3 Porro carnifices presidio noctis incogniti iam diffugerant; et cui crimen hoc intenderetur erat incertum, cum quidam, propter minas preteritas domum R(odulfi) quae erat aput nos suspectam habentes, repererunt in ea uernaculum quendam uestes suas et calciamenta lota siccantem. Ex quo signo coniectura^f incepta,4 cum ad causam huius lauacri dicendam homo acrius urgeretur, se facto de quo agebatur affuisse confessus est, socios prodidit, et ordinem rei gestae exposuit. Nos denique totum hoc alcius perscrutantes pro certo ita esse^g comperimus. Comperimus, inquam, inuidiae liuorem, fraudem maliciae, sacrilegii nefas, crudele, cruentum, et singulare facinus in occisione sanctissimi sacerdotis. Nunc ergo tanta causa, quia iudicacio eius obscura non est, solam (ut uides) ulcionem expostulat. Sed cum iuris sit ad utilitatem rei publicae cunctos punire maleficos, illos tamen uehemencius exturbare necesse est qui in Deum et sanctos eius tam impie tamque crudeliter audent. Quid enim mali ulterius, uel certe eque magnum excogitari queat? Multo nimirum leuius illi complices Chorae peccasse uidentur, quos tamen iudicio Dei terra uiuos obsorbuit.5 Nam si illi sanctos Dei contempserant, non utique trucidarant. Quod si tales socordia uel iniquitas iudicum reliquerit inpunitos, cum hoc facere conspirare sit in contumeliam Dei, et^h exponere

---

^{b} absentia . . . ignorari potuerit (*perhaps correctly*) B ^{c} quidem *om.* DR
^{d} presbiterum . . . rabidum *om.* DR ^{e} praedicantem LDR replicantem B
^{f} conceptura L ^{g} esse *om.* DR ^{h} et *om.* LDR

---

3 See Acts 7: 59: 'Lord, lay not this sin to their charge.'
4 Cf. Terence, *Ad.* 822.
5 See Num. 16: 1 ff.

replied that it was not suitable for him, as he was a bishop, or for his brother, as he was still of immature age and character. Then we chose one of our priests for that office, Evrardus, a man both learned and pious. This aroused R(alph), his mother, and his brother to such vindictiveness that they uttered terrible threats against that saintly man in the presence of many who can testify to it, and what they threatened came to pass. Some of their servants who were so important that their absence could not go unnoticed even for one day came from the city of Senlis to Chartres. During the day they remained in hiding; but going out in the dark of night, they butchered in the very forecourt of the cathedral that holy priest, who was coming to church as usual, with spears, falchions, and swords, as if he were a fierce wolf. His clerks, who were lagging behind as their master hurried along, found him still uttering the last words of Stephen, the proto-martyr.[3] The murderers had already fled, unrecognized under the cover of night; and to whom this crime should be attributed was uncertain, when some persons, because of R(alph's) earlier threats, became suspicious of a near-by house of his and found there a servant who had washed his clothes and shoes and was drying them. This discovery gave rise to conjecture;[4] and when the man was pressed more forcibly to tell why he had washed them, he confessed that he had been present at the crime in question, betrayed his companions, and told what had happened. Then we investigated the whole case more thoroughly and found that what he said was indeed true. We found, I say, jealous envy, deliberate treachery, monstrous sacrilege, and an outrage cruel, bloody, and unique, in the slaying of a most holy priest. Now since the results of the investigation are clear, such an enormous crime, as you can see, demands nothing less than vengeance. If it is right to punish all criminals for the sake of the common weal, then it is necessary to take even more vigorous measures in afflicting those who dare to commit such impious and cruel acts against God and his saints. What evil could be devised that would be greater than or even as great as this? Indeed, Corah's accomplices committed a much less grievous sin, but God still condemned them to be swallowed up alive by the earth.[5] Yet they but treated God's holy ones with contempt, they did not butcher them. But if out of negligence or wrongdoing the judges leave such men unpunished (which in itself is to conspire in contempt of God and to expose his servants

seruos eius ad cedem, quid restat nisi ut ipsius summi[i] iudicis ira
deseuiens et hos et illos inaudita mortis atrocitate disperdat?
Proinde nobis quibus idem Dominus ecclesiae suae tribunalia
commisit adprime necessarium est regem nostrum nosque inuicem
modis omnibus excitare, ne repente feriamur in huiusmodi
socordia oscitantes. Quod ego[k] te facere deprecor, magne pater,
cui Deus bene suadendi copiam incomparabilem dedit, simulque
ut ipse mecum predictos maleficos citra legitimam satisfactionem
excommunices, quos tamen usque in finem a communione pri-
uandos esse non nescis. Vale.

30

*Fulbert to Archbishop Leothericus of Sens: rejecting his
petition on behalf of Evrardus' murderers*[1]
21 Feb. 1018/19–5 Sept. 1019/20

Venerando Senonensium presuli L(eutherico) F(ulbertus) Carnotensium humilis sacerdos.

Litteras ex parte uestra suscepimus suadentes recipere quod
homicidae Silnectenses offerunt, ut mereantur absolui. Nos autem
in quibus oportet uobis ut patri semper obedire parati sumus; sed
in hoc ad presens ideo non oportet, quia neque iustum neque
commodum est. Et iustum non esse leges scriptae demonstrant.
Commodum uero non est ut mors sanctorum, quae in conspectu
Dei[a] pretiosa est,[2] apud homines uili precio constet. Quod siquis
instituerit, omnium sanctorum qui ea de causa perituri sunt reus
sanguinis erit. Sanctitas uestra ualeat semper et uigeat.

---

[i] supremi LDR   [k] ergo LDR (-r- *marked for deletion, in a later hand?* L)

30 LDRPB   [a] Domini DR

---

30. [1] See no. 29.   [2] Cf. Ps. 115: 15.

to slaughter), what remains except for the Supreme Judge himself in his furious wrath to destroy both judges and criminals with unprecedented cruelty and death? So it is especially necessary for us to whom the Lord has entrusted the courts of his church to do all that we can to bestir our king and each of ourselves so that we be not suddenly struck down idling in such negligence. I beg you to do this, eminent father, to whom God has given an incomparable talent for effective persuasion. I also ask you to join me in excommunicating these criminals until they make legal satisfaction, and even then you know that they must be deprived of communion until the very end. Farewell.

Fulbert to Archbishop Leothericus of Sens[1]
21 Feb. 1018/19–5 Sept. 1019/20

To the venerable archbishop of Sens, L(eothericus), from F(ulbert), humble bishop of Chartres.

We have received your letter advising us to accept what the murderers from Senlis are offering in order to receive absolution. We have always been ready to obey you as our father where this is proper; but in the present case it is not proper, since it is neither just nor fitting. That it is not just is proved by the written laws. Nor is it fitting that the death of saints, which is precious in the sight of God,[2] be held of little value by men. If anyone should set such a precedent, he will be guilty of the blood of all the saints who perish in the same way. My wishes for your holiness's long life and good health.

31

Fulbert to Bishop Ralph of Senlis and his family: calling on them to plead guilty or to stand trial for the murder of Evrardus[1]   *21 Feb. 1018/19–5 Sept. 1019/20*

F(ulbertus) Dei gratia [Carnotensium episcopus] siquidem fidelibus adhuc (ut aiunt) R(odulfo), G(uidoni), A.

Nec porta iustitiae nec ianua misericordiae uobis clausa est apud nos; neque uero de Briccio episcopo[2] fecimus hostiarium, qui uos (ut significatis) a nostris penitralibus arcet, sed utrumque aditum seruandum racioni commisimus. Si uultis intrare per portam iustitiae, defendite culpam. Si per ianuam misericordiae, agite penitentiam. Aliter enim uos racio non admittet. Haec breuiter rescribentes, uobis consentire[a] putamus, dum terminos sanctorum patrum nec ipsi transgredimur,[3] nec uobis transgredi suademus.

32

Fulbert to Bishop Ralph of Senlis: granting his request for a trial for the murder of Evrardus[1]
21 Feb. 1018/19–5 Sept. 1019/20

Venerabili Silnectensium episcopo R(odulfo) F(ulbertus) Dei gratia Carnotensium sacerdos.

Quia iudicio contendere magis quam ueniam postulare statuistis, restat uobis conuenire iudices, qui prefixo loco et tempore nos[a] in alterutrum legali racione iustificent. Non enim usurpamus officium iudicis in isto negocio sicut uos uelle dicitis, cum nullus esse possit suae causae et assertor et iudex.[2] Verum enim uero satis admirari nequimus quidnam mali est quod tam audacter ad iudicium properatis, nisi forte quod abhorrere humanum est publice dampnari eligitis, quam secreta[b] satisfactione purgari. Quid enim aliud in iudicio mereatur manifestae culpae odiosa

---

31 LDRKCPB   [a] uobiscum sentire LDRKP
32 LDRCPB   [a] uos LP   [b] sacrata L   secrata D, *ante corr.* R

Fulbert to Bishop Ralph of Senlis and his family[1]
21 Feb. 1018/19–5 Sept. 1019/20

F(ulbert), by grace of God [bishop of Chartres], to R(alph), G(uido), and A., if indeed they are, as they say, still faithful to him.

Neither the gate of justice nor the door of mercy is closed to you in our sight, nor have we made Bishop Briccius[2] a doorkeeper to prevent (as you claim) your entering into our presence; but we have entrusted the keeping of both entrances to Reason. If you wish to enter through the gate of justice, disprove your guilt; if through the door of mercy, do penance. Otherwise Reason will not let you in. In sending you this brief reply, we think you will agree that we ourselves are not transgressing the limits set by the holy fathers[3] nor advising you to do so.

Fulbert to Bishop Ralph of Senlis[1]
21 Feb. 1018/19–5 Sept. 1019/20

To the venerable bishop of Senlis, R(alph), from F(ulbert), by grace of God bishop of Chartres.

Since you have decided to stand trial rather than to ask for pardon, it remains for you to agree to the judges who, at a time and a place fixed in advance, will decide in favour of one or the other of us in accordance with the law; for we are not usurping the office of judge in this affair as you say you wish us to, since no one can be both advocate and judge in his own case.[2] But in truth, we cannot wonder enough what is wrong with you that you should hasten so boldly to stand trial, unless, perhaps, you prefer for a crime that all men naturally abhor to be publicly condemned rather than expiated by private penance. For what else might a detestable attempt to disprove obvious guilt gain from a trial?

31. [1] See nos. 29 f. G. and A. are apparently Ralph's brother Guido and their mother (cf. nos. 29, 36).
   [2] Identity unknown, perhaps a pseudonym.   [3] Cf. Prov. 22: 28.

32. [1] See no. 31.
   [2] Cf. *Cod. Theod.* ii. 10. 5 (= *Brev.* ii. 10. 2), *Inter.*

defensio? Et uestra quidem culpa sic manifesta[c] est, ut nullo excusacionis genere ualeat obumbrari. Vox enim sanguinis fratris uestri[d] et consacerdotis Eurardi, postquam ad aures supremi iudicis ascendit,[3] per totam Galliam uehementer infremuit. Qui, ut certo scimus, non est occisus ob aliam causam, quam ob uestrae cupiditatis iniustam calumniam. Viderint iudices utrum effectus referatur ad causam.

33

Fulbert to Bishop Ralph of Senlis: refusing to be drawn into further correspondence concerning his trial for Evrardus' murder   *21 Feb. 1018/19–5 Sept. 1019/20*

Venerabili Silnectensium episcopo R(odulfo) F(ulbertus) Dei gratia Carnotensium sacerdos.

Non oportet nostri ordinis uiros in superfluis scriptitacionibus occupari. Multa enim et magna negocia nobis expendenda[a] (si non dissimulamus) incumbunt. Sufficiant ergo uobis super his unde agimus litterae nuper a nobis missae, quarum erat extremitas: 'Viderint iudices utrum effectus referatur ad causam.'[1] Quae enim ibi scripta sunt, aut ipsi ea legitima assercione confirmabimus, aut uos infirmare et pernegare paciemur, si data fuerit concilii iudiciique occasio. Sin autem, contenti erimus ea premonuisse, quae uos[b] credimus emendare debuisse. Valete.

---

[c] manifestata LDRC   [d] nostri LDRC

33 LDRCPB   [a] expenda L   explenda DR   expetenda B   [b] quae
uos] quos LCP   quae DR

---

[3] Cf. Gen. 4: 10.

33. [1] See no. 32.

Indeed, your guilt is so obvious that nothing can justify or extenuate it; for the voice of the blood of your brother and fellow priest, Evrardus, after rising to the ears of the Supreme Judge,[3] has uttered loud groans throughout Gaul. We know for a truth that he was killed for no other reason than your greed and unjust claim. The judges will see whether the effect is matched to the cause.

Fulbert to Bishop Ralph of Senlis
21 Feb. 1018/19–5 Sept. 1019/20

To the venerable bishop of Senlis, R(alph), from F(ulbert), by grace of God bishop of Chartres.

It is not proper for men of our position to be taken up with unnecessary scribbling, for there are many important matters which, if we are honest, need our attention. So be satisfied in the present case with the letter that we recently sent which ends: 'The judges will see whether the effect is matched to the cause.'[1] What we have written there we shall either confirm by legal proof or let you refute and disprove it altogether, if there is an opportunity for a court and a trial. If not, we shall rest content with having admonished you as to what we think you ought to correct. Farewell.

34

Fulbert to Deodatus, bishop-designate of Soissons:[1] advising him to ask the bishop of Châlons-sur-Marne to consecrate him   6 Aug. 1019–5 Sept. 1019/20

F(ulbertus) Dei gratia Carnotensium episcopus D(eodato) episcopo designato quicquid sibi.

Sic estis per Dei gratiam in arbitrii uestri libertate positi, et finitimorum episcoporum copia fulti, ut in manus episcopi Silnectensis[2] incidere nulla uos necessitudo compellat. Sed ne ciuitati uel ecclesiae[a] Catalaunis suum derogetis honorem, meminisse uos decet quod in antiqua descripcione prouinciae Belgicae secundae, ipsa ciuitas a Remensi tercium locum habeat.[3] Sapienti[b] pauca.[c4] Valete intrando per hostium in ouile ouium.[5]

35

Fulbert to Bishop Guido of Senlis:[1] asking him to grant his protection to dependants of the church of Chartres, to set a date for settling matters left over from Bishop Ralph's pontificate, and to explain why he has not been consecrated at Senlis   5 Sept.–18 Nov. 1019/20

Dilectissimo fratri et consacerdoti suo G(uidoni) F(ulbertus) oracionis suffragium.

Rogamus caritatem uestram pro his seruis ecclesiae nostrae qui sub uestra potestate[a] degunt, ut eis patrocinari dignemini, et ut

---

34 LDRCPBVM   [a] uel ecclesiae *om.* DR   [b] Sapiencia LCB
[c] sufficiunt *add.* DR

35 LDRPB   [a] potestate *om.* LDR

---

34. [1] According to *DHGE* viii. 878, Bishop Fulk of Soissons died 6 August 1019 and was succeeded by his nephew Beroldus, who was not consecrated until 1021. However, an entry in a necrology of Saint-Étienne of Dijon lists Fulk, Deodatus, and Beroldus as bishops of Soissons (*GC* ix. 347); and Deodatus is also found among the witnesses to a charter of 1019 (?) which

Fulbert to Deodatus, bishop-designate of Soissons[1]
6 Aug. 1019–5 Sept. 1019/20

F(ulbert), by grace of God bishop of Chartres, to D(eodatus), bishop-designate, with his wishes for all that he could wish for himself.

By God's grace you are free to choose whom you wish, and you have the advantage of having a number of neighbouring bishops to choose from, so there is nothing that would necessitate your falling into the hands of the bishop of Senlis.[2] But so that you might not detract from the honour of the city or church of Châlons, you should bear in mind that in the ancient description of the province of Belgica Secunda that city held the third place after Rheims.[3] A word to the wise![4] My best wishes to one who is entering the sheepfold through the door.[5]

Fulbert to Bishop Guido of Senlis[1]
5 Sept.–18 Nov. 1019/20

To his very dear brother and fellow bishop, G(uido), from F(ulbert), with the support of his prayers.

We ask you in your charity to deem worthy of your protection these servants of our church who live in your diocese and to set

includes all the bishops of the province of Rheims except Senlis (Coolidge, p. 100 n.). The charter is known only from a later copy, and it presents some difficulties, especially as regards its date; but it does point to the existence of Bishop Deodatus of Soissons, and the date would not be unsuitable. Deodatus is also said to have left a legacy from his patrimonial inheritance to the church of Saint-Gervais (J. Saincir, *Le diocèse de Soissons*, i (Évreux, 1935), 57, but without giving a reference). See p. 53 n. 1.

[2] Ralph (see nos. 29 ff.).

[3] See 'Notitia Galliarum', *MGH AA* ix. 552 ff., especially 590 and the reference to Chartres MS. 193 (p. 566).

[4] A variation on the popular saying 'A word to the wise is sufficient', perhaps most easily known from Terence, *Phorm.* 541.

[5] Cf. John 10: 1 f.

35. [1] *c.* 1019–December 1042 (see E. Dhomme and A. Vattier, 'Recherches chronologiques sur les évêques de Senlis', *Comptes rendus et mémoires du Comité arch. de Senlis*, 1865, pp. 66 ff.; above, pp. lxxiv f.).

nobis constituatis terminum post octabas beati Martini[2] quando
et ubi nostri legati possint uobis occurrere ad definiendam causam
eorum, quae propter obitum antecessoris uestri indefinita reman-
sit. Rogamus etiam ne nobis scripto significare grauemini, cur
Siluanectis non fuerit sacracio uestra. Valete.[b]

36

*Fulbert to Archbishop Leothericus of Sens: refusing his
request for a hearing for Guido as regards his part in
Evrardus' murder*[1]   *after 5 September 1019/20*

Sancto ac[a] uenerabili archiepiscopo L(eutherico) F(ulbertus)
episcopus de uirtute in uirtutem progredi.[2]

De Guidone excommunicato nostro nos appellas, reuerende
pater, ut ei misereamur, dicens quod episcopali se uelit examinari
iudicio, et aecclesiastica satisfactione purgari.[3] At nos praecem
tuam seu uerba minime paruipendentes,[b] tibi respondemus,[c] nos
eius libenter misereri uelle, sed examinationem eius ultra non
curare. Apud nos enim iam de ipso sicut de manifeste[d] reo optime
factum est episcopale, hoc est canonicum ac decretale iudicium,
dum illum secundum auctoritatem canonum ac decreta sanctorum
patrum excommunicauimus. Dicimus autem illum[e] manifeste
reum propter rationes subscriptas: primo, quia causa cupiditatis
eius, fratris quoque ac matris ipsius occisus est immerito noster
subdecanus; deinde, quia sciuit insidias illi praetendendas, nec
michi patefecit; tercio, quod insidiatores eius quos disturbare
potuit non disturbauit, sed et praesentia sua domum, ex[f] qua
sanctae aecclesiae nostre seruire debuerat, eis receptandis dolose
uacuam fecit; quarto, quod malo eius consensit. His itaque modis
nobis aperte reus comprobatur. Vnde uocatus et per sex menses[g]
expectatus dum confessionis ac poenitentiae remedia a nobis

---

[b] Vale LDR

36 DRKCPBVH (L)   [a] ac *om.* D   [b] parui prudentes D
[c] respondimus DRK (respondemus L)   [d] manifesto DRKC (L)
[e] illum *om.* DRKC (L)   [f] ex] et D   [g] per sex menses *om.* BVH

---

[2] 18 November, St. Martin's feast falling on 11 November.

36. [1] See nos. 29 ff.   [2] Cf. Ps. 83: 8.
[3] This seems to refer to the procedure (later known as *purgatio canonica*)

for us a date after the octave of the feast of St. Martin[2] and a place where our representatives can meet you in order to conclude their case, which has remained unsettled because of your predecessor's death. We also ask if you will be so kind as to write and let us know why you have not been consecrated at Senlis. Farewell.

Fulbert to Archbishop Leothericus of Sens[1]
after 5 September 1019/20

To the holy and venerable Archbishop L(eothericus) from Bishop F(ulbert), with his prayer that he may advance from strength to strength.[2]

You appeal to us, reverend father, to have mercy on our excommunicated clerk Guido, saying that he wishes to be tried in a bishop's court and to clear himself in the manner prescribed by the church.[3] Though we do not take your request or message lightly, we answer that we are quite willing to have mercy on him, but no longer to be concerned with trying him; for we have already seen to it that he, as one who was obviously guilty, was properly tried in a bishop's court as provided by the canons and decretals at the time we excommunicated him in accordance with the prescriptions of the canons and the decrees of the holy fathers. We say that he is obviously guilty for the following reasons: first, because as a result of his greed and that of his brother and mother our subdean was unjustly killed; second, because he knew of the plot which had been laid for him, but did not reveal it to me; third, because he did not thwart the plotters when he could have done so, but even treacherously vacated the house from which he should have served our church so that they might hide there; fourth, because he consented to their crime. To us these reasons clearly prove him guilty. After he had been summoned and awaited for six months, during which he postponed asking us for the remedy of confession and penance, he received

whereby a defendant cleared himself by swearing to his innocence (cf. no. 13). It is, however, possible that it simply means that Guido wished to make satisfaction (i.e. 'to cleanse himself by performing the penance prescribed by the church'). As regards *crimina manifesta*, where no accusation was needed, and *purgatio canonica*, see P. Hinschius, *Das Kirchenrecht der Katholiken und Protestanten in Deutschland*, v (Berlin, 1893), 338 ff.

quaerere distulit, iure meritam excommunicationis sententiam pertulit. Cum ergo supradictis irrefragabilibus scilicet causis, plures enim earum ueri testes existunt parati[h] quemlibet resistentem conuincere,[i] cum ille, inquam, propter has causas indubitabili crimine teneatur obnoxius, quis curet[k] examinationem eius? An quia manifesta culpa examinari egeat? An forte crederetur[l] examinatus,[m] si[n] culpam se non habere[o] peiurando culpam accumularet?[p] Sed ut scientes aliquem peiurare sinant, ab animo sacerdotum religio prohibet. Iam uero tam[q] euidens peccatum quae purgatio maneat, nisi confessio et poenitentia? Hanc si expeteret audiens extra ciuitatem[r] sibi infestam[s] me esse, propter amorem Dei cuius misericordiae me commonefecisti adhuc apud me locum eius[t] reperiret, atque haec ei forsitan aliquando absolutionem pareret.[u] Quod si hoc noluerit, quando tu concilium statueris de maioribus et utilioribus tractaturus, cum illis et haec recensurus adero tecum si mandaueris. Et siquod in illum[x] actum est bene stat, astipulatione tua nitatur. Sin minus, corrigatur. Vale.

37

Fulbert to King Cnut of (England and) Denmark:[1] *thanking him for his gift*   *21 Feb. 1018/19–5 Sept. 1019/20*

Nobilissimo regi Danomarchiae Cnucio F(ulbertus) Dei gratia Carnotensium episcopus cum suis clericis et monachis oracionis suffragium.

Quando munus tuum nobis oblatum uidimus, sagacitatem tuam et religionem pariter admirati sumus. Sagacitatem quidem, quod homo nostrae linguae ignarus, longoque a nobis terrae marisque interuallo diuisus,[2] non solum ea quae circa te sunt strenue capessas, sed etiam ea quae circa nos diligenter inquiras. Religionem uero, cum te quem paganorum principem audieramus,

---

[h] pareat B   paret VH   [i] conuinci BVH   [k] quaerat DRKC (L)
[l] credetur DRK (L)   [m] examinato VH   [n] si *om.* BVH   [o] si *add.*
BVH   [p] accumulet DRKH (ac . . mularet L)   [q] tam *om.* BVH
[r] extra ciuitatem] contra ciuitatem C (L)   non contra ciuilitatem DRK

the sentence of excommunication which he rightly deserved. These are the causes, and irrefutable they are, for there are many witnesses to the truth of them ready to refute anyone who would deny it—these are the causes, I say, why he is held guilty of a crime which cannot be doubted, and so who would go to the trouble of trying him? Does obvious guilt require a trial? Or if he were tried, would he be thought to have cleared himself if, by forswearing his guilt, he added to it the crime of perjury? But that priests should consciously allow anyone to commit perjury is forbidden by their office. So now what expiation remains for such a flagrant sin except confession and penance? If he, hearing that I am out of the city, where he goes in fear of his life, should come and ask me for this, for the love of God, of whose mercy you have reminded me, he may yet find a place with me, and by this same mercy it may be that he will some day obtain absolution. But if he is not willing to do this, when you set up a council to treat of more important and useful matters, I shall meet with you, if you summon me, to consider the present case along with them. If the action taken against him is right, let it have your consent and support; if not, let it be corrected. Farewell.

Fulbert to King Cnut of (England and) Denmark[1]
21 Feb. 1018/19–5 Sept. 1019/20

To the most noble king of Denmark, Cnut, from F(ulbert), by grace of God bishop of Chartres, and his clerks and monks, with the support of their prayers.

When we saw the gift that you sent us, we were amazed at your knowledge as well as your faith: at your knowledge, because you, a man who does not know our language and who is separated from us by a great expanse of land and sea,[2] not only vigorously take care of your own affairs, but also diligently inquire into ours; at your faith, since you, whom we had heard to be a pagan

---

s infestum DRKVH corr. *to* repararet C	*t* eius *om.* VH *x* illo DRK (illum L)	*u* pararet DRK repareret

37 LDRCB

37. [1] See p. lxxv. This letter is cited by William of Malmesbury (see p. lxiv).
   [2] Cf. Gregory I, ep. v. 41 (*MGH Ep.* i. 332).

non modo Christianum, uerum etiam erga ecclesias atque Dei
seruos benignissimum largitorem agnoscimus. Vnde gratias
agentes regi regum ex cuius disposicione talia descendunt, rogamus
ut ipse regnum tuum in bonis prosperari faciat, et animam tuam
a peccatis absoluat, per coeternum et consubstancialem sibi unigenitum Christum dominum nostrum in unitate Spiritus sancti.
Amen. Vale memor nostri, non inmemorum[a] tui.

38

*Fulbert to Bishop G.: prescribing the penance for a deacon
who said mass*   c. *1019/20?*[1]

Caro patri et coepiscopo suo G. F(ulbertus).

De[a] diacono qui se presbiterum simulauit, missamque celebrare
presumpsit, modum poenitenciae in diuinis legibus proprie
statutum non inuenimus, per raciocinacionem[b] similium sic
estimare[c] possumus. Chore, Dathan, et Abiron, iudicio Dei
condempnati, et horribili morte multati sunt, eo quod Aaron
sacerdoti se comparare[d] eiusque officium usurpare presumpse-
runt.[2] Hic autem leuita more illorum[e] illicite sibi sacerdocium
usurpauit. Quis ergo in isto dubitet esse mortale commissum,
quod in illis Deo iudice uidet[f] morte punitum? At quia iam
Saluator noster, qui uenit saluare quod perierat, non uult mortem
peccatoris sed ut conuertatur et uiuat,[3] clementer agitur[g] ut
degradentur huiusmodi, et inter laicos penitenciam agant. Sed ne
nimis austeritatem ueteris legis haec raciocinacio sapere uideatur,
proponamus et nouam. Legitur in quodam capitulo: 'Statutum
sepissime et inhibitum est, ut missarum celebraciones in locis
incongruentibus omnino non fiant'; et quibusdam interpositis,
sequitur: 'Quia sicut non est concessum ut alii missam cantent
et sacrificia consecrent, quam illi qui ad hoc ab episcopis sunt
consecrati, ita non est licitum ut in aliis domibus uel altaribus aut
locis missas celebrare presumant, quam ab episcopis consecratis';
et in fine capituli: 'Siquis ergo post tot prohibiciones haec decreta
apostolica et synodali auctoritate renouata temerare presumpserit,

---

    [a] inmemoris B

38 LDRKCPBVH   [a] De *erased?* L *om.* C Si PB Sed VH (*omitting
the salutation and incorporating this letter with no. 23*)   [b] uero add. LDRK
(*supra* L) autem add. C   [c] exstimare LD existimare RK   [d] con-
parasse LDRK   [e] suorum LDRK   [f] uidetur VH   [g] agit VH

prince, we now know to be not only a Christian, but also a most generous donor to churches and God's servants. So we give thanks to the King of Kings, from whom, in his providence, all such things proceed, and we pray that he may make your kingdom prosperous and flourishing and absolve your soul from sin, through his coeternal, consubstantial, and only-begotten son, Christ, our Lord, in the unity of the Holy Spirit. Amen. Farewell, and remember us, as we remember you.

Fulbert to Bishop G. c. *1019/20?*[1]

To his dear father and fellow bishop G. from F(ulbert).

With regard to the deacon who posed as a priest and dared to celebrate mass, we have not found a specific penance prescribed in divine law, but we can judge as follows by reasoning from analogy. Corah, Dathan, and Abiron were condemned by God's judgement and punished with a horrible death because they dared to deem themselves equals of the priest Aaron and to usurp his office.[2] This deacon has illicitly usurped the priesthood just as they did. So who can doubt that a mortal sin has been committed in this case seeing that in theirs it was punished by God's judgement with death? But now that our Saviour, who came to save what was lost, does not desire the death of a sinner, but that he might be converted and live,[3] it is mercifully permitted for such persons to be degraded and to do penance among the laity. So that the way we are reasoning may not seem to savour too much of the severity of the old law, let us also set forth the new. One reads in a certain chapter: 'It has often been decreed and forbidden for mass to be celebrated in places which are unsuitable.' After a few lines, it continues: 'For just as it is not right for anyone to sing mass and to consecrate the sacrifices except those who have been ordained for this by a bishop, so it is not lawful for them to venture to celebrate mass in other buildings, on other altars, or at other places than those which have been consecrated by a bishop.' And at the end of the chapter: 'So if anyone, after so many prohibitions, should dare to violate these decrees which have been renewed by papal and synodal authority, he will be in

38. [1] See p. lxxv.   [2] See Num. 16: 1 ff.
[3] Cf. Matt. 18: 11; Ezek. 33: 11.

gradus sui periculo subiacebit.'[4] Videmus ergo capitulum nouae legis uetustae[h] congruere, nec opus[i] est amplius quid de illo diacono faciendum sit dubitare. Est enim procul dubio extra chorum deponendus,[k] penitencia plectendus. Quod si de longitudine penitenciae questio fiat, meminisse debemus illius sentenciae quae ad hanc questionem respondet hoc modo: 'Mensuram temporis in agenda penitencia idcirco non satis attente prefigunt canones pro unoquoque crimine, sed magis in arbitrio antistitis statuendum relinquunt, quia apud Deum non tam ualet mensura temporis quam doloris, nec abstinencia tantum ciborum sed mortificacio pocius uiciorum.'[5] In manu ergo uestra situm est penitenciam eius uel breuiare uel protelare, iuxta quod eum[l] in penitendo diligentem seu negligentem uideritis. Valeat sanctitas uestra.

39

Fulbert to Bishop Roger of Lisieux:[1] *explaining why his priests did not pay their synodal dues and asking that they be allowed to resume their duties*   *1014–22*

Venerando Lexouiensium pontifici R(ogerio) F(ulbertus) Carnotensium episcopus salutem et fideles oraciones.[a]

Presbiteri canonicorum nostrorum ex ecclesiis quas habent in episcopatu uestro uenerunt ad nos dicentes quod uos interdixistis eis ministerium suum, ideo quia de ipsis ecclesiis non ferunt uobis synodum.[2] Et nos quidem eam uobis iure soluendam esse non ignoramus; sed Tetoldus prepositus noster ac uester seruus[3] non bene rem intellexit hactenus, eo deceptus quod nulla ecclesiarum quas nostri canonici possident in episcopatu nostro

---

[h] uetustaeque LDRK (-que *supra* L)   [i] opus] episcopo VH   [k] et *add.* VH   [l] eum *om.* VH

39 LDRPBVH   [a] fideles oraciones] benedictionem LDR

---

[4] Benedictus Levita, iii. 431 (ed. Knust, p. 129).
[5] A fairly common passage, probably taken from Halitgarius of Cambrai, *De vitiis et virtutibus*, preface (*PL* cv. 657). See P. Anciaux, *La théologie du*

danger of losing his orders.'[4] Thus we see that the chapter of the new law conforms to the old, nor need one have any further doubt as to what should be done with regard to that deacon, for it is clear that he must be removed from choir and punished with penance. In case there should be a question concerning the length of his penance, we ought to bear in mind the answer that is given in the following maxim: 'The length of time for doing penance is not specified by the canons for each sin in particular, but instead is left to the judgement of the bishop, for the length of time is not as important in God's sight as the degree of sorrow, nor abstinence from food as much as mortification of vices.'[5] So it is in your hands to shorten or to lengthen his penance according to whether you see him diligent or negligent in carrying it out. My best wishes to your holiness.

Fulbert to Bishop Roger of Lisieux[1]   *1014–22*

To the venerable bishop of Lisieux, R(oger), from F(ulbert), bishop of Chartres, with his greetings and faithful prayers.

The priests who serve the churches which belong to our canons in your diocese came and told us that you had prohibited them from exercising their office because they did not pay you the synodal dues for these churches.[2] We are well aware that the law requires these to be paid to you; but Tetoldus, our provost and your servant,[3] did not understand it as he was misled by the fact that none of the churches which our canons possess in our own

---

sacrement de pénitence au XIIe siècle (Louvain, 1949), pp. 31 n., 259 n. The following sentence in Fulbert's letter is paraphrased from the same passage.

39. [1] Before 990–before late 1022 (*GC* xi. 765 f.; above, pp. lxxviii f., lxxxiii).

[2] The churches in question were probably those granted to Chartres by Duke Richard II of Normandy on 21 September 1014 (Fauroux, no. 15). The grant is also mentioned in Richard's obituary in the cathedral necrology (Merlet, pp. 173 f.). The *synodus* was a payment made at the time of a diocesan synod. With specific reference to Chartres see *Cart. S.-Père*, i, pp. cxxv–cxxvi; L. Merlet, 'Redevances au pays chartrain durant le moyen âge', *Mém. de la Soc. arch. d'Eure-et-Loir*, xii (1901), 222. There is no evidence that Bishop Roger remitted the *synodus* (he is not mentioned in the necrology), and his successor claimed a similar payment (cf. no. 66). See J.-F. Lemarignier, *Étude sur les privilèges d'exemption et de juridiction ecclésiastique des abbayes normandes depuis les origines jusqu'en 1140* (Paris, 1937), pp. 66 f., 89 f., 108 f.

[3] See nos. 65, 108.

obligata est huiuscemodi debito, remittente uidelicet eis[b] ante-
cessorum meorum piissima liberalitate. Sed ea quantalibet caritate
fulta, quantalibet laude digna, uestro tamen iuri minime pre-
iudicat. Nunc itaque serenitati uestrae supplicamus, ut concedatis
eis officium suum agendi licenciam, paratis amodo aut uestram
synodum uobis reddere, aut in usus fratrum nostrorum necessarios
retinere, si caritati uestrae placuerit sanctorum patrum meorum
supramemoratum remissionis exemplum obseruare. Si non merui
ut[c] causa mei aliquid faciatis, restat (spero) aliquando meritum
iri opitulante gratia Christi. Valete, carissime pater, et mementote
mei in oracionibus uestris.

40

*Fulbert to Bishop Thierry of Orleans: explaining that it will
not be possible to make the procession to Orleans*

late 1020–early 1021

Venerabili Aurelianorum episcopo T(heoderico) F(ulbertus)
Carnotensium sacerdos obsequium dilectionis sine fuco simula-
cionis.[1]

Grator[a] diligenciae tuae, licet inter multa aduersancia sua
strenue capessenti,[b] me quoque de negociis ad me pertinentibus
amice commonenti. At ego commonicionem tuam benigne sus-
cipio, in ceteris quidem quae mihi scripsisti libenter tibi prout
decuerit et tempus erit obtemperaturus. De processione uero
ecclesiae nostrae ad uestram fieri solita[2] clericos nostros conueniens,
audiui ab eis quod optime noueram, et teipsum aequo animo
concredere[c3] uolo, uidelicet quod dampnatis incendio[4] et ad
ecclesiae restauracionem inhiantibus aliisque plurimis seriis ualida
necessitate occupatis, processio non sit ad presens facilis, successu
uero prosperae facultatis, cum magno gaudio ac debita deuocione
se illam facturos. Vale cum beatissimo clero tuo et grege tibi
commisso, cohortans eos orare Deum, ut liberet nos ab aduersis
nostris.

<hr>

[b] eis *om.* BVH		[c] ut *om.* VH	
40 LDRKPBVH	[a] Gratulor BH	[b] capescenti L	[c] credere BVH

40. [1] Cf. Ambrose, *Expositio psalmi cxviii*, xiii. 27. 2 (ed. Petschenig, *CSEL*
lxii. 297).
   [2] The cathedral necrology contains an entry under 11 November com-
memorating Constantine, priest and canon of Saint-Euverte of Orleans, who
asked to wash the feet of the canons of Chartres in his house after the procession

diocese is obliged to pay them since they were remitted to them by my predecessors out of their generosity and devotion. But their action, however great the underlying charity and however praise-worthy in itself, by no means prejudices your rights. So we beg your eminence to permit them to exercise their office with the understanding that they are prepared for the future to pay you the synodal dues which belong to you or to keep them to defray the expenses of our brothers if it should please you in your charity to follow the example of my holy predecessors and to remit them. If I have done nothing to merit your doing anything for my sake, there still remains my hope that by the help of Christ's grace I may some day prove deserving. Farewell, dearest father, and remember me in your prayers.

Fulbert to Bishop Thierry of Orleans
late 1020–early 1021

To the venerable bishop of Orleans, T(hierry), from F(ulbert), bishop of Chartres, with his loving service, sincere and unfeigned.[1]

I thank you for your diligence in sending me friendly advice about my affairs although you yourself are striving amidst many difficulties to take care of your own. I am happy to receive your advice, and as regards the other matters about which you wrote, so far as is proper and time permits I shall gladly comply with your wishes. But as for the procession which is usually made from our church to yours,[2] I held a meeting with our clerks and heard from them what I myself knew quite well and what I want you to accept with equanimity:[3] that because of their losses from the fire,[4] their eagerness to rebuild the church, and their involvement in many other serious and pressing affairs, it would be difficult to make the procession at present, but that when they are in a better position to do so, they will make it with great joy and due devotion. My best wishes to you and the most blessed clergy and flock entrusted to your care, and please urge them to pray to God to deliver us from our adversities.

and left a bequest to his heirs with instructions that they were to continue *hoc exemplum dominicum et memoriale suum* (Merlet, pp. 181 f.).

[3] Fulbert is apparently using *concredere* almost in the judicial sense found from the Carolingian period on to mean the voluntary acceptance of a (legal) judgement (see Du Cange, s.v.).   [4] 7–8 September 1020 (see p. xx).

41

Fulbert to King Robert: explaining that it is not possible to make the procession to Orleans[1]   *late 1020–early 1021*

Dilectissimo domino[a] suo regi Francorum R(otberto) F(ulbertus) humilis episcopus sanctae uirtutis augmentum.

Si nobis omnes euagandi facultates simul cum uoluntate supeterent, interesset[b] uestrae pietatis leuitatem nostram arguere, et ad nostrae ecclesiae quae destructa est restauracionem assiduam reuocare. Nunc uero cum omnes eiusmodi facultates desint, et nos ad assiduitatem necessitudo magna coherceat, quomodo sapienciae uestrae dignum uideri possit, ut uel nos uel clerum nostrum de qualibet longa processione commoneat? Sustinete pocius, sancte pater, sustinete inbecillitatem nostram, supplete indigenciam nostram, ut Deus omni bono refocilet caram animam uestram. Valete[c] regaliter.

42

Fulbert to Archbishop Leothericus of Sens: justifying his ordination of Odolricus, bishop-elect of Orleans, to the priesthood[1]   *before 12 March 1021*

Sacro Senonensium archipresuli L(eutherico) F(ulbertus) Dei gratia Carnotensium episcopus uirtutem suae dignitatis excellenciae competentem.

Odolricum Aurelianensem ego quidem[a] ad episcopum non elegi sicut uobis dictum est, sed a clero et populo suae ciuitatis electum sacraui presbiterum. Quod autem eum Romam ire uelle audistis, et ibi creari episcopum, dissuasi uestri honoris gratia. Sed et ipse gratanter dissuadenti paruit, suggerentibus fidelibus suis Rodulfo scilicet et Herfrido.[2] Multis occupatus, pauca uobis rescribere cogor. Saluto uos quantum possum in Domino, paternitati uestrae deuotus suffraganeus.

41 LDRKPBVM   [a] domino *only in* B   [b] interesse deberet VM
[c] Vale L

42 LDRPBVM   [a] ego quidem *om.* DR

Fulbert to King Robert[1]   *late 1020–early 1021*

To his very dear lord, R(obert), king of France, from F(ulbert), a humble bishop, with his prayer that he may increase in holy virtue.

If we had all the means for wandering around and were inclined to do so, it would be your pious duty to accuse us of irresponsibility and to bid us return and persevere in rebuilding our church, which has been destroyed. But now, when all such means are wanting and we are forced by great necessity to be persevering, how can it seem right to you in your wisdom to remind us or our clergy of any long procession? But rather support us, holy father, support us in our weakness and provide for us in our need so that God may refresh your dear soul with all good things. May long life and royal splendour be ever yours.

Fulbert to Archbishop Leothericus of Sens[1]   *before 12 March 1021*

To the holy archbishop of Sens, L(eothericus), from F(ulbert), by grace of God bishop of Chartres, with his prayer that he may have the virtue which is proper to the eminence of his office.

I myself did not 'elect' Odolricus of Orleans to the bishopric as you were told; but after he was elected by the clergy and people of his city, I did ordain him to the priesthood. As for your hearing that he wanted to go to Rome and to be consecrated bishop there, I persuaded him against this for the sake of your honour, and he gladly yielded to my dissuasion at the prompting of his friends Ralph and Herfridus.[2] I am very busy and forced to send you a brief reply. My very best greetings in the Lord, father, as one who is your devoted suffragan.

41. [1] See no. 40.
42. [1] See pp. lxxvii–lxxix.   [2] See no. 23.

43

Fulbert to Archbishop Leothericus of Sens: justifying his consecration of Bishop Odolricus of Orleans[1]

before 9 June 1021

Patri ac primati suo L(eutherico) F(ulbertus) episcopus.

Gratias ago uigilantiae tuae quae meae simplicitati praemonitorium facit. Vere enim indigeo premoneri de multis propter meae indiscrecionis seu negligenciae morbum. Verum in hac causa qua de nunc agis, id est ne quibuslibet episcopandis cito[a] manus imponam,[2] opus non esse arbitror monitore.[b][3] Nam et si tu in isto negotio consilio meo (ut decuerat) hactenus uti uoluisses, et ordo noster et tua res aliter processisset. Sed omitto preterita; de futuris uero plurimum bonae spei capio ex eo quod nunc cum uiris sanctis ac sapientibus agis, patrem nostrum Odilonem[4] loquor et asseculas eius. Consilio enim illorum spero te non solum animae periculum euadere, sed etiam huius uitae gloriam et honorem posse recuperare. Vale memor mei, tibi in omnibus bonis obedire et opitulari parati.[c]

44

Fulbert to Bishop Franco of Paris: supporting him in his efforts to recover church revenues and agreeing to investigate a complaint against Count Galeran of Meulan

before 12 March 1021

Venerabili uiro et consacerdoti suo F(ranconi) F(ulbertus) ea quae sunt uerae pacis.

Tu, frater dilectissime, ex habundantia caritatis honore me nimio ac sapienciae laude dignaris; ego uero meam personam humilem uirtutisque inopem sicut est uideo et agnosco. Verum utcumque se habeat pusillitas mea, hoc tamen nefas inhumanitatis admittere nec uelle nec posse me fateor, ut te de erumpnis[a] sanctae aecclesiae sine compassione zeloque iustitiae audiam querelantem. At[b] quia compassio ubi corde concepta est mox

---

43 LDRKCPBVM   [a] cito *om.* LDRKC   [b] opus . . . monitore] non esse arbitror monitore LVM   non esse opus arbitror monitore DRK (opus

Fulbert to Archbishop Leothericus of Sens[1]
before 9 June 1021

To his father and primate, L(eothericus), from Bishop F(ulbert).

I thank you for your vigilance in sending me a forewarning, simple-minded as I am, for I truly need to be forewarned on many counts because of my tendency to be imprudent and negligent. But as to the matter in question, namely that I should not hastily lay my hands on whoever comes along to consecrate him to the bishopric,[2] I do not think I need anyone to admonish me;[3] for if you had only been willing earlier to accept my advice in this case as you should have done, the outcome would have been different for both the episcopate and your affairs. But no more of the past; and as for the future, I am very hopeful since you are now dealing with men who are holy and wise, I am speaking of our father Odilo[4] and his followers. By their counsel I hope that you will not only escape endangering your soul, but even be able to recover glory and honour in this life. Farewell, and remember that I am prepared to obey and to assist you in all good tasks.

Fulbert to Bishop Franco of Paris before 12 March 1021

To the venerable lord and his fellow bishop, F(ranco), from F(ulbert), wishing those things that make for true peace.

You, my very dear brother, out of the abundance of your charity deem me worthy of too much honour in praising my wisdom; I see and know myself as I am, humble and lacking in virtue. But though I cannot claim much, I confess that I am neither willing nor able to commit the inhuman crime of hearing your complaint about the hardships suffered by the holy church without feeling compassion and zeal for justice. As soon as compassion is conceived in the heart, it longs to bring forth consolation,

supra R)   non esse arbitror monitore opus C   *c* memor . . . parati *om.* VM

44 LDRKCPBVM   *a* te de erumpnis] de erumpnis se L   de erumnis te DRK
b Aut L

---

43. [1] See no. 42.   [2] Cf. 1 Tim. 5: 22.
   [3] Cf. Terence, *Heaut.* 171.   [4] Abbot of Cluny.

consolacionem edere gliscit, et plagam ulcionis infligere zelus,
nosque tamen ad primum quam ad secundum proniores esse
oportet, ego quoque priusquam zelum in tuos hostes exerceam,
consolatoria te racione conuenio. Rogo itaque, frater, ne ui
molestiarum inpulsus indiscrecius irascaris, ne forte ad inpacien-
ciam, inde ad arma prorumpas, et cum gladium alienum usur-
paueris, tuum facias non timeri. Rogo iterum ne fias ob multam
iniuriam tristis, turbulentus, et anxius, sed 'delectare semper in
Domino, et dabit tibi petitiones cordis tui'.[1] Vsum fructum uero
altarium, quae tui[c] antecessores laicis tradiderunt, te alendis debili-
bus publica uoce destinare suadeo, tum ne quis illis inde fraudet
aliquid interminari, et siqui in hanc fraudem irruperint, sicut
fures sacrorum et occisores pauperum anathemate condempnari.
Ne reuererearis[d] quaeso homines innocenter offendere propter
Deum, ut sis eo dignus quo, nisi patrem et matrem insuper et
animam tuam propter ipsum oderis,[2] iudicaris indignus. 'Si Deus
pro te, quis contra te?'[3] Est autem[e] pro te semper in sua causa
Deus, est etiam tecum ut ait: 'Ecce ego uobiscum sum omnibus
diebus usque ad consummacionem seculi.'[4] Quid ergo timeas
defendere Dei causam, cum ipse tecum sit ad cooperandum, pro
te sit ad tutandum? 'Confortare' itaque, frater, 'in Domino et in
potencia uirtutis eius.'[5] Confortare, inquam, confide et gaude,
exulta et tripudia, et alacri animo ad certamen eius prolude, cum
propheta dicendo: 'Congregamini,[f] populi, et uincimini; accin-
gite[g] uos, et uincimini; inite consilium, et dissipabitur; loquimini
uerbum, et non fiet, quia nobiscum Deus.'[6] Et quia certo scio
communem Dominum tibi in sua causa semper esse patrocinatu-
rum, me quoque seruulum eius non defuturum esse[h] polliceor siue
ad cohercendas[i] manus persequencium, siue ad ora contradicen-
cium obstruenda.[7] Ad summam autem securum te requiescere
iubeo inter medios cleros,[8] quamdiu te audiero persecutoribus
ecclesiae non cedentem. Gualerannum[9] uero ut petisti conueniam;
et causa discussa quid inde senciam uel quid te facere oporteat,
aut uerbis aut litteris innotescam. Vale.

---

    c tibi VM   *d* reuearis L   uerearis C   *e* autem] enim LDRK
f Congratulamini DRK   *g* accingimini LDRKC   *h* esse *om.* DRK
i coercendum DRK

---

44. [1] Ps. 36: 4.   [2] Cf. Luke 14: 26.   [3] Rom. 8: 31.
    [4] Matt. 28: 20.   [5] Eph. 6: 10.
    [6] Isa. 8: 9 f., with a slight omission.   [7] Cf. Ps. 62: 12.
    [8] Cf. Ps. 67: 14.   [9] Galeran I of Meulan (see nos. 27, 45 f.).

while zeal is eager to strike an avenging blow; but since we should be more inclined toward the one than the other, before I exercise my zeal against your enemies, I am writing to console you. I beg you, brother, not to let the force of these troubles drive you into a thoughtless rage, for fear that you burst forth into impatience and then into arms, and when you have usurped another's sword, bring it about that your own is not feared. Again, I beg you not to be saddened, disturbed, or troubled by this great injury, but 'delight in the Lord always, and he will give thee the requests of thy heart'.[1] As regards the usufruct of the altars which your predecessors alienated to laymen, I advise you to issue a public statement that you are setting it aside to support the needy, then to forbid anyone to deprive them of any of it under penalty of censure, and if any should dare to do so, to excommunicate them as sacrilegious robbers and murderers of the poor. Do not be afraid, I beseech you, to offend men through no fault of your own, but for the sake of God, that you may be worthy of him who will judge you unworthy unless you would hate both father and mother and even your own soul for his sake.[2] 'If God is for you, who is against you?'[3] But God is always for you when you are working in his behalf, and he is also with you as he says: 'Behold I am with you all days even to the consummation of the world.'[4] So why do you fear to support God's cause when he himself is there to work with you, there to protect you? 'Be strong, brother, in the Lord and in the power of his strength.'[5] Be strong, I say, be confident and joyful, rejoice and dance, and eagerly prepare yourself to do battle for him, saying with the prophet: 'Gather yourselves together, O ye people, and be overcome; gird yourselves, and be overcome. Take counsel together, and it shall be defeated; speak a word, and it shall not be done, for God is with us.'[6] Because I know that the Lord of all will always protect you when you are working in his behalf, I promise that I too, his humble servant, will not be wanting either to restrain the hands of your persecutors or to silence the mouths of your opponents.[7] Finally, I bid you rest secure amid those who are your lot[8] so long as I hear that you are not yielding to the church's persecutors. As for Galeran,[9] I shall summon him as you ask; and when I have gone into the case, I shall let you know by messenger or by letter what I myself think about it and what you should do. Farewell.

45

Fulbert to Bishop Franco of Paris: enclosing his letter admonishing Galeran to answer Franco's charges[1]

before 12 March 1021

Patri et coepiscopo F(ranconi) F(ulbertus).

Gualeranno misi litteras huiusmodi: 'Fulbertus episcopus G(ualeranno) plus boni quam sit meritus. Rogo, frater, et moneo, ut emendes culpas quas habes contra Deum et me et Parisiorum episcopum, qui conplanctum facit de te. Quod si non feceris ante mediam quadragesimam, abinde faciemus de te sicut de homine qui grauiter peccat et non uult emendare.' Si ergo Gualerannus se non iustificauerit uobis ante prescriptum terminum, tunc facite de illo ministerium uestrum. Valete*[a]* quamplurimum.

46

Fulbert to Bishop Franco of Paris: notifying him that Galeran cannot come to trial at present, but promises to do so later[1]

before 9 June 1021

F(ulbertus) Dei gratia Carnotensium episcopus uenerabilem patrem et coepiscopum suum F(ranconem) cum uenerit Dominus inueniri uigilantem.[2]

Commonitus a legato nostro Gualerannus de iustitia*[a]* prosequenda in diem et locum destinatum a uobis, respondit se esse premonitum ab Odone comite*[b]* sub nomine sacramenti de facienda expedicione contra Fulconem[3] circa*[c]* eundem diem, uerum infra octo dies ex quo illa expedicio uel facta erit uel omissa, uenturum se esse ad iustitiam pollicetur. Sed quando ille promissioni*[d]* suae adinplendae terminum fixum non statuit, et multae causae protelacionis incidere possunt, uel certe quae nobis conueniendi adimant facultatem, suademus (si honeste fieri possit) per uestros necessarios rem accelerare, et uestrum uobis casatum firmiter alligare.*[e]* Nescitis enim quid fortuna parturiat.*[f]*[4] Valete.

---

45 LDRKPBVM   *[a]* Vale L
46 LDRKCPBVH   *[a]* sua *add.* LDRK   *[b]* comite *om.* VH

Fulbert to Bishop Franco of Paris[1] *before 12 March 1021*

To his father and fellow bishop, F(ranco), from F(ulbert).

I have sent Galeran the following letter: 'Bishop Fulbert to Galeran, with better wishes, perhaps, than he deserves. I beg and admonish you, brother, to make amends for the wrongs that you have done to God, me, and the bishop of Paris, who has lodged a complaint against you. If you do not do so before mid Lent, we shall treat you from then on as one who has sinned gravely and is unwilling to make amends.' So if Galeran does not give you satisfaction before the prescribed date, do your duty as concerns him. All best wishes.

Fulbert to Bishop Franco of Paris[1] *before 9 June 1021*

F(ulbert), by grace of God bishop of Chartres, to his venerable father and fellow bishop F(ranco), with his prayer that when the Lord comes, he may be found keeping watch.[2]

When Galeran was summoned by our messenger to stand trial at the time and place that you set, he replied that Count Odo had already summoned him in the name of his oath to make an expedition against Fulk[3] about the same time; but he promises that within a week after the expedition is either completed or abandoned he will come to trial. Yet since he did not set a definite time for fulfilling his promise, and since many things can happen that would delay it or indeed deprive us of the opportunity to meet, we advise you, if you can honourably do so, to use your associates to speed the case up and to get a firm hold on your vassal, for you know not what fortune may bring forth.[4] Farewell.

---

[c] Fulconem circa *om.* LDRKCVH   contra Fulconem *om.* B   [d] pro-missionis PVH   [e] casamentum firmiter allegare DRK   [f] pariat BH

---

45. [1] See no. 44.
46. [1] See nos. 44 f.   [2] Cf. Luke 12: 37.
    [3] Counts Odo of Chartres and Fulk Nerra of Anjou.
    [4] Cf. Prov. 27: 1.

47

Fulbert to Bishop Adalbero of Laon: sending him some medicines   *before 12 March 1021*

Virtute magis predito quam predicato presuli A(dalberoni) F(ulbertus).

Vestrae sospitati amice gratulantes, ualitudini quoque uestri fidelis et amici nostri Ebali[1] (si diuina benignitas allubescat) quanta nouimus ope subuenire parauimus, mittendo gera Galieni pociones iii et totidem tiriacae diatesseron.[2] Quae quid ualeant, et modus acceptionis uel obseruacionis earum, in uestris anti-dotariis[3] facile reperitur. Vulgaginem[4] etiam petitam uobis mitti-mus, quamuis etatem uestram tali iam uomitu fatigari non suademus, sed eo pocius si opus sit alleuari, qui frequenter et sine periculo fieri possit, ex oximelle et rafanis, uel certe quod seniori magis conducibile est, morantem aluum laxatiuis pilulis incitari.[5] De quibus ultro uobis fere xc*a* oblatis, caetera omnia*b* bona uestra*c* putate. Valete.*d*

48

Hildegar to Ebalus:[1] directions for taking a laxative
before 12 March 1021

Quem purae dilectionis affectu colit seniorem suum E(balo)*a* H(ildegarius) plurimum saluere.

Potionem iera quam dominus presul tibi mittit sumes cum aqua calida ante crepusculum diei. Nocte qua debes eam accipere, non cenabis; et ipsa nocte positam pocionem in uasculo in quo dis-

---

47 LDRCPBVM   *a* cx DR   *b* omnia] nostra P   *om.* B   *c* uestra
om. LDR   *d* Vale LRPB
48 LDRCP   *a* G. LR

---

47. [1] Probably the future archbishop of Rheims (see no. 56), who is said to have been Adalbero's *secretarius* (*Gesta Pontificum Cameracensium*, iii. 25 (*MGH SS* vii. 473)).
    [2] *Hiera* (or *gera*) and *theriaca* are frequently found in early medieval medical handbooks and were composed of various ingredients and thought to cure many

Fulbert to Bishop Adalbero of Laon
before 12 March 1021

To Bishop A(dalbero), by whom virtue is possessed rather than professed, from F(ulbert).

As your friend we rejoice to hear that you are in good health; and as for the illness of your faithful servant and our good friend Ebalus,[1] we have taken steps to give him all the help in our power, if God in his mercy approves, by sending three doses of Galen's *hiera* and three of the four-in-one syrup.[2] What these are good for and how to take or to administer them can easily be found in your *antidotaria*.[3] We are also sending the wild nard[4] that you asked for, though we do not advise a man of your age to weaken himself by using this as a purgative, but rather, if it is necessary to be relieved, to stimulate sluggish bowels with oximel and radishes (which can be done frequently and without danger) or indeed, as is more suitable for an older man, with laxative pills.[5] We are taking the liberty of sending you about seven and a half dozen of them, and please consider as your own whatever else we have that might help you. Farewell.

Hildegar to Ebalus[1]
before 12 March 1021

To his lord, E(balus), whom he cherishes with sincere love and affection, from H(ildegar), with many greetings.

Take the dose of *hiera* which the bishop is sending you with warm water before twilight. On the evening when you are going to take it, do not eat supper. On that evening put the *hiera* in the

different ailments. See H. Sigerist, *Studien und Texte zur frühmittelalterlichen Rezeptliteratur* (Studien zur Geschichte der Medizin, xiii (Leipzig, 1923)), pp. 23, 30, 34, 43 f., and *passim*. See no. 48.

[3] For such handbooks of *materia medica* see L. C. MacKinney, 'Medieval Medical Dictionaries and Glossaries', *Medieval and Historiographical Essays in honor of James Westfall Thompson* (Chicago, 1938), pp. 251 ff.

[4] See Sigerist, op. cit., index, s.v. *asarum*.

[5] For oximel (a mixture of vinegar and honey) and radish, see Sigerist, op. cit., pp. 88, 135 f.; and for the use of pills, ibid., pp. 48 ff., 55 ff., and *passim*.

48. [1] See no. 47.

temperanda est asperges salis gemma, uel si haec non adest,[b] delicato sale ad pensum unius scripuli. Accepta pocione, sedeas ante focum absque ullo tumultu cauens tibi penitus a frigore; et si paululum cubueris, non nocebit, nolo tamen ut dormias. Cum primum sencies moueri tibi uentrem, deambula pedetemptim,[c] et sic ad secessum uade. Si propter solucionem tandem ceperit te sitis, nequaquam bibes, nisi paululum aceti cum aqua calida mixti, propter stomachum diluendum seu releuandum, quod etiam non urgente siti facere poteris, solucione propemodum uacante. Prandere differes, quousque sencies[d] catarticum nihil amplius operari uelle. Cum sederis ad mensam, uide ne quid nimis, neque manduces aliquid stipticum uel plus aequo salsum. Plura de obseruacionis modo notarem, nisi pauca sufficerent sapienti.[2] Hoc tandem scribere me iubet nescia simulari[e] caritas, ut talem pocionis huius sencias effectum,[f] quatenus semper incolumis perseueres. Vale.

49

Fulbert to Abbot Odilo of Cluny: thanking him for his greetings and his concern over his health and asking for his counsel   *before 9 June 1021*

Prudenter humili et preclare magnifico patri O(diloni) F(ulbertus) suus ut ait.[a]

Sic nunquam ab alio liberaliter acceptus, quas opere nequeo, affectu saltem gratias reconpenso. Tali enim apparatu in epistola tua dignatus sum, quali non festiuior expectetur in ferculo Salomonis.[1] Inter organa uatum et ardentes cicendelas uirginum angelicum mihi manna posuisti, non sine mistica dape columbarum ac[b] turturum. Propinabas[c] interea karitatis nectar, quo inhianter hausto et ad cordis interiora transmisso, si non prophetice ut Dauid uerbum bonum,[2] panagirice tamen (ut fit) et inprecatorie sicut filio refocilatus Israel[3] tibi patri filius eructare

---

  [b] est LDR   [c] pedetempti LC   [d] sencias LDRC   [e] simulare
DR   [f] effectum sencias LDRC

49 LDRPBVM   [a] ut ait *om.* VM   [b] aut DR   [c] Propinabis
LDR

[2] See p. 63 n. 4.

vessel in which it is to be mixed and sprinkle it with a crystal of
salt or, if this is not available, with one twenty-fourth of an ounce
by weight of clarified salt. After you take it, sit in front of the
hearth, away from any excitement, and guard yourself completely
from the cold. If you lie down for a little while, it will not hurt
you, but I do not want you to go to sleep. As soon as you feel
your bowels moving, walk slowly and go to the privy. If you
should become thirsty because of the purging, do not drink anything except a little vinegar mixed with warm water so as to wash
out and refresh the stomach. (You can do this, even if you are not
very thirsty, when the purging is almost over.) Do not eat until
you feel that the purgative has stopped acting. When you sit down
at the table, see to it that you observe moderation and eat nothing
sharp or more salty than average. I would set down more about
how to take this save that a few words are enough for a wise man.[2]
But I am writing this much at the bidding of charity, which cannot
be feigned, so that you may feel a good effect from this medicine
and remain in continual good health. Farewell.

Fulbert to Abbot Odilo of Cluny   *before 9 June 1021*

To his father O(dilo), in wisdom lowly, glorious in splendour,
from F(ulbert), his friend, as he calls him.

I have never been received by anyone so warmly as I was by
you when you called me your friend; and though there is nothing
I can do to repay you, I can at least offer you my thanks and affection. In your letter you deemed me worthy of all the splendour
and festivity that might be expected at Solomon's pavilion.[1] Amid
bards playing their instruments and maidens carrying burning
lamps you set before me the manna of angels and a mystical feast
of doves and turtle-doves. Meanwhile you gave me the nectar of
charity to drink; and after I had eagerly drunk it and it was carried
to my innermost heart, I rejoiced to speak to you as a son to his
father, if not, as did David, with the prophecy of a good word,[2]
yet with praise, as it were, and invocation, as Israel spoke to his
son who had given him refreshment.[3] Then you showed with

49. [1] Cf. Cant. 3: 9 ff.   [2] Cf. Ps. 44: 2.
    [3] Apparently an error for Isaac: cf. Gen. 27: 25 ff.

gaudebam. Paterna deinde cura significasti te meae ualitudinis
habitum sagaciter explorasse, atque ubi uitalis calor aliquod in
me dabat[d] sospitatis indicium gratulari, dolere autem morbi
signum, et formidare periculum. Nec uero tandem benignitas tua
plagam meam relinquere passa est suae curacionis exortem, quin
arte diuina mirabiliter[e] usus liquorem quendam instar uini Samyi
prius infudisti, qui indigestum uulneris humorem excoqueret,
dehinc alterum oliuo persimilem, quo[f] totus omnino tumor atque
dolor mitigatus abscederet. Nunc ergo tua curatus industria, tuis[g]
epulis recreatus dignum duco, ut omnes meae uires tuae uoluntatis
semper amminiculentur effectui,[h] nec aliquatenus a tua sententia
discrepatum ire statuo, quia te cum Deo quantum homini datur
idem uelle atque nolle confido.[4] Decet itaque, pater, ut tu quoque
uicissim me tuum seruulum de te pendentem, teque non sine
magna fiducia respectantem,[5] sacris intercessionibus adiuues. Sum
enim ualde miserabilis homo, qui cum ad propriam non sufficerem,
ad publicam curam (nescio qua seu racione siue temeritate)
perductus sum. Idque certe est, ne dissimules, quod te specialiter
mihi facit consilii atque auxilii debitorem, quod te suasore non
desero hunc laborem. Vale.[i]

50

*Abbot Odilo of Cluny to Fulbert: praising him for following
the Lord's example in inquiring about himself, but refusing
to sit in judgement on him*   *1021 or later*

Domino et uenerabiliter desiderabili et desiderabiliter uenerabili
sancto sancteque[a] carissimo fratri et compresbitero Fulberto
frater Odilo salutem in Domino.

O industrissime uir, quid sibi uult questio prolata nobis a
quodam uestro fideli clerico? Placuit,[b] ut ipse fatetur, paternitati
uestrae me licet indignum iudicem fieri uitae uestrae, mandando
mihi ut litteratim describerem uobis quid michi uideretur[c] de
uestra quantum dici fas est inreprehensibili conuersacione? Sed
oculi caligine caecitatis obtecti non ualent perspicue intueri
splendorem firmamenti et globos stellarum caeli. Splendorem uero

---

[d] dabit LDR   [e] mirabiliter *om.* DR   [f] qui LBM   [g] tuisque
LDR   [h] affectui PVM   [i] Valete LV

50 LDRC   C has some omissions and a large number of unique variants
which have only been noted where they might point to the original reading.
[a] sancteque *om.* DR   [b] clerico, placuit enim C   [c] uidetur C

fatherly care that you had knowingly examined the state of my health and that where the vital warmth in me gave some indication of soundness, you rejoiced, but that you grieved at a sign of illness and feared danger. Nor in your kindness did you permit my affliction to be left without proper treatment, but making wondrous use of the divine art you first administered a liquid like the wine of Samos to melt out the undigested humour and then another much like olive oil to soothe and take away all the swelling and pain. Now, cured by your diligence and refreshed by your banquet, I think it fitting that I should ever strive with all my strength to carry out your wishes, and I have resolved never to stray from your judgement, for I firmly believe that, so far as this is given to man, whatever God likes and dislikes, so do you.[4] So it behoves you in turn, father, to help me by your holy prayers, your little servant who depends on you and who looks to you with full confidence,[5] for I am a most pitiful wretch who could not manage his own affairs, and yet was induced, I know not whether reasonably or rashly, to enter on a public office. It is surely this, and you cannot deny it, that makes you especially obliged to give me counsel and aid: that with you as my adviser I shall not desert this task. Farewell.

Abbot Odilo of Cluny to Fulbert 1021 or later

To the lord whom he holds in loving reverence and reverent love, his holy and in all holiness very dear brother and fellow priest, Fulbert, from Brother Odilo, greetings in the Lord.

Most eminent bishop, what did you mean by the question that was put to us by one of your faithful clerks? Did you wish, as he stated, father, for me, unworthy as I am, to sit in judgement on your life when you enjoined me to write and send you advice about the state of your soul, which is, so far as this can rightly be said, irreproachable? But eyes that are shrouded and darkened by blindness cannot clearly see the splendour of the firmament and the starry spheres of heaven; for I shall call you the splendour of

---

[4] A paraphrase of the commonplace that friends like and dislike the same things, perhaps taken from Sallust, *Cat.* xx. 4.

[5] Cf. Horace, *Ep.* i. 1. 105.

firmamenti et stellam, stellam etiam matutinam te uocabo,
Danielis prophetae usus testimonio: 'Qui docti fuerint', inquit,
'fulgebunt sicut splendor firmamenti; et qui ad iustitiam erudiunt
multos, sicut stellae in perpetuas aeternitates.'¹ Vos enim,ᵈ qui
talis ac tantus estis quem nec quidem digne cogitare ualeo, nostro
debetis estimari iuditio? Nos enim, qui ignorantiaeᵉ tenebris
pressi nosmetipsos non possumus dinoscere, iustorum uitam
nostro arbitrio nullo modo debemus estimare. Vos omnis homo
adeo laude dignum merito iudicat, ut plus de uobisᶠ mirari libeat,
quam aliquid dicere liceat. Obrueretur intellectus nostrae paruita-
tis pondere uestrae questionis, nisi esset in promptu recordatio
diuini sermonis. Vt enim daret exemplum fidelibus auctor uitae
et salutis, ut ipse melius scitis utpote uir per omnia euuangelicus,
ueniens in partes Caesareae Philippi interrogabat discipulos suos:
'Quem dicunt homines esse filium hominis?'; et post pauca: 'Vos
autem quem me esse dicitis?'² Non idcirco interrogat quem nemo
nouit, et quem nihil latet, ueluti quid nesciat, sed ut prelatis
aecclesiae exemplum de se interrogandi prebeat.ᵍ Et ideo unus-
quisque prepositus ecclesiae a subditis debet exquirere cuius
famae cuiusue sit opinionis; et si aliquid de se boniʰ audierit, Deo
a quo siquid boni est habet gratias referat, etⁱ de uirtutibus in
uirtutem ipso annuente felici cursu perueniat, usquequo Deum
Deorum in Syon uidere queat.³ Si uero sinistrum aliquid de se
audierit, peniteat, et de cetero sollicite emendare satagat. Sed et si
uos monetᵏ exemplo doctorum de uobis interrogandi auctoritas,
predicanda a nobis est uestrae sapientiae claritas, uestrae fidei
puritas, uestraeque industriae probitas. Quippe quia caret omnino
silentio ueritas; sed ab homine idiota et sine litteris, non potest
predicari Deo amabilis, et mundo odibilis.⁴ Haec de uobis nunc
etˡ alias et in communi locutione non aliqua fraude adulacionis
deceptus, non alicuius muneris ᵐ laudis uel pecuniae cupidus
retuli; sed quod ueraciter credo, et quod ut fiat quam maxime
opto, dicere etiam non recuso, nec recusabo. Si autem me adula-
torem iudicaueritis, audite scripturam: 'Fili mi, si te lactauerint
peccatores, ne adquiescas illis.'⁵ Non est tamen culpabile si illos

---

ᵈ autem C   ᵉ ignomine C   ᶠ de uobis] a nobis C   ᵍ debeat C
ʰ boni *om.* DR   ⁱ et] ut DR   ᵏ manet C   ˡ et *om.* C
ᵐ numeris DC

50. ¹ Dan. 12: 3.
² Matt. 16: 13, 15. Odilo's interpretation is apparently based on a sermon
ascribed to Heiric of Auxerre and inserted in the homilies of Paul the Deacon
(*PL* xcv. 1477 f.). See H. Barré, *Les homéliaires carolingiens de l'école d'Auxerre*
(*Studi e Testi*, ccxxv (Rome, 1962)), p. 174, no. 23.
³ Cf. Ps. 83: 8.   ⁴ Source unidentified.   ⁵ Prov. 1: 10.

the firmament and a star, even the morning star, citing in evidence what the prophet Daniel says: 'They that are learned shall shine as the brightness of the firmament; and they that instruct many to justice, as stars for all eternity.'[1] Should you, whose excellence we cannot even worthily ponder, be weighed and judged by us? For we, who are oppressed by the darkness of ignorance and cannot see into ourselves, should in no way pass judgement on the lives of the just. All men rightly judge you so worthy of praise that one is more happy to admire you than free to make comments about you. Given our limited intelligence, we would have been overwhelmed by the weight of your question had God's word not come readily to mind. So as to set an example to the faithful, the Author of life and salvation (as you yourself well know, since you are in every respect a man of the gospels), as he was approaching Caesarea Philippi, asked his disciples: 'Who do men say that the Son of man is?'; and a little later, 'But who do you say that I am?'[2] He whom no one knew and from whom nothing is hidden did not ask as if he himself did not know, but rather that he might set an example to the leaders of the church to inquire about them-selves. Thus everyone who has charge of a church should ask his subjects what people say and think of him. If he should hear any-thing good about himself, let him give thanks to God, from whom he has whatever is good, and let him run from strength to strength, God willing, in his happy course until he can see the God of Gods in Sion.[3] But if he should hear anything bad about himself, let him repent and strive diligently to do better in the future. So if you are prompted by this counsel to follow the example of those who are learned and to inquire about yourself, we must praise the splendour of your wisdom, the purity of your faith, and the sincerity of your diligence. To be sure, truth will always out, but coming from an ignorant and unlearned man it cannot be pro-claimed so as to be pleasing to God and hateful to this world.[4] I have said these things about you now and on other occasions and said them openly, not because I have been deceived and beguiled by flattery, nor because I want to be rewarded with praise or money, but because I am not and never shall be reluctant to say what I truly believe and what I so greatly desire to happen. But if you should judge me a flatterer, listen to Scripture: 'My son, if sinners shall entice thee, consent not to them.'[5] Yet it is not sinful if we praise those whom we believe worthy of praise,

laudamus quos dignos laude credimus, dicente scriptura: 'Laudet te alienus, et non os tuum.'[6] Si autem aliquis uelit[n] opponere quod scriptura dicit: 'Ne laudes hominem in uita sua',[7] et ego assencio,[o] quia mortali uita uos mortuum existimo,[p] quia et ab apostolo audistis: 'Mortui enim estis, et uita uestra[q] absconditia est cum Christo in Deo';[8] et cum ipso et uerbis et operibus dicitis: 'Si enim uiuimus, Domino uiuimus; si uero morimur, Domino morimur.[r] Siue enim uiuimus siue morimur, Domini[s] sumus.'[9] De cetero, carissime, ut quidam sapiens ait: 'Omnia fugere poterit homo preter cor suum. Non enim potest a se quisque recedere; ubicumque enim abierit, conscientia sua illum non derelinquit.'[10] Et apostolus Paulus: 'Nemo scit quae sunt hominis, nisi spiritus hominis qui in ipso est.'[11] Dicerem tamen aliquid exhortandi gratia, sed quomodo debet docere indoctus, quem unctio spiritualis docet de omnibus?[12] Sed[t] illud recitem euuangelicum: 'Adhuc unum tibi deest.'[13] Quid illud sit, quam optime nosti. Vale et in contemplatiuis memor esto nostri.[u]

51

Fulbert to Duke William V of Aquitaine: setting forth the obligations between vassal and lord   before 9 June 1021

Glorioso[a] duci Aquitanorum W(illelmo) F(ulbertus) episcopus oracionis suffragium.

De forma fidelitatis aliquid scribere monitus, haec uobis quae secuntur breuiter ex librorum auctoritate notaui.[1] Qui domino suo fidelitatem iurat, ista sex in memoria semper habere debet: incolume, tutum, honestum, utile, facile, possibile. Incolume uidelicet, ne sit in dampnum domino de corpore suo. Tutum, ne

---

[n] uellet L   [o] assentior C   [p] uitae nos mortuum existunt C
[q] uestra uita L   [r] Domino morimur *om.* L   [s] Dei L   [t] ut *add.* C   [u] mei C

51 LDRCPBVMK   [a] Gloriosi L

---

[6] Prov. 27: 2.   [7] Ecclus. 11: 30.   [8] Col. 3: 3.
[9] Rom. 14: 8.   [10] Isidore, *Sententiae*, ii. 26. 2 (*PL* lxxxiii. 627).
[11] 1 Cor. 2: 11.   [12] Cf. 1 John 2: 27.   [13] Luke 18: 22.

51. [1] Although Fulbert's immediate sources are not certain, H. Mitteis, *Lehnrecht und Staatsgewalt* (Weimar, 1933), pp. 312 ff., has suggested that he was influenced by Isidore, *Etymologiae*, ii. 4. 4 (see above, p. xxxi), the writings

as Scripture says: 'Let another praise thee, and not thine own mouth.'[6] But if someone wishes to object that Scripture says: 'Praise not a man in his lifetime',[7] I myself agree, for I consider you dead to this mortal life, as you hear from the apostle: 'For you are dead, and your life is hid with Christ in God';[8] and you say with him both in words and in works: 'For whether we live, we live unto the Lord; or whether we die, we die unto the Lord. So whether we live or whether we die, we are the Lord's.'[9] As for the rest, my very dear friend, as a wise man says: 'A man can escape from everything except his own heart. No one can run away from himself; for wherever he goes, his conscience will be there with him.'[10] The apostle Paul says: 'No one knoweth the things of a man but the spirit of a man that is in him.'[11] Still I would say something by way of exhortation, yet how should one who is untaught teach him who is taught on all matters by his spiritual anointing?[12] But let me repeat what the gospel says: 'Yet one thing is wanting to thee.'[13] What that may be, you yourself know full well. Farewell, and remember us in your prayers.

Fulbert to Duke William V of Aquitaine
before 9 June 1021

To the glorious duke of Aquitaine, W(illiam), from Bishop F(ulbert), with the support of his prayers.

Since you have asked me to write a few words concerning the oath of fidelity, I have briefly set down the following for you based on what I have read.[1] He who swears fidelity to his lord should always keep these six terms in mind: safe and sound, secure, honest, useful, easy, possible. Safe and sound, that is, not to cause his lord any harm as to his body. Secure, that is, not to

of Hincmar of Rheims, and the Carolingian capitularies, though to be sure none of these contain a similarly comprehensive exposition. For the circumstances which perhaps prompted William's query see M. Garaud, 'Un problème d'histoire: à propos d'une lettre de Fulbert de Chartres à Guillaume le Grand, comte de Poitou et duc d'Aquitaine', *Études d'histoire du droit canonique dédiées à Gabriel Le Bras*, i (Paris, 1965), 559 ff.; G. Beech, 'A Feudal Document of Early Eleventh Century Poitou', *Mélanges offerts à René Crozet*, i (Poitiers, 1966), 203 ff.; J. Martindale, 'Conventum inter Guillelmum Aquitanorum comes et Hugonem Chiliarchum', *English Historical Review*, lxxxiv (1969), 528 ff. See pp. xli, lx f.

sit ei in dampnum de secreto suo uel de municionibus per quas tutus esse potest. Honestum, ne sit ei in dampnum de sua iustitia uel de aliis causis quae ad honestatem eius pertinere uidentur. Vtile, ne sit ei in dampnum de suis possessionibus. Facile uel possibile, ne id bonum quod dominus suus leuiter facere poterat faciat ei difficile, neue id quod possibile erat, reddat ei impossibile. Vt fidelis haec nocumenta caueat iustum est, sed non ideo casamentum meretur. Non enim sufficit abstinere a malo, nisi fiat quod bonum est.[b2] Restat ergo ut in eisdem sex supradictis consilium et auxilium domino suo fideliter prestet, si beneficio dignus uideri uult, et saluus esse de fidelitate quam iurauit. Dominus quoque fideli suo in his omnibus[c] uicem reddere debet. Quod si non fecerit, merito censebitur malefidus, sicut ille, si in eorum preuaricacione uel faciendo uel consenciendo deprehensus fuerit, perfidus et periurus. Scripsissem uobis lacius si occupatus non essem, cum aliis multis, tum etiam restauracione ciuitatis et ecclesiae nostrae, quae tota nuper horrendo incendio conflagrauit.[3] Quo damno etsi aliquantisper non moueri non possumus, spe tamen diuini atque uestri solatii respiramus.

52

Fulbert to Count Stephen of Troyes:[1] *admonishing him to abandon his support of Lisiardus for the bishopric of Meaux before 9 June 1021*

Nobili comiti S(tephano) F(ulbertus) Dei gratia Carnotensium episcopus fideles oraciones.

Si in eligendo uestrae ciuitatis episcopo regulariter ageretis, suffragium nostrae humilitatis non deforet iuxta modum racionis. Nunc autem palatinus ac publicus rumor est quod ille clericus quem eligere uultis fauorem uestrum sit aucupatus promissionum sibilis et pecuniae uisco. Dicunt etiam quod sine iussu regis et consensu episcoporum conprouincialium aedes et rem episco-

---

[b] Non ... est *om.* LDR   [c] in his omnibus *om.* DR

52 LDRKCPBVH

---

[2] Cf. Prosper, *Liber sententiarum*, c. lxxxvi (ed. Gastaldo, *CCL* lxviii[a]. 277).

[3] 7–8 September 1020 (see p. xx).

52. [1] *c.* 994/5–mid 1021 (see Newman, pp. 63 n., 64 n.; above, p. lxxxi). See no. 53.

endanger him by betraying his secrets or the fortresses which make it possible for him to be secure. Honest, that is, not to do anything that would detract from his lord's rights of justice or the other prerogatives which have to do with his honour. Useful, not to cause him any loss as regards his possessions. Easy and possible, not to make it difficult for his lord to do something that would be of value to him and that he could otherwise do with ease, or to render it impossible for him to do what was otherwise possible. That the vassal should avoid injuring his lord in any of these ways is only right, but this does not entitle him to a fief; for it is not enough to abstain from evil, it is also necessary to do good.[2] So it remains for him to give his lord faithful counsel and aid as regards these six points if he wishes to be considered worthy of his benefice and secure as to the fidelity that he has sworn. The lord, in turn, should be faithful to his vassal in all these matters. If he does not do so, he will rightly be considered unfaithful, just as the vassal, if he is caught violating any of them by his own actions or by giving his consent, will be considered perfidious and perjured. I would have written you at greater length if I were not taken up with many other matters and especially with rebuilding our city and church, which not long ago was totally destroyed by a terrible fire.[3] Although it is impossible for us not to be concerned for some time over this loss, yet now we are breathing again in the hope of comfort from God and you.

Fulbert to Count Stephen of Troyes[1]   *before 9 June 1021*

To the noble Count S(tephen) from F(ulbert), by grace of God bishop of Chartres, with the faithful service of his prayers.

If in electing a bishop for your city you were proceeding in accordance with the law, you would have our humble support so far as is just and proper. But now it is rumoured both in the court and outside that the clerk whom you wish to elect has lured your favour with the whistling of promises and the bird-lime of money. These rumours also have it that he has seized control of the bishop's palace and possessions though the king has not ordered it and the bishops of the province have not given their consent.

palem inuaserit.[a] Quae si sunt uera, non sunt regularia; nec me uel uobis uel aliis contra ius et fas opitulari oportet. Valete.[b]

53

Fulbert to King Robert: advising him as regards Lisiardus' usurpation of the bishopric of Meaux[1] *before 9 June 1021*

Dilectissimo domino suo regique R(otberto) F(ulbertus) humilis episcopus humilitatem in prosperis, fidenciam[a] in aduersis.

De Lisiardo clerico, qui Meldensis episcopii res odiosa inportunitate inuasit, tale consilium damus. Precipite archiepiscopo Senonensi[2] ut uel ipse episcopium uisitet, uestraeque et suae dicioni reuocet ut dignum est, uel si id facere prohibeatur, mandet predicto Lisiardo per litteras ex sua et nostra (suorum uidelicet suffraganeorum) parte conscriptas, ut cedat loco et rebus stulte peruasis, et de presumptione sua nobis satisfacere studeat ante proximam festiuitatem sancti Petri apostolorum principis.[3] Quod si facere neglexerit, ex tunc in antea a nobis omnibus excommunicatus sit. Valete.

54

Fulbert to Bishop T(hierry of Orleans?):[1] *explaining that it would be better not to excommunicate those who have injured him*   *before 9 June 1021*

Dilectissimo fratri et coepiscopo suo T(heoderico) F(ulbertus).

Illatam uobis iniuriam uere meam facio conpassionis affectu, in eos qui sacro ordini fecere contumeliam zelo feruens. Sed quia nec uobis utile esse uideo nec mihi tutum ut zelus noster ad uindictam excommunicacionis erumpat, expectandum et commonitoriis utendum esse reor, donec illos aut penitentia corrigat, aut summi iudicis sententia multet. Valete.

---

[a] euaserit L   [b] Vale L
53 LDRKPBVH   [a] fiduciam BH
54 LDRKCPBVH

If these things are true, they are unlawful; and it is not fitting for me to aid you or others in matters contrary to human and divine law. Farewell.

Fulbert to King Robert[1]   *before 9 June 1021*

To his very dear lord and king, R(obert), from F(ulbert), humble bishop, with his wish for humility amid prosperity, confidence amid adversity.

As regards the clerk Lisiardus, who has acted with detestable violence in seizing control of the bishopric of Meaux, we advise you to do as follows. Instruct the archbishop of Sens[2] to go in person to the bishop's palace and to bring it back under your control and his as it should be, or, if he cannot do this, to write a letter to Lisiardus in his name and ours (namely, as his suffragans), ordering him to surrender the office and possessions which he has foolishly usurped and to undertake to make satisfaction to us for his presumption before the next feast of St. Peter, Prince of the Apostles.[3] But if Lisiardus should refuse to do this, let him be excommunicated by all of us forthwith. Farewell.

Fulbert to Bishop T(hierry of Orleans?)[1]
before 9 June 1021

To his very dear brother and fellow bishop, T(hierry), from F(ulbert).

In my warm sympathy for you I have made the wrong done to you my own, and I am burning with zeal against those who have committed a shameful crime against the episcopate. But since I do not see that it would be useful to you or safe for me if we let our zeal break forth and take vengeance by excommunicating them, I think we should rest content with sending them letters of warning until they are corrected by doing penance or punished by order of the Supreme Judge. Farewell.

53. [1] See no. 52.   [2] Leothericus.   [3] 29 June.
54. [1] See p. lxxviii.

55

Fulbert to Archbishop Leothericus of Sens: suggesting that he postpone a synod because of local warfare

before 9 *June 1021*

Venerabili Senonensium archiepiscopo L(eutherico) F(ulbertus) Carnotensium humilis episcopus oracionis suffragium.

Vides, pater, et audis quanta bellorum incendia nostris in partibus exardescunt. Vnde periculosum esse timeo nos ad metas[a] destinatae synodi conuenire. Quid autem super hoc tuae prudenciae uideatur, cito mihi remanda.

56

Fulbert to Bishop G.:[1] advising him as regards the consecration of Archbishop Ebalus of Rheims

5 *March–9 June 1021*

Egregie dilecto coepiscopo suo G. F(ulbertus).

Amor iustitiae qui tuam, pater, animam inbuit abnormitati fecit eam offensam et ab excessibus cautam. Cuius rei fidem cum ex aliorum dictis, tum ex litteris tuis euidenter accepi. Sed ab ordinacione Ebali[2] non ualde tibi metuendum esse puto, si est (ut dicitur) ab infancia Christianus, sano sensu, sacris litteris eruditus, sobrius, castus, amator pacis et dilectionis, nullo crimine, nulla infamiae nota turbatus,[a] tandemque a clero et populo suae ciuitatis electus.[3] Magni etenim uiri ut optime nosti, Ambrosius

---

55 LDRKPBVH   [a] metam DRK   *The 's' superscribed over '-a' in* L
in a different hand
56 LDRKCPBVH   [a] turpatus PVH

---

56. [1] The addressee cannot be identified with certainty; but if, as seems probable, he was a suffragan of Rheims, it was Guido of Senlis (see p. 63), Garin of Beauvais (see p. 223 n.), or Gerard of Cambrai (see T. Schieffer, 'Ein deutscher Bischof des 11. Jahrhunderts: Gerhard I von Cambrai (1012–1051)', *Deutsches Archiv*, i (1937), 323 ff.).

Fulbert to Archbishop Leothericus of Sens
before 9 June 1021

To the venerable archbishop of Sens, L(eothericus), from F(ulbert), humble bishop of Chartres, with the support of his prayers.

You see and hear, father, what great flames of war are flaring up around us, and so I fear it is dangerous for us to gather for the synod as planned. But quickly let me know what you in your wisdom think best in this matter.

Fulbert to Bishop G.[1]   *5 March–9 June 1021*

To his very dear fellow bishop G. from F(ulbert).

The love of justice with which your soul is imbued, father, has made it a stumbling-block to irregularity and wary of transgressions. I have received clear evidence of this both from what others have said and from your letter. But as regards consecrating Ebalus,[2] I do not think you need have any serious fear if, as is said, he has been a Christian from infancy, is of sound mind, and is learned in sacred doctrine, if he is sober, chaste, a lover of peace and charity, and unsullied by any crime or mark of infamy, and finally if he has been elected by the clergy and people of his city;[3] for indeed, as you well know, great men such as Ambrose of

---

[2] Whether the Ebalus who became archbishop of Rheims was Count Ebalus of Roucy is disputed. It is rejected by H. Moranvillé, 'Origine de la maison de Roucy', *BEC* lxxxiii (1922), 39 ff., and Newman, p. 71 n., and accepted by Pfister, *Robert*, pp. 183, 238, and Coolidge, pp. 67 f., 85 ff., largely on the basis of nos. 47 f. in the present collection and an entry in the thirteenth-century chronicler Alberic des Trois Fontaines. Ebalus was put forward by Bishop Adalbero of Laon (see no. 47), but opposed by Bishop Gerard of Cambrai on the grounds that church law forbade a layman to be raised directly to the episcopate (*Gesta Pontificum Cameracensium*, iii. 25 (*MGH SS* vii. 473 f.)). There had been notable exceptions to this including the two whom Fulbert mentions. These may indicate that he was acquainted with Paulinus' life of Ambrose and Constance of Lyon's life of Germanus or Stephan's life of Germanus' predecessor, Amator.

[3] Though Fulbert does not seem to be drawing on any one source, cf. *Statuta ecclesiae antiqua*, prologue (ed. C. Munier (Strasbourg, 1960), pp. 75 ff.)=c. 1 (Mansi, iii. 949 f.; Hinschius, p. 303). Such formulations ultimately derive from 1 Tim. 3: 1 ff.; Titus 1: 7 ff. Cf. 2 Tim. 3: 15; Jerome, ep. liii. 3, lxx. 3 (ed. Hilberg, *CSEL* liv. 447, 704).

Mediolanensis, et Germanus Autisiodorensis, aliique nonnulli, quia tales in laico habitu extiterunt, subito nobis sancti presules exierunt.[b] Dominus uero papa, cuius animaduersionem te reuereri significasti, non est quod tibi merito debeat succensere, si te grauiter collapsae sanctae Remensi aecclesiae aliquam spem resurrectionis audierit prouidisse. Vale inperpetuum memor mei, uere fidelis tui. Illi quoque ualeant qui tuam memoriam mihi commendauerunt.

57

Fulbert to Bishop Franco of Paris: enclosing his letter rebuffing Azelinus' efforts to regain the bishopric of Paris[1]

mid 1021–1022

Venerabili fratri et coepiscopo F(ranconi) F(ulbertus) salutem.

Superfluum duxi longam fabulam nostri senis transcribere et mittere tibi cum totam[a] racionem eius (siqua est) ex mea breui responsione facile percipere possis, quae fuit huiusmodi: 'Fratri in Domino et consacerdoti suo A(zelino) F(ulbertus). Absit, frater, ut credatur uerum esse quod scripsisti, meum archipresulem[2] et me tuam confessionem publicasse, non est enim uerum; tuque dum talia scribis, bene meritis de te[b] ingratus es, et iniuste contumeliam facis. Siqua enim honesta tua nouimus aut sperauimus, fideliter ea publicauimus ad testimonium tuae probitatis, contra illos maxime qui discessionem tuam ab episcopatu auaritiae[c] uel ignauiae uel turpitudini ascribere nitebantur. Siqua uero occulta quae penitenda forent nostrae fidei credidisti, caute celata sunt. At si talia confessus es quae prius et postmodum ore uulgi uentilata sint, ea nos occultare nequimus. Comperi autem ex litteris tuis tibi molestum esse quod te monasticae uitae diximus amatorem. Quod, quia nocere non intelligo, molestum esse demiror. Amor namque religionis episcopali gradu quem repetis dignum te pocius quam indignum efficeret, si nihil aliud inpediret. Vtrum autem sit uel quid sit quod inpediat, sagacitatem tuam non arbitror ignorare. Si quedam grauis causa quam dissimulas non

[b] exierunt *corr. to* extiterunt L   extiterunt DRKVH   effulserunt C

57 LDRKP BVH contain only part of the letter and are not used here.
[a] totam *om.* DR   [b] de te *om.* DR   [c] auaritiae episcopatu *with*
auaritiae *marked for deletion* LK   auaritiae *om.* DR

57. [1] See no. 28.

[2] Leothericus of Sens.

Milan, Germanus of Auxerre, and several others, since they possessed these qualities as laymen, suddenly rose in our midst to be saintly bishops. As for your fear of being censured by the pope, there is no just reason for him to be angry with you if he hears that you have provided the holy church of Rheims, which has fallen into utter ruin, with some hope of recovery. Farewell, now and always, and remember me, your true and faithful servant. My best wishes to those who conveyed your regards to me.

Fulbert to Bishop Franco of Paris[1]   *mid 1021–1022*

To his venerable brother and fellow bishop, F(ranco), from F(ulbert), with his greetings.

I have not thought it necessary to make a copy of our elderly friend's long story and to send it to you since you can easily grasp his whole case (such as it is) from my brief reply, which was as follows: 'To his brother in the Lord and fellow bishop, A(zelinus), from F(ulbert). Heaven forbid, brother, that what you wrote be believed to be true, namely that my archbishop[2] and I made your confession public; for it is not true, and when you write such statements, you are being ungrateful to those who deserve well of you and abusing them unjustly. If we knew of or hoped for anything honourable concerning you, we faithfully made it public as evidence of your integrity, especially against those who were trying to attribute your leaving the bishopric to greed, sloth, or immorality. If you entrusted to our confidence any secret matters that called for penance, they were carefully concealed. But if you confessed matters that might have been bandied about as common talk both before and since, these we could not conceal. I also learned from your letter that you are upset at our saying that you loved monastic life. Since I do not see how this can harm you, I am astonished that it upsets you, for love of the religious life would make you worthy rather than unworthy of the episcopal office that you are trying to regain, provided nothing else stood in the way. Whether there is something else and if so, what it is, I do not think that you in your wisdom are unaware. If a certain serious matter that you are hiding does not block your path, the

obstaret, ea est huiusmodi. Si de repetendo episcopio querimoniam incipere uelis, non satis apparet cui eam iure intendere possis. Nullus enim te expulit, nullus cathedram tuam te renitente peruasit; sed tutemet ultro causa egritudinis (ut aiebas) curam episcopalem simul et cathedram reliquisti (ut perhibent), et siue Franconem tunc decanum Parisiacensis ecclesiae, siue quemlibet alium subrogari tibi uerbis et scriptis a rege petisti. Quod si ita est, et sic tibi consequenter substitutus est Franco eligente clero, suffragante populo, dono regis, approbacione Romani pontificis, per manum metropolitani Senonensis, fulcitur itaque[d] substitucio et consecracio eius fauore quoque et auctoritate beati Gregorii papae, qui scriptis suis sicut nulli pontificum non petenti pro qualibet egritudine succedendum fore docuit, ita uoluntarie renuncianti sedi suae[e] successorem nullo modo denegauit.[3] Siquid aliud est quare te episcopatu carere oporteat, tute noueris. Sin autem, hoc tanti nobis esse uidetur, ut te facere ualeat recuperacionis exortem. Quapropter desine curiosos instigatores audire, desine reges et presules inefficacis querimoniae tediosis scriptitacionibus fatigare, et ecclesiae Parisiacensi te inportune obtrudere uelle, quae (ut fatetur) nec ut[f] patronum te habuisse gauisa est, nec doluit amisisse, quippe cum[g] neque ex presencia tua doctrinae profectum, neque ex absencia senserit detrimentum.' Viue memor nostri.

58

Fulbert to Archbishop Ebalus of Rheims: informing him that he has persuaded Count Odo of Chartres to make amends and advising him to bear up[1]   mid *1021–1022*

Venerando Remorum archipresuli Ebalo F(ulbertus) Carnotensium humilis episcopus.

Angustiae tuae compaciens, Odonem comitem arguendo conueni. Respondit tandem quod in te deliquerat emendare se uelle, et ad tollendam animi tui egritudinem, adiuuare quod maxime desideras, ut Remensis ecclesia respiret ad pristinam dignitatem.

---

[d] utique P   [e] suae sedi LDRK   [f] ut *om.* P   [g] tum P

58 LDRKCPB

[3] e.g. ep. xi. 29; xiii. 7, 8 (*MGH Ep.* ii. 299 f., 372 ff.).

58. [1] See pp. lxxix f.

case is as follows. If you wish to initiate a complaint to regain your bishopric, it is not altogether clear against whom you can bring a legal charge; for no one drove you out, no one seized your episcopal throne against your will. But you yourself on grounds of ill health (so you said) voluntarily relinquished your episcopal charge along with your throne (as they say), and you asked the king by word of mouth and in writing to have Franco, then dean of Paris, or someone else chosen to succeed you. If this is the case, and if as a result Franco was put in your place by the election of the clergy, with the support of the people, by the grant of the king, with the approval of the Roman pontiff, and through the hand of the archbishop of Sens, then his election and consecration are supported and approved by the authority of the blessed Pope Gregory; for in his writings, just as he taught that a bishop is not to be replaced by reason of illness unless he requests it, so he in no way prohibited choosing a successor to one who voluntarily renounces his see.[3] If there is another reason why you should not have a bishopric, you yourself should know it; and even if there is not, this seems to us to be enough to keep you from regaining it. So stop listening to meddlesome trouble-makers, stop wearying kings and bishops with tiresome scribblings about an unsupportable suit, and stop wishing to force yourself by violence upon the church of Paris, which, so it confesses, was neither happy to have had you as its protector nor sorry to have lost you, since to be sure it felt neither increase of learning from your presence nor loss from your absence.' Farewell, and remember us.

Fulbert to Archbishop Ebalus of Rheims[1]   mid 1021–1022

To the venerable archbishop of Rheims, Ebalus, from F(ulbert), humble bishop of Chartres.

In my sympathy for your distress, I confronted Count Odo and took him to task. At length he replied that he was willing to make amends for the wrong he had done to you and, in the hope of raising your flagging spirits, to help you realize your fondest desire, namely to restore the church of Rheims to its former

Si haec tibi facere uoluerit, recipere*a* suadeo, ut quamprimum expeditus redeas ad officium tuum. Deinde suggero etsi non indiges, ut ad pacem pauperum componendam*b* tota mente satagas,*c* quos sui reges et principes uehementer affligunt.[2] Preterea*d* Beroldo episcopo[3] referente audiui sic te merore affectum, ut curam gregis Domini relinquere uelis. Quod ego acriter et amice redarguo, testans te, si hoc egeris, non fuisse pastorem. Vale memor mei peccatoris in oracionibus tuis.

59

Fulbert to King Robert: telling of his efforts to support him and of the injuries inflicted on himself   mid *1021–1022*

Dilectissimo domino suo R(otberto) regi F(ulbertus) episcoporum humillimus consilium et fortitudinem a Deo.

Cum presentia mea nequeo, saltem litteris te reuiso, mi domine, sciscitans de fortunis tuis, et exponens aliqua eorum quae geruntur in partibus nostris. Carnotenses adhuc plerosque detineo ne in tuum nocumentum erumpant, sed Herbertum et Gausfridum[1] nullo interdicto refrenare potui. Faciunt tibi mala quae possunt, minantur quae non possunt.[2] Virtus altissimi conterat et disperdat superbiam eorum. Quidam autem uernaculi tui qui ab eisdem malefactoribus iniuriam passi sunt (Martinus scilicet de Villeri monte[3] et filii eius) iram suam retorquent in terram sanctae sanctarum*a* dominae nostrae, diripientes fruges et cetera bona nostra quae in uicinia sua sunt. Nos uero haec inulta*b* patimur propter te, expectantes et deprecantes iustitiam tuam. Sunt haec et alia multa,

---

a respicere L   resipiscere DRK   *b* pacem . . . componendam] pauperum componendam LC (C *has a blank space after* pauperum)   pauperum componendam causam DRK   *c* sagacitas L   *d* Propterea L Praetereat D

59 LDRCPB   *a* sanctarum *om.* LDRC   *b* multa DC

---

[2] Perhaps a reference to the peace movement, though the letter is too early to connect it with the events of 1023 (Hoffmann, p. 56).

[3] Of Soissons, 1021–27 October 1052 (*DHGE* viii. 878 f.; above, p. 62 n.).

dignity. If he should be willing to do this for you, I advise you to accept so that you may be free as soon as possible to return to your duties. Then I suggest (though you do not need the hint) that you strive with all your heart to bring about peace for the poor, who are suffering terribly at the hands of their own kings and princes.[2] I have also heard from Bishop Beroldus[3] that you are so cast down and discouraged that you wish to abandon the care of the Lord's flock. As your friend I strongly urge you not to do it; and if you do so, I am witness that you have not been a shepherd. Farewell, and remember me, a sinner, in your prayers.

Fulbert to King Robert   mid 1021–1022

To his very dear lord, King R(obert), from F(ulbert), most humble bishop, with his prayer for the counsel and strength that comes from God.

While I cannot visit you in person, my lord, I can at least do so by letter, inquiring how things are going with you and telling you some of the events that have happened in our neighbourhood. I am still keeping most of those who live in the area of Chartres from breaking out and injuring you; but as for Herbert and Geoffrey,[1] enjoin them as I will, I have not been able to restrain them. They are doing all they can to harm you and threatening what they cannot do.[2] May the power of the Most High trample them down and destroy them in their pride. Some of your servants who have been injured by these evil-doers (namely, Martin of *Mons Villeri*[3] and his sons) are venting their wrath against the land of our most holy Lady, plundering our crops and other possessions in their neighbourhood. We are bearing with these injuries and not taking vengeance for your sake, waiting and praying for you to do us justice. There are these and many other

59. [1] Neither can be identified; and if my identification of Geoffrey, vicomte of Châteaudun, is correct (see p. lxxxi n.; nos. 98 ff.), he could hardly be the Geoffrey here.

[2] Gregory I, *Hom. in ev.* xviii. 2 (*PL* lxxvi. 1151).

[3] Martin is otherwise unknown; and the place-name cannot be identified with certainty, the closest forms being Monvilliers and Villermon, neither of which is attested until much later (L. Merlet, *Dictionnaire topographique du département d'Eure-et-Loir* (Paris, 1861), pp. 124, 191).

mi domine, quae me nimis angustiant. Satis olim honeri esse uidebatur aduersa corporis ualitudo; sed tamen illud egrius tolerabam quod res ecclesiae in superfluorum domesticorum uictualia sic expendere conpellebar ex praua consuetudine precessorum[c] meorum, ut offitium hospitalitatis et elemosinae sicut mea interest administrare non possem. Nunc autem ipsas res, quantulae erant, passim inimici diripiunt. Additur his malis incendium ecclesiae nostrae,[4] quam cum unde restaurem sicut decet non habeo, mihi quoque necessarios sumptus indulgeri detrecto. His itaque et pluribus aliis difficultatibus circumuentus, quas uel pudoris lex uel breuitatis enumerare uetat,[5] multa mecum agito, non ut erumnas in hac uita euadere coner (quod est impossibile), sed ut[d] aliquo labore quamuis arduo ualeam restaurandae ecclesiae opem ferre. Huius uero consultacionis meae finem tibi domino meo reuelatum iri disposui, cum Deus dederit tui oportunitatem alloquii. Vale perhenniter.

60

Fulbert to Bishop Odolricus of Orleans: declining his offer of assistance in going to a council   *mid 1021–1022*

Dilectissimo coepiscopo suo O(dolrico) F(ulbertus) ex animo quicquid uerus amicus.

Primum gratias ago, karissime, quod nobis ad concilium et comitatum et obsequium pollicemini. Quod dum facitis, ingenita benignitate uestra multum nos hylaratis. Et nobis quidem desiderium esset memorato concilio interesse, sicut etiam uenerabili archiepiscopo nostro Leutherico in audientia uestra nos dixisse meminimus; sed difficultates ex malitia huius temporis obortae non sinunt. Quod etiam uos illi[a] notum facere precamur, ne sit nostra expectacione suspensus. Ceterum exobtabilis colloquii uestri oportunitatem ad presens non habemus, nisi forte uobis Nouigentum[1] placeat propinquare. Valete.[b]

---

[c] praedecessorum DR   [d] ut *om.* L
60 LDRKPB   [a] illi uos LDRK   [b] Vale LB   *om.* P

troubles, my lord, which I find most distressing. Once I thought it quite enough to be burdened with poor health. Then I found it even harder to bear that I was forced by the evil custom of my predecessors to use so much of the church's resources to support unneeded servants that I was unable to fulfil my duties of hospitality and almsgiving as I should. Now even these resources, little as they were, are plundered by enemies on one side and the other. To these troubles is added the burning of our church;[4] and since I do not have the means to rebuild it as I should, I am refusing to spend anything on myself, even for necessities. Beset by these and many other difficulties which the law of propriety or of brevity forbids me to recount,[5] I am turning over a number of schemes in my mind, not in an effort to avoid hardships in this life (which is impossible), but rather so as to be able to contribute something, however difficult it may be, to rebuilding our church. After I have thought this over and decided what to do, I intend to tell you, my lord, when God gives me the chance to speak with you. Farewell, now and always.

Fulbert to Bishop Odolricus of Orleans   mid 1021–1022

To his very dear fellow bishop, O(dolricus), from F(ulbert), with the cordial wishes of a true friend.

First I thank you, my dear friend, for promising us an escort and assistance in going to the council, for your inborn kindness in doing this makes us very happy. In truth we wanted to attend this council, as we remember telling our venerable Archbishop Leothericus in your presence; but difficulties arising from the evils of these times will not permit it. We ask you to inform him of this so that he will not be kept waiting for us. As for the rest, there is no chance at present for us to meet you as we should very much like to do, unless, perhaps, you are willing to come to Nogent.[1] Farewell.

---

4 7–8 September 1020 (see p. xx).
5 Cf. Horace, *Ars poetica* 135.

60. 1 Probably Nogent-le-Roi (Eure-et-Loir, *arr.* Dreux), of which Odolricus was lord (see J. Devaux, 'Essai sur les premiers seigneurs de Pithiviers', *Annales de la Soc. hist. et arch. du Gâtinais*, iv (1886), 107 and *passim*).

61

Fulbert to King Robert: expressing his surprise that Count Odo intends to leave the decision concerning the bishop of Meaux up to him late 1021–1022

Serenissimo regi Francorum R(otberto) F(ulbertus) humilis Carnotensium episcopus quod decet et prodest.

Gratulor*a* tibi, domine mi, quod fonte bonitatis, ut semper irriguus, negocium Dei mandasti mihi tractare ut expedit. Talia denique te regem precipere decus est, subditosque tibi capessere*b* tutum.[1] Sed illud miror quod Odonem comitem in mea deliberacione uel posuisse uel positurum esse dixisti quid facere debeat de recepcione Meldensis episcopi,[2] cum abhinc anno fere dimidio nec ipsum uiderim nec de tali negocio legacionem eius acceperim. Attamen si aspirante Deo ad nos uenire, et consiliis meis adquiescere uoluerit, desinet procul dubio predictam aecclesiam lacerando diuinam ulcionem in se prouocare, tuisque sacris ordinacionibus contraire.*c*

62

Fulbert to King Robert: informing him that he has abandoned his journey as instructed, but would like to confer with him in person 1021 or later

Regi sacerdos, R(otberto) F(ulbertus) fidelia pronus.*a*

Accepta legacione uestra per Rodulfum sanctae Crucis aechononum,[1] destinatam peregrinacionem iterum intermisi. Nunc ergo quid me uelit serenitas uestra colloquio magis, si fieri possit, quam legatis aut litteris cupiam edoceri. Venirem autem ipse protinus ad uos huius rei gratia, si commode possem. Sed uenire in armis sacrum tempus abnuit ac religio nostri ordinis; uenire inermes longa uia interminatur ac malicia secularis. Est enim mihi Olricus coluber in uia, Rodulfus cerastes in semita.[2] Ceterum ex arbitrio

---

61 LDRKCPB *a* Grator LDC Grator *corr. to* Gratulor R
b capescere LRK capesere *corr. to* capessere D capesscre C *c* Valete *add.* P Vale *add.* B

62 LDRB *a* promis L promissa DR *cf. the salutation to no.* 65

Fulbert to King Robert   late 1021–1022

To his highness, King R(obert) of France, from F(ulbert), humble bishop of Chartres, with his wishes for what will redound to his honour and his profit.

I congratulate you, my lord, for having instructed me from the springs of your bounty, which are overflowing as always, to handle God's affairs as they should be. It does honour to you as king to issue such commands, and it is the part of prudence for your subjects to carry them out.[1] But I am astonished at your saying that Count Odo had placed or was going to place in my hands the decision as to whether he should accept the bishop of Meaux,[2] for it has been almost a half-year since I have seen him, and I have not received a message from him concerning it. Be that as it may, if by God's inspiration he were willing to come to us and to accept my advice, he would certainly stop calling down divine vengeance on himself by injuring the church of Meaux, and he would stop opposing your highness's commands.

Fulbert to King Robert   1021 or later

To the king from his bishop, to R(obert) from F(ulbert), who kneels and offers his faithful services.

I have received the message that you sent by Ralph, *economus* of Sainte-Croix,[1] and once again I have given up the journey I had planned. Now I should like to be told what your highness wishes of me in a conference, if possible, rather than by messenger or letter. I myself would come at once to confer with you if I could suitably do so. But to come bearing arms is prohibited by the holy season and due regard for our state of life; and to come unarmed is forbidden by the long journey and the evil of this world, for Olricus is a serpent in my way, and Ralph a horned viper in my path.[2] As for the rest, it is in your hands from now on

61. [1] Cf. Virgil, *Aen.* i. 76 f.
   [2] Probably Bernerius, though the earliest evidence for him dates from 1028 (Appendix C, no. 12). See pp. lxxix, lxxxi; nos. 52 f.

62. [1] See p. lxxvi.
   [2] Cf. Gen. 49: 17. Their identities are unknown.

uestro pendeat amodo quo pacto uoluntatem uestram mihi placeat indicare, quoniam apud me definitum est[b] uoluntati uestrae quae uobis non noceat conuenire.[c] Valete regaliter.

63

Fulbert to Abbot Odilo of Cluny: informing him that he has had to postpone his visit   *1021 or later*

Venerabili patri suo Odiloni F(ulbertus) sacerdos non meriti confidencia sed pietatis affectu presumptum orationis suffragium.

Magnum mihi desiderium fuit et adhuc quidem est ad uos ueniendi, sed obortae nuper in nostro episcopatu dissensionum causae propositum iter omittere coegerunt. Quod uobis quamprimum his pauculis apicibus significare curaui, ne sublimitas uestra sit ad praesens de meae pusillitatis expectacione suspensa. Veniam autem aliquando (si licuerit) ad uos quos uere Deus inhabitat saluti meae consilium diuini oraculi petiturus.[a] Valete in Domino semper, iterum dico ualete.[1]

64

Fulbert to the monk O.: explaining why he has not written earlier and asking him to convey his greetings to Abbot Odilo of Cluny   *1021 or later*

Dilecto suo O. F(ulbertus).

Quod uobis olim, karissime, per ueredarium uestrum[a] litteras non remisi, id causae fuit quia uos quamprimum uisere destinabam; idque etsi diu distuli, desiderare non destiti. Sed interim uos scire uolo quod utique uelle scio, me scilicet ad presens Dei gratia bene ualere, uestris[b] obsequiis spiritualiter instantem, corporaliter apparatum, sicut nemo fidelius excepto illo sancto monachorum archangelo[1] Odilone, cui me in nullo comparare presumo.[c]

---

[b] est *om.* B   [c] uobis noceat conuenire L   nobis noceant non uenire DR
63 LDRPB   [a] petiturum L

as to how it pleases you to let me know your wishes, for I have resolved to comply with those that cannot harm you. May long life and royal splendour be ever yours.

Fulbert to Abbot Odilo of Cluny   *1021 or later*

To his venerable father, Odilo, Bishop F(ulbert), not from confidence in his just deserts, but out of filial affection ventures to send the support of his prayers.

I have very much wanted to visit you, and indeed I still do, but the troubles which have recently arisen in our diocese have forced me to give up the journey that I had planned. I have tried to let you know of this as soon as possible by sending you these few lines so that your eminence might not be kept waiting at present for my humble self. But some day, if it is ever permitted, I shall come to visit you in whom God truly dwells to ask your advice, as God's oracle, concerning my salvation. Farewell in the Lord always, again I say farewell.[1]

Fulbert to the monk O.   *1021 or later*

To his dear O. from F(ulbert).

I did not send you a reply by your courier, my dear friend, as I had planned to visit you as soon as possible; and though I have postponed this for a long time, I still want to do so. But meanwhile I want you to know what I know you undoubtedly wish, that at present, thanks to God's grace, I am quite well and both eager in mind and ready in body to serve you more faithfully than anyone except that holy archangel of monks,[1] Odilo, to whom I in

---

64 LDRPB   *a* nostrum LDR   *b* nostris LP   *c* Odilone . . . presumo *om.* LDR

---

63. [1] Cf. Phil. 4: 4.

64. [1] Fulbert's epithet is expressly cited by Odilo's biographer, Jotsoldus, *De vita et virtutibus sancti Odilonis abbatis*, i. 11 (*PL* cxlii. 906). See p. 175 n. 3.

Cuius etiam caritas siqualiter afficiat animam meam aggrediar
dicere, rem inenarrabilem uidear uelle narrare. Plura me scribere
prohibuit tam multiplex negociorum occupatio quam etiam
legatus morarum inpaciens. Sed hoc unum tandem apud uestram
benignitatem deprecor, ut cum nostrum archangelum*d* uice nostra
salutaueritis, cum simplicitate*e* monastica hylaritatem angelicam
quae uobis presto est induatis. Valete prospere in uirtute Dei.

65

The canons of Chartres to Archbishop Hugh of Tours:[1]
asking for his aid while Fulbert is on a pilgrimage to Rome
late 1022–early 1023

Clarissimo Turonensium archiepiscopo H(ugoni) A(lbertus)
decanus[2] et tota congregacio canonicorum sanctae Mariae Carnotensis prona atque deuota fidelitatis obsequium et oracionum
suffragia.

Nuper antequam Romanum iter agere cepisset*a* beatissimus
pater noster F(ulbertus) episcopus, uestro (ut scitis) dulci usus
est colloquio. Vnde reuersus, dum quadam die in conuentu nostro
resideret de ipso itinere nobiscum agens, conquerentibus nobis
post abscessum eius multa nos a pluribus aduersa passuros,*b* et
nominatim a Fulcherio eiusque nepotulo suorum quoque mani-
pulis furum,[3] ille constanter et confortatorie ut solet in talibus
respondit: 'Malorum iniurias boni aequanimiter ferre deberent.*c*
Vt enim ipsi legitis in quadam omelia beati papae Gregorii, bonus
non fuit quisquis malos non tolerauit.'[4] Adiecit preterea se uobis
inde fuisse locutum, uos etiam illi et nobis proposse de ipsis malefactoribus adiutorium promisisse. Quod si necessitas urgeret,
praecepit statim uestrae paternitatis solacium nos adire. Quod
nunc facimus, potentissime pater, uariis pulsi tribulacionibus.
Nam ut alias omittamus, illi anathematizati quorum supra meminimus, postquam dilectissimus pastor*d* noster uiam suam tenuit,

---

d angelum LDR   *e* supplicitate LP

65 LDRP   *a* Romam iter aggrederetur LDR   *b* *marked for corr. to*
passos L   *c* debent LDR   *d* pator (-er?) *corr. to* pastor L   pater DR

---

65. [1] 1 January 1005–10 June 1023 (see Newman, p. 25 n.; Boussard, pp. 174 ff.).

no way presume to compare myself. If I were to try to tell what
his love has done for my soul, I should seem to be attempting to
express the inexpressible. I am kept from writing more by my
many time-consuming affairs as well as a messenger who is
anxious to be on his way. But I beg you in your kindness for this
one last favour: when you greet our archangel for us, please clothe
with monastic simplicity the angelic gaiety which comes so
readily to you. Farewell and good fortune in the strength of God.

The canons of Chartres to Archbishop Hugh of Tours[1]
late 1022–early 1023

To his eminence, Archbishop H(ugh) of Tours, from A(lbert),
the dean,[2] and all the community of canons of St. Mary's of
Chartres, who devoutly kneel and offer the service of their fidelity
and the support of their prayers.

Not long ago, before our most blessed father Bishop F(ulbert)
set out on his journey to Rome, he had, as you know, the pleasure
of conversing with you. After he returned from visiting you,
while he was sitting in our chapter one day talking with us about
his approaching journey, we complained that after he left we
would suffer many wrongs from several persons and in particular
from Fulcher and his nephew and their bands of thieves.[3] But he,
in the calm and comforting way with which he usually handles
such matters, replied: 'Good men should patiently bear the
wrongs committed by evil ones; for as you yourselves read in one
of the blessed Pope Gregory's homilies, no one is good who does
not bear with those who are evil.'[4] He added that he had spoken
to you about this and that you had promised to do whatever you
could to help him and us against these evil-doers. But if there were
pressing necessity, he instructed us, father, to seek your aid at
once. We are doing so now, most mighty father, beset as we are
by many troubles. Not to speak of other matters, after our beloved
shepherd went his way, those excommunicated malefactors whom
we mentioned unjustly plundered our estates which lie in the

[2] Dean and procurator of the cathedral and then monk and abbot of Marmoutier, 1032–64 (Merlet, p. 164; *DHGE* i. 1432 ff.).
[3] Cf. Terence, *Eun.* 776. Fulcher's identity is unknown.
[4] *Hom. in ev.* xxxviii. 7 (*PL* lxxvi. 1286).

terras nostras quae sunt in ministerio Heruei et Tetoldi,[5] quasi
lupi caulas ouium irrumpentes, nobis inmerentibus predati sunt;
neque etiam rabidis eorum morsibus ouium dampna suffecerunt,
immo uero ad uastandam quandam pastoris ipsius potestatem
quae dicitur Ermenulfi uilla[6] se conuerterunt. Proinde rogamus
uos, iustissime pater, ut propter amorem sanctae sanctarum
dominae nostrae cui seruimus licet indigni, ipsius quoque dilectis-
simi uestri qui in uobis plurimum confidit, et nos abiens uestro
patrocinio commisit, predam suam et nostram reddere[e] faciatis,
cum nepote uestro Gausfrido[7] magnopere satagendo, quatenus
ipsi lupi res domni praesulis et nostras deinceps non diripiant,
uel donec ipse annuente Deo redeat.[f] Valete et nos supplices
uestros quicquid de his egeritis mandando rescire dignamini.[g]

66

The canons of Chartres to Bishop Herbert of Lisieux:[1]
explaining why they have not paid their visitation dues and
asking him to wait until Fulbert returns from Rome
                                    late *1022–early 1023*

Venerabili[a] Lexouiensium pontifici Herberto congregatio canonicorum[b] sanctae Mariae Carnotensis[c] plurimum saluere et orationum suffragia.

Iubes, inclite presul, nos dare tibi circadas pro[d] aecclesiis
nostris quae sunt in episcopio tuo. At nos serenitati tuae uerum
quiddam intimare uolumus, scilicet quod episcopi beatae memoriae in quorum diocesi possedimus aecclesias hunc semper
amoris et reuerenciae cultum exibuerunt sanctae sanctarum
dominae nostrae, ut a nobis eius licet indignis famulis nequaquam
exegerint[e] id obsequii quod requiris. Vnde quesumus ne inportuni
uocemur dum rogamus te, benigne pater, ut honesta sanctorum
patrum sequens uestigia, nos huius pensionis angaria nullatenus
obliges, ne in hac parte nobis officiendi primus auctor ipse noteris.

        [e] reddi LDR   [f] annuente Deo ipse credat P   [g] Valete . . .
dignamini] et nos supplices uestros quicquid egeritis mandato rescire dignamini.
Valete. LDR

66 LDRCP   [a] Venerando LDR   [b] canonicorum *om.* DR
  [c] Carnotensium LDR   [d] de DR   [e] exigerent DR

archdeaconries of Hervé and Tetoldus[5] like wolves breaking into the sheepfold. Nor was the harm done to the sheep enough for their rabid bites, but instead they turned and ravaged one of our shepherd's domains called Ermenonville.[6] So we beg you in your great justice, father, for the love of our most holy Lady, whom we serve, though unworthy, and for the love of him who is most dear to you, who is relying very much on you, and who, as he was leaving, entrusted us to your protection, to recover what they have stolen from him and from us and with your nephew Geoffrey[7] to take forceful measures against them so as to keep these wolves from plundering the possessions of our bishop and ourselves for the future or until he himself (God willing) returns. Farewell, and please let us, your suppliants, know what action you are taking in these matters.

The canons of Chartres to Bishop Herbert of Lisieux[1]
late 1022–early 1023

To the venerable bishop of Lisieux, Herbert, from the community of canons of St. Mary's of Chartres, with many greetings and the support of their prayers.

You order us, your excellency, to pay you the visitation dues for our churches which lie in your diocese. But we wish to inform your eminence of the truth of the matter, namely that the bishops of holy memory in whose diocese we have churches have always shown their loving and reverent devotion to our most holy Lady by not exacting from us, her unworthy servants, the payment that you demand. So we beg you not to accuse us of being unreasonable when we ask you in your kindness, father, to follow in the honourable footsteps of the holy fathers and not to make us pay these dues for fear that you yourself might be blamed as the one who was first responsible for the loss that this causes us. We

---

[5] Both are commemorated in the necrology as archdeacon and provost (Merlet, pp. 159, 175). See nos. 39, 108.

[6] Probably Ermenonville-la-Grande (Eure-et-Loir, *arr.* Chartres).

[7] Possibly the vicomte of Châteaudun (see nos. 98 ff.).

66. [1] Before late 1022–1049/50 (see *GC* xi. 766; above, p. lxxxiii). For the churches and payment in question see no. 39.

Optamus etenim potius non paruo tuae ipsius utilitatis amore
ducti in albo felicis ordinis benefactorum nostrorum te recenseri,
ut cum pro illis, tum etiam pro te iuge Domino sacrifitium
offerentes, ac humanitatis tuae benefitia coram illo recitantes,
dignum te libro quoque uitae celestis inseri predicemus.[2] Preterea
non arbitramur notitiae tuae amplitudinem preterisse dominum
nostrum[f] F(ulbertum) episcopum, cui te ualde carum esse scimus,
Romam pergere. Quod ideo memoramus, quia[g] si liberalitati tuae
placuerit nostrae petitioni fauere, nos id illi cum redierit innote-
scemus tibi quidem pro hoc bene et sapienter facto nimium gratu-
laturo. Quod si non, oramus saltem expecta nos supplices tuos
illum reuersum super hoc consultum ire debentes, a cuius nutu
pendent nostra consilia, neque interim ullum interdictum facias
aecclesiis nostris. Bene agendo ualeas, et de sacrario tui pectoris
quid oraculi super haec egrediatur nobis rescribere ne graueris.
Iterum iterumque ualeas et semper ualeas.

67

Hildegar to Siegfried:[1] *reminding him that he promised to
send him a horse*   *late 1022–early 1023?*

Amicus amico, Hildegarus Sigefrido, totius boni sufficienciam.

Dum apud nos morareris inter primos amicorum meorum
habitus, quid mihi tuis obsequiis plerumque dedito pollicitus sis,
memorem te esse puto. Ipse tamen eius rei te commonefaciens,
rogo ut secundum promissionem tuam mittas mihi equum
ambulatorium qualem te dare, me quoque recipere deceat.[2] Cum
illis equidem adhuc[a] sentio, qui amicitiam non propter se tantum
sed et propter utilitatem censent expetendam.[3] Diu uiuens et
bene agens, premio pociaris aeterno.

<table>
<tr><td>f meum L</td><td>g quia] ut DR</td></tr>
<tr><td>67 LDRCP</td><td>a adhuc om. P</td></tr>
</table>

---

[2] The names of benefactors of a religious foundation and their grants were
customarily entered in a book often entitled (as would appear to be indicated
here) *Liber vitae*. These were sometimes read in commemoration during the
celebration of mass, and the book itself placed on the altar. The particular
volume in use at Chartres at this time is apparently lost, having been replaced
by the necrology which has been repeatedly cited and of which the basic part

are inspired even more than this by no small desire for your own welfare, and we hope to see you entered in the list of benefactors of our blessed community, so that as we continually offer sacrifice to the Lord for them, and thus also for you, and recount in his presence your kind good works, we may declare that you too are worthy of being included in the book of heavenly life.[2] Moreover, we do not think that it has escaped you, given the breadth of your knowledge, that our lord, Bishop F(ulbert), to whom we know that you are very dear, has gone to Rome. We mention this, for if it should please you in your generosity to grant our petition, we shall tell him about it when he returns, and he will be very grateful for your good and judicious kindness. But if it should not please you to do so, we beg you at least to give us, your humble servants, time, since we are bound in this matter to seek the advice, on his return, of him on whose good pleasure our plans depend, and we also beg you in the meantime not to place our churches under any censure. May a long life of good works be yours, and please be so kind as to write and let us know the answer that comes from the oracle in the sanctuary of your breast. Again and again, may you fare well, now and always.

Hildegar to Siegfried[1]   *late 1022–early 1023?*

From one friend to another, from Hildegar to Siegfried, with his wish that he may have all good things that he needs.

While you were staying with us, I treated you as one of my very best friends; and what you promised me for having devoted most of my energies to serving you, I think you yourself remember. Be that as it may, I am reminding you of it, and I ask you to send me as you promised a horse that can travel and that you will not be ashamed to give nor I to accept.[2] For indeed I still agree with those who think that friendship is to be desired not only for its own sake, but also for what one gains from it.[3] May a long life of good works be yours, and so may you receive an eternal reward.

---

was copied probably in 1027 (Merlet, p. 100). There is no entry for Bishop Herbert.

67. [1] Possibly chaplain to Duke Richard II of Normandy (see no. 68; p. lxxxii) .
  [2] Cf. Seneca, *De beneficiis* ii. 16.
  [3] Cf. Cicero, *De officiis* iii. 33. 118; *De finibus* ii. 26. 82 ff.

68

*Hildegar to Siegfried: again reminding him that he promised
to send him a horse*[1]   *late 1022–early 1023?*

Hildegarius domini Fulberti discipulus Sigefrido Richardi comitis[2]
capellano adhuc salutem.

Verbis tuis fidem minime seruans, diu me fefellisti. Vnde cum
me deceptum esse doleam, tum pro mendacio tuo pudor mihi
maximus ingeritur. Non enim deceret talem[a] tantamque personam probrosum falsitatis nomen subire. Horrendum etiam
esset[b] in sacrilegii crimen incidere,[3] quia sicut legitur: 'Verba
sacerdotis aut uera sunt aut sacrilega.'[4] Obsecro itaque per
sanctam amititiam quae inter nos esse debet, ut honestae ueritatis
famae te reconcilies, mittendo mihi ad presens per Gualterium
monachum olim meum merito mihi promissum[c] abs te caballum.
Quod nisi feceris, noueris te funditus ab amore nostro decidisse.
Teste conscientia mea dixerim in hoc quod ego[d] te rogo non
magis utilitatem meam, quam tuam simul et honorem exopto.

69

Hildegar to W(illiam V, duke of Aquitaine?):[1] *asking him
to carry out his promise*   *late 1022–early 1023?*

H(ildegarius) G(uillelmo) uerba transformare in actus.

Tuae, mi domine, karitatiuae promissionis nuncium hactenus
sustinens laboraui nimium. Sollicitus namque quid tuae celsitu-
dini meae paruitati placuisset designare, percunctabar unde sese
reciperent uiatores quosque[2] pendens ab urbis uallo huc respici-
ente; nemine uero dante responsum tui de parte, mestus redibam
domum iam facta nocte.[3] Sed quia in humanis perfectum nihil
extat ex toto,[4] humano parcimus ingenio. Pacto[a] tamen tali ne

68 LDRP   [a] talem *om.* P   [b] est DR   [c] meum . . . promissum]
non inmerito promissum mihi LDR   [d] ego *om.* LDR

69 LDRCP   [a] Paeto P

68. [1] See no. 67.
     [2] Possibly Duke Richard II of Normandy.

Hildegar to Siegfried[1]　　　　　　*late 1022–early 1023?*

Hildegar, Bishop Fulbert's disciple, to Siegfried, Count Richard's[2] chaplain, even now with his greetings.

By not keeping faith with your words, you have deceived me for a long time, and I am distressed at finding myself deceived and overwhelmed with shame by your lies. It is not fitting for a person of your eminence and position to suffer the disgrace of being called a liar, and it would be a dreadful thing to fall into the sin of sacrilege,[3] for as one reads: 'A priest's words are either true or sacrilegious.'[4] So I beg you by the holy friendship that ought to exist between us to begin living up to your reputation for truthfulness and honesty by sending me now by the monk Walter the horse that you once promised me and rightly. Unless you do so, know that you will have utterly fallen from our love. With my conscience as my witness let me say that in asking you for this I am no more desirous of my own advantage than of yours, and of your honour too.

Hildegar to W(illiam V, duke of Aquitaine?)[1]
　　　　　　　　　　　　　　late 1022–early 1023?

From H(ildegar) to W(illiam), with his wish that he might transform his words into deeds.

Until now, my lord, I have tried hard to wait for the message that you in your kindness promised. In my anxiety to know what it may have pleased your highness to tell my lowly self, I have asked every traveller[2] where he comes from as I hang over the city wall that faces this way; but no one has brought a reply from you, and I have gone home at night disappointed.[3] As nothing that involves mankind is perfect,[4] we are making allowances for

---

[3] Cf. Heb. 10: 31.
[4] Hincmar, *Opusculum lv capitulorum*, c. xlv (*PL* cxxvi. 456).

69. [1] Although the addressee cannot be identified with certainty, William is the only one mentioned in the present collection who seems suitable (see p. lxxxii).
[2] Cf. Job 21: 29.　　　　　　　　　　　　[3] Cf. Terence, *Heaut.* 122.
[4] Cf. Priscian, *Inst. gram.*, preface (ed. H. Keil, *Grammatici Latini*, ii (Leipzig, 1855), 2).

proruas in uerba excusacionis, quin quod pollicitus es adimplere studeas sine fuco dilacionis.⁵ Igitur ut cerciorem*b* reddas, mando et*c* deprecor quatenus innuere digneris quid me agere iubeas. Nolo, mi domine, hesites in calamo, bonum opus habens in animo, quoniam in perfectione erit ex Dei auxilio.⁶ Vale.

70

*W(illiam V, duke of Aquitaine?)*¹ *to Hildegar: explaining that he cannot fulfil his promise at present*
late 1022–early 1023?

H(ildegario) G(uillelmus) bene optata consequi.

Tantam*a* apud me tua prudens simplicitas² inuenit gratiam, ut quod a me petisti non magis ipse fieri quam ego uelim. Sed quoniam inpresenciarum facultas non suppetit, angitur*b* animus meus, uerens me tibi suspectum esse, quasi uerba dare molientem. Quod non esse meum credas per fidem quae inter nos est obsecro, rogans te modicum tempus adhuc sustinere, donec grauissimis quibus nunc*c* impedior officiis expeditus, operam tibi dare queam. Quod si forte morarum impaciens mox ad me ueneris,*d* si uotis tuis minus respondero, nequaquam id mihi causam predoctus iure succensebis. Vale nunc et semper.

71

*Archbishop Hugh of Tours to Bishop Hubert of Angers:*¹ *answering his charge that he had rashly excommunicated him and admonishing him as regards the health of his soul*
before 10 June 1023

H(uberto) And(egauensium) presuli H(ugo) Tur(onensium) archiepiscopus salutem.

Quamuis tua nuper ad me directa*a* epistola sibi condigna mereatur rescripta, satius*b* tamen existimaui responsis interim suae

b te *add.* P   *c* ac LDRC

70 LDRCP   *a* Tanquam P   *b* angitur *om.* P   *c* nunc *om.* P
d adueneris P

71 LDRCP (see pp. xlviii n.; lvi n.).   *a* ad me directa nuper LC   nuper *om.*
DR   *b* satis P

human nature. But since this was our agreement, do not rush forth with excuses, but rather strive to carry out what you promised without pretending to be delayed.[5] So that I may have a better idea of what you want me to do, I beg and entreat you to deign to let me know. With good work in mind, let not your pen fall behind, my lord, for you will have God's help in carrying it out.[6] Farewell.

W(illiam V, duke of Aquitaine?)[1] to Hildegar
late 1022–early 1023?

To H(ildegar) from W(illiam), with the wish that he may obtain what he rightly desires.

You in your wise simplicity[2] have found such favour in my sight that you cannot be more anxious than I am to see your request fulfilled. But since I do not have the means to do so at present, I am upset and worried that you will suspect me of trying to put you off with words. By the faith that is between us, I beg you to believe that this is not my intention, and I ask you to hold out a little longer until I have settled the very troublesome affairs in which I am now involved and can turn my attention to you. But if you should get tired of waiting and come to me now, you will have no just reason to become angry with me if I should fail to satisfy your requests, since you will already be acquainted with my circumstances. Farewell, now and always.

Archbishop Hugh of Tours to Bishop Hubert of Angers[1]
before 10 June 1023

To Bishop H(ubert) of Angers from Archbishop H(ugh) of Tours, with his greetings.

Although the letter that you recently sent me ought to be answered in kind, I have thought it better for the time being to

---

[5] Cf. no. 40, salutation.
[6] Cf. Gregory I, *Hom. in ev.* xxi. 1 (*PL* lxxvi. 1170).
70. [1] See no. 69.   [2] Cf. Matt. 10: 16.
71. [1] Hubert of Angers, 13 June 1006–2 March 1047 (*Cartulaire noir de la cathédrale d'Angers*, ed. C. Urseau (Documents historiques sur l'Anjou, v (1908)), p. xxvi; Boussard, pp. 166 ff.). See pp. lxxx, lxxxiii.

contumaciae debitis supersedere, quam tuae saluti quantum ad
nos non consulere, et inter consulendum quibusdam eiusdem[c]
epistolae locis discrete et humiliter non respondere. Medicorum
enim est melancolicis siue maniacis seu qualibet alia ualitudine
laborantibus licet ingratis et conuitiis artificem lacessentibus[d]
nihilominus tamen suae artis experimenta impendere, et ut
curentur attentius insistere. Vnde et me non professum[e] quidem
medicum, quippe imperitissimum, sed[f] tamen ad hoc ita[g] prela-
cionis utcumque prouectum, qui te, si exorbites, debeam corrigere,
oportet ex coemptis sanctorum patrum medelis tibi licet ingrato
medicari, et ut[h] cureris uelis nolis insistere. Sed priusquam ad
hoc ueniam, libet (ut dixi) quibusdam tuae epistolae locis obuiare;
nam cetera quae plurimam partem illius occupant pretereunda
censeo. Quod ergo me inconsultae concepcionis fuisse, et temere
ac sine culpa te non uocatum a diuino officio separasse criminaris,
certa et inexpugnabili contraditione destruo. Inconsulta namque
concepcio non fuit, quae tibi conditionem[i] quid potius uelles
eligendum proposuit. Quod si bene aduertisses, inconsultum non
dixisses. Inconsultius igitur fecisti qui te (ut post clarius liquebit)
in peiorem partem flexisti.[k] Non temere uero ac[l] sine culpa te et
tuos fuisse interdictos testantur reliquiae uinearum in quibus
uestra fixistis[m] castra. Quod in exemplo[n] datum ceteris quibus
acerrime culparis fidem facit. Te quoque uocatum esse qui tibi
missas a me sciat litteras, quis uel insanus non asserat? Te igitur,
frater, racionabiliter[o] pro tua culpa et canonice uocatum et a
diuino offitio separatum recognoscendo plange, et plangendo ad
satisfactionem reuertere. Quod si quadragenario uocationis spacio
lege canonum te defendere niteris, scito[p] quia singulares causae
uel personae non preiudicant legi.[2] Nam te in furorem uersum
et ex presule ducem tot armatorum factum, totam nostram
patriam crudeliter uastare cernens, ferrum, ignes, diuersasque
nobis mortes minatum, imminentique plagae quadragenariae

---

[c] eiusdem *om.* P   [d] lacescentibus L   [e] professus sum L   [f] si P
[g] ita] iure DR   *om.* C   [h] ut *om.* P   [i] conditione LP   [k] ·i· (=id
est ?) *add.* L *with a corrector's mark in mar.*   [l] non *add.* P   [m] fixisti P
[n] exemplum P   -o *sup. ras.* L   [o] racionabiliter *om.* DR   [p] scio P

---

[2] See p. 41 n. 6. As regards the delay given a defendant, the canons
usually stipulated only that a reasonable time should be allowed (see Gratian,
C. V q. 2 (*Corpus Iuris Canonici*, ed. E. Friedberg (Leipzig, 1879–81), i. 545 ff.));
however, a delay of forty nights was prescribed by Salic law (see H. Brunner,
Deutsche Rechtsgeschichte, ed. C. von Schwerin, ii (2nd edn., Munich, 1928),
446).

refrain from answering you as your arrogance deserves and instead to attend to my duty as regards your salvation and while doing this to make a reasoned and humble reply to certain passages in your letter. It is a physician's duty to offer those who are suffering from depression, insanity, or any other illness what he has learned in the exercise of his art and to apply himself with all diligence to the task of curing them even if they are ungrateful and insult his skill. Similarly it is my duty—though I do not claim to be even the most unskilled of physicians, but only somehow to have advanced to where I have an obligation as your archbishop to correct you if you should go astray—to administer to you, ungrateful as you may be, the remedies I have acquired from the holy fathers and to apply myself to the task of curing you whether you want me to or not. But before I do so, I wish, as I have said, to refute certain passages in your letter, for I think that the other matters, which form the larger part of it, are best passed over.

With regard to your charge that I was ill-advised and acted rashly in severing you from divine worship since you were not guilty and had not been duly summoned, this I shall destroy with clear and irrefutable proof. It was not ill-advised to offer you terms you yourself ought to have chosen. If you had given sufficient thought to it, you would not have called it ill-advised. So you have been even more ill-advised, as will appear more clearly later on, in having gone from bad to worse. That you and your followers were not excommunicated rashly and without having deserved it is shown by the remains of the vineyards in which you placed your camp, and the evidence afforded by this lends conviction to the other charges of which you are so bitterly accused. As for your having been duly summoned, is there anyone, sane or not, who knows of the letters which I sent you who would not vouch for this? So admit, brother, that as reason demanded in return for your sin you were canonically summoned and severed from divine worship; in admitting it, lament; and in lamenting, return and make satisfaction. But if you should attempt to defend yourself on the grounds that canon law gives you forty days to answer the summons, know that individual cases and persons do not prejudice the law.[2] For when I saw you turned into a raging maniac and changed from a bishop into the leader of a substantial army, cruelly ravaging all our land, and threatening us with the sword, fire, and death in one way and

uocacionis spacium ut desisteret nihil uidens prodesse, uenabulum mox tibi excommunicationis opposui, ut eo saltim uiso territus et[q] te et tuos uel ad momentum refrenares, et presulem quem amiseras recognosceres. Sed tu maluisti illo excommunicationis uenabulo confodi, quam accepta[r] tirannide uel ad punctum refrenari. Nam quod dicis te regis hoc iussu fecisse, nec nego nec affirmo, nec quid te hoc leuet intelligo. Cuiuscumque enim hoc iussu feceris, eadem culpa ac si nullus iusserit urgeris. Nam ad exaggerationem tuae culpae ista satis transgressio sufficit, quod preter mea tua archiepiscopi consulta contra canonicam auctoritatem tale aliquid incipere presumpsisti, quodque etiam me iubente non debuisses facere, hoc te ipso consultore fecisti. Quod autem ais te in malum Odonis[3] a rege[s] inpulsum, nec etiam unam[t] ei palmitem destruxisti, sed uineas canonicorum sancti Mauritii[4] preter cetera quae in tuam matrem aecclesiam iussu tui diui Fulconis[5] intulisti opprobria radicetenus comminuisti. His de causis excommunicatorias tibi litteras, quas contra ius et fas audaciae notas (non enim te oportuit tuum magistrum et dominum tam temere reprehendere), ut a tuo incepto resipisceres transmisi, non ut te uellem flecti in eam partem qua corruisti. Quod discrete an indiscrete fecerim, tua[u] iuriditialis libra penset, qui me consultorem quaerere mones. At si indiscrete ac sine causa temerariam in te (quod absit) excommunicationem intorsissem, sustineres tamen iuditium tui pastoris, et a sacra celebracione cessares. Quod quia non fecisti, et consultrice superbia tui magistri interdicta paruipendisti, prudens in uoraginem te excommunicationis praecipitasti. Accipe quid super hoc beatus papa Gregorius dicat: 'Vtrum', inquit, 'iuste an iniuste obliget pastor, pastoris tamen

---

[q] et *om.* P   [r] acẹpta (=a coepta?) DRP   [s] a rege] agere P
[t] unum DR   [u] tui DR

---

[3] Count of Chartres.   [4] The cathedral of Tours.
[5] Count of Anjou.

another, and when I did not see that there was anything to gain from giving you forty days' grace to put an end to the danger that was already upon us, I immediately countered with the spear of excommunication, hoping that the sight of this might at least frighten you into restraining your followers and yourself, if only for the moment, and into recognizing the pastor you had lost. But you preferred to be run through by that spear of excommunication rather than to restrain yourself, even for an instant, from the lawlessness on which you had embarked. As for your saying that you did this by order of the king, I neither deny nor affirm it, nor do I see how it can in any way lighten your responsibility; for it does not matter who ordered you to do it, you are just as guilty as if no one had done so. To establish your guilt, your sin in this regard is quite enough: that without consulting me, your archbishop, you have dared to venture on a monstrous violation of canon law, and that what you ought not to have done even if I had ordered it, you have done without consulting anyone save yourself. As to your claim that you were pushed by the king into injuring Odo,[3] you have not destroyed a single branch of a vine belonging to him, but you have trampled down to the very roots vineyards of the canons of Saint-Maurice,[4] not to mention the other reproaches which you have heaped on your holy mother, the church, by the order of your own god, Fulk.[5]

These were the reasons why I sent you the letter of excommunication which you brand as rash, thus violating human and divine law, since you should not be so quick to reprove your master and lord; and I sent it to make you come to your senses and abandon what you had begun, and not because I wanted to make you turn on to that path along which you have been rushing to your ruin. As to whether I have acted wisely or not, you can weigh this in the scales of your own judgement, you who are admonishing me to seek counsel. But even if (heaven forbid) I had been imprudent and rash and had hurled an excommunication against you without grounds, you should still have borne with the judgement of your pastor and refrained from celebrating mass. But since you have not done this, and since with Pride as your counsellor you have paid no attention to what your master has prohibited, you have acted with full knowledge in throwing yourself into the abyss of excommunication. Listen to what the blessed Pope Gregory says concerning this: 'Whether a pastor binds a

sentencia gregi timenda est, ne is qui subest, et cum iniuste forsitan
ligatur, ipsam obligationis suae sentenciam ex alia*x* culpa mereatur.
Pastor ergo uel absoluere indiscrete timeat uel ligare. Is autem
qui sub manu pastoris est ligari timeat*y* uel iniuste, nec pastoris
sui iuditium temere*z* reprehendat, ne etsi iniuste ligatus est ex
ipsa tumidae reprehensionis superbia culpa quae non erat fiat.'*6*
Hactenus beatus Gregorius. Hac igitur, frater, cornuta argumenta-
tione conuictus excommunicatum te recognoscendo iterum plange,
et plangendo ad satisfactionem reuertere; atque his tuae epistolae
locis tantum nos respondisse suffitiat. Ceteris aliquis otiosus
respondeat; nam ego illa quae magis sunt necessaria et*a* pollicitus
sum prosequar. Contemplor enim, frater, ex motibus tui corporis
diuersa genera passionum tuam germinare animam.*7* Quibus si
aliquo medicamine priusquam in uires prodeant non occurritur,
miserabilem tuae animae generabunt mortem. Sed congrua cuique
passioni ignorabitur medicina, nisi origenes et (ut ita dicam)
radices earum intentissima discrecione fuerint exploratae. Omnium
itaque passionum animae unus fons atque principium est; secundum qualitatem uero partis quae in anima uitiata fuerit, una-
queque passio uocabulum sortitur. Quod et corporalium mor-
borum docetur exemplo. Si enim uis noxii humoris obsederit*b*
caput, cephalargica passio nuncupatur; si pedes, podagrica; si
manus, ciragrica nominatur. Totque uocabula unius humoris
sortitur incommoditas, quot membrorum obsederit porciones. De
uisibilibus ergo ad inuisibilia transeuntes, uniuscuiusque animae
partibus uim cuiusque uitii inesse credamus. Quam sapientissimi
quique tripertitae diffinierunt esse uirtutis; nam et racionabilis
est et irascibilis et concupiscibilis. Secundum qualitatem ergo
uitiatae partis, infectio cuiusque pestis nominatur. Nam si racionabilem partem infecerit, cenodoxiae, elationis, inuidiae, superbiae,
presumptionis, contemptionis,*c* hereseos uicia procreabit. Si
irascibilem uulnerauerit, furorem, inpacientiam, tristitiam, acci-
diam, pusillanimitatem, crudelitatemque parturiet. Si concupi-

---

x aliqua LDR   *y* metuat P   *z* temere *om.* DR   tenere C
a et] ut DR   *b* obsidet DR   *c* contentionis DR *and similarly*
throughout the following passage; likewise Cassian, with no mention of contemptio
as a variant, though the context indicates that it is the correct word here

---

6 *Hom. in ev.* xxvi. 6 (*PL* lxxvi. 1201).
7 The following passage is based on, and in large part copied from Cassian,
Conlationes, xxiv. 14–16 (ed. Petschenig, *CSEL* xiii. 690 ff.).

sin justly or unjustly, his flock should still stand in awe of his judgement, for otherwise a subject who is perhaps unjustly bound may deserve to be bound by the same sentence as a result of committing another sin. So let the pastor stand in fear of making a mistake in absolving or binding a sin; and let him who is under the pastor's power be afraid of being bound, even unjustly, and let him not take it on himself to reprove his pastor's judgement, for fear that even though there was no reason for him to be bound, yet as a result of his being so swollen with pride as to reprove his pastor he commits a sin where he had not committed one before.'[6] Thus far St. Gregory. On the evidence presented here, brother, you stand convicted. Once again admit that you have been excommunicated and lament; and in lamenting, return and make satisfaction. As regards these passages in your letter, let this answer be sufficient; as for the rest, let someone who has time to do so answer them, for I have more important matters to pursue as I have promised.

I can tell from what you are doing, brother, that your soul is fostering various disorders.[7] If these are not counteracted by some remedy before they grow to full strength, they will result in your soul's dying a miserable death. But the proper remedy for each disorder cannot be known unless their origins and, as it were, their roots are examined with care and discernment. All disorders of the soul have the same source and origin, but each has its own proper name in accordance with the nature of the part of the soul which is diseased. This is also shown by the diseases of the body. If a harmful humour should attack the head, the illness is known as a headache; if it should attack the feet, it is known as gout-of-the-feet; if the hands, it is called gout-of-the-hands. Thus it is that a disease caused by a single humour has as many different names as the parts of the body that it attacks. Moving from the realm of the visible to the invisible, we think that the power of each vice dwells in different parts of the individual soul. Now philosophers distinguish three faculties in the soul: the rational, the irascible, and the concupiscible; and it is in accordance with the nature of the diseased part that each infection receives its name. If it should infect the rational part, it will produce the vices of vainglory, self-elation, envy, pride, insolence, scorn, heresy. If it should afflict the irascible part, it will bring forth anger, impatience, depression, spiritual sloth, faint-heartedness, and cruelty.

scibilem infecerit portionem, castrimargiam, fornicationem, filargiriam, auaritiam, et desideria noxia terrenaque generabit. Animaduerto igitur, frater, ex motibus tui (ut dixi) corporis tuam animam
suam germinare*d* mortem. Nam cum tu*e* tantam in me tuum
presertim magistrum superbiam, contemptionem, et presumptionem demonstrares, apparet racionabilem tuae animae partem
miserabiliter esse corruptam. Certis enim inditiis haec tria in te
notantur: superbia uidelicet, quod tam superbe tuo archiepiscopo
respondes; contemptio, quod sua interdicta paruipendis, quae
licet iniusta (quod absit) essent, tamen (sicut superius probatum
est) timenda tibi esse debuissent; praesumptio quoque, quod iuste
an iniuste interdictus, ad sacram celebracionem accedis. Quorum
trium*f* inditia racionabilem (ut dixi) tuae animae partem praedicant esse uiciatam. Reliquas*g* autem siquid in te germinent, tu
ipse uideris; nam huic ego parti quam tam horribiliter corruptam
cerno quiddam ex sanctorum patrum coemptis (sicut pollicitus
sum) medelis, quo reuocetur ad salutem procurabo. Sed haec
procuratio nihil tibi proderit, si prius uulneri quo ad mortem
inflexus*h* es satisfactionis medela non subuenerit.*i* Quo (ut dico)
per satisfactionem sanato, tumores ilico superbiae, contemptionis,
et presumptionis, quos in tuam animam induruisse suspicor, falce
discretionis amputabis. Deinde amputationis illius uulnera recentia, ne aliquam aliam passionem generent, penalis cauterio*k*
timoris ustulabis; quam usturam ne frigus impietatis tangat,
caritatis ardore et oleo fouebis misericordiae. Quod si ita feceris,
et superbia illa qua instigante responsa in me tam torua iaculatus
es, et contemptio qua meum interdictum paruipendis, et presumptio qua excommunicatus ad sacram celebracionem accedis
peribunt, et racionabilis pars tuae animae ex magna parte ad
incorruptionem reuertetur. Post hoc*l* autem has uirtutis speties,
humilitatem, pacientiam, et obedientiam, in unum melle diuinorum
eloquiorum confities, et in buxtula tuae mentis hoc antidotum
diligenter recondes. Vnde cotidianam tua anima dietam sumens
non solum has pestes inperpetuum non germinabit, sed etiam a
caeteris omnibus incorrupta fulgebit. His te, frater, monens, non
fastu doctoris efferor, sed offitium meae prelationis trepidus

---

d generare P   *e* tuam LC   *f* tria LC   *g* Reliqua P
h influxus *corr. to* inflexus L   infixus P   inflexus es] influxisses C   *i* subueneris LDR   *k* cautio LC   *l* haec P

If it should infect the concupiscible part, it will engender gluttony, fornication, greed, avarice, and harmful and worldly desires.

So, brother, as I have said I can tell from what you are doing that your soul is fostering that which will kill it. In showing such monstrous pride, scorn, and insolence toward me, your especial master, you reveal that the rational faculty of your soul is dreadfully diseased. That you possess these three vices is clearly proven: pride, by the haughtiness of your answer to your archbishop; scorn, by your having no regard for his injunctions, which, as was shown above, you should have feared even if (heaven forbid) they were unjust; insolence, by your having ventured to celebrate mass when you were excommunicated, whether justly or not. These three vices are clear proof, as I have said, that the rational part of your soul is diseased. As to whether the other parts of your soul have fostered any vice, you must see to it yourself; for to this part, which I see to be so horribly diseased, I shall, as I have promised, administer one of the remedies acquired from the holy fathers so as to restore it to health. But what I administer will not do you any good unless the remedy of penance is first applied to heal that wound which will lead to your death. As soon, I say, as this has been healed by penance, use the scalpel of prudence to cut away the tumours of pride, scorn, and insolence, which I have reason to believe have already become hardened in your soul. Then cauterize the raw wounds that this produces with the hot iron of holy fear so as to prevent their fostering some other disorder; and keep the places you have cauterized warm with the fire of charity and the oil of mercy that they may not be chilled by the touch of impiety. When you have done this and have destroyed that pride which moved you to assail me with such savage replies, that scorn which prompted you to have no regard for my injunctions, and that insolence which led you to venture to celebrate mass when you were excommunicated, the rational part of your soul will in large part be restored to good health. Then take the virtues of humility, patience, and obedience, and mix them with the honey of the divine word, and carefully store this remedy in the cupboard of your mind. By eating some of this daily, not only will your soul never foster these same disorders, but it will shine forth untarnished by any others.

In sending you this warning, brother, I am not being haughty and lording my teaching office over you, but rather carrying out

exequor. Quibus si annueris, tuae (ut arbitror) saluti prouidebis. Si autem (quod absit) aliter senseris, non erit culpa monentis. At[m] si idcirco his quae precipio parere neglexeris, quod meis repugnent factis, ab hoc te errore dominica uoce reprimo qua ait: 'Super cathedram Moysi sederunt scribae et pharisaei. Quecumque ergo[n] dixerint uobis, seruate et facite; secundum opera uero[o] eorum nolite facere, dicunt enim et non faciunt.'[8] Scribis et pharisaeis (ut tu[p] ipse melius nosti) commissa erat doctrina legis, ut eam exponerent auditoribus suis. Ideo Dominus dixit: 'Super cathedram Moysi sederunt scribae et pharisei', id est super doctrinam legis. Quorum dictis, postpositis factis, auditores obtemperare iussit cum ait: 'Quecumque ergo dixerint uobis seruate et facite; secundum opera uero[q] eorum nolite facere.' Pharisaei enim[r] quod bene[s] docebant, malis operibus destruebant, quod Dominus subsequenter adiunxit: 'Dicunt enim et non faciunt.' Tales sunt modo in sancta aecclesia episcopi, presbiteri, et abbates, qui bene docent et male uiuunt; de quorum etiam numero et me esse confiteor. Sed tamen quia super cathedram doctrinae et prelationis licet indignus et inperitus nec dicta factis conpensans sedeo, siquid boni a me in illa cathedra sedente preceptum tibi fuerit, dominica (ut audis) ammonicione obseruare debebis. Quod si neglexeris, dominicis preceptis apertissime contraibis. Vale.

72

Fulbert to Count Fulk Nerra of Anjou: calling on him to do penance for his attack on Archbishop Hugh of Tours[1]

before 10 June 1023

F(ulbertus) Carnotensium episcopus humilis F(ulconi) comiti salutem.

Doleo super te, nobilis homo, cum audio te errare et periclitari. Errare dico, quia cum debeas Deum timere, sanctos honorare,

---

[m] *apparently marked for deletion* L   [n] ergo *om.* DR   [o] uero opera LDRC   [p] tu *om.* LDRC   [q] uero opera LDRC   [r] autem LDR
[s] bene *om.* P

72 LDRKCPBV

---

[8] Matt. 23: 2 f. The interpretation here is apparently based on Haimo,

in all trepidation my duty as your archbishop. If you agree to do as I have said, you will, I think, be taking thought for your salvation; but if (heaven forbid) you should be of a different opinion, the fault will not be mine, for I have warned you. As for your refusing to heed my teachings on the grounds that they are at variance with my deeds, I would keep you from making this mistake by quoting the Lord's words, where he says: 'The scribes and the pharisees have sat on the chair of Moses. Whatsoever they should say to you, observe and do; but according to their works, do ye not, for they say and do not.'[8] The scribes and the pharisees, as you yourself know quite well, were entrusted with teaching the law and were to expound it to their disciples. Hence the Lord said: 'The scribes and the pharisees have sat on the chair of Moses', that is, they are charged with teaching the law. He commanded their disciples to follow their teachings and to disregard their deeds when he said: 'Whatsoever they should say to you, observe and do; but according to their works, do ye not'; for the pharisees undid their good teachings by their evil works, as the Lord added afterwards: 'For they say and do not.' Their counterparts in the holy church at present are those bishops, priests, and abbots, who give good instruction, but whose lives are evil, and I confess that I am one of them. Be that as it may, since I hold the office of teacher and archbishop, despite my unworthiness, my lack of skill, and the discrepancy between my words and deeds, if in the exercise of this office I should enjoin you to do anything that is good, you ought to heed the Lord's admonition and to obey. But if you should refuse, you will quite clearly be violating the Lord's own commands. Farewell.

Fulbert to Count Fulk Nerra of Anjou[1]

before 10 June 1023

F(ulbert), humble bishop of Chartres, to Count F(ulk), with his greetings.

I grieve for you, count, when I hear that you are going astray and are in danger. I say that you are going astray, because when

---

Homelia cxxxiii (*PL* cxviii. 707 f.). Cf. H. Barré, *Les homéliaires carolingiens de l'école d'Auxerre* (*Studi e Testi*, ccxxv (Rome, 1962)), p. 157, no. 39.
72. [1] See no. 71.

aecclesiam defendere, contempnis Deum, sanctos inhonoras, res ecclesiae inuadis et aufers. Periclitari dico, quoniam qui talia agunt, non habent partem in regno Dei. Propter haec peccata monuit archiepiscopus Turonensis omnes episcopos nostros et inter alios me pusillum ut te excommunicaremus. Sed ego censui pium esse ut te prius monerem et deprecarer ut habeas misericordiam de anima tua, placans Deum.[2] Iam enim prope est tuus finis.[a] Festina igitur, queso, reconciliari Christo saluatori nostro, quia non est salus homini nisi per ipsum.[3] Tene in memoria uerbum hoc: 'Qui confitendo et penitendo finem facit peccatis suis antequam moriatur, finem habebit in altero seculo pena ipsius; et qui peccatis mortalibus penitendo non facit finem, pena ipsius erit sine fine.'[4] Euigila igitur propter temetipsum sicut homo in proximo moriturus, et reconciliare Christo, ne moriaris apostolica auctoritate dampnatus. Vale et remanda michi uelociter atque ueraciter uoluntatem tuam.

73

Fulbert to Archbishop Gauzlin of Bourges: informing him that the abbot of Bonneval has resigned and left
before 27 July 1023

Sancto et sapienti uiro G(auzlino) abbati et archiepiscopo F(ulbertus) humilis episcopus uerae dilectionis affectum.

Nouerit prudencia uestra, sancte pater, quod domnus T(etfridus)[a] abbas[b1] discedens tristitiam nobis reliquit et lacrimas, non quod innocenciam eius (si esset) nequiremus facere tutam, sed quia culpam nec purgare nec tegere poteramus. Vnde si uestro ducatu quasi ad examinacionem uenire affectat, cum periculo sui gradus et communi dedecore sacerdotum, conatus eius inefficaces sagaci racione conpescere uos oportet, seruantes illud apostolicum: 'Si preoccupatus fuerit homo in aliquo delicto, et caetera.'[2]

---

[a] finis tuus LDRKC

73 LDRCPBV   [a] T.] I. LDR   [b] abba LPV

[2] Cf. Ecclus. 30: 24.   [3] Cf. Acts 4: 12.
[4] Cf. Fulgentius, *De remissione peccatorum*, ii. 17, 21 f. (ed. Fraipont, *CCL* xci[a]. 700, 705 ff.).

you ought to fear God, honour the saints, and defend the church, you treat God with contempt, dishonour the saints, and seize the church's possessions and carry them off. I say that you are in danger, since those who commit such sins have no share in God's kingdom. Because of these sins, the archbishop of Tours has called on all our bishops, including my humble self, to excommunicate you. But I considered it my duty to admonish you first and to entreat you to have mercy on your soul and to make your peace with God,[2] for your end is at hand. So hasten, I beg you, to be reconciled to Christ our Saviour, for there is no salvation for man except through him.[3] Keep this saying in mind: 'If anyone puts an end to his sins by confessing them and doing penance before he dies, his punishment in the next world will have an end; but if anyone does not put an end to his mortal sins by doing penance, his punishment will not have an end.'[4] So take care for yourself as a man who is to die tomorrow, and be reconciled to Christ, so that you may not die condemned by apostolic authority. Farewell, and let me know what you intend to do quickly and truthfully.

Fulbert to Archbishop Gauzlin of Bourges
before 27 July 1023

To the holy and wise abbot and archbishop, G(auzlin), from F(ulbert), a humble bishop, with his true love and affection.

May you in your wisdom know, holy father, that Abbot T(etfridus')[1] departure left us sad and sorrowful, not because we were unable to maintain his innocence (such as it was), but because we could not disprove or conceal his sin. So if he comes to your province saying that he wishes to be examined, to the peril of his orders and the general dishonour of the priesthood, you ought to restrain his ventures by wise advice and bring them to naught in keeping with the apostolic precept: 'If a man be overtaken in any fault, and so forth.'[2]

73. [1] Of Saint-Florentin of Bonneval (Eure-et-Loir, *arr.* Châteaudun). See nos. 74 f. His case is otherwise unknown.
[2] Gal. 6: 1, continuing: 'you, who are spiritual, instruct such a one in the spirit of meekness, considering thyself, lest thou also be tempted.'

74

Fulbert to Archbishop Gauzlin of Bourges: informing him that he has notified the monks of Bonneval that they will have to appear at a hearing against Abbot Tetfridus and justifying his blessing Abbot Solomon[1]   before 27 July 1023

Venerabili Bituricensium presuli G(auzlino) F(ulbertus) Carnotensium humilis episcopus incrementa uirtutum.

Legatum uestrum diu detinui, quia Salomon abbas[2] cum quibusdam monachis aberat, sine quorum consultu uobis responderi non oportebat. Quos ubi redierunt commonui, ut sese ad audienciam presentarent contra domnum Tetfridum. Ipsi uero responderunt se messiuo tempore occupatos, lites ad presens agitare non posse, sed idibus Octobris in Aurelianensi concilio quod futurum esse destinauimus, constituent uobis proximum audienciae et diem et locum, tantummodo fratrem suum Dodonem (qui est apud uos) reddatis eis infra predictum terminum. Interea oblatae sunt nobis*[a]* quaedam litterae sub uestro nomine conscriptae ad domnum Arnulfum abbatem sancti Petri,[3] significantes uos excommunicasse monachos nostros; sed auctoritatem qua uobis id liceat me uidisse non memini. At si apud uos habetur, nobis eam debetis ostendere, ne forte si non ostendatur, aut temere aut minime excommunicati esse dicantur. In litteris etiam quas mihi nuperrime direxistis confictam inueni reprehensionem meam de ordinacione Salomonis abbatis hoc modo: 'Miramur qua*[b]* auctoritate fieri potuit, ut sine audiencia subditus prelato prepositus sit.' Quod (ut puto) mirari non debetis, quia non est, sed illud pocius attendere quod est. Non enim hoc sine audientia factum est, neque subditus Salomon Tetfrido adhuc prelato praepositus est. Domnus T(etfridus) a suis monachis criminatus (ut scitis) apud me de infamia sua querimoniam fecit, eorumque maliciam se ferre non posse dicens, sub audiencia mea et eorum qui mecum erant prelacioni suae perpetualiter renunciauit, astruens abbatem monachorum Bone Vallis ulterius se non esse futurum. Sicque petita a nobis migrandi licencia transiuit ad uos. Monachi uero qui in

---

74 LDRCPBV KF contain only the last half of the letter beginning with *In litteris* and have not been used here.   *[a]* nobis *om.* PV   *[b]* quia L

Fulbert to Archbishop Gauzlin of Bourges[1]
                                    before 27 July 1023

To the venerable archbishop of Bourges, G(auzlin), from F(ul-bert), humble bishop of Chartres, with his prayer that he may grow in virtue.

I detained your messenger for a long time as Abbot Solomon[2] and some of his monks were away, and I needed to consult them before I replied to you. When they returned, I notified them that they would have to appear at a hearing and plead their case against Tetfridus. They replied that it was harvest time and that they were too busy to be involved in lawsuits at present, but that at the council which we have called to meet at Orleans on 15 October they will set for you the earliest possible day and place for the hearing provided you send their brother Dodo, who is with you, back to them before then. Meanwhile a letter was brought to us written in your name to Abbot Arnulf of Saint-Père[3] which stated that you have excommunicated our monks. I do not recall having seen anything that authorizes you to do this. If you have such authorization, you ought to show it to us, for otherwise it may be said that they have been excommunicated rashly or not at all. Moreover, in the letter that you recently sent me, I found myself reproved as follows for having blessed Abbot Solomon: 'We wonder on what legal grounds a subject can be set over a superior without a hearing.' I do not think you ought to wonder at this, for it is not the case; but instead you should attend to what is. This was not done without a hearing, nor was Solomon, as a subject, set over Tetfridus while he was still abbot. As you know, after T(etfridus) was accused by his monks, he complained to me that he had been publicly disgraced and said that he could not continue to cope with their ill will. In the presence of my companions and myself he renounced his prelacy for ever and declared that he was no longer abbot of the monks of Bonneval. Then he asked for our permission to leave and went to you. The

74. [1] See no. 73.
    [2] The new abbot of Bonneval, of whom nothing else is known except that he attended a church dedication in 1040 (*GC* viii. 1238 f.).
    [3] *c.* 1013–33. His life in J. Mabillon, *Acta Sanctorum ordinis sancti Benedicti*, vi. i (Paris, 1701), 315 ff., consists of excerpts from *Cart. S.-Père* and his epitaph (see p. xliii n.).

Bona Valle remanserant, hoc scientes, alium quendam ex fratribus suis electum eo quod inreprehensibilis esse uidebatur obtulerunt Odoni comiti[4] abbacia donandum ut mos erat, michique deinde consecrandum. Is interim locum pastoris tenet. Siquis ergo est qui me super hoc facto presumpcionis arguat, nouerit me respondere paratum, et hoc (si opus sit) tam racione quam auctoritate approbare, quod siquis abbatum uel animi uel corporis egritudine molestatus prelacionem suam inperpetuum renunciando deserat, episcopus ipsius diocesis in loco eius alterum debeat ordinare.[5] Valete.

75

Fulbert to Archbishop Gauzlin of Bourges: consenting to his request for a hearing for Abbot Tetfridus of Bonneval[1]
                                    c. *mid 1023*

Vitae pariter et doctrinae meritis uenerando abbati et archiepiscopo[a] G(auzlino) F(ulbertus) humilis episcopus utriusque officii praemia gloriosa.

Si de mea dilectione confidis, pater, sicut litterae tuae significant, securus esto quia rem tenes, non te fallit opinio. Proinde quicquid a me conpetenter exposcis facile impetras, et nunc quidem specialiter de audiencia domni T(etfridi) uenerabilis sacerdotis, ne[b] queratur diucius se fraudari oportunitate iudicii. Quod ego sibi hactenus (Deum testor) non insidiando distuli, sed prouidendo dissuasi, sciens quia causa eius in fine turpitudinis est, et sentinae modo quo amplius agitatur, eo dirius fetet. Nec uero turpis tantum, sed et[c] periculosa est adeo ut si uenerit ad iudicium, aut ipse aut accusator eius cum magna sit contumelia degradandus. Hoc itaque preuidens,[d] et illud euuangelicum mente reuoluens: 'Nolite iudicare, nolite condempnare, et caetera',[2] herebam timorate suspensus, et expectans ut Dominus tantum dedecus ecclesiae suae sine publica discussione uel insultacione piaret. Nunc autem inpaciencia domni T(etfridi) non permittit hoc fieri,

---

75 LDRCPBV   *a* suo *add.* LDR   *b* nec PB, *ante corr.* L   *c* et
om. CP   *d* prouidens BV

monks who remained in Bonneval, knowing this, elected another of their brothers who seemed to be irreproachable, presented him to Count Odo[4] to be invested with the abbey as was the custom, and then to me to be blessed. Since then he has been their pastor. So if anyone wishes to accuse me of having acted rashly in this matter, let him know that I am prepared to answer and, if necessary, to prove by reason and on the basis of competent authority that if any abbot is afflicted with an illness of mind or body and abandons his prelacy and renounces it for ever, the bishop of his diocese should bless another to take his place.[5] Farewell.

Fulbert to Archbishop Gauzlin of Bourges[1]   c. *mid 1023*

To Abbot and Archbishop G(auzlin), who deserves to be honoured for his life and his learning, from F(ulbert), a humble bishop, with his wish that he may be gloriously rewarded for his excellence in both.

If you are relying on my love, father, as you say in your letter, you may rest assured that you are right and that you have judged correctly. Hence if you ask me for anything that is suitable, you easily obtain it, and now in particular a hearing for the venerable priest T(etfridus), so that he may no longer complain that he is being cheated of the chance for a trial. I call God to witness that I did not postpone this till now out of treachery, but that I advised him against it out of foresight; for I knew that his case involved immorality, and like filth the more it is stirred up, the worse it smells. Indeed, not only does it involve immorality, it is also dangerous, so much so that if he comes to trial, either he or his accuser must be degraded to his great dishonour. Foreseeing this and turning over in my mind the evangelical precept: 'Judge not, condemn not, and so forth',[2] I held off, anxiously waiting and hoping that the Lord would rid his church of such a great disgrace without public discussion or derision. But now in his impatience T(etfridus) will not let me do this. Instead he obstinately insists

---

[4] Of Chartres.   [5] Cf. p. 100 n. 3.

75. [1] See nos. 73 f.

[2] Luke 6: 37: 'Judge not, and you shall not be judged. Condemn not, and you shall not be condemned. Forgive, and you shall be forgiven.'

sed[e] pertinaciter instat, ac pie dissimulantes ad iudicium bestius[f] urget.[3] Tandem ergo quamuis inuitus et coactus cedo, diemque et locum (ut rogasti) constituo, iam non audens relinquere indiscussum, quod Deum puto nolle preterire inultum.[4] Inperpetuum uale.

76

Fulbert to Archbishop Ebalus of Rheims: commending a student   before 27 July 1023

Diligendo semper ac uenerando Remorum archiepiscopo E(balo) F(ulbertus) Carnotensium humilis episcopus communicare fontem intimae caritatis.

De uestra bonitate non de nostro merito confidentes, deprecamur, obtime pater, ut notum habere dignemini hunc carum nostrum nomine Hubertum, qui de patria sua causa discendae honestatis egressus, et apud nos aliquandiu demoratus, talem se nobis exibuit, ut non minus quam frater uterinus amari et honorari meruerit. Nunc uero eadem causa permotus, monasterium beati Remigii[1] quod uestrum est uisitare disposuit. Vbi si in aliquo fuerit indigus uestrae opis, sentiat, quesumus, uiscera[a] pietatis. Valete.

77

Fulbert to Archbishop Leothericus of Sens: advising him as regards an impediment of spiritual relationship   before 27 July 1023

Venerabili Senonensium archiepiscopo L(eutherico) F(ulbertus) Carnotensium humilis episcopus a summo Domino 'euge, boni serui'.[a1]

Placuit excellenciae uestrae sciscitari a nobis quid agendum sit de quodam uiro qui, filium suum tenendo ad confirmacionem,

---

[e] sed *only in* P   [f] uehementius B instantius V
76 LDRCPBV   [a] uestrae add. LDR (*supra* L)
77 LDRCPBVKF   [a] bone serue (*perhaps correctly*) B

and unreasonably demands[3] that those who are dutifully keeping silent come to trial. So I am finally forced against my will to give way and to set a day and a place as you asked, for now I do not dare to leave untried what I think God is unwilling to let pass unpunished.[4] Farewell, now and always.

Fulbert to Archbishop Ebalus of Rheims
before 27 July 1023

To Archbishop E(balus) of Rheims, who is always to be loved and revered, from F(ulbert), humble bishop of Chartres, with his wish that he may share in the fount of inmost charity.

Trusting in your goodness and not in our just deserts, we beg you, dear father, to deign to consider our good friend Hubert, bearer of this letter, as your friend too. Having left his homeland for the sake of acquiring a sound education, and having stayed with us for some time, he has shown himself as deserving of our love and honour as if he were our born brother. Now the same reason has led him to make arrangements to visit your monastery of Saint-Remi.[1] If he should in any way need your help there, we beg that he may feel the kindness of your heart. Farewell.

Fulbert to Archbishop Leothericus of Sens
before 27 July 1023

To the venerable archbishop of Sens, L(eothericus), from F(ulbert), humble bishop of Chartres, with his wish that he may hear from the most high Lord: 'Well done, good servant.'[1]

It has pleased your excellency to ask us what should be done with regard to a man who acted as his son's sponsor at confirmation

---

[3] Cf. Persius, vi. 37 f., where Bestius (as in Horace, *Ep.* i. 15. 37) is cast as the relentless critic of extravagance. It is impossible to tell whether Fulbert understood it as a proper name, and the copyists of B and V seem to have been troubled by it. The word is otherwise found (see Du Cange, s.v.) in the sense of 'beast-like', and Fulbert is apparently using it to denote one who makes persistent and unreasonable demands.   [4] Cf. Job 24: 12.

76. [1] Of Rheims.

77. [1] Cf. Matt. 25: 21; Luke 19: 17.

factus est de patre patrinus: uidelicet utrum ab uxore sua matre eiusdem pueri*b* sit separandus an non. Nos uero quod sancti patres de tali causa statuerunt, id censemus esse tenendum. Inuenitur ergo statutum in concilio Liptiniensi, capitulo vii, sub Zacharia papa, sub principe Karlomanno, hoc modo: 'Siquis filiastrum aut filiastram suam ante episcopum ad confirmacionem tenuerit, separetur ab uxore et alteram non accipiat. Simili modo et mulier alterum non accipiat.'*c* Item in eodem: 'Nullus proprium filium uel filiam de fonte baptismatis suscipiat, nec filiolam nec commatrem ducat uxorem, nec illam cuius filium uel filiam ad confirmacionem tenuerit.*d* Vbi autem factum fuerit, separentur.'[2] Credo ista sufficere pauca sapienti.[3] Valete.

78

Fulbert to King Robert: notifying him that he will not meet him at Tours as instructed[1] *before 27 July 1023*

Regi sacerdos, domino fidelis, R(otberto) F(ulbertus).

Vt uobis proximo sabbato Turonis occurrerem, quia sero commonitorium accepi, non parui. Siquae aliae causae sunt, tacentur ad presens, quia minus uos tacitae quam expositae ledunt. Valete nunc et semper.

79

Fulbert to Bishop Franco of Paris: explaining why he has not excommunicated an enemy, advising him as to a rebellious archdeacon, and notifying him of his action as regards a complaint *before 27 July 1023*

Venerando Parisiorum antistiti F(ranconi) F(ulbertus) Dei gratia Carnotensium episcopus tocius prosperitatis munus.

Laudonensem illam sacrilegam res ecclesiae uestrae diripientem propter has causas excommunicare distulimus: primo, quia defuit

---

b pueri *om.* KF   *c* Simili . . . accipiat *om.* CV   *d* confirmacionem tenuerit] contenuerit LP

78 LDRCPBV   It is copied twice in C.

79 LDRKP

---

[2] The attribution to the council of Estinnes (743) is erroneous. Fulbert's source was apparently Benedictus Levita, i. 7, 167 (ed. Knust, pp. 47, 54),

and so changed his relationship to him from father to god-father: should the man be separated from his wife (the boy's mother) or not? We think that you should hold to what the holy fathers decreed in such a case. One finds the following decreed in chapter seven of the council of Estinnes, held under Pope Zachary and Prince Carloman: 'If anyone acts as sponsor for his stepson or stepdaughter when he is confirmed by the bishop, let him be separated from his wife and not take another; and likewise let the woman not take another husband.' Also in the same council: 'Let no one receive his own son or daughter from the baptismal font or marry his goddaughter or fellow-sponsor or her whose son or daughter he sponsored for confirmation. Where this happens, let them be separated.'[2] I think these few words are enough for a wise man.[3] Farewell.

Fulbert to King Robert[1]   *before 27 July 1023*

To the king from his bishop, to a lord from his vassal, to R(obert) from F(ulbert).

Since I was late in receiving your instructions to meet you at Tours next Saturday, I have not obeyed. As for any other reasons, I am saying nothing for the present, since they will give less offence if I leave them unsaid than if I should tell you. Farewell, now and always.

Fulbert to Bishop Franco of Paris   *before 27 July 1023*

To the venerable bishop of Paris, F(ranco), from F(ulbert), by grace of God bishop of Chartres, with his wish that all may prosper.

With regard to the woman from Laon who is committing sacri-lege by ravaging your church's possessions, we have put off

where the first canon is cited shortly after a reference to that council. Fulbert was apparently misled by this and their similarity into attributing both canons to it. They actually come from the councils of Compiègne (757), c. 15 (*MGH Leges*, ii. i (1883), 38), and Mainz (813), c. 55 (ibid. iii. ii (1906), 273). See A. Werminghoff, 'Zu den fränkischen Reformsynoden des 8. Jahrhunderts', *Neues Archiv*, xxxii (1907), 230 f.; E. Brouette, *DHGE* xv. 1064 ff., who, however, accepts their attribution to Estinnes.   [3] See p. 63 n. 4.

78. [1] See p. lxxxiv.

qui ipsi ferre auderet nostram excommunicacionem; deinde, quia
parum uobis aut nihil fortasse prodesset, si illa nesciens excom-
municaretur in ecclesia nostra; tercio, quia expectauimus ut in
conuentu nostrorum conprouincialium episcoporum utilius hoc
fieret. Quod etiam adhuc expectandum nobis uidetur, si animi
uestri serenitas adquiescat. De Lisiardo autem archidiacono uestro,[1]
quem scripsistis in uos superbum ac rebellem esse, non opus est
nos consulere, cum optime nouerit prudencia uestra quid de
huiusmodi lex diuina sanciat, neque nos[a] oporteat quemquam
absentem et causa indiscussa iudicare. Volumus autem uos scire
quod Adroldus[b] noster de Nouigento,[2] cui anathematis sentenciam
intentatis propter querelam quam habent contra eum monachi
sancti Dionisii, dicit se paratum esse ad iustificandum in audiencia
uestra atque nostra. Proinde si litem hanc cito iustoque fine deter-
minare uultis, constituite diem quo uobis et monachis sancti
Dionisii apud sanctum Arnulfum[3] occurrere ualeamus, qui locus
nobis ad conueniendum oportunior esse uidetur. Valete.

80

*Archbishop Leothericus of Sens and Fulbert to the clergy
of Paris: exhorting them to support Bishop Franco in his
struggle against his archdeacon Lisiardus[1]*   c. *mid 1023*

L(euthericus) Senonensium archiepiscopus, et F(ulbertus) Carnotensium[a] episcopus, clero[b] Parisiacensis ecclesiae temperanciam
in prosperis, fortitudinem in aduersis, caritatem ubique.

Audiuimus, carissimi, famam iniuriarum quas patitur episcopus
uester, et corde compatimur. Vos quoque illas ita sentire credimus,
sicut fideles filios, et bono capiti bene coherencia membra. Sed
miramur quare in tanto merore constituti, nec ad nos petendae
consolacionis causa uenistis, nec saltem litteras direxistis. Nam

---

[a] uos L   [b] Rodulfus LDRK (*initial* ad- *erased* L)

80 LDRCPBVKF   [a] Carnotensis R   Carnot KF   [b] sanctae *add.*
BKF

---

79. [1] Apparently the archdeacon who is the subject of no. 80 and whose name
appears in a charter of Franco (*Cartulaire de l'église Notre-Dame de Paris*,
ed. B. Guérard, i (Paris, 1850), 325).

excommunicating her for the following reasons: first, because there was no one who would dare to notify her that we had excommunicated her; second, since it would be of little or perhaps no profit to you if she were excommunicated in our church without knowing it; third, because we believe that this could be done to better advantage in a provincial council of our fellow bishops. I think that we should wait until then, if you with your usual long-suffering will concur. As for your archdeacon Lisiardus,[1] who you wrote was arrogant and rebellious toward you, there is no need to consult us, since you in your wisdom well know what divine law prescribes in such cases, and since we should not judge anyone who is absent and whose case has not been heard. We also want you to know that our vassal, Adroldus of Nogent,[2] whom you are threatening to excommunicate because of a complaint that the monks of Saint-Denis have made against him, says that he is prepared to defend himself in court before both of us. So if you wish to bring this case to a rapid and just conclusion, set a day when we can meet you and the monks of Saint-Denis at Saint-Arnoul,[3] which seems to be the most convenient place for us to come together. Farewell.

Archbishop Leothericus of Sens and Fulbert to the clergy of Paris[1]   c. mid 1023

L(eothericus), archbishop of Sens, and F(ulbert), bishop of Chartres, to the clergy of the church of Paris, with their wishes for moderation amid prosperity, fortitude amid adversity, charity at all times.

We have heard, dear friends, a report of the injuries suffered by your bishop, and in our hearts we suffer with him. We believe that you share our feelings in this regard as faithful sons and members closely joined to a good head. But we wonder why in the midst of your great sorrow you have not come to ask us for consolation or even sent us a letter, for your affliction is not so

---

[2] Probably the vicomte of Nogent-le-Roi (Eure-et-Loir, *arr.* Dreux), who witnessed Appendix C, nos. 11 f.

[3] Perhaps Saint-Arnoult-en-Yveline (Seine-et-Oise, *arr.* Rambouillet), where Saint-Maur-des-Fossés had recently received a grant (Appendix C, no. 7).

80. [1] See no. 79.

neque plaga uestra tanta est ut inuenire*c* nequeat consolacionis remedium, neque uerus medicus ille dereliquit aecclesiam, qui se nobis 'omnibus diebus usque ad consummacionem seculi'[2] promisit affuturum. Miramur iterum cur impios homines qui diuinis sanctionibus aduersantur, et in uestrum pastorem contumaces existunt, in communionem recipitis contra canonicam legem, quam uobis et ignorare nefas est et periculum soluere. Quod si putatis eos tandiu uobis in communione habendos, quousque ab episcopo uestro palam excommunicentur, corrigit hanc estimacionem Petrus apostolus in sermone habito ad Romanos de ordinacione Clementis his uerbis: 'Quedam', inquit, 'fratres ex uobis*d* intelligere debetis, siqua sunt quae uester episcopus propter insidias malorum hominum non possit euidencius et manifestius*e* proloqui: uerbi gratia, si inimicus est alicui pro actibus suis, uos nolite expectare ut ipse uobis dicat, sed prudenter obseruare debetis,*f* uoluntati eius absque commonicione obsecundare, et auertere uos ab eo cui ipsum sentitis aduersum.'*g*[3] Haec et plura huiusmodi beatus Petrus in predicto sermone. Nos autem, fratres, dum talia uobis proponimus, nolite estimare*h* (absit enim) ut sinistrum aliquid de uobis suspicemur; sed officium nostrum facimus, cum aut uos aut alios fratres nostros ad cautelae uigilanciam excitamus. Non enim sine causa*i* scriptum est propheticum illud de pennatis animalibus quod se inuicem alarum commocione contingant.*k*[4] Vnde nos quoque uicem nobis rependi postulantes, agili penna exhortacionis uos ad haec*l* excitare cupimus, ut sitis in lege Domini studiosi, ad obedienciam et suffragium uestri pastoris pio amore deuoti, ad resistendum uero aduersariis eius sagaciter instructi, fideliter animati. Inter quos uidelicet aduersarios*m* unus est (ut audiuimus) nomine*n* Lisiardus, olim quidem archidiaconus, qui cum esse deberet oculus episcopi sui, dispensator pauperum, catecizator insipiencium,[5] apostatauit ab omnibus his et factus est episcopo suo quasi clauus in oculum, praedo pauperibus, dux erroris insipientibus. Quia superba et contumeliosa maledicta in episcopum suum iaculans, serenitatem speculacionis eius turbat; decimas et oblaciones altarium (stipem uidelicet pauperum) suo episcopo inconsulto seculari miliciae

---

c uenire L   *d* ipsis *add.* BKF   *e* et manifestius] manifestiusque LDR (-que *add. supra* L) atque manifestius P   *om.* V   *f* et *add.* LDRBKF (*supra* L)   *g* auersum KF   *h* exstimare L   existimare DR
i causa *om.* L   *k* commocio·ē· (= est) contingantur L   *l* hoc BKF
m aduersarius LDRCK   *n* nomine *om.* LDRC   omne V

[2] Matt. 28: 20.
[3] Pseudo-Clement, ep. i. 17 (Hinschius, p. 36).

great that it cannot find consolation and relief, nor has that true Physician abandoned the church who promised to be with us 'all days even to the consummation of the world'.[2] We also wonder why you receive into communion impious men who are opposed to divine law and disobedient toward your pastor, for this is contrary to canon law, which it is wrong for you not to know and perilous for you to violate. But if you think they should remain in communion with you until they are publicly excommunicated by your bishop, the apostle Peter refutes this notion in his sermon to the Romans on Clement's consecration as follows: 'Brothers, there are certain matters you should know for yourselves in case your bishop cannot talk about them plainly and openly because of treacherous and wicked men. For example, if his actions show that he disapproves of someone, you should not wait for him to tell you, but you should watch carefully and comply with his wishes without having to be told and turn away from him to whom you feel he is opposed.'[3] This and more to the same purpose were said by St. Peter in that sermon. But in our pointing this out to you, brothers, do not think (heaven forbid) that we suspect you of anything evil. We are but doing our duty in rousing you or our other brothers to watch and take care, for it was not without reason that the prophet wrote as regards the winged creatures that they touch one another by moving their wings.[4] So while asking you to do the same for us in return, we wish to rouse you by the nimble wing of exhortation to be zealous for the law of the Lord, to obey and support your pastor with filial love and devotion, and to be armed with wisdom and inspired with fidelity to resist his enemies. Among them there is one (so we have heard) named Lisiardus, who was once an archdeacon. When he should have been the eye of his bishop, the steward of the poor, and the instructor of the unlearned,[5] he deserted all these and became, as it were, a beam in his bishop's eye, a robber of the poor, and a leader in wrongdoing to the unlearned. For by assailing his bishop with haughty, insolent, and slanderous abuse, he disturbs his peace of mind; he takes the tithes and offerings of the altars (that is, the alms for the poor) and without consulting his

[4] Cf. Ezek. 3: 13. According to Gregory I, *Hom. in Ez.* i. x. 30 ff. (*PL* lxxvi. 898 ff.), the animals who touch each other in moving their wings signify holy men who rouse each other to further spiritual progress by the sight of their virtues.

[5] Cf. Pseudo-Clement, ep. i. 12 (Hinschius, p. 34).

tradit; et cum talia facit, dat insipientibus erroris et perdicionis exemplum, quibus inpendere debuerat uerae scienciae cathecismum. Quid dicemus de iuramento fidelitatis quod ita contaminat, ut episcopo suo nec corde nec uerbo nec opere fidelis existat? Non autem temere de corde*o* iudicamus,[6] cum ueraciter in sacro poemate dictum sit: 'Ex operum specie clarescunt intima cordis.'[7] Is itaque pro contumacia sua qua poena dignus sit, si ruina angeli non sufficit ad exemplum, contumacis Chore manifestat interitus.[8] Pro perfidia uero sua et contumeliosa maledictione quid meruerit, suspendium Iudae et sororis Aaron lepra testatur.[9] O hominem infelicem nimium, cui tam horrenda tempestas diuinae ulcionis incumbit! Condempnat illum testamentum uetus his uerbis: 'Qui maledixerit patri, morte moriatur.'[10] Condempnat illum lex Christianorum iudicum hac sentencia: 'Siquis episcopo aliquam iniuriam aut iniustam dehonoracionem fecerit, de uita componat, et omnia quae habere uisus fuerit ecclesiae cui praeesse dinoscitur integerrime socientur.'[11] Excommunicat illum Gangrense concilium capitulo septimo et octauo;[12] degradat illum Cartaginiense concilium capitulo lvii;[13] sed et alia plura.*p* Quapropter et nos a sanctorum patrum sentencia discrepare nolentes, consequenter illum a communione separamus, quantum nostrae potestati conceditur, donec resipiscat, et episcopo suo digne humiliatus satisfaciat. Et nisi cito resipiscens ad satisfactionem uenerit, in plenaria synodo perpetuo anathemate ferietur. Mandamus autem uobis, karissimi, ut ipsi L(isiardo) has litteras*q* ostendatis, ut tam horrenda pericula uel grauiter admonitus exire meminerit. Patet etenim*r* adhuc euadendi locus dicente Domino per Hiezechielem: 'Si impius egerit poenitenciam ab omnibus peccatis*s* quae operatus est, et custodierit uniuersa precepta mea, et fecerit iudicium et iustitiam, uita uiuet et non morietur';[14] et per Iohannem: 'Filioli, haec scribo uobis ut non peccetis; et*t* siquis peccauerit, aduocatum habemus apud patrem iustum

---

o ipsius *add.* BKF   *p* plurima KF   *q* litteras has LDRC   *r* enim RCBVKF   *s* suis *add.* BKF   *t* Sed et DR

[6] Cf. Prosper, *Liber sententiarum*, c. xxi (ed. Gastaldo, *CCL* lxviii[a]. 262), which was taken up in Pseudo-Zepherinus, ep. i. 7 (Hinschius, p. 132).
[7] Source unidentified.   [8] See Isa. 14: 12 ff.; Num. 16: 1 ff.
[9] See Matt. 27: 5; Num. 12: 1 ff.   [10] Exod. 21: 17; Lev. 20: 9.
[11] Benedictus Levita, ii. 99 (ed. Knust, p. 78).

bishop uses them to wage impious warfare; and in so doing, he shows the unlearned the way of sin and damnation when he should have offered them instruction in true knowledge. What shall we say as to his oath of fidelity, which he violates to the point of being unfaithful to his bishop in thought, word, and deed? Nor are we making a rash judgement as to his thoughts,[6] for the Christian poet rightly says: 'In the way a man acts the secrets of his heart are revealed.'[7] The punishment he deserves for his arrogance is clearly shown, if the ruin of the angels is not a suitable example, by the destruction of Corah for wilful defiance.[8] What he deserves for his faithlessness and insolent curses is attested by Judas's hanging himself and the leprosy of Aaron's sister.[9] O wretched, wretched man on whom falls such a dreadful storm of divine vengeance! The Old Testament condemns him in these words: 'He that curseth his father shall die the death.'[10] The law of Christian judges condemns him with this pronouncement: 'If anyone commits an injury against a bishop or in any way unjustly dishonours him, let him pay with his life, and let all that he has be given to the church of which that bishop has charge.'[11] The council of Gangres, chapters seven and eight, excommunicates him;[12] the council of Carthage, chapter fifty-seven, degrades him;[13] and there are many more. So since we do not wish to differ from the judgement of the holy fathers, we too sever him from communion so far as in us lies until he comes to his senses, is suitably humbled, and makes satisfaction to his bishop; and unless he quickly comes to his senses and makes satisfaction, he will be stricken and permanently excommunicated in a full synod. We also ask you, dear friends, to show this letter to L(isiardus) himself, so that having been so solemnly admonished he may take thought as to how to escape such dreadful perils. For the way to escape still lies open, as the Lord says through Ezekiel: 'If the wicked do penance for all his sins which he hath committed, and keep all my commandments, and do judgement and justice, living he shall live, and shall not die';[14] and through John: 'My little children, these things I write to you that you may not sin. But if any man sin, we have an advocate with the Father, Jesus the just,

[12] Mansi, ii. 1111; Hinschius, p. 265.
[13] *Statuta ecclesiae antiqua*, c. 57 (Mansi, iii. 956; Hinschius, p. 305) = c. 44 (ed. C. Munier (Strasbourg, 1960), p. 87), traditionally ascribed to Carthage IV.
[14] Ezek. 18: 21.

Ihesum;[u] ipse est exoracio pro peccatis nostris.'[15] Et ipse Dominus
ait: 'Gaudium est angelis Dei super uno peccatore penitenciam
agente quam super[x] xcviiii iustis qui non indigent penitencia.'[16]
Certum enim habet catholica fides, ut uerbis beati Fulgencii utar,
quia 'quocumque tempore homo egerit penitenciam, quamlibet
iniquus,[y] quamlibet annosus, si toto corde renunciauerit peccatis
preteritis[z] et pro eis in conspectu Dei non solum corporis sed
aetiam cordis lacrimas fuderit, et malorum operum maculas bonis
operibus diluere curauerit, omnium peccatorum indulgenciam
mox habebit.'[17] Verum ut ait pater Augustinus: 'Qui ueniam
penitenti promisit, dissimulanti diem crastinum non spopondit.'[18]
Rogamus etiam, fratres, ut domnum F(ranconem) uenerabilem
episcopum uice nostra salutare et confortare memineritis, certo
scientes suam tristitiam nostram[a] esse, nostra prospera sua.
Valete cum ipso.

81

*Fulbert to King Robert: explaining why he cannot attend a
conference with the Emperor Henry II*[1]

before 27 July 1023

Domino suo R(otberto) regi benignissimo F(ulbertus) humilis
sacerdos inperpetuum uigere.

Sacram maiestatis uestrae nuperrime[a] suscepi monentem me
vi kalendas Augusti uestro et H(einrici) imperatoris interesse
colloquio, non solum uestri obsequii sed et nostrae commoditatis
causa. Vnde suppliciter uobis pro tanta erga me pietatis affectione
gratulans, rescribo me iamdiu infirmatum, egritudinem hoc tempore maxime reuereri, longum iter aggredi non audere, successu
uero temporis oportunioris, annuente Deo libenter uos eo siue
alias comitaturum esse; quamquam ad presens si ualitudo non
obsisteret, longe tamen ante premoneri me tanti itineris oporteret.
Valete feliciter.

[u] et *add.* DR   [x] supra LDR   [y] quamlibet iniquus *om.* PB
[z] praesentis L   [a] sua tristicia nostra CPBKF (tristia KF)

and he is the propitiation for our sins.'[15] The Lord himself says: 'There is more joy among the angels of God over one sinner that doth penance than over ninety-nine just who need not penance.'[16] The catholic faith holds it for certain, to quote St. Fulgentius, that 'at whatever time a man does penance, however wicked, however old he may be, if he renounces his past sins with all his heart and in the sight of God pours forth tears for them not only from his body, but also from his heart, and takes care to wash away the stain of evil deeds with good works, he will immediately obtain forgiveness for all his sins'.[17] But as St. Augustine says: 'He who promised pardon to the penitent did not give to the hypocrite the assurance of a morrow.'[18] We also ask you, brothers, to remember to greet and comfort your venerable bishop F(ranco) for us. You may rest assured that his sadness is ours and our good fortune his. Our best wishes to you and him.

Fulbert to King Robert[1]   *before 27 July 1023*

To his very kind lord and king, R(obert), from F(ulbert), a humble bishop, with his wish that he may flourish for ever.

I have just received your majesty's letter summoning me in the name of the service that I owe you as well as for our common good to attend a conference between you and the Emperor H(enry) on 27 July. While I humbly thank you for showing me such fatherly affection, I am writing to let you know that I have been in poor health for some time and am very much afraid of becoming ill now, and so I do not dare to undertake a long journey, but that when I am better able to do so, I shall (God willing) accompany you there or elsewhere. But even if I were not held back by ill health at present, I should have been notified of such a long journey far in advance. Farewell, and good fortune.

---

81 LDRKCP   It is copied twice in P.   *a* nuperrime *om.* DRK

---

[15] 1 John 2: 1 f.   [16] Luke 15: 7, 10.
[17] *De fide*, c. xxxix (ed. Fraipont, *CCL* xci[a]. 737).
[18] Actually Prosper, *Liber sententiarum*, c. lxxi (ed. Gastaldo, *CCL* lxviii[a]. 274).
81. [1] See pp. lxxx, lxxxii–lxxxiv.

82

Fulbert to Bishop Bonibertus of Fünfkirchen:[1] thanking him for his letter and sending him a copy of Priscian

c. *mid 1023*

Sancto ac uenerabili coepiscopo suo Boniberto F(ulbertus) fidelitatis obsequium et summi pastoris benedictionem.

Primum quidem benedicimus Deum Patrem ingenitum, filiumque suum unigenitum Ihesum Christum dominum nostrum,[a] et Spiritum sanctum paraclitum, unum uerum Deum qui cuncta creauit, qui te quoque, dilectissime pater, multa sapiencia inlustrauit ad docendum populum suum, et decore sanctitatis ad prebendum bonae uitae exemplum decenter ornauit. Deinde magnas tibi referimus[b] grates, quod nos licet inmeritos atque ignotos salutacionis tuae pariterque munere gratiae dignatus es preuenire. Vnde profecto nos in amorem tuum sic animasti, ut perhennem tui memoriam in intimo cordis nostri uigere uelimus, ut saltem per crebra oracionum suffragia, si aliter facultas non suppecierit, tuae benignitati uicem rependere satagamus. Significauit autem nobis filius noster tuusque fidelis Hilduinus[2] tuae caritatis erga nos insignia, fideliter asserens unum de nostris Priscianis te uelle, quem et per eundem libenter mittimus, quicquid etiam de nostro pecieris hilarissime tibi (si possibile fuerit) transmissuri, ipsam quoque presenciam nostram, si tibi opus esset ac uoluntas, nobisque[c] potestas, obsequentissime prestaturi. Ad ultimum saluere te semper obtamus, precantes ut illam nouam ac gloriosam adoptionis prolem summi regis, regem uidelicet Stephanum, ex nostri parte salutes, intimans excellenciae suae ex nostra parte[d] et uniuersarum congregacionum quae sunt in episcopatu nostro, canonicorum scilicet ac monachorum, oracionum fidelia.

---

82 LDRKP   [a] Ihesum . . . nostrum] dominum Ihesum Christum LDRK
[b] referimus tibi LDRK   [c] nobis quoque LDRK   [d] salutes . . . parte
om. P

Fulbert to Bishop Bonibertus of Fünfkirchen[1] c. mid 1023

To his holy and venerable fellow bishop, Bonibertus, from F(ulbert), with his faithful service and the blessing of the Most High Pastor.

First we bless the unbegotten God the Father and his only-begotten Son, our Lord Jesus Christ, and the Holy Spirit, the Paraclete, one true God, who created all things and illumined you, my dear father, with great wisdom so that you might teach his people and suitably adorned you with the beauty of holiness that you might show them how to live rightly. Then we thank you very much for having deigned to take the first step in sending our undeserving and unknown selves the gift of your greeting and friendship. In doing this you have inspired us with such love for you that we wish ever to cherish your memory in our inmost heart so that we may strive to repay you for your kindness, if in no other way, at least with the support of our constant prayers. Our son and your faithful servant Hilduinus[2] has told us of your gestures of charity toward us and dutifully stated that you would like one of our copies of Priscian. We are happy to send this by him, and whatever else you should ask of us we shall be most delighted to send you if we can; and if you should need and want us to, and if we are able, we ourselves shall most obediently attend you in person. In closing we send our wishes for your continual well-being, and we ask you to convey our greetings to that new and glorious adopted son of the Most High King, namely King Stephen, and to assure his excellency on behalf of us and all the communities in our diocese, both canons and monks, of our faithful prayers.

---

82. [1] The first bishop of Fünfkirchen (Pecs, in southern Hungary), who resigned in 1036 and died in 1042 (*Annales Posonienses* (*MGH SS* xix. 572)). Pilgrims to the Holy Land began to use the land route through Hungary about this time, and King Stephen (997–1038) became known for his generosity to them (see Raoul Glaber, iii. 1 (ed. Prou, p. 52); the letter to Stephen from Abbot Odilo of Cluny in Bibliothèque Nationale, latin 9376, f. 60 (see p. xlviii n.), from which it was printed in Pfister, *Fulbert*, pp. 53 f.).

[2] Perhaps the Hilduinus mentioned in no. 105 and possibly the son of the vidame Reginald (see no. 121) and subdeacon and canon of Chartres (Merlet, p. 179).

83

Fulbert to Duke Richard II of Normandy:[1] *asking him not to impose new burdens on the lands he gave to Chartres*
c. *mid 1023*

Venerando Normannorum principi R(icardo) F(ulbertus) Dei gratia Carnotensium episcopus salutem et oracionum suffragia.

Multa bona fecistis ecclesiae sanctae Mariae dominae nostrae. Retribuat uobis Deus per intercessionem ipsius. Nos quoque pro illis animae uestrae corporique uestro et fideles sumus, et semper esse ualeamus.[a] Sed nuper ad nos insperata uenit legacio, quod ipsam terram quam nobis dedistis[2] Baldricus minister uester[b] reuocauerit, nostro ministro quem ibi prefeceramus[c] aliquid disponendi potestatem interdixerit, suas etiam res inuaserit, nostris hominibus nouam angariam induxerit, banniendo scilicet ut irent ad molendinum sancti Audoeni,[3] quinque leugis (ut ferunt) ab eorum hospiciis remotum. Si haec, obtime princeps, uestro iussu (quod minime credimus) facta sunt, plurimum uestri causa dolemus, et ut corrigantur suppliciter postulamus. Quin etiam iubeat prudencia uestra ministris uestris, ne ulterius inquietent nostros homines, et deinceps terram predictam ita libere nos possidere sinant, ut eam a benignissima uestra manu[d] suscepimus. Vigeat diutissime incolumitas et potencia uestra.

84

Fulbert to Bishop R.: advising him as regards the bond of betrothal
mid 1023–early 1024

F(ulbertus) humilis episcopus uenerabili consacerdoti suo R. boni propositi finem optimum.

Mulier illa, de cuius causa nostram humilitatem consulere uoluistis, impedita est uinculo iuramenti, nec potest inire conubium sine crimine peiurii,[a] nisi per consensum aut post obitum illius cui se tali iuramento condicionaliter obligauit. Valete.

---

83 LDRKP   [a] uolumus DRK   [b] uester minister LDRK
[c] perfeceramus L preferamus P   [d] manu uestra LDRK
84 LDRPBVKF   [a] *corr. to* periurii L

Fulbert to Duke Richard II of Normandy[1]   c. *mid 1023*

To the venerable prince of Normandy, R(ichard), from F(ulbert), by grace of God bishop of Chartres, with his greetings and the support of his prayers.

You have performed many good services for the church of our Lady, St. Mary. May God reward you through her intercession. In return for them we too are faithful vassals of your soul and body, and we hope that we can always be so. But recently we received an unexpected message that your servant Baldricus has recalled the land that you gave us,[2] forbidden the servant whom we placed in charge there to exercise any authority and seized his possessions, and imposed a new *banalité* on our men by ordering them to use the mill at Saint-Ouen,[3] which (so they say) is five leagues away from their holdings. If these things, most excellent prince, were done at your command (which we by no means believe), we are very much grieved on your account, and we humbly beg that they may be corrected. May you in your wisdom instruct your servants not to give our men any further trouble and from now on to let us hold this land on the same terms as we received it from your most kind hand. May good health and strength be yours for many years.

Fulbert to Bishop R.   *mid 1023–early 1024*

F(ulbert), a humble bishop, to his venerable fellow bishop R., with his wish that what he has resolved may meet with every success.

With regard to the woman about whose case you consulted our humble selves, she is held back by the bond of her oath and cannot enter into marriage without committing perjury except with the consent or after the death of him to whom she bound herself under the terms of her oath. Farewell.

83. [1] November 996–23 August 1026 (D. Douglas, 'Some Problems of Early Norman Chronology', *English Historical Review*, lxv (1950), 289 ff.).

[2] See p. 71 n. 2. A 'Baldricus procurator' was one of the witnesses to the charter cited there.

[3] A fairly common place-name which cannot be identified with certainty. The only mill of that name listed in Le Marquis de Blosseville, *Dictionnaire topographique du département de l'Eure* (Paris, 1877), pp. 203 f., is apparently too distant.

85

Fulbert to O(dilo, abbot of Cluny?): informing him that he cannot meet him as planned   *mid 1023–early 1024*

Sanctissimo atque dilectissimo patri O(diloni) F(ulbertus) humilis sacerdos oracionis suffragium.

Volebam uobis occurrere, pater, ut mandaui per R. diaconem meum; sed domestici mei nouo quodam rumore permoti, nec me iter ad presens agere, nec se itineris mei fore comites adquiescunt, donec tutius id fieri posse perpendant. Valete.

86

Count Odo II of Chartres to King Robert: explaining why he did not come to trial and calling on him to do him justice[1]
mid 1023–early 1024

Domino suo regi R(otberto) comes Odo.

Pauca tibi, domine, dicere uolo si audire digneris. Comes Ricardus[2] tuus fidelis monuit me uenire ad iustitiam aut ad concordiam de querelis quas habebas contra me. Ego uero misi causam hanc totam in manu ipsius. Tum ille ex consensu tuo constituit mihi placitum, et ubi hoc perfici posset. Sed instante termino cum ad hoc peragendum paratus essem, mandauit mihi ne me fatigarem ad condictum placitum ueniendo, quia non erat tibi cordi aliam iustificacionem seu concordiam recipere, nisi hoc tantum ut faceres mihi defendere quod non essem dignus ullum beneficium tenere de te, nec sibi competere dicebat, ut me ad tale iudicium exhiberet sine conuentu parium suorum. Haec causa est cur tibi ad placitum non occurri. Sed de te, domine mi, ualde miror, qui me tam prepropere causa indiscussa tuo beneficio iudicabas indignum. Nam si respiciatur ad condicionem generis, claret Dei gratia quod hereditabilis sim. Si ad qualitatem beneficii quod mihi dedisti, constat quia non est de tuo fisco sed de his quae mihi per tuam gratiam ex maioribus meis hereditario iure

85 LDRPBV
86 LDRPBV

Fulbert to O(dilo, abbot of Cluny?) mid 1023–early 1024

To his most holy and very dear father O(dilo) from F(ulbert), a
humble bishop, with the support of his prayers.

I wanted to meet you, father, as I told you through my deacon
R.; but my servants are disturbed by a new rumour and will not
consent to my travelling at present or to accompany me on my
journey until they consider it safer to do so. Farewell.

Count Odo II of Chartres to King Robert[1]
mid 1023–early 1024

To his lord, King R(obert), from Count Odo.

I wish to say a few words to you, my lord, if you will deign to
listen. Your vassal Count Richard[2] called on me to stand trial or
to come to an agreement with you as regards the charges you made
against me. I placed the whole case in his hands. Then with your
consent he set up for me a court where this could be done. But
when the time came and I was ready to go through with it, he
sent me word not to bother going to the court that he had con-
vened since you did not intend to accept any other judgement or
agreement, but only to charge me with being unworthy to hold
any benefice from you, and he said that it was not right for him
to bring me to trial on this charge except before a court of his
peers. This is why I did not meet you at that court. But as regards
you, my lord, I am exceedingly astonished that so hastily and
without hearing my case you have judged me unworthy to hold
a benefice from you. For if it is a question of my birth, it is clear
that by God's grace I am able to enter on an inheritance. If it is a
question of the nature of the benefice you gave me, the fact is
that it does not come from your domain, but from the estates
which come to me with your consent by hereditary right from

86. [1] See pp. lxxix ff., lxxxiv, and especially the article by Halphen cited there
whose interpretation I have largely followed.
    [2] Duke Richard II of Normandy.

contingunt. Si ad seruicii meritum, ipse profecto nosti donec tuam gratiam habui quomodo tibi seruierim domi et miliciae et peregre. At postquam gratiam tuam auertisti a me, et honorem quem dederas mihi tollere nisus es, si me et honorem meum defendendo aliqua tibi ingrata commisi, feci hoc lacessitus iniuriis et necessitate coactus. Quomodo enim dimittere possum, ut non defendam honorem meum ?[3] Deum et animam meam testor, quod magis eligerem honoratus mori, quam uiuere dishonoratus. At si me dishonorare uelle desistas, nihil in mundo est quod magis quam gratiam tuam uel habere uel promereri desiderem. Discordia enim tua mihi quidem molestissima est, sed tibi, mi domine, tollit officii tui radicem et fructum, iustitiam loquor et pacem. Vnde suppliciter exoro clementiam illam quae tibi naturaliter adest, si maligno consilio non tollatur, ut iam tandem a persecucione mea desistas, meque tibi siue per domesticos tuos seu per manus principum reconciliari permittas.[a]

87

Fulbert and Bishop Avesgaudus of Le Mans to Archbishop Ebalus of Rheims: asking him to support Avesgaudus in his struggle against Count Herbert of Le Mans

mid 1023–early 1024

Gloria et honore digno patri et archiepiscopo Ebalo F(ulbertus) humilis episcopus cum uenerabili Cinomannensium episcopo Auisgaudo salutem.

Scientes uos habere zelum diuinae legis, nec minus opitulari uelle quam debere fratribus uestris, sed et plurimum posse, fiducialiter a uobis auxilium petimus in necessitatibus nostris, ac[a] nunc quidem singulariter in precursorem antichristi[b] Herbertum comitem Cinomannis,[1] qui sedem episcopalem eiusdem ciuitatis

---

[a] Vale *add.* B   Valete *add.* V

87 LDRPBV   [a] at RB   [b] Christi L   persecutorem Christi DR

---

[3] Throughout this passage the writer is playing on 'honour' in its double meaning of benefice and respect.

87. [1] 1014/15–1032/5 (R. Latouche, *Histoire du comté du Maine pendant le Xe et XIe siècle* (Paris, 1910), pp. 22 ff.). There was continual friction between

my ancestors. If it is a question of what I deserve in return for my service, you yourself know how as long as I had your favour I served you at home, in the field, and in foreign parts. But after you withdrew your favour from me and tried to dishonour me by taking away the benefice you had given me, if in defending myself and my benefice I in any way offended you, I did so because I was provoked by the wrongs done to me and forced by the circumstances. For how can I honourably forgo defending my benefice?[3] I call God and my soul to witness that I would prefer to die with honour while defending it than to live dishonoured by its loss. But if you would stop trying to dishonour me in this way, there is nothing in the world that I should like more to have or to deserve than your favour. The discord that you have caused is indeed very troublesome to me, but as for you, my lord, it takes away the root and fruit of your office, that is to say justice and peace. So I humbly beg you, in that clemency to which you are by nature inclined unless you are dissuaded from it by bad advice, now, at last, to stop persecuting me and to let me be reconciled to you through your servants or by the mediation of the princes.

Fulbert and Bishop Avesgaudus of Le Mans to Archbishop Ebalus of Rheims   mid 1023–early 1024

To their father and archbishop Ebalus, who is worthy of glory and honour, from F(ulbert), a humble bishop, and the venerable Bishop Avesgaudus of Le Mans, with their greetings.

Since we know that you are a zealous supporter of God's law, that you wish to help your brothers no less than you should, and that you can help them very much, we confidently ask you for aid in our necessities and now in particular against a precursor of the antichrist, Count Herbert of Le Mans,[1] who is trying to destroy

---

Avesgaudus and Herbert. On the present occasion, according to the *Actus pontificum Cenomannis in urbe degentium*, c. xxx (ed. G. Busson and A. Ledru, Archives historiques du Maine, ii (1901), 358 f.), which quotes from a lost letter by Fulbert to Herbert ('. . . misit epistolam sale satis conditam, et scripsit in ea: nisi ab hac malitia se temperaret et rectum ei faceret, excommunicatum omninoque damnatum a Domino se crederet'), Avesgaudus fled and took refuge with Fulbert. At Count Herbert's request Fulbert went to Le Mans and arranged a settlement.

euertere nititur. Episcopum enim predictum (uidelicet Auis-
gaudum) in ea cum pace manere non sinit, domus eius et terras
et fruges et omnia uictualia insuper et prebendas canonicas
ecclesiae peruasit. Haec itaque uos ad uiuum sentire uolumus
nisuque indissimulato propellere. Et ut facilem modum habeat
petitio uestra,[c] precamur uos illi commonitorium scribere, ut iam
dicto episcopo sua reddat, et eum in pace uiuere sinat; alioquin,
ut pro certo nouerit se a uobis et suffraganeis uestris excommunicatum[d] iri, ex illo die quo eum excommunicauerit Auis-
gaudus episcopus. Commonitorium autem quod illi sacrilego
uestra dignacio mittet, nobis[e] transcribi postulamus et mitti.
Valete in[f] infinitum.

88

*Fulbert to Hildegar: advising him on the administration of
Saint-Hilaire and sending him an excerpt from Amalarius
on liturgical vestments*   *before 5 April 1024*

F(ulbertus) episcoporum humillimus H(ildegario) suo salutem.

Absencia tua sepe commemoror[a] quam necessarius eras presens.
Sed hoc me consolor, quod obsequia tua tali[1] delegauerim qui sit
dignus[b] recipere, et utrique[c] remunerare paratus. Spero enim ut
michi quoque de tuis benemeritis (siqua Deo dante fuerint) aliqua
tecum mercedis porciuncula cedat. Opitulabor itaque tibi[d] ad bene
promerendum ex animo; sed ueniendi ad uos diem statuere dubito,
quia et ibi[e] uictualia michi puto deesse, et in mea diocesi multis
occupor. Fac tu interim quod te facere opto et credo. Lectioni,
oracioni, et erudicioni fratrum operam tuam cum alacritate
diuide, animae simul et corporis curam gerens, ne propter secundi[f]
lassitudinem primi[g] uigor euanescat.[2] De re sancti patris H(ylarii)
et nostra fideliter disponenda, scio te non indigere monitis, dummodo fures caueas. Vestes et caetera ornamenta ecclesiae quae

----

[c] nostra DR   [d] excommunicaturum LDR   [e] uobis PV   [f] in
om. LBV

the episcopal see of that city. He will not let Bishop Avesgaudus remain there in peace and quiet and has seized his houses, lands, crops, and all his provisions, as well as the prebends of the canons of the church. We want you to take these matters to heart and to make an honest effort to put an end to them. So that your case may turn out successfully, we ask you to write to Count Herbert, admonishing him to return Bishop Avesgaudus's possessions and to let him live in peace and quiet, and notifying him that otherwise he will be excommunicated by you and your suffragans from the day Bishop Avesgaudus excommunicates him. We also ask your excellency to have a copy made and sent to us of the letter that you send to that sacrilegious sinner. Farewell, now and always.

Fulbert to Hildegar   *before 5 April 1024*

F(ulbert), most humble bishop, to his H(ildegar), with greetings.

Your absence often reminds me how important was your presence. But I take comfort in the thought that I have transferred your services to one[1] who is worthy to receive them and prepared to reward us both, for I hope that some small portion of your reward for your good works (God granting there be any) may also fall to me. So I shall sincerely help you to be truly deserving, but I hesitate to set a date to visit you, since I do not think that there are adequate provisions for me there, and since I am very busy with my own diocesan affairs. Meanwhile do what I hope and trust you are doing. Divide your energy and your diligence between reading, praying, and teaching the brothers, and take care of both your soul and your body so that the one may not lose its strength because of the other's weariness.[2] As a faithful steward of St. H(ilary's) possessions and ours, I know that you do not need any advice from me, provided you are on your guard against thieves. As for the vestments and other furnishings of the

---

88 LDRKCPBV   *a* commemorat BV   *b* et dignus LDRK
indignus P   *c* utrimque P   utrumque BV   *d* tibi *om.* BV   *e* tibi
LCPV   *f* seculi RCBV   *g* praemii CB   premia V

---

88. [1] Namely, St. Hilary (cf. no. 121).
    [2] Cf. Cassian, *Conlationes*, xii. 16 (ed. Petschenig, *CSEL* xiii. 360).

lauari uolunt, procura ut festa paschalia suo[h] candore uenustent. Laurus nostrae et totum pomerium gaudeant suo cultu. Vinitorem quoque et agricolam te esse memineris.[3] De uario numero psalmorum qui adiciuntur a quibusdam in tempore ieiunii per singulas horas canonicas in fine post oracionem dominicam et capitula quae secuntur,[4] regulam non inuenio. Ex[i] meo quidem arbitratu[k] superflui essent, nisi eos tutaret psalmistarum deuocio. Finitis enim capitulis post oracionem dominicam ubi dicitur 'Domine, exaudi oracionem meam', statim esset[l] subdenda oracio, quae ex libro sacramentario recitatur. Patere tamen[m] aecclesiam retinere suum usum ad presens. De significacione clericalis ornatus, Amalarius[5] sic: 'Breuiter desideramus recapitulare omnem ornatum clericorum. Caput clerici in superiore parte discoopertum, mens est ubi est imago Dei, in inferiore parte circumdatum capillis, quasi aliquibus cogitacionibus de presenti necessitate. Amictus est castigacio uocis. Alba, caeterorum inferiorum sensuum, presidente magistra racione et interius per disciplinam continenciae constringente quasi quodam cingulo uoluptatem carnis. Calciamenta, prohibicio pedum ad malum festinare.[n] Sandalia, ornatus ad iter praedicatoris, qui caelestia non debet abscondere, neque terrenis inhiare. Secunda tunica, opera mentis sunt. Casula, opera corporis pia. Stola, iugum Christi, quod est aeuuangelium. Dalmatica[o] diaconi (id est ministri), cura proximorum est. Sudarium, pie et mundae cogitaciones quibus detergimus molestias animi ex infirmitate corporis. Pallium archiepiscoporum, torques deuotissimae praedicacionis et in ueteri testamento et in nouo.' Hactenus Amalarius. Mitto tibi Ciprianum, Porphyrium, et Vitas patrum, cum psalterio[p] ut petisti. Moneo aetiam ut cum Donatum construxeris, nihil admisceas ineptae leuitatis ut sit causa ioci, sed omnia seria. Spectaculum enim factus es,[6] caue. Vide etiam ne tui asseculae

---

[h] suo *om.* DRK   [i] Ex] Et P   Psalmi BV   [k] arbitrio C   arbitratui B   arbitratus V   [l] esset(?) *corr. to* est L   est DRK   [m] enim LDRKC   [n] festinantium LDRKC (-tium *sup. ras.* L)   [o] Dalmacia LPV   [p] et psalterio *corr. to* -ium L   et psalterium DRK

---

[3] Cf. Isa. 61: 5. Though Fulbert's allusion is obscure, he is apparently telling Hildegar not to concentrate on some of his duties to the neglect of others.

[4] As regards such additions to divine office, see E. Bishop, *Liturgica Historica* (Oxford, 1918), pp. 211 ff.; P. Salmon, *L'Office divin au moyen âge* (Paris, 1967), pp. 101 ff., 110 ff.

church which need washing, see to it that they are white and clean so as to adorn the Easter festivities. Tend our laurel and the whole orchard as they deserve and make them flourish, and remember that you are both a vine-dresser and a farmer.[3] As regards your question concerning the different number of psalms which some add during Lent at the end of each canonical hour after the Lord's prayer and the little chapter that follows,[4] I find no rule. I should think they are superfluous unless those who say the office wish to keep them for the sake of devotion; for after the little chapter and the Lord's prayer where 'O Lord, hear my prayer' is said, the collect which is read from the sacramentary ought to follow immediately. But let the church continue its usual practice for the present. As to what is signified by the dress of the clergy, Amalarius[5] says this: 'We wish to sum up briefly all that has been said as to the dress of the clergy. The clerk's head, which is bare in its upper part, typifies the mind, wherein is God's image; in its lower part it is beset by hair as if by thoughts concerning our daily needs. The amice signifies the disciplining of the voice; the alb, that of the other inferior senses, with reason presiding as the mistress and like a cincture inwardly restraining the desires of the flesh by the teaching of continence. Stockings are a restraint to keep the feet from hastening to evil; sandals, the dress for the journey of the preacher, who should neither lose sight of heavenly things nor long for earthly. The tunicle is works of the mind; the chasuble, pious works of the body. The stole is the yoke of Christ, which is the gospel; the deacon's (that is, the servant's) dalmatic, care of one's neighbours; the maniple, pious and pure thoughts by which we cleanse the mind of troubles arising from the body's weakness; the archbishop's pallium, the intertwined collar of very devout preaching on both the Old Testament and the New.' Thus far Amalarius. I am sending you copies of Cyprian, Porphyry, and the *Lives of the Fathers* along with a psalter as you asked. I also wish to remind you when you are construing Donatus not to mix in any unseemly levity by way of amusement, but keep everything serious. Remember that you are on show,[6] and take care. Also see

[5] Of Metz, the ninth-century liturgist whose writings on liturgical practice and symbolism were very popular. The following passage in which he summarizes his exposition of the symbolism of liturgical vestments is taken from his *Liber officialis*, ii. 26 (ed. J. M. Hanssens, *Studi e Testi*, cxxxix (Rome, 1948), 253 f.).

[6] Cf. 1 Cor. 4: 9.

inedia uel nuditate laborent. Saluta mihi[q] fratres nostros in Domino, et tute uale.

Presbitero benedicenti os[r] non alligabis nisi ex precepto episcopi sui.[7] Quod oblitus fueram; prohibetur tamen Agatensi canone.[8]

89

Fulbert to Archbishop Arnulf of Tours:[1] *advising him not to resign merely because he has not received the pallium*
early–mid 1024

Venerabili Turonensium archipresuli A(rnulfo) F(ulbertus) humilis episcopus semper agere prudenter ac simpliciter.

Et nunc quidem gratia Dei sic agitis, cum licet non inconsulti fratrum tamen consilia captatis. Respondemus itaque uobis quia si pallium requisistis a Romano pontifice,[2] et ipse uobis illud sine causa legitima denegauit, propter hoc non est opus dimittere ministerium uestrum. Et[a] si uestra tarditate nondum est requisitum, cautela est expectare donec requiratur, ne uos ex inprouiso praesumpcionis arguere possit. Continentur quedam reuerenda nobis in priuilegiis Romanae ecclesiae, quae propter negligenciam nostram[b] non facile inueniuntur in armariis nostris. Valete.[c]

---

[q] Salutamus BV	[r] os *om.* LDR (Presbitero . . . canone *om.* K)
89 LDRCPBV	[a] At BV [b] uestram L [c] Vale LDRPV

---

[7] Cf. 1 Cor. 9: 9, 1 Tim. 5: 18 (citing Deut. 25: 4).

[8] Fulbert is apparently referring to Agde (506), c. 47 (*Concilia Galliae*, ed. C. Munier, *CCL* cxlviii. 212; Mansi, viii. 332; Hinschius, p. 335), which prescribed that the people were not to leave mass before the *benedictionem sacerdotis* and were to be publicly reproved by the bishop if they did. In earlier centuries the blessing at mass had been reserved to the bishop, but by Fulbert's time it had become accepted (partly because of the ambiguous term *sacerdos*) that it could also be given by just a priest. See J. Lechner, 'Der Schlußsegen des Priesters in der heiligen Messe', *Festschrift Eduard Eichmann* (Paderborn, 1940), pp. 651 ff.; J. A. Jungmann, *Missarum Sollemnia*, ii (5th edn., Vienna, 1962), 544 ff.

89. [1] Arnulf succeeded his uncle Hugh as archbishop of Tours on 25 November

to it that your disciples are not troubled by want of food or clothing. Please convey my greetings to our brothers in the Lord; and as for you yourself, farewell.

You may not bind the mouth of a priest who is giving a blessing except on the instructions of his bishop.[7] I had forgotten this, but it is prohibited by a canon of Agde.[8]

Fulbert to Archbishop Arnulf of Tours[1]   *early–mid 1024*

To the venerable archbishop of Tours, A(rnulf), from F(ulbert), a humble bishop, with his wish that he may always act wisely and without guile.

Now indeed by God's grace you are acting as I would wish, for though you are not without wise counsel yourself, you are still seeking the advice of your brothers. So in answer to your question, if you have asked the Roman pontiff[2] for the pallium and he has refused to send it to you without a lawful reason, this does not mean you need resign your archbishopric; but if you have been slow and not yet asked for it, it is common prudence to wait until you have done so, so that you cannot be accused of acting hastily and with presumption. Among the prerogatives of the Roman church there are some that we must honour which as a result of our negligence are not easily found in our book-chests. Farewell.

1023 (*Annales Vindocinenses* (*Recueil d'annales angevines et vendômoises*, ed. L. Halphen (Paris, 1903), p. 60)) and died after 20 September 1052 (*DHGE* iv. 623 f.). See Boussard, p. 176.

  [2] Probably Benedict VIII, who died 9 April 1024 (Zimmermann, no. 1276) and was succeeded by John XIX in April or May (L. Santifaller, *Zur Geschichte des ottonisch-salischen Reichskirchensystems* (2nd edn., *SB Wien*, ccxxix. 1 (1964)), p. 198). If Arnulf had requested the pallium, the delay may have been connected with Benedict's death.

90

Fulbert to Bishop Odolricus of Orleans: advising him that impotence is grounds for annulment   early–mid 1024

Venerabili coepiscopo suo O(dolrico) F(ulbertus).

De causa unde simplicitatem nostram consulere uoluistis, in vi*a* libro capitularium aera[1] xci ita scriptum inuenimus: 'Si uir et mulier coniunxerint se in matrimonio, et postea dixerit mulier de uiro*b* non posse nubere cum ea, si poterit*c* probare quod uerum sit, accipiat alium eo quod iuxta apostolum[2] non potuit illi reddere uir suus*d* debitum.'[3] De profectione autem nostra ad sanctum Hylarium, prefixum adhuc terminum non habemus. Viuite feliciter in Christo Ihesu domino nostro.

91

Fulbert to Bishop Franco of Paris: reproving him for suggesting that he enfeoff laymen with church revenues
early–mid 1024

Venerabili Parisiorum episcopo F(ranconi) F(ulbertus) humilis sacerdos.

Doleo super te, karissime, cum te a pristina uirtute apostatare uideo. Olim apud me*a* conquerebaris de tuo antecessore qui sacrilega temeritate altaria laicis in beneficium dederat,[1] nunc mihi suades ut ego similiter faciam. O caelum, O terra, quid clamem,[2] aut quo tuis meritis digno modo te obiurgare possim? Sed conpesco nunc feruentes animi mei fluctus, donec te presencialiter exquisitis increpacionum tormentis excruciem. Vale interim.

90 LDRCPBV   *a* iii LDR   au P   u V   *b* suo *add.* LDRC
c potuerit LDR   poterat V   *d* suum DR
91 LDRCPBV   *a* te LDRC

Fulbert to Bishop Odolricus of Orleans   early–mid 1024

To his venerable fellow bishop O(dolricus) from F(ulbert).

As regards the case about which you consulted our simple-minded selves, in book six of the capitularies, chapter[1] ninety-one, we find this prescribed: 'If a man and a woman unite in matrimony, and the woman later says that her husband is not able to have intercourse with her, if she can prove that it is true, she may take another husband, for according to the apostle[2] her husband was not able to give her her due.'[3] As for our journey to Saint-Hilaire, we have not yet set a date. May long life and good fortune be yours in Christ Jesus, our Lord.

Fulbert to Bishop Franco of Paris   early–mid 1024

To the venerable bishop of Paris, F(ranco), from F(ulbert), a humble bishop.

I grieve for you, my dear friend, when I see you falling away from your former virtue. Once you complained to me about your predecessor, who with sacrilegious rashness had given altars as benefices to laymen.[1] Now you advise me to do likewise. Heaven and earth, what can I say,[2] or how can I rebuke you as you deserve? But I am restraining the waves of my mind, raging as they are, until I can chastise you face to face with well-wrought torments and reproaches. Until then, farewell.

90. [1] See H. Mordek, 'Aera', *Deutsches Archiv*, xxv (1969), 216 ff.
    [2] 1 Cor. 7: 3.
    [3] Actually Benedictus Levita, ii. 91 (ed. Knust, p. 78). See p. xxiv n.
91. [1] See no. 44.
    [2] Cf. Terence, *Ad.* 789 f.

92

Fulbert to Hildegar: sending him messages for Duke William of Aquitaine, news and advice for himself, and excerpts from the fathers concerning Solomon's salvation
c. summer 1024

F(ulbertus) humilis episcopus fratri*ᵃ* H(ildegario).

Dic karissimo nobis principi G(uillelmo) perpetuam*ᵇ* fidelitatem*ᶜ* cum oracionibus ex parte nostra et totius cleri ac populi nostri propter elemosinam quam misit ad restauracionem ecclesiae nostrae; deinde uero nos predicasse publice (sicut ipse mandauit) uirtutem Dei per meritum sancti Iohannis ostensam in districtione Gausberti, cum gaudio et exultacione omnium qui audierunt;[1] monuisse quoque Bituricensem archiepiscopum per quendam monachum suum ut sese pacare*ᵈ* non negligat cum ipso domno Guillelmo et episcopis eius, priusquam sibi exinde scandalum oriatur;[2] tibi etiam misisse sibi exponendas sentencias Bacharii, Bedae, et Rabani de fine Salomonis unde fecerat questionem; sed et de prebenda quae uacat sicut et de omni bono, uoluntati eius me prebere consensum. Preterea scias me propter te magistro S(igoni)[3] ueniam indulsisse. Ceterum Tigrinus[4] submonebat ut mitterem uobis aliquem procuratorem ad colligendas fruges; sed ego totum hoc curae uestrae*ᵉ* committo, te exercitans, illum probans. Adiutorem scolarum nolo tibi mittere, qui nondum assecutus sit maturitatem aetatis et grauitatem morum. Vtere interim clientelae tuae qualicumque subsidio, donec causam communi consilio pertractemus. Vale. Cum audio te facere quod debes, letor quamuis trepidus de futuris. Vnde

---

92 LDRCPBV   KF contain only the last part of the letter and have not been used here. See pp. lxi f.   *ᵃ* fratri *om.* DR   *ᵇ* salutem uel *add.* LDRC
ᶜ felicitatem DB   *ᵈ* peccare LPV   *ᵉ* tuae curae BV

---

92. [1] The head of St. John the Baptist is said to have been discovered in the early eleventh century at the monastery of Saint-Jean d'Angély, which became a popular centre for pilgrims and was patronized by Duke William (see Adémar, iii. 56, 58 (ed. Chavanon, pp. 179 ff., 184); Richard, i. 169 ff., ii. 593 f.). According to the *Miracula sancti Leonardi*, c. vi (*AASS*, Nov. iii. 158), there were some who doubted its authenticity, and Gausbertus was apparently one such opponent whose punishment was interpreted as a vindication of the relic.
[2] Presumably a reference to the controversy concerning Bishop Jordan of Limoges, the details of which are reported only by Adémar, iii. 57 (ed. Chavanon, pp. 182 ff.). After the death of Bishop Gerald on 11 November (Adémar, iii. 50 (ed. Chavanon, p. 174)), Jordan of Laron, provost of the church

Fulbert to Hildegar   c. *summer 1024*

F(ulbert), a humble bishop, to Brother H(ildegar).

Please tell our dear prince W(illiam) on behalf of us and all our
clergy and people that he has our continual fidelity and prayers
for the alms that he sent for rebuilding our church; that we
publicly announced, as he asked, that God has shown his power
through the merits of St. John in punishing Gausbertus, and that
all who heard it rejoiced and were glad;[1] that we have warned the
archbishop of Bourges through one of his monks not to put off
making peace with Duke William and his bishops before it causes
him serious trouble;[2] that we have sent to you excerpts from
Bacharius, Bede, and Rabanus as regards his question concerning
Solomon's salvation so that you may expound them to him; and
that as to the vacant prebend or any other suitable request, I am
complying with his wishes. You may also wish to know that for
your sake I have forgiven the master S(igo).[3] Tigrinus[4] has hinted
that I should send someone to you as procurator to collect the
first-fruits; but I am entrusting this entirely to your care, thus
giving you the experience and putting him to the test. As to your
request for an assistant in the schools, I do not want to send anyone who is not of mature age and proven character. Use your
students to help you as best you can until we can discuss the
matter together. Farewell. When I hear that you are doing what
you should, I rejoice, though I am uneasy for the future. I pray

of Saint-Léonard, was chosen. He was consecrated without the consent of
Archbishop Gauzlin of Bourges, who placed Limoges under interdict and
forbade Jordan to exercise his office. Jordan later submitted and was accepted by
Gauzlin. The dates are disputed. Richard, i. 179 ff., places Gerald's death in
1022 and Jordan's election and consecration in 1023. The latest authority,
however, is not so certain, but would date them 1022/3 and 1023/4 respectively
(R. Limouzin-Lamothe, *Le diocèse de Limoges des origines à la fin du moyen âge*
(Strasbourg, 1951), p. 71). According to a twelfth-century interpolation in
Adémar, iii. 57 (ed. Chavanon, p. 183), Gauzlin's censure was promulgated at a
synod held in northern France at Pentecost and attended by seven archbishops
and their suffragans and King Robert. There is no other evidence for this
synod, and it seems unlikely that it would have been so well attended; but the
date would not be unsuitable here (2 June 1023 or 24 May 1024). Jordan's case
was still pending in the summer of 1025 (see nos. 107 f.), but was settled before
late 1025–early 1026 (see no. 114).

[3] See pp. xxxv, xxxviii.

[4] Perhaps a pseudonym. The name does not appear in the cathedral necrology.

summam bonitatem deprecans ut te dignetur regere, te quoque
moneo ut habenis*f* preceptorum eius obtemperare memineris.
Iterum dico uale. Bachario insertam inuenies sentenciam Bedae
et Rabani, quorum tamen trium sentencias hic quoque subnotare
non piguit. Bacharius*g* ait: 'Salomon ille mirabilis, qui meruit
assistrici*h* Deo*i* sapienciae⁵ copulari, in alienigenarum mulierum
incurrit amplexus; et in uinculo libidinis laqueatus, etiam
sacrilegii*k* errore se polluit quando simulacrum Camos
Moabitarum idoli*l* fabricauit.⁶ Sed quia per prophetam culpam
erroris agnouit, numquid misericordiae caelestis extorris est? At*m*
forsitan dicas: "Nusquam eum in canone lego penituisse, neque
misericordiam consecutum." Non*n* ambigo, frater, de penitencia
eius quae non inscribitur publicis legibus; et fortasse ideo acce-
ptabilior iudicatur, quia non ad faciem populi sed in secreto con-
scienciae Deo teste penituit. Veniam autem ex hoc consecutum
esse agnoscimus: quia cum solutus*o* fuisset a corpore, sepultum
illum inter regum Israhelitarum corpora scriptura commemorat.⁷
Quod tamen alibi peccatoribus regibus abnegatum esse cogno-
scimus, qui usque in finem uitae suae in propositi peruersitate
manserunt.⁸ Et ideo quia inter reges iustos meruit sepeliri, non
fuit alienus a uenia. Veniam autem ipsam sine penitencia non
potuit promereri.'⁹ Beda in opusculo super librum Regum capitulo
xxviiii premissis paucis ait: 'Vbi hoc quoque (ni*p* fallor) palam
ostenditur quod utinam non ostenderetur: quia uidelicet Salomon
de admisso*q* idolatriae scelere numquam perfecte penituit. Nam
si fructus poenitenciae dignos faceret, satageret ante omnia ut
idola quae aedificauerat de ciuitate sancta tollerentur; et non in
scandalum stultorum quae ipse cum fuisset sapiens erronea
fecerat, quasi sapienter ac recte facta relinqueret.'¹⁰ Rabanus sic
sub persona Isidori in exposicione eiusdem libri: 'Iam porro de
aliis operibus Salomonis quid dicam, quae uehementer arguit
sancta scriptura et dampnat, nihilque de poenitencia eius uel in

---

f habens L, *ante corr.* C   habens praeceptum B   habens preceptis V
g Bacharius *om.* LDRC   *h* assistrui LP   astitrici DR   astrici *corr. to*
asistrici C   astrui BV   *i* Dei DR   *k* sacrilegi LPV   sacrilego DR
l idola L   idolum C   idolo PBV   *m* Aut CP, *ante corr.* L   *n* Nam
LC   *o* consolutus LDC   *p* nisi CB   *q* commisso BV

---

⁵ Cf. Wisd. 9: 4.   ⁶ Cf. 3 Kgs. 11: 1 ff.

that God in his most high goodness may deign to guide you, and
I caution you to heed the reins of his precepts with all care. Again
I say farewell. In the quotation from Bacharius you will find what
Bede and Rabanus say, but it is no trouble to copy the statements
of all three. Bacharius says: 'Solomon, that wondrous man who
deserved to share in the wisdom that sits next to God,[5] rushed
into the embraces of foreign women; and once he was entangled
in the bond of lust, he also defiled himself by committing sacrilege
when he made an image of Chamos, the idol of the Moabites.[6]
But since he was led by the prophet to acknowledge the error of
his ways, is he banished from the mercy of heaven? Perhaps you
will say: 'Nowhere in the canon do I read that he repented or
obtained mercy.' I have no doubt, brother, as to his repentance,
though this was not recorded in the public laws; and he may have
been judged all the more acceptable because he did penance, not
in front of the people, but in the secrecy of his conscience with God
as his witness. That he obtained pardon we know from this: that
when he was released from his body, Scripture states that he was
buried among the bodies of the kings of Israel.[7] From other
passages we know that this was refused to kings who sinned and
who obstinately persevered in their wickedness to the end of their
life.[8] So since he deserved to be buried among the just kings, he
had received pardon; and he could not have obtained pardon
unless he had repented.'[9] Bede, in his commentary on the books
of Kings, chapter twenty-nine, a few lines from the beginning,
says: 'Here also, unless I am mistaken, is clearly shown what I
wish were not: namely, that Solomon never fully repented for
having committed the sin of idolatry. For if he had brought forth
fruits worthy of repentance, he would have striven above all else
to have the idols that he had made removed from the holy city;
and the abominations which despite all his wisdom he had yet
made he would not have left standing as though they had been
made wisely and rightly and thus to be a stumbling-block to the
foolish.'[10] Rabanus, quoting Isidore, says in his exposition of the
same book: 'What shall I say as to Solomon's other works, for
which holy Scripture violently charges and condemns him and

---

[7] Cf. 3 Kgs. 11: 43; 2 Para. 9: 31.
[8] Cf. 2 Para. 21: 20; 24: 25; 28: 27.
[9] Bacharius, *Liber de reparatione lapsi*, c. xii (*PL* xx. 1048).
[10] Bede, *In regum librum xxx quaestiones*, c. xxix (ed. Hurst, *CCL* cxix. 320).

eum indulgenciae Dei omnino commemorat, nec prorsus occurrit quid saltim in allegoria bene significet? Haec est[r] flenda submersio.'[11]

93

Fulbert to Archbishop Robert of Rouen:[1] *telling him of Count Galeran of Meulan's request to remarry*

mid–late 1024

Venerabili Rotomagensium archipraesuli R(otberto) F(ulbertus) humilis episcopus siqua ualet oracionum suffragia.

Procacitas G(ualeranni), cuius mihi mencionem fecistis, satis superque fatigauit me de nouis conubiis expetendis; sed ego semper obstiti dicens non licere ei sua uxore uiuente alteram usurpare. Nunc ergo tandem rogauit me seu callide siue simpliciter, ut sibi aut uxorem suam fugitiuam redderem, aut eam si reniteretur excommunicarem. Alioquin, diceret quod ego et illa pariter faceremus eum mechari.[2] Conuenta igitur de hac causa mulier respondit mihi nunquam se redituram ad illum; et quia certo nouerat mores suos cum moribus G(ualeranni) conuenire non posse, uelle se pocius[a] renunciare seculo et monacham deuenire, tantum si Gualerannus sibi uel centum libras nummorum Carnotensium ferendas ad monasterium daret. Ego uero inter haec monacham illam fieri nec prohibeo nec compello, sed nec ut ad uirum odientem peritura redeat coartare presumo. Gualerannus autem sepe mittit ad me licenciam ineundi noui conubii petens, illam se gurpisse, suamque pecuniam recepisse, licet non uere protestans. Ego uero interdico ei licenciam istam donec uxor eius aut monacha facta sit aut defuncta. Quorum utrum prius futurum sit nescio.[3] Si ergo de hac causa meum consilium uultis, quod ego facio idem uos facere suadeo,[b] hoc adiciens, ut si causam hanc acri censura pertractare uelitis, ex mea parte non contradiccionem sed suffragium uos habere sciatis.

---

[r] significet haec eius DRB

93 LDRCPBVKF   [a] melius KF   [b] suadeo facere LDR   suadeo uos facere B

makes no mention of his repentance or God's pardoning him, nor do we find anything that might be a favourable sign even allegorically? This is a lamentable ruin.'[11]

Fulbert to Archbishop Robert of Rouen[1] mid–late *1024*

To the venerable archbishop of Rouen, R(obert), from F(ulbert), a humble bishop, with the support, such as it is, of his prayers.

In his shamelessness, G(aleran), whom you mentioned to me, has wearied me time and again with asking to enter into a new marriage. I have always refused, saying that while his wife is alive he is not allowed to take another. But now he has asked me, either out of cunning or innocence, to make his wife (who has run away) return to him or, if she should refuse, to excommunicate her. Otherwise he will say that the two of us are forcing him to commit adultery.[2] When his wife was summoned to present her side of the case, she replied that she would never return to him, and that since she knows that she and G(aleran) are incompatible, she would prefer to renounce the world and become a nun provided Galeran will give her at least a hundred pounds in the coinage of Chartres to take to the convent. For my part I am neither forbidding nor compelling her to become a nun, but neither am I venturing to force her to return to a husband who hates her and so to her death. Galeran often sends to me, asking permission to enter into a new marriage and protesting that she has left him and has received her money, though it is not true. But I refuse to let him do so until his wife has either become a nun or died. Which will happen first, I do not know.[3] If you want my advice as regards this case, I recommend that you do the same thing, adding that if you wish to handle it by sharply censuring him, know that so far as I am concerned you will meet not with objections, but with

---

[11] Rabanus, *Commentaria in libros iv regum*, iii. 11 (*PL* cix. 199), taken from Isidore, *Quaestiones in vetus testamentum: in regum tertium*, vi. 1 (*PL* lxxxiii. 417).

93. [1] 989/90–16 March 1037 (E. Vacandard, 'La liste chronologique des archevêques de Rouen', *Revue catholique de Normandie*, 1904, p. 196; D. Douglas, *William the Conqueror* (London, 1964), p. 39).

[2] Cf. Matt. 5: 32.

[3] She became a nun at Notre-Dame de Coulombs (E. Houth, *BPH*, 1959, p. 157 n.).

Capitula canonum ad hanc causam pertinencia nobis subscribere non uacauit ad presens, hostium persecucione turbatis. Scribemus autem et haec et alia libenter in obsequium uestrum, si Deus concesserit nobis salutem et pacem. Valete.

94

Fulbert to King Robert: advising him not to hold a council at Orleans unless it is first reconciled by Bishop Odolricus before Christmas 1024

Excellentissimo regi et caro domino suo R(otberto) F(ulbertus) Carnotensium*a* humilis episcopus cursum honesti continuum ad beatitudinis finem.

Inter multas sollicitudines meas, cura tui, domine mi, non mediocriter afficit. Cum enim te prudenter agere accipio, letor. Sin aliter, tristor et timeo. Audito igitur inter alia quod proxima sollempnitate natalis Domini consilium*b* habiturus sis*c* cum principibus regni de pace componenda, gaudeo. Sed audito quod Aurelianis, in ciuitate uidelicet incendio uastata, sacrilegiis profanata, et insuper excommunicacione dampnata, nec post reconciliata, miror et paueo. Quanto enim dolore putas afficiendos esse sacerdotes fideles tuos, qui ad honorificenciam Dei et tuam ipso die congregandi sunt, si in eo loco fuerint ubi nec ipsis sacrificare liceat, nec tibi sacrosanctam eucharistiam absolute percipere? Absit hoc a te, karissime domine, ut tu in tanta sollempnitate aut diuinis officiis careas, aut inlicite uel indigne te sciente usurpari permittas. Quod ideo te premonere curaui, ut uel illum locum facias reconciliari, aut ubi melius sit sollempnitatem celebrare memineris. Velim autem suadere tibi si possim, ne dimittas propter iram quae iusticiam Dei non operatur,[1] quin episcopo tuo treguam des, polliceare iustitiam, insuper et conductum prebeas (si uelit) ad reconciliandas ecclesias suas.[2] Quod si detrectauerit, ipse in periculo, tu nauigabis importu.[3] Ceterum quia tuis obsequiis

---

94 LDRCPBV   *a* Carnot̄ (*add. supra*) L   Carnotensis D   *b* consilium *om.* LDR   *c* colloquium *add.* DR

---

94. [1] Cf. Jas. 1: 20.
   [2] The legal terminology here suggests that Fulbert is referring to an otherwise unknown dispute between King Robert and Bishop Odolricus, perhaps occasioned by Odolricus's laying Orleans under interdict. Robert seems to have

support. As for the appropriate chapters of canon law, we do not have time at present to set them down, as we are troubled and persecuted by enemies. But we shall gladly copy these and others in obedience to your commands if God will grant us safety and peace. Farewell.

Fulbert to King Robert   *before Christmas 1024*

To the most excellent king and his dear lord, R(obert), from F(ulbert), humble bishop of Chartres, with his wish that he may always follow the path of honour until he reaches the goal of blessedness.

Among my many cares, my lord, my concern for you is very close to my heart. When I hear that you are acting wisely, I rejoice. But when I hear otherwise, I am disturbed and frightened. Thus when I hear among other matters that you are going to hold a council next Christmas with the princes of the realm for the sake of establishing peace, I am delighted. But when I hear that it is to be at Orleans, a city ravaged by fire, desecrated by sacrilege, laid under interdict, and not reconciled thereafter, I am amazed and frightened. Do you not think that it will be a most grievous affliction to your faithful bishops who are to gather on that day to honour God and you if they are in a place where they are not allowed to celebrate mass and you are not at full liberty to receive the most holy Eucharist? Heaven forbid, my dear lord, that on such a solemn feast you should either be deprived of divine worship or knowingly permit it to be celebrated illicitly or unworthily. I have taken care to warn you of this in advance so that you may have Orleans reconciled or arrange to celebrate the feast at a more suitable place. I should also like to persuade you, if I can, not to let your anger, which does not conduce to the working of God's justice,[1] keep you from granting a delay to your bishop, promising him justice, and offering him a safe-conduct, if he wishes, so that he may reconcile his churches.[2] But if he rejects your offer, he will be sailing in dangerous waters, while you are safe in the harbour.[3] As for the rest, since you have instructed me

summoned Odolricus to appear forthwith, and Fulbert is asking him to grant a delay. See p. lxxxv.   [3] Cf. Terence, *And.* 480

me tunc adfuturum esse^d mandasti, apud sanctum Maxi-
minum[4] hospitari postulo, quod nec monachis quidem ipsius loci
fore ingratum puto, ut ibi^e natalicia nocte celebratis uigiliis,
sequenti mane in tuum seruicium possim esse paratus. Vale
semper et prosperare^f in Domino.

95

Hildegar to Fulbert: asking forgiveness for his quick temper
late 1023–mid 1025

Domino seruus, magno presuli F(ulberto) H(ildegarius) suorum
minimus quod potis erit strenuum^a fidelitatis obsequium.

Ex hoc, domine mi reuerentissime, quod te propter mores tuos
matura sanctitate suauissime redolentes erga tibi subditos eo
animo esse intelligo, ut bonos sinceri amoris gratia conplectaris,
malis pii cordis miserationem impendas, ullum^b uero odisse uelud
nocentissimam pestem horreas, magnae releuationis^c solatium
mihi comparatur ualde metuenti eo quod nimis sum ad irascendum
properus gratia tua etsi non funditus, aliquatenus tamen caruisse.
Cui enim etiam grauioribus delictis obnoxio apud tam bonae
moralitatis uirum desperanda sit uenia, considerato quod delin-
quenti potius conpateris quam odis, conpacientem uero ad
ignoscendum minime esse difficilem, ipsum quidem dummodo
correptionem^d exhibeat maioris abs te usumfructum dilectionis
habiturum? Tanta itaque ui bonitatis animatus, supplico ut cum
mihi pro meis offensis miserescas, tum etiam eis renuntiatum ire
conanti ueniamque postulanti parcens, amoris sinum amplius
relaxes. Vnde absit ut te remoretur illa cogitatio me scilicet irae
uicio perhennem fecisse dediationem quandoquidem multis astan-
tibus necnon etiam in presencia tui, cui plus omnibus cultum
reuerentiae debeo, aliquotiens irasci non omittam. Certe quanto
crebrius huiusmodi uitium manifestatur, et maiore hominum
frequentia redarguitur, tanto celerius hinc euasurum, qui uere
captiuus eius effici noluerit, auctore^e abbatis Serapionis^f collacione[1]
crediderim. Quare cum alios mihi succensere cupiam, te potis-
simum ut id sedulo agas oro. Te enim super cunctos mortales,

---

^{d} esse *om.* DR ^{e} ubi L ^{f} properare *ante corr.* L, V   sperare D
prosperate C   prospere PB
95 LDRCP ^{a} pro *add.* LDR ^{b} nullum DR ^{c} reuelationis
RCP ^{d} correctionem DR   correptionem *corr. to* correctionem P
^{e} auctoritate LDR ^{f} et *add.* LDR (*supra* L)

to be on hand to serve you, I ask to stay at the monastery of Saint-Mesmin,[4] which I do not think will be unacceptable to its monks, so that after I have celebrated the vigils of Christmas night there, I may be ready on the following morning to serve you. Farewell, now and always, and good fortune in the Lord.

Hildegar to Fulbert   *late 1023–mid 1025*

To a lord from his servant, to the mighty Bishop F(ulbert) from H(ildegar), the least of his disciples, with the most vigorous service of his fidelity.

Since I know, my most reverend lord, that you, whose virtues emit the sweetest fragrance of mature holiness, are so disposed toward your subjects that you sincerely love and cherish those who are good, that you offer the compassion of a father's heart to those who are bad, and that you recoil from hatred for anyone as from a most dangerous pestilence, I am greatly comforted and relieved, for I very much fear that since I am so prone to anger I have lost your favour, if not altogether, yet in part. But should one who is addicted to even more serious sins despair of obtaining pardon from a man of such excellence once he has reflected that you pity rather than hate the offender, that pity easily leads to forgiveness, and that provided he shows the effect of the rebuke he has received he will have the benefit of your loving him all the more? Inspired by the force of such great goodness, I beg you to take pity on me in proportion to my offences and to forgive one who is striving to renounce them and asking for pardon, opening to him more fully the bosom of your love. Heaven forbid that you should hold back because you think that I have for ever abandoned myself to the vice of anger since on several occasions when there was a large gathering and even when you were there whom I ought to honour and revere above all others, I let myself give way to anger. Indeed, on the authority of Abbot Serapion's conference[1] I should rather think that the more frequently such a vice comes to light and the more publicly it is rebuked, so much the quicker will he escape from it who is truly unwilling to be its slave. So while I welcome

---

[4] Saint-Mesmin de Micy, a short distance from Orleans.

95. [1] Cassian, *Conlationes*, v. 4 (ed. Petschenig, *CSEL* xiii. 124).

quod simplicitas adulacionis ignara fatetur, animae meae uisceribus diligendum mandaui. Sum namque diuina procurante gratia disciplinae tuae uernaculus a puero; nec ulli[g] unquam tanta[h] meae conscientiae secreta, nam aliis quaedam, tibi omnia detexi. Quaeso ergo te perfusus lacrimis faciem mentis, ne mei cura posthabita necessariam castigationis uel admonitionis elemosinam mihi subtrahas. Nam si hoc (auertat autem diuina pietas) egeris, nunquam ita merore frangar ullius incommodi, quam cum me uidero sic a te neglectum iri. Rogatus opusculum meum corrigere, uale summa spes consilii mei post Deum. Amen.

96

Duke William V of Aquitaine to Abbot Aribertus:[1] *asking for monks to reform the monastery of Charroux*

late 1023–mid 1025

Domno Ariberto sancto ac uenerabili abbati G(uillelmus) Dei gratia dux Aquitaniae prospera cuncta.

Caritatem uestram iam secundo interpellaui, ut mitteretis ad Carroficum[a] monasterium quosdam ex monachis uestris qui essent feruentes in obseruanda regula sancti Benedicti, quorum sancta conuersatio fratribus ipsius loci bonum preberet exemplum, et eorum abbatem fasce regiminis leuaret. Quoniam uero petitioni meae nondum adquieuistis, nunc quoque tertio ad hostium uestrae caritatis pulso, instar illius euuangelici petitoris amicum[2] obnixe rogantis, ut si non propter amicitiam, saltem propter improbitatem meam accommodetis mihi quotquot habeo necessarios. Obsecro igitur uos in nomine sanctae Trinitatis quae Deus unus est, ut uel decem fratres ex collegio uestri angelici ordinis[3] mihi transmittatis,

---

[g] illi LDR   [h] tanta *corr. to* tacita L   tacui DR

96 LDRCP   [a] Corroficum LDR   Corofitum C

---

96. [1] Aribertus's identity is not known. According to Adémar, iii. 58 (ed. Chavanon, p. 184), William expelled Abbot Peter of Charroux (Vienne, *arr.* Civray), who had obtained his office by simony, and made Gunbaldus of Saint-Savin abbot. Hence it has usually been presumed that Aribertus was abbot of Saint-Savin (Vienne, *arr.* Montmorillon). The suggestion of P. de Monsabert, *Chartes et documents pour servir à l'histoire de l'abbaye de Charroux* (Archives

the resentment of others against me, I especially beg you to be zealous in rebuking me. I confess with a simplicity that is free of flattery that I have enjoined my inmost soul to love you above all mortals; for by the care of God's grace I have been subject to your teaching since my childhood, nor to anyone have I ever revealed so many secrets of my conscience, for though to others I have revealed some, to you I have revealed all. With the face of my mind streaming with tears, I beg you not to neglect your care of me by withholding the alms of chastisement and admonition that I need. For if (which the mercy of heaven forbid) you should do this, no blow will ever strike me as cruelly as seeing myself so much neglected by you. In asking you to correct my little writing, I bid you farewell, you who are my highest hope for counsel after God. Amen.

Duke William V of Aquitaine to Abbot Aribertus[1]
late 1023–mid 1025

To the holy and venerable Abbot Aribertus from W(illiam), by grace of God duke of Aquitaine, with his wish that he may prosper in every respect.

I have asked you in your charity twice to send to the monastery of Charroux some of your monks who are fervent in their observance of the Rule of St. Benedict and whose holiness of life will set a good example to the monks there and lighten the burden of their abbot's office. But since you have not yet consented to my request, I am for a third time knocking at your door and, like that man in the Gospel who persevered in calling on his friend,[2] asking you in your charity, if not for the sake of friendship, yet at least because of my persistence, to give me what I need. So I beg you in the name of the Holy Trinity which is one God to send me at least ten brothers who follow the angelic life[3] in your community,

---

hist. du Poitou, xxxix (1910)), pp. 90 f., that the addressee might actually have been Abbot Albert of Marmoutier (see p. 111 n.), and that consequently the letter should be attributed to William VI or VII, must be rejected if only because it is included in Hildegar's correspondence.

   [2] Luke 11: 5 ff.

   [3] On the notion of monastic life as *vita angelica* see J. Leclercq, *La vie parfaite* (Turnhout, 1948), pp. 19 ff. For similar terms see nos. 64, 98.

memores tandem illius apostolici dicti: 'Alter alterius honera portate, et sic adimplebitis legem Christi.'[4] Valete cum omnibus uestris.

97

Fulbert to King Robert: sending messages from William of Bellême and Count Odo of Chartres mid *1024–early 1025*

Dilectissimo domino suo regi R(otberto) F(ulbertus) humilis episcopus omnia decencia regem.

Dignum est scire te negocia regni tui. Nouerit ergo prudencia tua quod Guillelmus de Bellissimo,[1] ultus perfidiam filii sui, coniecit eum in carcerem, unde non egredietur (ut ait) sine consilio nostro. Mandat autem se esse paratum ad facienda que mandasti[a] per Hildradum monachum. Ceterum ut a tuae sanctitatis presencia me rediisse cognouit Comes Odo, qui tunc Turonis agebat, mandauit ut post duos dies Blesis sibi[b] occurrerem, ad audiendum quid dicerent legati Romanorum.[2] Sed quoniam id mea parum intererat, ualitudine quoque prohibente, non parui. Mandat autem et obnixe precatur maiestatem tuam ipse comes ne te properanter ingeras in suum nocumentum, sed mittas ad eum Milonem de Caprosis[3] qui tibi referat uerba Romanorum, et Guillelmi ducis Aquitanorum, et sua. Vale.

98

Fulbert to Abbot Odilo of Cluny: telling of the injuries inflicted on him by Geoffrey, vicomte of Châteaudun

c. *early 1025*

F(ulbertus) indignus episcopus ineffabiliter caro patri et domino suo O(diloni) cum cherubin et seraphin odas loqui.[1]

Quantas animo concipere possum tibi gratias[a] habeo, sancte pater, qui meo arbitratu tediosam et uix tolerabilem importunitatem

---

97 LDRKCPBV   [a] mandastis LRKC   mandatis D   [b] sibi *om.*
LDRK

98 LDRKCPBV   [a] grates LDRKC

[4] Gal. 6: 2.

and thus at last to be mindful of the apostolic precept: 'Bear ye
one another's burdens, and so you shall fulfil the law of Christ.'[4]
My best wishes to you and all yours.

Fulbert to King Robert   *mid 1024–early 1025*

To his very dear lord, King R(obert), from F(ulbert), a humble
bishop, with his wish for whatever is proper to a king.

Since you ought to be aware of what is happening in your
kingdom, may you in your wisdom know that William of Bellême[1]
took vengeance on his son's treachery by throwing him into
prison, from which he will not release him (so he says) unless we
advise it. He sends word, however, that he is prepared to carry
out the instructions you sent by the monk Hildradus. As for other
matters, when Count Odo (who was then at Tours) learned that
I had returned from your holiness's presence, he sent word for
me to meet him at Blois to hear what the envoys of the Romans
had to say.[2] But since that was of little importance to me, and
since I was also held back by ill health, I did not go. Count Odo
asks, however, and vigorously entreats your majesty not to rush
forth to injure him, but to send Miles of Chevreuse[3] to him so
that he can report to you what is said by the Romans, Duke
William of Aquitaine, and Count Odo himself. Farewell.

Fulbert to Abbot Odilo of Cluny   *c. early 1025*

F(ulbert), an unworthy bishop, to his inexpressibly dear father
and lord, O(dilo), with his wish that he may sing praises with the
cherubim and seraphim.[1]

I thank you, holy father, from the very depths of my heart,
for you regard my persistent demands, which to my thinking are

97. [1] William was lord of Bellême *c.* 1005–*c.* 1028 (G. H. White, 'The First
House of Bellême', *Transactions of the Royal Historical Society*, Fourth Series,
xxii (1940), 76 ff.; see above, p. 25 n. 3). The incident mentioned here is
otherwise unknown.   [2] See pp. lxxxv–lxxxvii.
    [3] Miles is otherwise unknown except for his signature on a charter in 1031
(Newman, no. 88).

98. [1] See p. 175 n. 3.

meam quasi pro deliciis habes, seruoque se et sua tibi debenti omnia uersa uice dominus obsequia paras. Vere uiuit hic et fulgorat illa fortis ac speciosa caritas, quae iuxta apostolum paciens est, benigna est, et cuius uigor numquam excidit.[2] Hac denique presencialiter fruendi desiderio maceror, sed graui ad presens difficultate detineor. Malefactor enim ille Gausfridus[3] quem pro multis facinoribus excommunicaueram, incerto utrum desperatus an uersus in amenciam, collecta multitudine militum quo ducendi essent ignorancium, uillas nostras inprouiso incendio concremauit, nobisque quantas potest machinatur insidias. Super his itaque, ne tantae causae indiscussae uel inultae remaneant, necessario michi conueniendus est primitus Odo comes; qui[b] si dissimu-lauerit, restabit regis et Richardi[4] rogare patrocinia. Quod si isti quoque opitulari neglexerint, quid melius mihi restet non uideo, quam haec missa facere,[5] et Christo secrecius deseruire. Vale.

99

Fulbert to King Robert and Queen Constance: informing them of the injuries inflicted on him by Geoffrey, vicomte of Châteaudun[1]　　　　　　　　　　　　　　c. early 1025

Dilectissimo domino suo R(otberto) regi ac reginae C(onstantiae) utinam in Domino constantissime F(ulbertus) humilis Carnoten-sium episcopus fidelitatis obsequium et oracionum suffragia quan-tum scit ac potest.

Cognita per nuncium uestrum alacritate uestra gaudio magno[a] repleti sumus Deo gratias agentes. Vobis enim incolumibus, nos bene ualituros per Dei gratiam et uestram speramus. Quoniam autem placuit bonitati uestrae consulere nos super habitu nostro, scribimus uobis multis nos ad presens incommodis urgeri quae nobis infert Gausfridus uicecomes de castro Dunensi. Refecit

---

[b] quod PB

99 LDRCP　　　　　[a] magno *om.* DR

[2] Cf. 1 Cor. 13: 4, 8.
[3] Probably the vicomte of Châteaudun of nos. 99 ff. Hugh, who was later archbishop of Tours, is attested as vicomte of Châteaudun between 997 and 1003; and Boussard, p. 175, has suggested that he resigned as vicomte in favour of either his brother-in-law Guérin of Domfront or ('L'origine des familles seigneuriales dans la région de la Loire moyenne', *Cahiers de civilisation médiévale*, v (1962), 312 n.) his brother Geoffrey. The reference to Geoffrey in

tiresome and almost impossible to bear, as though they were a delight, and reversing our positions, you who are the master obey the servant who owes you himself and his all. Here there truly lives and shines forth that vigorous and splendid charity which according to the apostle is long-suffering and kind and whose strength never falleth away.[2] I am tormented by the desire to enjoy this charity face to face, but I am kept from doing so at present by a serious difficulty. That evil-doer Geoffrey,[3] whom I excommunicated for his many crimes, I know not whether from desperation or madness collected a number of knights who did not know where they were being led, burned down some of our farms without warning, and is treacherously plotting to do us all the harm that he can. So that such serious injuries may not remain unheard and unavenged, I must first summon Count Odo to my aid. If he puts me off, I shall still be able to ask the king and Richard[4] for protection. But if they too should fail to help me, I do not see that I have any other choice than to abandon such ideas[5] and to serve Christ in greater seclusion. Farewell.

Fulbert to King Robert and Queen Constance[1]

c. early 1025

To his very dear lord, King R(obert), and to Queen C(onstance) (and may she ever be most constant in the Lord) from F(ulbert), humble bishop of Chartres, with the service of his fidelity and the support of his prayers so far as in him lies.

When we learned from your messenger of your strenuous pursuits, we were filled with great joy and gave thanks to God; for since you are safe and sound, we hope that through God's grace and yours we too may prosper. As it has pleased you in your goodness to ask how matters stand with us, we are writing to inform you that we are hard pressed at present by the many troubles inflicted on us by Geoffrey, vicomte of Châteaudun.

no. 65, however, suggests that the vicomte here might be Hugh's nephew. If so, it would almost certainly prevent his being identified with the Geoffrey in no. 59. See Merlet, pp. 191 ff.

    [4] Count Odo of Chartres; Duke Richard of Normandy.
    [5] Cf. Terence, *Ad.* 922, 906.

99. [1] See no. 98.

enim ante natale Domini castellum de Galardone*b* quod olim destruxistis; et ecce tercia die post Epiphaniam Domini coepit facere alterum castellum apud Isleras*c2* intra uillas sanctae Mariae. Vnde legatos nostros misimus ad filium uestrum regem H(ugonem) et O(donem) comitem incerti utrum illorum assensu tanta mala presumpserit; aliter enim haec illum aggredi uix opinabile est. Sed si illi nos in tantis aduersitatibus non adiuuerint, ad uos post Deum respicimus, ut per uos ab huiusmodi oppressione liberemur. Dolemus autem uos ita nunc in aliis partibus occupatos, ut uestro succursu de presenti respirare nequeamus. Quod si cito nobis a filio uestro subuentum non fuerit, communi nostrorum consilio diuinum officium desiturum in toto episcopatu nostro noueritis. Si comes Odo apud uos est, monete illum ut subueniat nobis propter Deum et fidelitatem uestram. Valete.

100

Fulbert to King Robert: repeating his account of the injuries inflicted on him by Geoffrey, vicomte of Châteaudun, and asking for his aid[1]   c. *early 1025*

Domino suo R(otberto) regi serenissimo F(ulbertus) humilis Carnotensium episcopus in gratia regis regum semper manere.

Gratias referimus benignitati uestrae quod nuper misistis legatum uestrum ad nos, qui et uestram nobis*a* sospitatem nuncians nos letificaret, et fortunae nostrae modum sciscitatus*b* a nobis uestrae maiestati renunciaret. Ac tunc quidem scripsimus uobis de malis quae inrogat ecclesiae nostrae G(ausfridus) uicecomes, qui nec Deum nec excellenciam uestram se reuereri satis superque indicat, cum et castellum de Galardone*c* a uobis olim dirutum restituit, de quo dicere possumus 'Ecce ab oriente panditur malum ecclesiae nostrae'; et rursus alterum edificare presumpsit apud Isleras intra uillas sanctae Mariae, de quo et reuera dici potest 'En ab occidente malum'.[2] Nunc quoque de eisdem malis necessario scribentes conquerimur apud misericordiam uestram, consilium et auxilium petentes ab ea, quoniam a filio uestro

---

b Gualardone LDR   *c* Isleris LCP   *cf. no. 100*

100 LDRCP   B breaks off shortly after the beginning and is not used here.
a nobis *om.* LDRC   *b* suscitatus LC   *c* Gualardone LDRC

Before Christmas he rebuilt the fortress of Gallardon which you had earlier destroyed, and on the third day after Epiphany he began to build another at Illiers[2] among the estates belonging to St. Mary's. We have sent messengers to your son King H(ugh) and to Count O(do) to inquire about this, as we did not know whether they had consented to his venturing upon such monstrous evils, for it is hard to believe that he would otherwise have done so. If they should not bring us aid in our great distress, we look to you after God to free us from this affliction. We are grieved that you are so involved in other regions that we cannot at present take hope in the thought that you are hastening to help us. But if some relief should not be quickly forthcoming on the part of your son, know that by our common consent divine worship will be discontinued throughout our diocese. If Count Odo is with you, enjoin him to come to our aid for the sake of God and his fidelity to you. Farewell.

Fulbert to King Robert[1]   c. *early 1025*

To his lord and most high king, R(obert), from F(ulbert), humble bishop of Chartres, with his prayer that he may always remain in the grace of the King of Kings.

We thank you for your kindness in having recently sent your messenger to gladden us with the news that you were safe and sound and to inquire how matters stood with us and to report this to your majesty. At that time we wrote to you about the injuries inflicted on our church by the vicomte G(eoffrey), who shows beyond all doubt that he has no regard for God or your excellency. For he has rebuilt the fortress of Gallardon which you earlier destroyed and of which we can say 'Behold, from the east shall evil break forth on our church'; and he has ventured to build another at Illiers among the estates belonging to St. Mary's, of which it can be said and in truth 'Lo, evil from the west'.[2] Once again we are forced to write to you about these same injuries and to lay our complaint before you in your mercy, from this very mercy begging for counsel and aid, since we have not received

---

[2] Both places are in Eure-et-Loir, *arr.* Chartres (cf. no. 100).

100. [1] See nos. 98 f.   [2] Cf. Jer. 1: 14; no. 99.

H(ugone) super hec mala nil opis uel consolacionis accepimus. Pro quibus tacti dolore cordis intrinsecus,[3] iam in tantum merorem nostrum prodidimus, ut signa nostra, iocunditatem et letitiam significare solita, ab intonando desinere et tristitiam nostram attestari quodammodo iusserimus, officiumque diuinum, hactenus in ecclesia nostra per Dei gratiam cum magna cordis et oris iubilacione celebrari solitum, depressis modo miserabiliter uocibus et pene silencio proximis fieri. Vnde pietatem uestram cum fletu[d] cordis et mentis genua flexi precamur, succurrite sanctae Dei genitricis ecclesiae cui nos fideles uestros quantum possumus licet indignos preesse uoluistis, quorum a uobis solummodo post Deum in his quae ingeruntur molestiis consolacio et respiracio funditus pendet. Cogitate ergo qualiter ab his liberemur, et ut merorem nostrum conuertatis in gaudium,[4] obsecrando comitem O(donem) et ei uestra regali auctoritate uiuaciter imperando, ut predictas diabolici instinctus machinas uero animo destrui iubeat, uel ipse destruat propter Deum et fidelitatem uestram, et sanctae Mariae honorem, et nostri adhuc sui fidelis amorem. Quod si nec per uos nec per illum irrita fuerit haec quasi perpetua nostri loci confusio, quid restat aliud nisi ut penitus interdicamus agi diuinum officium in toto episcopatu nostro, ipsi inde heu inuiti et maxima necessitate coacti aliquo exulantes, nec oculis nostris uidere diucius sanctae Dei ecclesiae conculcacionem ferentes? Quod ne[e] facere cogamur, uestram misericordiam iterum iterumque flebiliter oramus, ne et illud (quod absit) apud extraneum regem uel imperatorem fateri compellamur a uobis exules, noluisse uos uel non ualuisse sponsam Christi sanctam ecclesiam uobis regere commissam tueri.[f]

101

Fulbert to King Robert: explaining why King Hugh has not sent him aid and interceding in his behalf[1]   c. *early 1025*

Domino suo R(otberto) regi benignissimo F(ulbertus) Dei et sui gratia Carnotensium episcopus statum plenae felicitatis.

Postquam transmisimus uobis litteras per Ragenfridum clericum querimoniae nostrae de oppressione quam ecclesia **nostra**

---

[d] confletu L   conflexu C   [e] nec *ante corr.* L, P   [f] intueri P
101 LDRP

[3] Cf. Gen. 6: 6.   [4] Cf. Jas. 4: 9.
101. [1] See nos. 98 ff.

any help or consolation from your son H(ugh) in our distress. As a result of these injuries, our heart is inwardly stricken with grief,[3] and in our great sorrow we have already announced that we have ordered that the bells, which usually signify our joy and gladness, are to give some evidence of our sadness by their silence, and that divine worship, which in the past by God's grace has usually been celebrated in our church with great joy of heart and voice, is now to be performed mournfully, with low voices and almost in silence. With weeping heart and in our mind on bended knee, we beg you in your piety to come to the aid of the church of the holy Mother of God, of which you placed us in charge, your unworthy, though faithful, servants so far as in us lies. On you alone after God totally depends our consolation and recovery from the troubles with which we are afflicted. So take thought as to how we may be freed from them; and that you might change our sorrow into joy,[4] entreat Count O(do) and earnestly command him in the name of your royal authority to order in all honesty that those hell-inspired devices be destroyed or to destroy them himself for the sake of God, his fidelity to you, honour to St. Mary, and love for us who are still his faithful servants. But if this well-nigh continual disorder in our neighbourhood is not brought to an end by one of you, what remains except for us to prohibit all celebration of divine worship throughout our diocese, and then (alas) for us ourselves, forced against our will by the greatest necessity, to go somewhere into exile and no longer to have to endure seeing with our own eyes God's holy church being trampled down? So that we may not be forced to do this, we piteously beg you again and again to have mercy on us. Heaven forbid that you should compel us as exiles to confess to a foreign king or emperor that you were unwilling or unable to protect the spouse of Christ, the holy church which was entrusted to your guidance.

Fulbert to King Robert[1]   c. *early 1025*

To his lord and most kind king, R(obert), from F(ulbert), by God's grace and his bishop of Chartres, with his wish that he may prosper in every respect.

After we sent the letter by the clerk Ragenfridus in which we laid our complaint before you as regards the affliction with which

patitur, locuti sumus cum domino rege H(ugone) filio uestro sciscitantes ab eo cur nobis in tanta necessitate non succurrerit. Qui se contra nos humiliter purgans, respondit, quia procul a nobis erat, ideo facultatem sibi ueniendi in auxilium nostrum non fuisse, immo copiam uirorum qui se comitarentur non habuisse. Cuius nos purgacioni*a* minime discredentes, pro illo uestram clemenciam oramus, ne fiat aliena*b* uestro genito paternitatis uestrae gratia, si sanctae ecclesiae non prestitit*c* opem quae impossibilis erat ei prestari.*d* Ad*e* uos tandem, dilectissime domine, nostri adiutorii summa redit, cuius gratuita bonitate presulis honore fungimur, et tutela cuius*f* posse eripi a malorum iniuriis omnino confidimus. Sed ab his quae modo nobis*g* incumbunt, sine multo*h* labore uestro speramus erui, dummodo prece et obsecracione cum Odone comite obnixe agatis, quatenus idem nos ab illis expediat. Ceterum serenissimam pietatem uestram appellamus pro eodem rege filio uestro, qui satis superque desolatus incedit; neque enim in domo uestra cum securitate uel caritate licet ei manere, neque foris est ei unde uiuat cum honore regi competente.[2] Vnde uos oportet aliquid boni consilii reperire, et illi impendere, ne dum ille quasi peregrinus et profugus agit, paterni animi fama uobis depereat.

102

Bishop Isembertus of Poitiers[1] to Bishop Hubert of Angers: declining his invitation to attend the dedication of his cathedral before 16 August 1025

Sancto ac uenerabili Andegauensium episcopo H(uberto) I(sembertus)*a* humilis Pictauorum sacerdos suffragium orationis et fidelitatis obsequium.

Cum mihi constans dilectionis uestrae sit habitus, eo magis gauderem, presul optime, quo sepius uobis placitura facerem.

a purgationis P   *b* a *add.* LDR (*supra* L)   *c* prestat LDR
d prestare LDR   *e* At per DR   *f* redit . . . cuius *om.* LDR
g nobis *om.* DR   *h* inculto L

102 LDRP   *a* I(sembertus) *om.* P

our church is oppressed, we spoke with your son King H(ugh) and asked him why he had not brought us help when we very much needed it. He humbly cleared himself in our sight by replying that he was far away from us and did not have the means to come to our aid or even enough followers to accompany him. We are quite satisfied with his explanation, and in his behalf we beg you in your clemency not to deprive your son of your paternal favour because he did not offer the holy church the aid which it was not possible to offer it. So now it devolves on you, my lord, to be our help and mainstay, for it is by your freely given kindness that we exercise the office of bishop, and by your protection we are fully confident that we can be rescued from the injuries of evil-doers. From our present afflictions we believe that we can be delivered without much effort on your part if you will only be resolute in enjoining and entreating Count Odo to free us from them. As for the rest, we appeal to your highness's paternal affection on behalf of your son King Hugh, who is going about in utter wretchedness, for he cannot stay in your household in safety or with charity, and there is no other place where he can live with the honour that befits a king.[2] Hence you ought to work out some satisfactory arrangement and to offer it to him so that you may not lose your reputation for fatherly affection as a result of his living as an exile and a fugitive.

Bishop Isembertus of Poitiers[1] to Bishop Hubert of Angers before 16 August 1025

To the holy and venerable bishop of Angers, H(ubert), from I(sembertus), humble bishop of Poitiers, with the support of his prayers and the service of his fidelity.

Since you are unwavering in your affection for me, dear bishop, my joy should increase with every chance that I have to give you

---

[2] See the account in Raoul Glaber, iii. 9 (ed. Prou, pp. 81 ff.), of Hugh's early promise and of how Queen Constance forced him to leave the royal court.

102. [1] Before 1023/4–c. 1047 (*GC* ii. 1162 ff., where, however, the date of Bishop Jordan of Limoges's consecration needs to be corrected (see p. 165 n.)). The bishopric of Poitiers was virtually hereditary in his family (see M. Garaud, *Les châtelains de Poitou et l'avènement du régime féodal* (Mém. de la Soc. des Antiquaires de l'Ouest, Fourth Series, viii (1964)), pp. 65 ff.).

Nouerit ergo serenitas uestra quod libentissime uenirem ad preciosissimam dedicationis[b] templi uestri sollempnitatem,[2] nisi detineret me causa huiusmodi. Domnus noster Guillelmus comes, habito consilio cum Italis, precepit mihi et domnis meis Isloni atque Rohos coepiscopis[3] sua quaedam seria procurare, quae nullatenus sunt nobis postponenda. Hac de causa quia caritatem uestram[c] inuitatus adire nequeo, non paruus animum meum occupauit egritudinis affectus. Sed hoc consolor, quia spero me per Dei gratiam alias offitiis uestris alacriter affuturum. Valete coram Deo in sanctitate condigna.

103

Duke William V of Aquitaine to Bishop Leo of Vercelli:[1]
asking for his help in securing the Italian crown

c. mid 1025

G(uillelmus) Dei gratia dux Aquitaniae domno Leoni Vercellensium episcopo salutem.

Itali suaserunt mihi et filio meo intromittere de regno Italiae, facientes nobis sacramentum et ipsius regni et Romani imperii[a] adquirendi per rectam fidem quantum poterunt.[b2] Vnde mando uobis et precor uestram gratiam,[c] ut adiuuetis nos de hac causa sicut melius scitis et potestis. Modo pareat si uerum est quod semper mihi dixistis, uos amicum meum esse et rerum mearum curam habiturum si opus esset. Hoc scitote quia si nostris partibus faueritis, numquam uidistis tam bonos dies quam illos quibus nos in illum honorem mittetis. Nam omnia nostra procul dubio uestra erunt. Remandate mihi quam bene possum confidere in amore uestro et adiutorio. Valete.[d]

---

[b] dedicationem P	[c] uestram caritatem LDR

103 LDRP   [a] sacramentum . . . imperii] sacramento et ipsius et Romanum per id P   [b] potuerunt P   [c] praecorum uestram bonitatem P   [d] Vale LR

---

[2] The cathedral of Saint-Maurice, which was consecrated 16 August 1025 (*Cartulaire noir de la cathédrale d'Angers*, ed. C. Urseau (Documents historiques sur l'Anjou, v (1908)), pp. xxi–xxii).

[3] Islo of Saintes, before 18 January 1000–1032 or later (J. Depoin, 'Chronologie des évêques de Saintes de 268 à 1918', *BPH*, 1919, p. 48); Roho of Montaigu, bishop of Angoulême, after 28 January 1018–1031/8 (Newman, p. 172 n.). See pp. lxxxv–lxxxvii.

pleasure. So I should like your eminence to know that I would be delighted and esteem it a great privilege to attend the solemn consecration of your church[2] if I were not prevented from doing so for the following reason. Our lord, Count William, having met with the Italians, has instructed my fellow bishops Islo and Roho[3] and myself to take care of some serious matters which we cannot postpone. Since this makes it impossible for me to attend despite your kind invitation, I am quite overwhelmed with disappointment. But I take comfort in the hope that on another occasion, by God's grace, I may be on hand and eagerly serve you. Farewell, and may you possess in God's sight all the holiness that is properly yours.

Duke William V of Aquitaine to Bishop Leo of Vercelli[1]
c. *mid 1025*

W(illiam), by grace of God duke of Aquitaine, to Bishop Leo of Vercelli, with his greetings.

The Italians have persuaded my son and myself to intervene in the affairs of the kingdom of Italy and have sworn that in all good faith they will do what they can to secure for us that kingdom and the Roman Empire.[2] So I am writing and asking your grace to aid us in this matter to the utmost of your knowledge and power. Now let us see if what you have always told me is true: that you are my friend and will give me your support if I should need it. You may rest assured that if you will promote our cause, you will never have seen such good days as those in which you help us to attain that honour, for all that is ours will indeed be yours. Write and let me know to what extent I can rely on your love and aid. Farewell.

---

103. [1] 998/9–after 10 April 1026. Leo was one of the foremost supporters of the German emperors in northern Italy. See H. Bloch, 'Beiträge zur Geschichte des Bischofs Leo von Vercelli und seiner Zeit', *Neues Archiv*, xxii (1897), 13 ff.; M. Uhlirz, 'Die italienische Kirchenpolitik der Ottonen', *Mitteilungen des österreichischen Instituts für Geschichtsforschung*, xlviii (1934), 278 ff. and *passim*; J. Fleckenstein, *Die Hofkapelle der deutschen Könige*, ii (*MGH, Schriften*, xvi. 2 (Stuttgart, 1966)), pp. 90 ff. and *passim*. See above, pp. lxxxv f.
[2] Cf. nos. 104, 109. Pabst, p. 351 n., has called attention to the verbal similarity here and suggested that this pointed to Hildegar as their author or perhaps to a common documentary source.

104

*Count Fulk of Anjou to King Robert: asking him on behalf
of Duke William of Aquitaine to intervene in Lorraine*[1]
                                                    c. *mid 1025*

Domino suo regi R(otberto)[a] F(ulco) Andegauorum comes salutem et fidele seruitium.

G(uillelmus) Pictauorum comes herus meus[2] locutus est mihi
nuper, dicens quod[b] postquam Itali discesserunt a uobis diffisi
quod uos regem haberent,[c] petierunt filium suum ad regem.
Quibus ille inuitus coactusque[d] respondit, tandem adquiescere se[e]
uoluntati eorum, si consentirent illis cuncti marchiones Italiae et
episcopi ac ceteri meliores. Illi promiserunt quod recta fide face-
rent illos consentire si possent. Nunc ergo mandat uobis postulans
suppliciter gratiam uestram, ut detineatis homines de Lotharingia
et Fredericum ducem[3] atque alios quos poteritis ne concordent
cum rege Cono,[4] inflectendo eos quantum quiueritis ad auxilium
eius. Dabit uobis pro hoc negotio mille libras denariorum et c
pallia,[f] et dominae reginae Constantiae quingentas libras nummorum. Orat uos ut ipse eam salutetis et filium uestrum regem[5]
ex parte sua; et ego precor significari mihi litteris uestris[g] aut
nunciis quid animi uobis sit super hoc quod ipse uos rogat, ut
renuntiem illi. Valete.[h]

105

*Hildegar to Fulbert: explaining why he cannot visit Chartres
and sending a book to be copied*   c. *mid 1025*

Domino suo carissimo F(ulberto) presuli H(ildegarius) omnium
expetendorum summam.

Quod ante uindemias non reuiso uos, pater dilectissime, fratris
B. morbus me[a] detinet, cum oportunum fuerit (annuente Deo)

104 LDRP   [a] R(otberto) *om.* P   [b] quod *om.* DR   [c] habere P
[d] coactus L   [e] se *om.* P   [f] pallias P   [g] uestris *om.* P
[h] Vale L

105 LDRP   [a] me *om.* LDR

Count Fulk of Anjou to King Robert[1]   c. mid 1025

To his lord, King R(obert), from Count F(ulk) of Anjou, with his greetings and faithful service.

My lord, Count W(illiam) of Poitiers,[2] spoke with me recently and told me that after the Italians left you, since they had lost hope of getting you to be their king, they asked for his son. Much against his will he finally gave in and replied that he would agree to their request if this was acceptable to all the Italian marquises, bishops, and other nobles. They promised that in all good faith they would do what they could to secure their consent. So now he sends word and humbly asks your grace to keep the Lotharingians, Duke Frederick,[3] and such others as you can from coming to terms with King Conrad[4] and to persuade as many of them as possible to shift their support to him. In return he will give you a thousand pounds in pennies and a hundred cloaks, and Queen Constance five-hundred pounds in pennies. He asks you to convey his greetings to her and to your son the king;[5] and for my part I beg you to let me know by letter or messenger what you intend to do as regards his request so that I may pass it on to him. Farewell.

Hildegar to Fulbert   c. mid 1025

To his very dear lord, Bishop F(ulbert), from H(ildegar), with his wish for every blessing.

I cannot visit you before vintage-time, my dear father, as I am detained by Brother B.'s illness; but when I can, I shall (God

---

104. [1] See pp. lxxxv f.

[2] As regards the feudal relationship between William and Fulk, see no. 109; Halphen, pp. 54 ff.; Guillot, i. 39 ff.

[3] Frederick II, duke of Upper Lorraine, who was ruling along with his father since at least 1019 and who seems to have died 18 May 1026/7 (A. Hofmeister, *Mitteilungen des Instituts für österreichische Geschichtsforschung*, xxxviii (1920), 503 ff.; and following him, G. Tellenbach, 'Vom karolingischen Reichsadel zum deutschen Reichsfürstenstand', *Adel und Bauern im deutschen Staat des Mittelalters*, ed. T. Mayer (Leipzig, 1943), p. 36).

[4] The Emperor Conrad II. On the use of the names Cuno and Conrad see Bresslau, i. 348.   [5] King Hugh.

libentissime id acturum. Scripto uestro interim queso mihi innotescere quomodo uos agatis, et qualiter condiscipuli mei se gerant[b]
in scolis, et an melius solito celebrent canonicas horas. Mitto
uobis unum ex duobus libellis quos amicus uester comes G(uillelmus) rogauit transcribi. Immissum cuidam libro maiori[c] in archa
mea celabat eum obliuio, putante me illum uobis esse delatum.[d]
Si uos uel uestros in querendo laborare feci, mea culpa. Salutate,
precor, uice mea domnum meum Sigonem et Hilduinum, priorem
animum meum, alterum animae meae dimidium.[1] Ceteri uestri
omnes salui sint in Christo, summa omnium salute uos protegente.
Amen.

106

Hildegar to Ebrardus:[1] *asking about his success as school-*
master   c. *mid 1025*

Fratri E(brardo)[a] H(ildegarius) omne bonum.

Volo scribas mihi, carissime, quam bene tibi procedat scola-
sticum offitium a domino meo presule rogatu meo nuper tibi commissum, quantum eius gratiam inieris, qui te demulceant, qui
mordeant, quam incolumis tute consistis.[b] Prosperitas tua salus
mihi est, aduersitas[c] egritudo. Valeas semper in Christo.

107

Fulbert to Duke William V of Aquitaine: declining his
invitation to attend the consecration of the cathedral of
Poitiers and informing him of his efforts to settle the case of
Bishop Jordan of Limoges   c. *summer 1025*

Clarissimo duci Aquitanorum G(uillelmo) F(ulbertus) humilis
episcopus utile et honestum.

Gauderem, dilectissime princeps, ad dedicationem aecclesiae
uestrae[1] deuotus occurrere, nisi me aecclesiae nostrae nullo modo

---

  [b] generent P   [c] maiori *om.* P   [d] dimissum P
106 LDRP   [a] G. LDR   [b] consistat P   [c] et *add.* P
107 PB

willing) most gladly do so. I beg you in the meantime to write and let me know how you are doing, how my fellow students are getting along in the schools, and whether they celebrate the hours of divine office better than they used to. I am sending you one of the two little books that your friend Count W(illiam) asked to have copied. It was hidden by a larger book in my chest, and I had forgotten about it, since I thought I had sent it to you. If I put you or yours to any trouble in searching for it, forgive me. Please convey my greetings to Sigo and Hilduinus, the one is my soul, the other half my life.[1] To all the rest of yours my best wishes in Christ, and may he, the most high Saviour of all, protect you. Amen.

Hildegar to Ebrardus[1]   c. mid 1025

To Brother E(brardus) from H(ildegar), with his wish that all may be well.

Please write, my dear friend, and let me know how you are doing in your office as schoolmaster to which the bishop recently appointed you at my request, how well pleased he is with you, who are favourable to you, who attack you, and how well you are yourself. Your prosperity is my happiness; your adversity, my sorrow. Farewell in Christ, now and always.

Fulbert to Duke William V of Aquitaine   c. summer 1025

To the most illustrious duke of Aquitaine, W(illiam), from F(ulbert), a humble bishop, with his wish for what is useful and honourable.

I should be happy, my dear prince, to attend the consecration of your church[1] with due devotion if I were not detained by the

---

105. [1] Cf. Horace, *Carm.* i. 3. 8. See pp. xxxviii, 149.

106. [1] Probably the Ebrardus who witnessed Appendix C, no. 10, as *grammaticus*. He may be the Ebrardus commemorated in the necrology as deacon, subdean, and chancellor and renowned for his learning and eloquence (Merlet, p. 150) or the canon and chancellor of Chartres and later abbot of Breteuil (ibid., p. 162; cf. no. 108). *Cart. S.-Père*, i. 110, mentions a sacristan of this name who was celebrated for his learning and was consulted by King Robert on his way to the council of Orleans in 1022 (see p. lxxxv).

107. [1] The cathedral of Saint-Pierre of Poitiers, which was consecrated 17 October 1025 (see p. lxxxvii; no. 110).

negligenda necessitas detineret. Gratia namque Dei cum adiutorio
uestro criptas nostras peruoluimus, easque priusquam hiemalis*a*
inclementia ledat cooperire satagimus. Volo autem uos scire quia
littere quas priores episcopo Azolino[2] misistis regi relate sunt, qui
aetiam ualde contristatus est de sua uilitate quam ibi scriptam
inuenit, fecissetque Bituricensis episcopus[3] iuxta*b* consilium nostrum (ut ait)*c* de Lemouicensi episcopo,[4] nisi eum regalis irae
formido distineret.*d* Sed quia rex proximo rugitu (ut dicitur)[5]
uenire habet in siluam Legium, quae uicina est (ut scitis) mona-
sterio sancti Benedicti,[6] ego quoque (Deo fauente) illuc ire disposui, sciturus quales inueniam erga uos et regem et archiepiscopum uel quales reddere possim. Et quod interim effecero, aut ipse
uobis referam, aut litteris innotescam. Valete feliciter.

108

*Fulbert to Hildegar: explaining why he has delayed his
journey and sending him news and advice* c. summer 1025

Caro suo H(ildegario) F(ulbertus) humilis episcopus.

Scio te, fili, meum desiderare aduentum; sed retardant templi
restauratio, mandata regis, praedonum instantia, messiuae feriae,[1]
Lemouicensis episcopi causae pacandae difficultas,[2] uia scrupulosa.
Egre fero moras meas, satiusque michi fuisset rem sancti patris
Hilarii non suscepisse curandam, quam tali modo tractare. Sed
hac consolatione respiro, quia quod potes uice mea facis. Precor
ergo ut propositum urgeas[3] strenue tam in spiritualibus quam in
secularibus agens. Si Robertum praepositum[4] indiligenter uilicari
nosti, fer causam ad notitiam ducis nostri ut eius arbitratu uel
corrigatur uel mutetur. Saluta caros nostros R., A., Hu., Dur.[5] et

---

a hiemalis *om.* P   *b* iuxta *om.* P   *c* ait *om.* P   *d* detineret B
108 P

---

[2] Adalbero of Laon. As regards the name Azelinus, see Coolidge, p. 7 n.
Whether *sua* in the following clause refers to King Robert or to Adalbero, who
was notorious for his treachery, is not certain; and no further information concerning the present incident seems to be available.   [3] Archbishop Gauzlin.
[4] Jordan (see pp. 164 f.).   [5] i.e. the autumn mating-season
[6] Fleury-sur-Loire. For the name *Silva Legium* see P. Domet, *Histoire de la
Forêt d'Orléans* (Orleans, 1892), pp. 1 ff.
108. [1] See Du Cange, s.v. *Feriae messivae*, where this passage is cited for the
meaning *vacationes autumnales*.
[2] See pp. 164 f.   [3] Cf. Horace, *Sat.* ii. 7. 6 f.

pressing necessities of our own church; for by God's grace and
with your aid we have been hard at work on our crypts and are
trying to put roofs on them before they are damaged by the
rigour of winter. However, I want you to know that the letter you
earlier sent to Bishop Azelinus[2] was brought to the king, who was
very upset by the account of his base conduct which he found
there, and that the bishop of Bourges[3] would have followed our
advice (so he says) as regards the bishop of Limoges,[4] if he had
not been restrained by fear of arousing the king's anger. But
since at the next rutting-time (as it is called)[5] the king plans to go
to the forest of Orleans, which is (as you know) near the monastery of Saint Benedict,[6] I too have made arrangements to go there
(God willing) to see how I find the king and the archbishop
disposed toward you or what I can do to change them. What I
accomplish in the meantime I shall either tell you myself or let
you know by letter. Farewell, and good fortune.

Fulbert to Hildegar   c. *summer 1025*

To his dear H(ildegar) from F(ulbert), a humble bishop.

I know, my son, that you are eager for me to come; but I am
held back by the rebuilding of the church, the tasks imposed on
me by the king, the constant menace of robbers, the harvest days,[1]
the difficulty of settling the bishop of Limoges's case,[2] and the
rough journey. I find these delays hard to bear, and it would have
been better for me not to have taken charge of Saint-Hilaire than
to care for it like this. But I am consoled and take hope in the
thought that you are doing what you can in my place. I beg you to
stick to your task[3] and to be vigorous in handling both spiritual
and secular affairs. If you have evidence that the provost Robert[4]
is neglecting his stewardship, bring the matter to our duke's
attention so that he may be corrected or removed as he thinks
best. Give our greetings to our dear R., A., Hu., Dur.,[5] and the

---

[4] Robert is not mentioned in any of the early eleventh-century charters in
Rédet.

[5] R. is perhaps the Raino of nos. 120 ff. Dur. may be the Durand who witnessed several charters concerning Saint-Hilaire about this time (Rédet, xiv.
80, 82, 84), and Hu. the Ugo who witnessed the same charters and perhaps
several earlier ones.

alios tam clericos quam laicos.*a* Frater Tetoldus obiit; frater Ebrardus monachus euasit.[6] Scolarum ferulam et cancellarii tabulas tibi seruo, bona parans, meliora deuotans. Tu quoque pro nobis orans, feliciter uale.

109

Hildegar to Fulbert: informing him that Duke William of Aquitaine is setting out for Italy and asking whether he still intends to visit Poitiers   c. *autumn 1025*

Quem iugiter in precordiis animae suae fouet domino et patri suo F(ulberto) H(ildegarius) perpetuo uigere.

Dux noster G(uillelmus) uobis amicissimus profecturus est in Italiam die Iouis proxime uenturo sciscitari de causa filii sui si cum honore et incolumitate sua fieri queat. Itali enim elegerunt eum sibi ad regem, facientes ei sacramentum et Italiae regnum concedendi et Romanum imperium adquirendi per rectam fidem quantum possint. Hac de causa precessurus est prudens pater filium, quod*a* supra dixi cum ipsis deliberaturus. Nunc ergo prudentiae uestrae sit*b* decernere utrum ad nos illo absente ueniatis iuxta condictum. Si ueneritis, uictualia uobis Deo largiente non deerunt. Vnde quidlibet*c* uobis placuerit, litteris mihi rogo significari. Interim et semper cum omnibus uestris bene ualeatis, sanctissime pater, uitae nobis dulcedo pariter et gloria.[1] Si transieritis Bituricas, cum Odone de Dolis[2] amice loquimini. Inueni illum*d* in Romano itinere[3] prudentem uirum, et spero uobis obsequentissimum fore, siquid obsequii uultis ab eo. Est etiam comiti nostro G(uillelmo) satelles fidissimus*e* et familiarissimus. Fulco comes[4] appellatus a comite G(uillelmo) ne uobis tegnam inter uias moliatur, respondit in uera fide (sicut nobis*f* uisum est) nullam se moliturum, uelle etiam sibi premandari uestrum aduentum, ut conducat uos per sua. Prosperum iter faciat uobis Deus salutarium nostrorum.

a Tedoldus *add.* P

109 LDRP   *a* quam LDR   *b* sit *om.* P   *c* quodlibet P
d eum LDR   *e* fidelissimus LDR   *f* uobis P

[6] See nos. 65, 106.

others, both clerks and laymen. Brother Tetoldus has died; Brother Ebrardus (the monk) has gone.[6] I am keeping the schoolmaster's rod and the chancellor's place for you, with good things in store and better to follow. For your part, pray for us. Farewell, and good fortune.

Hildegar to Fulbert   c. *autumn 1025*

To his lord and father, F(ulbert), whom he always cherishes in the depths of his soul, from H(ildegar), with his wishes for his continuous prosperity.

Your very dear friend, our Duke W(illiam), is going to leave for Italy next Thursday to see if the plan for his son can be carried out honourably and safely. The Italians have chosen him to be their king and sworn that in all good faith they will do what they can to grant him the kingdom of Italy and to secure for him the Roman Empire. So the boy's father is wisely going there first to discuss this with them. Hence it is for you in your wisdom to decide whether you are going to visit us as planned even though he will not be here. If you do come, there will (God granting) be adequate provisions for you. Whatever you decide to do, please write and let me know. In the meantime and always, my best wishes to you and all yours, most holy father, who are the sweetness and glory of our life.[1] If you go through Bourges, make friends with Odo of Déols.[2] On the journey to Rome[3] I found him to be a man of wisdom, and I believe that he will be most ready to serve you if you should need his help. He is also a very faithful and close follower of Count W(illiam). When Count Fulk[4] was called on by Count W(illiam) not to give you any trouble on your journey, he replied in all good faith (or so it seems to us) that he would not do so and that in fact he wishes to be told of your coming in advance so that he himself may escort you through his land. May the God of our salvation grant you a safe journey.

109. [1] Cf. Macrobius, *Com. in Somn. Scip.* i. 1.
    [2] Indre, *arr.* Châteauroux. On Odo and the house of Déols, see J. Wollasch, 'Königtum, Adel und Klöster im Berry während des 10. Jahrhunderts', *Neue Forschungen über Cluny und die Cluniacenser*, ed. G. Tellenbach (Freiburg, 1959), pp. 48 ff.
    [3] Perhaps in connection with these same negotiations?   [4] Of Anjou.

110

Bishop Isembertus of Poitiers to Archbishop Arnulf of Tours: thanking him for accepting his invitation to attend the consecration of his cathedral, but informing him that he cannot send an escort before 16 October 1025

A(rnulfo) archipresuli I(sembertus) humilis episcopus eternam salutem.

Magnas gratias referimus uestrae caritati petitionem nostram explere sub racionabili conditione promittenti. Cui conditioni uelle nos alacriter deseruire, sed minime posse magnitudini uestrae notum facimus. Ductores enim itineris ipsi multis occupati mittere uobis non possumus, nec ab ipso comite W(illelmo) querere ualemus, quoniam abest in expeditionem profectus, ut aiunt non rediturus usque*a* xvii kalendas Nouembris cum sequenti*b* die simus dedicaturi ecclesiam nostram.[1] Nolumus ergo uestram excellentiam fatigatum iri, ne forte cum uelimus*c* presentia uestra gaudere, aliquo uestri incommodo obiter uobis illato turbemur. Quod si accideret, letitia nostrae*d* sollempnitatis in maximum uerteretur merorem.[2] Sic autem beatus Petrus et nos cum ipso uobis gratulamur, cuius obsequio interesse uolebatis, ac si interessetis. Valete*e* feliciter.

111

Duke William V of Aquitaine to Marquis Manfred of Turin and his wife:[1] informing them that it seems best to abandon the effort for the Italian crown and asking for their aid c. late 1025

M(aginfrido) marchioni clarissimo et uxori suae B(ertae) prudentissimae G(uillelmus) Dei gratia dux Aquitanorum inperpetuum uigere.

Quod ceptum est de filio meo non uidetur mihi ratum fore nec utile nec honestum. Gens enim uestra infida est, insidiae graues

---

110 LDRP *a* ad *add.* DR *b* consequenti *ante corr.* L, D
c uolumus P *d* uestrae P *e* Vale L

111 LDRCP

Bishop Isembertus of Poitiers to Archbishop Arnulf of Tours
before 16 October 1025

To Archbishop A(rnulf) from I(sembertus), a humble bishop, with eternal greetings.

Thank you very much for your kindness in promising to comply with our request and for the reasonableness of what you stipulate in return. We are writing to inform your eminence that despite our eagerness to do our part, we can in no wise do so. We have many commitments and cannot send anyone to escort you on your journey; nor can we ask Count W(illiam) to do so since he has gone on an expedition from which he is not expected to return until 16 October, and the consecration of our church is set for the next day.[1] So we do not want to put your excellency to this trouble, for fear that when we wish to have the pleasure of your presence, we might instead be distressed because you met with some harm on the way. If this should happen, our joy on that solemn occasion would be turned into the greatest sorrow.[2] Yet Saint Peter and ourselves thank you just as much for wishing to be here to serve him as if you were here to do so in person. Farewell, and good fortune.

Duke William V of Aquitaine to Marquis Manfred of Turin and his wife[1]
c. late 1025

To the most illustrious Marquis M(anfred) and his most wise wife B(ertha) from W(illiam), by grace of God duke of Aquitaine, with his wishes for their continuous prosperity.

I do not think that the plan for my son can be carried out with profit or honour; for your fellow countrymen are not to be trusted,

110. [1] The cathedral of Saint-Pierre of Poitiers (see p. lxxxvii; no. 107).
    [2] Cf. Jas. 4: 9.

111. [1] Oldericus Manfred II, before 1001–1033/5. He was married to Bertha, daughter of the Marquis Otbertus II, by 1014. See Bresslau, i. 361 ff., especially 373 ff.; C. W. Previté-Orton, *The Early History of the House of Savoy* (Cambridge, 1912), pp. 166 ff.; above, p. lxxxvi.

contra nos orientur. Si eas*a* uel cauere uel superare non possumus, regnum nobis minime proderit, fama nostra periclitabitur.*b* In nostris etiam partibus diuersi diuersa iam inceptant, nouis rebus quibus nos ad presens intentos uident et in futuro artius occupari putant*c* animati. Quae fieri nec posse*d* reprimi nobis*e* alias intentis, uos ipsi turpe et inutile decernitis. Quocirca per fidem et amiciciam quae inter nos est obsecramus uos operam*f* dare qualiter absque nostro et uestro dedecore ab incepto desistatur, cauentes ne filius meus uel quilibet alius hoc resciscat donec inuicem secreto loquamur. Quod si (Deo disponente) non dimittitur quin fiat, curate ut consensu archiepiscopi Mediolanensis et episcopi Vercellensis[2] et aliorum quorum interest effectum optineat. Valete.*g*

112

Bishop Leo of Vercelli to Duke William V of Aquitaine: exhorting him not to be discouraged by the failure of his Italian venture and alluding to an earlier agreement
c. *late 1025*

Domno G(uillelmo) duci frater Leo seruitium.

Ne tristeris, amice karissime, si Longobardi te deceperunt. Ego certe optimum tibi*a* dabo consilium si mihi credere uolueris. Esto uir fortis;[1] et de preteritis ne cures, de futuris caueas. Per tuum fidelissimum hominem mihi manda quid uelis facere, et ego optimum tibi dabo consilium. Mitte mihi mulam mirabilem et frenum preciosum*b* et tapetum mirabile pro quo te rogaui ante sex annos.[2]

---

a ṫ *add.* L   tandem *add.* DR | *b* periclitabatur L   *ante corr.* D?
c putant *om.* LDRC   *d* possem P | *e* uobis P   *f* date *add.* P
g Vale LP

112 LDRCP   *a* tibi optimum LDRC   *b* mirabile DR

---

[2] Aribertus II, archbishop of Milan 1018–45 (see H. E. J. Cowdrey, 'Archbishop Aribert II of Milan', *History*, li (1966), 1 ff.), and Leo of Vercelli, both ardent supporters of German rule.

112. [1] Cf. 1 Kgs. 18: 17; 2 Kgs. 10: 12.

[2] Cf. no. 113. It appears that William and Leo had engaged in some scheme six years earlier which they did not wish to discuss openly and of which no further details are known. It may have concerned German–Italian relations, for the Emperor Henry II had difficulty in controlling Lombardy and was

and it will give rise to dangerous plots against us. If we are unable to forestall or to overcome them, it will not be of any advantage to us to have the kingdom, and our reputation will be endangered. In our own land several persons have already been roused to embark on schemes of their own as a result of seeing our interest in this new venture at present and of thinking that we shall be more deeply involved in the future. For this to happen and for us to be unable to prevent it because we are busy elsewhere would, as you yourself see, be dishonourable and dangerous. So I beg you by our mutual faith and friendship to try to work out an honourable way for both of us to abandon this enterprise and to take care that neither my son nor anyone else learns of it until we have a chance to confer in private. But if by divine providence it is decided to go through with it, please see to it that this is done with the consent of the archbishop of Milan, the bishop of Vercelli,[2] and the others who are involved. Farewell.

Bishop Leo of Vercelli to Duke William V of Aquitaine
c. *late 1025*

To Duke W(illiam) from Brother Leo, with the offer of his service.

Do not be disheartened, my dear friend, if the Lombards have deceived you. For my part, I shall counsel you as best I can if you will trust me. Be strong and play the man.[1] As regards the past, put it out of your mind; and as for the future, be on your guard. Send one of your most trustworthy servants to let me know what you wish, and I shall counsel you as best I can. Send me the wonderful mule, the precious bridle, and the marvellous hangings for which I asked you six years ago.[2] Amen I say to

largely dependent on the loyalty of the churchmen and some secular nobles (cf. the terms which William says in no. 113 the Italians tried to impose on him). The only event I can find which might bear directly on this matter is the meeting which Henry held with the leading churchmen and nobles of northern Italy at Strasbourg in the autumn of 1019 (*Die Regesten des Kaiserreiches unter Heinrich II*, ed. T. Graff (Regesta Imperii, ed. J. F. Böhmer and others, ii. 4 (2nd edn., 1971)), no. 1957[a]; H. Bloch, *Neues Archiv*, xxii (1897), 101 f.); but throughout Leo was one of Henry's most faithful supporters. According to Adémar iii. 41 (ed. Chavanon, p. 163) William went to Rome almost every year (cf. Richard, i. 196 n.), and he may have met Leo on one of his journeys there.

Amen dico tibi non perdes mercedem tuam,[3] et quicquid uolueris dabo tibi.[c] Vale.[d]

113

Duke William V of Aquitaine to Bishop Leo of Vercelli: answering his letter and explaining why he abandoned his efforts for the Italian crown[1]   c. late 1025

Domno L(eoni) Vercellensium episcopo G(uillelmus) Pictauensis amicus eius karissimus salutem et seruitium.

Minime tristor, karissime,[a] super Longobardorum decepcione; non enim deceperunt me, qui nequaquam habui fidem[b] promissis eorum. De preteritis eorum fallaciis non curo, de futuris per Dei gratiam mihi cauebo. Non parum autem miror de te, qui et multam[c] preteritorum habes memoriam, et non minorem futurorum iactaris habere prouidentiam, quod illius C(ononis) partibus consensisti, qui nec in sua terra aliquid tibi umquam[d] donauit, neque posse donare fertur nec aliquid auferre in regno Italiae. Sed quamuis in hac causa non bene tibimet consuluisse uidearis, et mihi amicos meos probanti suffragium nullum prebueris, expectabo tamen illud optimum consilium quod mihi te daturum promittis, si tibi credere uoluero. Manda ergo mihi per litteras quomodo uis ut tibi credam et que benefitia mihi proueniant per tuum consilium ex dono illius C(ononis) si regnum Italiae, quod mihi promittitur, et quod adipisci possem (Deo uolente) si multum curarem, quaerere desiero.[e] Mulam quam rogasti non possum ad presens tibi mittere, quia non habeo talem qualem ad opus tuum uellem, nec repperitur in nostris partibus mula cornuta, uel quae tres caudas habeat, uel quinque pedes, uel alia huiusmodi, ut congrue possis eam dicere mirabilem. Mittam uero tibi quam cicius potero unam optimam ex melioribus quas repperire possim in nostra patria cum freno pretioso. Ceterum tapetum possem tibi mittere nisi fuissem oblitus quantae longitudinis et latitudinis tapetum iamdudum requisisti. Rememora ergo, precor, quam longum et latum esse uelis, et mittetur tibi si inuenire potuero.[f] Sin autem, iubebo tibi fieri quale uolueris, si consuetudo fuerit

---

[c] tibi dabo LDR   [d] Vale *om.* P

113 LDRCP   [a] karissime *om.* DR   [b] fidem habuissem LDR (fidem *supra* L)   [c] multum P, *ante corr.* L   [d] numquam P   [e] desiero *om.* P   [f] potero LDRC

you, you will not lose your reward,[3] and whatever you should want of me, I shall give you. Farewell.

Duke William V of Aquitaine to Bishop Leo of Vercelli[1]
c. late 1025

To Bishop L(eo) of Vercelli from his very dear friend W(illiam) of Poitiers, with his greetings and the offer of his service.

I am by no means disheartened, my dear friend, at being deceived by the Lombards, for they did not deceive me since I had no faith in their promises. As regards their intrigues in the past, I have put them out of my mind; and for the future, I shall, by God's grace, be on my guard. I am, however, very much astonished at your having so much regard for the past and at your claiming to have as much foresight for the future in supporting C(onrad), who has never given you anything in his own land and who is said to be unable to give or to take away anything in the kingdom of Italy. But though you would seem to have been ill-advised here as concerns your own interests, and though you did not support me when I was putting my friends to the test, I shall still look forward to the excellent advice that you promise to send me if I would trust you. So write and let me know how you want me to trust you and what benefits you will advise C(onrad) to give me if I abandon my efforts to obtain the kingdom of Italy, which has been promised to me and which I might be able to secure, God willing, if I really wanted to. As to your request for a mule, I cannot send it to you at present because I do not have one that I would want you to use, and there is none to be found in our land that has horns, or three tails, or five feet, or any other feature that would warrant your calling it wonderful. But I shall send you as soon as I can the very best one that I can find in our land along with a precious bridle. As for the hangings, I could send them to you if I had not forgotten the length and width of those you asked for earlier. So I beg you to refresh my memory as to the length and width you want, and I shall send them to you if I can find them. Otherwise I shall have them made for you if

---

[3] Cf. Matt. 10: 42; Mark 9: 40.

113. [1] See no. 112.

illud texendi*g* apud nostrates. Nec pro his quero*h* mercedem illam quam polliceris, ut dones mihi quaecumque*i* uoluero, quod fieri non potest. Peto autem ut etiam si nihil tibi dedero,*k* memor sis mei in orationibus tuis, et ores pro me, 'ut inhabitem in domo Domini omnibus diebus uitae meae, ut uideam uoluntatem Domini, et protegar a templo sancto eius,'[2] et illud optimum consilium quod mihi spondes ne differas. Promissiones tuae excitant me habere in te multam fidutiam, quia meum est amico credere, et de promissis eius non diffidere, et meum est aut nunquam promittere, aut promissa adimplere. Superius sermone nostro lusimus tecum, domine L(eo) frater carissime; nunc seria uerba dicemus. Longobardos non arguo deceptionis quam in me exercere uellent. Quantum enim*l* in ipsis fuit partum erat mihi*m* regnum Italiae si unum facere uoluissem quod nefas iudicaui, scilicet ut ex uoluntate eorum episcopos qui essent Italiae deponerem, et alios rursum illorum arbitrio eleuarem. Sed absit a me rem huiusmodi facere, ut pastores aecclesiae quibus mei patres semper*n* honorem exibuerunt, et*o* quos ipse quantum ualui semper exaltaui, sine crimine inhonorem. Sub hac conditione uellent quidam primorum Italiae me seu filium meum regem facere. Non laudauit mihi hanc uituperabilem conditionem prudens marchio Maginfridus, nec frater eius Alricus bonus episcopus,[3] quorum me sanissimo plerumque uti consilio nunquam penitui.*p* Quos supra omnes Italos prestantioris ingenii, fidei, bonitatis esse censeo. Siquid rerum mearum tibi pro certo placuerit quod mittere possim aut debeam, non te frustrabitur spes tua. Aequam mihi, queso, repende uicem, ut et ipse uotis meis imparem te non effitias. In proxime uentura festiuitate sanctae Dei genitricis Mariae litteras tuas opto uidere, quibus animi tui secreta mihi*q* amico tuo fidissimo pandantur. In Christo uiuas, ualeas, uiuendo, ualendo.

g texi LDRC *h* a te *add.* LDRC *i* quodcumque LDRC
k dedero tibi LDR *l* enim *om.* LDRC *m* mihi erat LDRC *n* super L
o et *om.* P *p* penituit LDRC *q* mihi *om.* LDRC

[2] Ps. 26: 4 (Roman Psalter).
[3] Manfred of Turin (see no. 111); Alricus of Asti, 1007/8–1035 (Bresslau, i. 373).

there is anyone here who can make them. In return I am not asking for the reward that you promise, namely that you would give me whatever I might want; for you cannot do so. But I am asking you, even if I should not send you anything, to remember me in your prayers and to pray for me 'that I may dwell in the house of the Lord all the days of my life and that I may see the goodwill of the Lord and be protected by his holy temple,'[2] and not to postpone sending the excellent advice that you promise me. Your promises move me to have great confidence in you, for I am accustomed to believe my friends and not to distrust their promises and either to make no promises myself or to carry out what I do promise.

In the preceding part of our letter, we have been jesting with you, my dear friend Bishop L(eo); now we shall speak in all earnest. I am not accusing the Lombards of trying to deceive me; for so far as they were concerned, the kingdom of Italy was mine if I had only been willing to do what I judged monstrously wrong: namely to depose the bishops in Italy whom they wanted me to and to raise to the episcopate those whom they chose. But heaven forbid that I should do anything that would unjustly dishonour the shepherds of the church whom my ancestors have always honoured and whom I myself have done all that I could to exalt. This was the condition on which some of the Italian nobles would make my son or myself king. This infamous stipulation was not commended to me by the wise Marquis Manfred nor his brother, the worthy Bishop Alricus,[3] whose very sound advice I have usually followed and never regretted it. In innate goodness, trustworthiness, and virtue, they are, I think, the very best of the Italians. If I have anything that you would like and that I can or ought to send you, your hope will not be in vain. I beg you to repay me like for like, for thus you yourself will be doing all that I might pray for. On the next feast of God's holy mother Mary I hope to see a letter from you in which you disclose the secrets of your mind to me, your very faithful friend. Long life and good health to you, living and flourishing in Christ.

114

Hildegar to Fulbert: expressing his regret that he cannot visit Poitiers and sending various greetings

late 1025–early 1026

Domino suo F(ulberto) H(ildegarius) fidelis eius ad uotum omnia bene contingere.

Priorem tuae penitentiae causam super honore beati Hylarii suscepto iustam esse noui, pater, sequentem gratiae tuae potius quam iusto reputans. Cum sim tuorum minimus neque necessarii nomine dignus,[1] illud dumtaxat conpetenter dixerim, quod tua*ᵃ* presentia carere multum mihi sit incommodum, ut puta rudi cotidie tuis eruditionibus egenti, necnon ab obsequio almae Dei parentis iam diu uacanti. Ferre tamen hoc et tuas licet graues ad nos ueniendi protelaciones quia sic iubes utcumque satagerem, dum certus essem ecclesiam sancti Hylarii a te in proximo frequentandam*ᵇ* aliquatenus exaltari. Tanti esse mihi exinde prouentura tibi coram Deo et hominibus gratia, cuius spe uehementer captus mirum in modum clientelae tuae tandiu me absentari et a supradictae dominae seruitio quasi emancipari*ᶜ* pertulerim. Tanti esset mihi preterea quandam famae tuae minorationem abigi, quam ingruentem*ᵈ* uideo, nisi quid*ᵉ* tu ipse loco suscepto profueris. Sed cum te plus biennio detinuerit hinc sollicitudo pastoralis, hinc principum discordia, nescio quando nisi illis obeuntibus conponenda, orturis*ᶠ* forsitan aliis pluribus causis te itidem remoraturis, uix ausim sperare te uel semel Pictauorum fines reuisere, et prout geris animo illi egregio confessori Christi deseruire. Sperabo tamen etiam adhuc sicut promittis, uice tua quod potero seruiens interim, letum rei exitum mihi tibique annuere Deum assiduis uocibus et hanelis precibus orans. Dic, queso, pater, quis unquam tyro sine duce militauit? Quis alto mari sine remige credere se uoluit? G(uillelmus) comes amicus tuus et canonici nostri te resalutant adhuc fideliter. Iordanis etiam Lemouicensis episcopus, cui olim suffragium prestitisti apud archiepiscopum Bituricensem, plurima te salute impertiens, rogat suppliciter ut mittas ei uitam sancti Leonardi in episcopatu suo quiescentis (ut aiunt), sicubi*ᵍ*

---

114 LDRP   *ᵃ* tui LDR   *ᵇ* certus . . . frequentandam *om.* P   *ᶜ* mancipari LDR   *ᵈ* incongruentem LDR   *ᵉ* quod DP   quidem R   *ᶠ* orituris DR   *ᵍ* sicubi] sic *corr. to* si L   si DR

Hildegar to Fulbert   *late 1025–early 1026*

To his lord, F(ulbert), from H(ildegar), his faithful servant, with his wish that all may turn out well as he has prayed.

I know that the first reason why you regret having taken charge of Saint-Hilaire is just, father, but I think that the next is due more to your good will than is right. Though I am the least of your servants and not worthy to be called your friend,[1] yet I can truly say that I find your absence very troublesome; for I am inexperienced and need your instructions daily, and I have not been there to serve God's loving mother for a long time. But since you ask me to bear with this and with the disappointment of your oft-postponed visits, I would try as best I can to do so if I were certain that you were soon going to visit Saint-Hilaire and bring it some relief. The favour that you would thus find in the eyes of God and men would mean so much to me that once the wonderful hope that you might come had taken forceful hold of me, I might endure my long absence from your protection and, as it were, release from serving our Lady. It would also mean much to me to defend your reputation against the disparagement that I see attacking it unless you yourself do something for the church you have received. But since you have been detained for more than two years by your pastoral duties and by the struggle among the princes (and I know not when it will be settled as long as they are alive), and since many other matters may also arise to delay you, I hardly dare to hope that you will even once return to Poitiers and serve Christ's illustrious confessor as you have in mind. But I shall still hope that you will do as you promise. Meanwhile I am doing what I can to serve in your place and constantly praying and begging God to grant that this may turn out well for both of us. Please tell me, father, what recruit ever fought without a captain, or who was ever willing to venture on the high seas without a coxswain? Your friend Count W(illiam) and our canons still send you their faithful greetings. Bishop Jordan of Limoges, whom you earlier supported in his struggle with the archbishop of Bourges, also sends you his best wishes and humbly asks you to send him a life of St. Leonard (who is said to be

114. [1] Cf. 1 Cor. 15: 9.

repperire poteris.[2] Pulchre dicas hoc tibi feneratum esse.[3] Ex mea
quoque parte non uos peniteat (te dico dominum meum karissi-
mum, tuumque[h] Sigonem probis moribus et artibus[i] magnum)
centenas millenas excipere salutes. Ne te scripti mei tedeat,
ineptiarum quaedam legatis[k] dicere iussi quae audire poteris cum
uolueris. Vale, karissime pater.[l]

115

*Hildegar to Fulbert: informing him of the reaction to his
stand as regards King Henry's election*[1]   c. *spring 1026*

Dilectissimo domino suo F(ulberto) episcopo H(ildegarius) eius
fidelis iuxta Domini preceptum serpentinam prudentiam colum-
bina simplicitate preditam.[2]

Quod tuo, beatissime pater, aliorumque multorum relatu per-
ceperam, id ipsum nuper domno Beraldo Suessionis episcopo
referente cognoui, scilicet incurrisse te grauissimum reginae
odium fauentem potius marito suo de constituendo rege maiore
filio, quem dicunt simulatorem esse, segnem, mollem, in negli-
gendo iure patrissaturum, fratri suo iuniori attribuentes his con-
traria. Te quoque plurimi coepiscoporum mordent clanculum,[3]
uel ab eis uel[a] a ceteris quasi quintum malleum a quatuor Pita-
goricis pro hac causa dissonantem.[4] Vnde quantum ex uerbis
supradicti presulis aduerti sententiam coepiscoporum tuorum
Francigenarum super hoc agendum negotium intimare tibi non
me piguit, ut si forte sanior est, ei ne refrageris,[b] et a periculo tibi
caueas. Est autem haec eorum ad componendam utrinque[c] litem
sententia: patre uiuente nullum regem sibi[d] creari; quod si acrius
institerint in uita patris hoc fieri, quem meliorem senserit[e] ad
regem debere sublimari. Videas, pater prudentissime, ne sis plus

---

[h] tuum quoque P   [i] actibus DR   [k] legatos P   [l] Vale . . . pater]
Valete P

115 LDRC   [a] ab . . . uel] ab eis L   ut ab eis C   [b] refrangeris L
[c] utrique *ante corr.* L   utrumque C   [d] sibi regem C   [e] censeat C

---

[2] Jordan had been provost of the church of Saint-Léonard (see pp. 164 f.).
The cult of St. Leonard first began to spread outside Limoges about this time,
and Jordan may be responsible for the writing of the oldest extant life (see
A. Poncelet, *AASS*, Nov. iii. 139 ff.).

[3] Cf. Terence, *Phorm.* 493.

buried in his diocese) if you can find one somewhere.[2] You can truly say that your help has been repaid with interest.[3] For my part, I hope it will not displease the two of you (I mean you, my very dear lord, and your friend Sigo, who is powerful in holiness and learning) to accept a hundred thousand greetings each. So that you may not tire of my scribbling, I have instructed the messengers to tell you some trivial matters which you can hear at leisure. Farewell, dearest father.

Hildegar to Fulbert[1]   c. *spring 1026*

To his very dear lord, Bishop F(ulbert), from H(ildegar), his faithful servant, with his prayer that he may follow the Lord's counsel in combining the wisdom of the serpent with the simplicity of the dove.[2]

What I had heard from you, most holy father, and from many others, I also recently learned from Bishop Beroldus of Soissons: namely that you have incurred the queen's bitterest hatred by opposing her and supporting her husband in making the elder son king. They say he is a hypocrite, lazy, weak, and ready to take after his father in having no regard for what is lawful, and attribute the opposite qualities to his younger brother. You are also being secretly attacked[3] by many of your fellow bishops who say that by differing from them and the others in this matter you are causing discord like a fifth hammer striking with Pythagoras' four.[4] Having learned this from Bishop Beroldus, I think I ought to tell you how your fellow bishops in France have decided to handle it so that if it should be the wiser part, you would not oppose it and thus avoid exposing yourself to danger. This is how they think the controversy between them should be settled: while the father is alive, they themselves would have no one made king over them; but if they should press on in demanding that it be done during the father's lifetime, the one who he feels is better qualified should be raised to the throne. See to it, father, that in

115. [1] See pp. lxxxviii f.
    [2] See Matt. 10: 16.   [3] Cf. Terence, *Eun.* 411.
    [4] Cf. Boethius, *De musica*, i. 10 (*PL* lxiii. 1178). The four Pythagorean hammers produced intervals of the fourth, fifth, and octave, and the interval produced by any other note was considered dissonant.

aequo iustus, nec a sanctis consacerdotibus tuis perperam dissideas.*f*

> Insani nomen sanus feret, aequus iniqui,
> ultra quam satis est uirtutem si petat ipsam.[5]

> Inuidiam nimio cultu uitare memento;
> quae si non ledit, tamen hanc sufferre molestum est.[6]

Adsit tibi in omnibus magni consilii angelus,[7] mihi quoque tribuat uidere faciem tuam desiderantissimam.*g* Siquid forte insolenti*h* susurro tecum ago, facilem, queso, apud te ueniae locum obtineam, cum magis ex prompta fidelitate quam improba temeritate peccauerim. Vale.

116

Duke William V of Aquitaine to Fulbert: inviting him to Poitiers and informing him of his position as regards King Henry's election   *19–29 May 1026*

Domino F(ulberto) uenerabili Carnotensium episcopo G(uillelmus) Dei gratia dux Aquitaniae salutem et caras amicicias.

Cum primum ad nos Pictauim, presul optime, uenire dignatus es, et nostrae petitioni ut curam loci sancti Hylarii gereres adquiescere, gaudium magnum fuit nobis. Sed huic gaudio multa*a* intercedit*b* egritudo[1] quod ad nos redire*c* dissimulas. Vnde tuam precamur gratiam, noli dimittere quin uenias, si fieri potest in octauis Pentecosten, sin autem, uel octo diebus ante natiuitatem sancti Iohannis Baptistae.[2] Tutum iter paciscimur*d* tibi ambulanti cum clericis et domesticis tuis. Apud nos satis militum habebis. Si non manseris nobiscum plus quam triduo, in ipsius temporis articulo plurimum nos recreabis. O si uenisses in proxime preteritis rogacionibus, quantam nobis et episcopis nostris et obtimatibus consolacionem et letitiam fecisses, tempestiue si uelles Carnotum ad diem festum Pentecosten reuersurus, uel si te subducere uelles

---

f dissileas C   *g* desideratissimam *post corr.* L, DR   *h* Sed quid forte insoliti C

116 LDRP   *a* multa *om.* P   *b* intercidit DR   *c* uenire P
d pasciscimur LDR   paciscismur P

[5] Horace, *Ep.* i. 6. 15 f.   [6] *Disticha Catonis*, ii. 13.
[7] Cf. no. 132.

your great wisdom you are not being more just than is reasonable and that you are not making a mistake in disagreeing with your fellow bishops.

> Call the wise man mad, the just unjust,
> If even for virtue's self he strives unduly.[5]

> Hatred avoid with all possible care;
> It may do no harm, but 'tis painful to bear.[6]

May the Angel of Great Counsel[7] be always with you, and may he grant that I may see your face as is my heart's desire. If I seem in any way impertinent in running to you with these tales, I beg that I may easily obtain your forgiveness, since I shall have sinned because of my eagerness to be faithful rather than from impudent rashness. Farewell.

Duke William V of Aquitaine to Fulbert 19–29 May 1026

To F(ulbert), venerable bishop of Chartres, from W(illiam), by grace of God duke of Aquitaine, with his greetings and loving friendship.

When you first deigned to visit us at Poitiers, dear bishop, and to comply with our request to take charge of Saint-Hilaire, we were filled with great joy, but our joy is giving way to great disappointment[1] at your failure to return. So we beg your grace not to abandon your plan to come here, if possible during the octave of Pentecost, but if not, at least for the week before the Nativity of St. John the Baptist.[2] We shall see to it that the road is safe for you to travel with your clerks and servants. While you are with us, you will have sufficient protection. Even if you stay with us only three days, in that brief time you will greatly refresh us. If you had only come for the last Rogation days, how much comfort and joy you would have brought us and our bishops and nobles! You could have returned to Chartres in good time for Pentecost if you so wished, or you would have had an honourable

---

116. [1] Cf. Terence, *And.* 961.

[2] i.e. 17 June, the Nativity of St. John (apparently a great feast-day for Duke William (see p. 164 n. 1)) being 24 June. Pentecost in 1026 fell on 29 May.

ne ires ad curiam domini regis, satis honestam causam habiturus.[3]
Quam inpresenti adire dimitto, minores inimicicias me susce-
pturum putans ob meam absentiam, quam si essem cum domno
rege uel regina non consensurus in ordinando rege absque[e] meo
fratre Odone comite.[4] Quem enim ipse regem fieri uoluerit,[f] ipsum
et me uelle pro certo noueritis.[g] De eius cum domino[h] rege con-
cordia quicquid audieris, et ubi sit si nosti, peto rescribe, et si
noui regis erit sacracio aut non, et cuius. Vale.

117

*Hildegar to Fulbert: advising him as regards the treasurer-
ship of Saint-Hilaire and setting a date for his visit to
Chartres*   *19–29 May(?) 1026*

Domino suo F(ulberto) episcopo H(ildegarius) seruulus eius
gaudium perpetuae salutis.

In litteris amici tui G(uillelmi)[a] comitis multam deprehendere
potes erga te benignitatem, familiaritatem, amititiam, sustinen-
tiam, quae non opus est mihi exponere tibi optime scienti. Vita
tua ac illius comite non amittes susceptum honorem si tenere
uolueris. Suadeo ergo ne facias uel scribas eius[b] repudium si
intelligis fore tibi utilem[c] et ecclesiae tuae restauracioni, et si est
tibi animus et facultas ad ipsum ueniendi ut rogat, et mihi uicarium subrogandi, uel socium addendi.[d] Nullatenus enim ferre
possum nisi iussione tua coactus uel absentari penitus me[e] uel[f]
abesse diutius obsequiis alme Dei genitricis et tuis, desiderans ut
ceruus ad fontes aquarum[1] tuis plenius instrui documentis, omni
auro et argento ipsa etiam uita mihi[g] carioribus. Volo interim
mandes mihi, bone pater, quid mercedis erit labori meo tantulo,
scilicet utrum iubeas ad presens non obturari[h] os bouis triturantis,[2]
an uelud Ysaac Iacob filium suum benedicens, caligantibus oculis
prophetans, inpresentique filium non uidens,[3] multa mihi bona
inposterum preuideas. Feria secunda post octabas Pentecosten

---

  [e] atque LD, *ante corr.* R?   [f] noluerit L   [g] noueris LDR
[h] domino *om.* P

117 LDRCP   [a] G.] et P   [b] eius *corr. to* ei L   ei DR   [c] utilem
corr. to utile L   utile DR   [d] uel . . . addendi *om.* P   [e] me penitus
LDRC   [f] uel *om.* LP   [g] mihi *om.* DR   [h] obturaris P

excuse if you wanted to put yourself out of reach so as to avoid going to the king's court.[3] I myself am staying away from there for the present, since I think that I shall incur less enmity by my absence than if I should not consent to the wishes of the king or the queen in making a king unless my brother Count Odo[4] does so too. You may be sure that his choice for king will also be mine. Whatever you hear as regards his reaching an agreement with the king and when it will take place, if you know, please write and tell me, and also whether a new king is to be consecrated or not, and if so, who. Farewell.

Hildegar to Fulbert   *19–29 May(?) 1026*

To his lord, Bishop F(ulbert), from H(ildegar), his humble servant, with his wishes for the joy of eternal salvation.

In your friend Count W(illiam's) letter you can perceive his great kindness, warmth, friendship, and loyalty toward you, and there is no need for me to dwell on these matters, since you are well acquainted with them. During your lifetime and his you will not lose the position you have received if you wish to keep it. So I advise you not to resign it either by word or in writing if you think it might be of some benefit to you and the rebuilding of your church, and if you intend and are able to visit him as he asks and to appoint a vicar for me or to give me a colleague. Unless you force me to, I can in no wise bear being permanently absent or away any longer from serving God's loving mother and you; and as the hart panteth after the fountains of water,[1] so I long to be more fully instructed by your teachings, which are more precious to me than all gold and silver and even life itself. Meanwhile, dear father, please write and tell me how I shall be rewarded for my meagre efforts: that is, whether you will order the mouth of the ox who is threshing to be left unbound for the present,[2] or whether like Isaac, who blessed his son Jacob and prophesied when he was blind and could not see his son at the time,[3] you foresee many good things coming to me later on. On Monday

---

[3] See pp. lxxxviii f.; no. 115.
[4] William and Odo of Chartres were cousins (Guillot, i. 39 n.).
117. [1] Cf. Ps. 41: 2.
    [2] Cf. p. 160 n. 7.   [3] Cf. Gen. 27: 1 ff.

proficiscar ad te si potero, resciturus utrum uenias ad comitem in
natale sancti Iohannis.[4]

118

*Fulbert to Hildegar: reproaching him for delaying his visit
to Chartres*[1]   *after 6 June 1026*

F(ulbertus) humilis episcopus H(ildegario) suo salutem.

Diu sustinui sperans te esse uenturum ut dixeras. Vnde iam
nimia dilacione commotus, arguo te apud te solum. Cur enim te
mendacem mihi et ingratum exibuisti, cum tibi dulce esse
debuisset paratos (siqui forent) de uenacione tua cibos seni patri
inferre, ut aliquam benedictionem merereris accipere?[2] Noli iam
morari diucius, si gaudere uis de humili gratia nostra. Vale, et
ueni aut rescribe mihi quid pro certo sperare debeam de te.

119

*Fulbert to Duke William V of Aquitaine: thanking him for
his kindness as regards Saint-Hilaire and informing him
that Hildegar wishes to stay longer at Chartres*

c. *late 1026*

Nobilissimo ac piissimo duci Aquitanorum G(uillelmo) F(ulbertus)
Dei gratia Carnotensium episcopus salutem et oracionum fidelia.

Vestram, obtime princeps, erga me beniuolenciam expertus sum
cunctis amicorum meorum beniuolenciis affectu mihi dulciorem,
effectu quoque utiliorem. Nam alii quidem amici mei uix[a] parem
aliquando meritis meis uicem rependunt. Vobis autem me licet
immerentem gratuitis beneficiis accumulare mira caritatis abun-
dancia placet. Iam fere tercio anno preterito quod sic agitis,
erubescerem munera uestra gratis suscepisse ni certus[b] essem
Dominum Ihesum Christum et sanctam Mariam genitricem eius

118 LDRKCPBV

119 LDRCPB   *a* beniuolenciis *add.* LDRC   *b* ni certus] incertus
CB

after the octave of Pentecost I shall, if possible, set out for
Chartres to learn whether you are coming to visit the count for
the Nativity of St. John.[4]

Fulbert to Hildegar[1]   after 6 June 1026

F(ulbert), a humble bishop, to his H(ildegar), with greetings.

I have waited for a long time in the hope that you would come
as you said, and I am moved by your excessive tardiness to bring
this as a charge against you with you alone as judge. Why have
you shown yourself to be untruthful and ungrateful toward me
when you should have been happy to bring your aged father a
meal which was prepared (if possible) from your hunting so that
you might deserve to receive a blessing?[2] Come at once if you
wish to enjoy our humble favour. Farewell, and come or write
and let me know for sure what to expect of you.

Fulbert to Duke William V of Aquitaine   c. late 1026

To the most noble and pious duke of Aquitaine, W(illiam), from
F(ulbert), by grace of God bishop of Chartres, with his greetings
and the faithful service of his prayers.

I have found from experience, dear prince, that your kindness
towards me surpasses that of all my friends in its tender affection
for me and in what it does to help me; for my other friends hardly
ever repay me as I deserve, but it pleases you in the wonderful
abundance of your charity to heap your freely given favours upon
my undeserving self. Now that you have been doing so for almost
three years, I would be ashamed to have accepted your gifts
without making any return unless I were certain that the Lord
Jesus Christ and his holy mother Mary, in whose service they

[4] See p. lxxxix; no. 116.
118. [1] See no. 117.
[2] Cf. Gen. 27: 1 ff., especially 25.

in cuius officio expensa sunt mercedem uobis reddituros. Preterea non defuit mihi animus uos adeundi et in uestra regione uobis obsequendi; sed multae causae difficultatis obstiterunt. Ob quod gerendum, pro certo noueritis cuncta me difficilia postpositurum, siquomodo*c* fuerit possibile. Hoc dicens, releuare cupio mirabilem affectus uestri erga me dulcedinem, in cuius litteris nuper legi quod gauderetis me superstitem esse in regionibus nostris, quasi desperantes numquam in uestris me uidere. Vnde auctori*d* tocius boni supplico, ut et uos in hac uita longum tempus superesse faciat, et me uobiscum superstitem adhuc beato Hylario uobisque deseruire concedat. Fratrem Hyldegarium uestrum et nostrum fidelem rogastis nos uobis remittere, sed deplorat quasi iam diu nostri pectoris mamillas non suxerit.[1] Quibus aliquandiu refici serenitatem uestram humiliter postulat, ut aspiracione dulciori uobis ac uestris postmodum complaceat. Valeatis feliciter cum omnibus uestris.

120

Fulbert to Duke William V of Aquitaine: offering to resign the treasurership of Saint-Hilaire   late 1026–early 1027

Piissimo duci Aquitanorum G(uillelmo) F(ulbertus) humilis episcopus fidelitatem ex corde.

Non est mirum, serenissime princeps, siquid moueris animo contra me de hoc quod sanctissimo ac sapientissimo patri nostro Hylario tibique debita seruicia non rependo. Magnam enim honorificenciam exhibuisti mihi, largosque dedisti munificenciae fructus, pro quibus nihil presentis emolumenti recepisse uideris. Sed est quod te reconfortare plurimum*a* potest, hoc uidelicet quod tuas gazas in aecclesiae beatae Mariae restauracionem expensas, non solum integras, uerum etiam multiplicatas ab ipsa recipies. Ex parte uero mea quamuis perexilis porcio mercedis estimari possit, tamen quicquid sum et possum tuum est. Si autem de malitia seculi ortae difficultates meum iter inpediunt ut te frequentare non possim, et dilaciones meas expectare tedet, fac, benignissime atque dilectissime princeps, de illa dignitate quam mihi commiseras, quicquid animae tuae beneplacitum fuerit,

---

c siquoquo modo LDR (-quo *supra* L)   *d* auctoritati L

120 LDRCP   *a* plurimum *om.* DR

were expended, would reward you themselves. I have wanted to visit you and to serve you in your land, but many difficulties have stood in the way. You may be sure than in order to do so I would put all of them to one side if it were in any way possible. In telling you this I want to revive the wondrous sweetness of your affection for me, for I recently read in a letter from you that you would be delighted if I were still alive in our own land, as though you had lost hope of ever seeing me in yours. So I pray the Author of all goodness to vouchsafe that you may have many years left in this life and to grant that I too may live and even yet serve you and St. Hilary. You ask us to send Brother Hildegar, your faithful servant and ours, back to you; but he complains that it has been a long time since he has, so to speak, fed at our breasts.[1] He humbly asks your highness for time to be thus refreshed so that by his sweeter breath he may then be pleasing to you and yours. Farewell, and good fortune to you and all yours.

Fulbert to Duke William V of Aquitaine
late 1026–early 1027

To the most pious duke of Aquitaine, W(illiam), from F(ulbert), a humble bishop, with his sincere fidelity.

It is no wonder, your highness, if you are exasperated with me for not performing the services that I owe to our most holy and wise father Hilary and to you, for you have shown me great honour and bestowed on me lavish fruits of your generosity for which you have received no immediate return. But there is one point that you should find very heartening, namely that you will get back the treasures you have laid out for rebuilding St. Mary's church not only undiminished, but even multiplied by her. As for my own contribution towards your reward, however little it might seem, yet all that I am and can do is yours. But if difficulties arising from the evils of the times keep me from travelling and from being able to visit you, and if you are tired of waiting for my oft-postponed arrival, most kind and very dear prince, do whatever you wish with the office you entrusted to me, and rest

---

119. [1] Cf. 1 Cor. 3: 1 f., and Heb. 5: 12 f., where the instruction given to the Christian neophyte is compared to the milk given to children.

certo sciens quod ea causa beniuolenciam meam erga te nunquam
sencies inminutam. Caetera quaedam quae scribere nolui, legato
nostro*b* (domno uidelicet Rainone)[1] referente cognosces. Vale.

121

*Hildegar to R(aino?),[1] dean of Saint-Hilaire: informing him
that he cannot return and asking him to convey Fulbert's
offer to resign and various greetings*

late *1026–early 1027*

Domno R(ainoni) uenerando atque amabili decano sancti Hylarii
H(ildegarius) aeternam salutem.

Multae uobis gratiae referantur ex parte Dei et domini mei
episcopi et mea, si (ut dicitis) rem sancti Hylarii bene custodistis;
hinc profecto uos eius*a* fidelem et amicum nostrum quorum uicem
exequi studueritis certissime probatis. Quia uero nobis*b* inpresenti
uos adire non licet, de quibus nos interrogastis significare cura-
uimus, ut triginta quinque libras et alias quas uobis dimisi in opus
sancti Hylarii per consilium boni ducis G(uillelmi) expendatis,
nullam mihi partem reseruantes. Non enim possum me intromittere amplius de offitio sancti Hylarii, cum etiam uia sit mihi
dominoque meo episcopo difficilis propter seculi malitiam quam
nostis, et ita sanctae Mariae seruitio tenear astrictus, ut ab hoc
sine dampno uel culpa dimoueri nequeam. Sed et ipsius Dei
genitricis eminentiam apud sanctum Hylarium siqua ex me est
huius rei deprecari posse reor offensam. Nec enim illum cuilibet
inferiorum postposuerim, sed clientelae matris Domini, quae
etiam archangelorum omnium dignitati prelata est, iure ut puta
eius alumnus quantuluscumque me reddiderim. Dicetis ergo illi
prudentissimo duci ex parte domini mei episcopi, ut tali rectori
committat locum sancti Hylarii*c* quem nec difficultas itineris nec
inperitia aecclesiastici ordinis ab eius obsequio detineat. Et hae
sunt raciones de quibus Ragenaldus uicedominus[2] ad seniorem

---

b meo C   uestro P

121 LDRP   *a* esse *add.* LDR   *b* uobis P   *c* locum . . .
Hylarii] sancti Hylarii L   sanctum Hilarium DR

---

120. [1] Raino is again mentioned in no. 122, and Fulbert's statement there
suggests that he may be the addressee of no. 121 and so dean of Saint-Hilaire.
Only a few of the documents in Rédet date from the late 1010s or 1020s, and

assured that you will never sense any lessening of my good will toward you because of it. There are some other matters I do not wish to put in writing which you will learn from our legate Raino.[1] Farewell.

Hildegar to R(aino?),[1] dean of Saint-Hilaire
late 1026–early 1027

To R(aino), dean of Saint-Hilaire, who is worthy to be revered and loved, from Hildegar, with eternal greetings.

May you receive many thanks from God, my bishop, and myself if, as you say, you are taking good care of Saint-Hilaire; for thus you are indeed very clearly proving yourself a faithful servant to him and a friend to us whose duties you are striving to carry out. Since we cannot visit you at present, we have written to tell you, in answer to your questions, that the thirty-five pounds and other money I have given you is to be used to defray the expenses of Saint-Hilaire as Duke W(illiam) thinks best and none of it is to be kept for me. I am not going to be able to resume my duties at Saint-Hilaire, since it is hard for my bishop and myself to make the journey because of the evil of this age which you know full well, and since I am so tied down by my duties at St. Mary's that I cannot leave them without incurring loss or guilt. I also think that God's own exalted mother can intercede with St. Hilary if I am in any way offending him in this, not that I would place him below anyone who is inferior to him, but since I am one of her nurslings, however lowly, I would rightly return to the patronage of the Lord's mother, whose grandeur surpasses even that of all the archangels. So on behalf of my bishop will you please tell the duke in his great wisdom to appoint someone to take charge of Saint-Hilaire who will not be prevented from serving him by a difficult journey or lack of experience in church affairs? These are the matters about which the vidame Reginald[2]

no mention is made of a dean whose name begins with 'R'; however, a subdean named Raino figures prominently in the charters concerning Saint-Hilaire from 985 to 1016 (Rédet, xiv. 54 ff.).

121. [1] See p. 216 n. 1.
   [2] Of Chartres. He died c. 1035 (Merlet, pp. 116 f., 159).

meum episcopum locutus est, et unde talem uobis finem mandamus. Nunc uestram caritatem quae mihi semper fuit prestantissima[d] rogo, dilectissime, ut omnes clericos domni nostri dulcissimi ac beatissimi patris[e] Hylarii a paruo usque ad maiorem ex meo nomine salutetis, et omnibus orationum fidelia dicatis. Ipsi etiam comiti centenas millenas salutes ex mea parte conferatis, quem pre omnibus laicis diligo, memoriam eius in orationibus meis ad Deum[f] faciens, qualescumque ei pro amore et benefitiis quae mihi exhibuit indesinenter gratias agens. Similiter autem et domnum meum Isembertum episcopum[3] salutare[g] obsecro, cuius in me benignitatis ac hilaritatis quanta fuerit gratia, nullatenus dicere me sinit probitatis eius inmensa magnitudo. Sed et filium comitis et domnam[h] comitissam,[4] necnon alios,[i] quorum beniuolentia etsi inmeritus gaudebam, eodem salutis munere cunctos impertiri ne pigeat. Ad summam uos ipsum bene ualere optans, finem orationis facio.

122

Fulbert to Duke William V of Aquitaine: resigning the treasurership of Saint-Hilaire   *May–June 1027*

Dilecto semperque diligendo domino et duci Aquitanorum G(uillelmo) F(ulbertus) Carnotensium humilis episcopus in hac uita se et sua omnia, in altera gaudia sempiterna.

Doleo, uir obtime, quod nuper in conuentu regis atque nostro loquendi tecum oportunitatem non habui, non de seculari negocio, sed de loco sancti patris nostri Hilarii, cuius rectorem me esse[a] bonitas tua uoluit; sed huius temporis malicia non permittit. Mando itaque tibi et precor absens id quod tunc presens intimare uolebam, uidelicet ut secundum beneplacitum cordis tui constituas ibi[b] alium thesaurarium et capiciarium de bonis clericis qui sunt in tua uicinia, quos uia longa et periculosa non disturbet ab officio, sicut me et meos hactenus disturbauit. Nec me putes, obsecro, ita prauum, ut propter hoc uidear tibi minus esse fidelis. Agnosco enim me perpetuum debitorem esse fidelitatis animae

---

[d] presentissima LDR   [e] nostri *add.* LDR   [f] semper *add.* LDR
[g] salutate LDR   [h] dominam *post corr.* L, DR   [i] bene *add.* P

122 LDRKPBV   [a] rectorem . . . esse] me rectorem (me *supra*) L   me esse
rectorem DRK   [b] tibi LDRK

spoke to my lord the bishop, and we are asking you to settle them in this way. Now in that pre-eminent charity which you have always shown me, I ask you, my dear friend, to convey my greetings to all the clerks of our most sweet lord and blessed father Hilary from the lowest to the highest, and to assure them all of my faithful prayers. Please present a hundred thousand greetings for me to the count himself, whom I cherish above all other laymen and whom I remember in my prayers and shall never cease to thank as best I can for the love and kindnesses he has shown me. Likewise, I beg you to give my greetings to Bishop Isembertus,[3] whose immense integrity in no wise permits my telling of the great kindness and joy with which he bestowed his favour on me. Also please present these same greetings to the count's son, the countess,[4] and all the others whose good will I enjoyed albeit undeserving. Finally, in closing my letter, my best wishes to you yourself.

Fulbert to Duke William V of Aquitaine May–June 1027

To his dear lord, who is ever to be loved, Duke W(illiam) of Aquitaine, from F(ulbert), humble bishop of Chartres, with his offer of himself and all that is his in this life and his wishes for eternal joy in the next.

I am grieved, my dear duke, that at our recent meeting with the king I did not have an opportunity to speak with you, not about secular affairs, but about the church of our father St. Hilary, of which you in your goodness wished me to have charge; but the evil of this age does not permit it. So in my absence I am writing to ask of you what I wanted to suggest when I was present, namely for you to appoint someone else whom you would like to be treasurer and sacristan there from the excellent clerks in your neighbourhood who will not be hindered in performing their duties by a long and dangerous journey as my clerks and I have been in the past. Please do not think that in doing this I am so corrupt as to be wanting in fidelity toward you, for I am well

---

[3] Of Poitiers.
[4] Agnes, daughter of Otto William of Burgundy. Which of William's four sons is meant cannot be determined.

tuae et corpori, propter benignitatem quam mihi inmerito exhibuisti. Vnde certo scias quia si tibi aut populo tuo mei ministerii necessitas inmineret, et hoc mihi mandare dignum duceres, subuenirem tibi Deo duce, si non possem aliter, uel in habitu pauperis peregrini. Precor autem bonitatem tuam ut domno Rainoni[1] releuare digneris dampnum quod pertulit in seruicio nostro. Vale nunc et semper, piissime atque benignissime;[c] ego uero nunquam obliuiscar te.

123

Fulbert to Ralph, economus *of Sainte-Croix of Orleans:*[1] *advising him as regards a priest who celebrated mass without receiving communion* late 1026–early 1027

F(ulbertus) Carnotensium humilis episcopus R(odulfo) sanctae ecclesiae Aurelianensis aechonomo.

Quod me scribere mones utilia clerico,[a] quodque de sciencia magnipendis, facis amice, facis[b] ut Christianae philosophiae cultor inuidiae purus. Ego uero etsi gnarus mei moduli non presumo grandia, tamen debiti memor, in quo parere possim exortacioni sanctae deesse non uolo. Scripsi itaque sicut monuisti[c] quid mihi uideatur agendum de presbitero illo qui missas celebrasse[d] et non communicasse compertus est in hunc modum. Videtur nanque diligenter inquirenda esse causa, qua sacrosanctam communionem subterfugerit: uidelicet utrum[e] heretica infidelitas sit, an timor ex consciencia plane mortalis criminis, an timor ex consciencia ebriositatis aut libidinis (quae quidem[f] miseri sacerdotes mortalia peccata esse aut nesciunt aut scire dissimulant, remordente tamen consciencia mala), an sit tedium ex multa celebracione missarum, an[g] timor indiscretus quo pusillanimes afficiuntur interdum pro leuibus culpis, an[h] morbus reumatizantis[i] et nauseantis stomachi, an passio cerebri mentem ledens. Si ergo infidelitas in causa inuenta fuerit, aut aliud plane mortale crimen, deponendus est auctoritate canonica usque ad legitimam satisfactionem. Si autem appetitus ebriositatis aut libidinis (quandoquidem et ipsae mortiferae sunt), ab officio remouendus est et tandiu abstinencia

[c] atque benignissime *om.* LDRK

123 LDRKFCPBV   [a] clero LDRKFC   [b] etiam *add.* LDRKFC
[c] nouisti KF   [d] caelebrare CB   [e] utrum *om.* LD; si R   [f] quidam LDRKFC   [g] sit *add.* KF   [h] aut KF   [i] reumazantis LDC

aware that I must always be faithful to your soul and body for the kindness you have shown my undeserving self. You may be sure that if you or your people should urgently need my services and should think it proper to let me know, I would come to your aid, God leading, and if no other way were possible, even in the guise of a poor pilgrim. I beg you in your goodness to repay Raino[1] for the loss he has incurred in serving us. Farewell, now and always, most pious and very kind duke. I shall indeed never forget you.

Fulbert to Ralph, economus *of Sainte-Croix of Orleans*[1]
late 1026–early 1027

F(ulbert), humble bishop of Chartres, to R(alph), *economus* of the holy church of Orleans.

In calling on me to write of matters that will help a clerk, and in having high regard for knowledge itself, you are acting as a friend and as an ungrudging admirer of Christian wisdom. Though I know my own limitations and do not venture upon great matters, yet I am conscious of my obligations and so far as I am able I wish to meet your pious request. I have set down as you asked what I think should be done as regards the priest who was found celebrating mass without receiving communion, and this is as follows. The reason why he refrained from receiving holy communion should be carefully investigated: that is, whether it was from heretical infidelity, fear because he knew that he was guilty of an obvious mortal sin, fear due to guilt of drunkenness or lust (which to be sure some wretched priests do not know are mortal sins or pretend not to know, despite the torments of a bad conscience), weariness as a result of repeatedly celebrating mass, the inordinate anxiety concerning venial sins that some-times troubles the scrupulous, an illness that upsets and nauseates the stomach, or a mental disorder that affects the understanding. If heresy or another obvious mortal sin should be found to be the cause, he should be degraded as is prescribed in the canons until he makes proper satisfaction. If an addiction to drunkenness or lust (since these too are mortal sins), he should be removed from

122. [1] See p. 216 n. 1.
123. [1] See p. lxxvi.

castigandus, quousque relicto uicio et per Dei gratiam superato[k]
reuocari uideatur idoneus. At[l] si ex frequenti missarum celebracione tedium, ita corripiendus est et per annum integrum a communione pellendus, sicut scriptum est in xiii concilio Toletano,
capitulo v.[2] Si uero indiscretus timor de leui culpa, castigandus
esse uidetur cum pietate, sicut legitur in capitularium libro primo,
capitulo vi.[3] At si prenotata passio stomachi uel cerebri fuerit in
causa, quiescere debet a ministerio donec recuperet sospitatem.
Si autem preter supradicta aliud aliquid in causa inuentum fuerit,
ex ipsorum comparacione per raciocinacionem facile tractabitur.
His breuiter assignatis saluto te[m] in Domino Ihesu Christo, uir
obtime, qui me multosque alios iugiter et interrogatus[n] et dum
prudenter interrogas bene doces.[4] Vale.[o]

124

*Fulbert to Bishop G.:[1] asking him to act as his proxy at
King Henry's consecration*　　　　　*before 14 May 1027*

Venerabili patri et coepiscopo suo G. F(ulbertus).

Ad benedictionem Heinrici regiae prolis uoto quidem rapior,
sed aduersa me corporis ualitudo retardat. Temptarem tamen
utcumque moderatis equitacionibus eo peruenire, si non abster-
reret seuicia matris eius,[a] cui satis creditur cum mala[b] promittit,
fidem facientibus multis et memorabilibus gestis eius. Qua difficultate prohibitus, rogo uestram caritatem, dilectissime, ut uice
mea suadeatis domno archiepiscopo Remensi[2] ceterisque primori-
bus, ne qua occasione differant benedictionem iuuenis supradicti.
Spero enim illum Deo et bonis omnibus placiturum. Valete.

---

[k] sperato L　　[l] Aut KF　　[m] salueto PB　saluatore V　　[n] interrogas DRKF　　[o] Valete LBV
124 LDRKPBV　　[a] eius *om.* DR　　[b] male LDRK

---

[2] Apparently Toledo XII, c. 5 (Mansi, xi. 1033; Hinschius, p. 416).

office and corrected by abstinence until with the help of God's
grace he has abandoned and overcome his vice and seems worthy
to be recalled. If it should be weariness as a result of repeatedly
celebrating mass, he should be rebuked and forbidden to receive
communion for one year, as is prescribed in the Thirteenth Council
of Toledo, chapter five.[2] If inordinate anxiety concerning a venial
sin, he should be corrected gently, as one reads in the first book
of the capitularies, chapter six.[3] But if it should be an illness of
the stomach or brain as described above, he should give up his
duties until he regains his health. If something else should be
found to be the cause, it can easily be handled by comparing it
with these and reasoning by analogy. At the close of this brief
exposition, I greet you in the Lord Jesus Christ, my good friend,
who by your answers to our questions and by the wise questions
that you yourself ask are continually teaching me and many
others.[4] Farewell.

Fulbert to Bishop G.[1]   before 14 May 1027

To his venerable father and fellow bishop G. from F(ulbert).

If my prayer were answered, I would indeed hasten to attend
Prince Henry's consecration, but I am kept back by ill health.
Yet I would try to go there as best I could by travelling a little at
a time if I were not frightened away by the savagery of his mother,
who is quite trustworthy when she promises evil, as is proved by
her many memorable deeds. Since I am held back by this obstacle,
I beg you in your charity, my dear friend, to act for me in urging
the archbishop of Rheims[2] and the other bishops not to postpone
consecrating that youth for any reason, for I believe that he will
prove pleasing to God and all good men. Farewell.

---

[3] Apparently Ansegisus, *Capitularia*, i. 6 (*MGH Leges*, ii. i (1883), 398),
though no mention is made of any penalty.

[4] Cf. Jerome, ep. liii. 3 (ed. Hilberg, *CSEL* liv. 449).

124. [1] Probably either Garin of Beauvais, 24 June 1016/9 June 1017–10 November 1030/4 (Newman, p. 168 n.), or Geoffrey of Chalon-sur-Saône, before 1015–
1039 (ibid., p. 65 n.), the only bishops whose name begins with 'G' to witness
a charter (the former signing as 'Warin', but cf. no. 129) granted at Henry's
consecration, 14 May 1027 (Newman, no. 68). See pp. lxxxviii f.

[2] Ebalus.

125

Fulbert to King Robert: explaining what is portended by a rain of blood   c. *late June 1027*

Pio regi R(otberto) F(ulbertus) humilis episcopus omnia fidelia.

Sacra uestra[a] monitus sum[b] inquirere festinanter et scribere uobis siqua historia sanguinem pluisse referat, et si factum fuit,[c] quid[d] futurum portenderit.[1] Liuium,[2] Valerium,[3] Orosium,[4] et plures alios huius rei relatores inueni; de quibus ad presens solum Gregorium Turonensem episcopum testem esse productum[e] sufficiat, propter auctoritatem religionis suae.[5] Ait ergo Gregorius idem in sexto libro historiarum, capitulo xiiii: 'Anno igitur vii Childeberti regis, qui erat Chilperici et Gunthranni uicesimus et primus,[f] mense Ianuario, pluuiae, choruscaciones, atque tonitrua grauia[g] fuerunt. Flores in arboribus ostensi sunt. Stella quam cometen superius nominaui apparuit,[h] ut in circuitu eius magna nigredo esset; et illa, tanquam si intra foramen aliquod posita,[i] ita inter tenebras[k] relucebat, scintillans spargensque comas. Prodibat autem ex ea radius mirae magnitudinis, qui tanquam fumus magnus[l] incendii apparebat a longe. Visa est autem ad partem occidentis in hora noctis prima. In die autem sancti paschae apud Suessionis[m] ciuitatem caelum ardere uisum est, ita ut duo apparerent incendia; et unum erat maius, aliud uero minus. Post duarum uero horarum spacium, coniuncta sunt simul, factaque in farum magnum euanuerent. In Parisiaco uero termino uerus sanguis ex nube defluxit, et super uestimenta multorum hominum cecidit, et ita tabe maculauit, ut ipsi propria indumenta horrentes abnuerent. Tribus enim locis in termino ciuitatis illius hoc prodigium apparuit. In Siluanectensi uero territorio hominis cuiusdam domus, cum ille mane surgeret, sanguine respersa[n] ab intus apparuit. Magna autem[o] eo anno lues in populo fuit. Vali-tudines uero uariae, melinae cum pustulis et uesicis multum

---

125 LDRKFCPBV See p. lxi.   [a] quaestione *add.* KF   [b] sum *om.*
LDRC   [c] fuerit LDRKC   [d] quod FC   [e] productum esse
LDRKFC   [f] uicesimus et primus] xx KF   [g] grandia KF
[h] ita *add.* DR   [i] esset *add.* LDRK (*supra* L)   [k] in tenebras LC
in tenebris DR   [l] magni DR   [m] Suessionas LDRKF   Suessiones
V   [n] aspersa KF   [o] enim LDR

---

125. [1] Robert's letter to Fulbert is not extant, but see his letter on the same occasion to Archbishop Gauzlin of Bourges and the latter's reply (Appendix B, nos. 2 f.).

Fulbert to King Robert   c. *late June 1027*

To the pious King R(obert) from F(ulbert), a humble bishop, with all the services of his fidelity.

Your highness enjoined me in your letter to make a rapid search and to write and tell you if in any historical work it is reported to have rained blood and if so, what it portended.[1] I have found that Livy,[2] Valerius,[3] Orosius,[4] and several others report its happening. Of these let it be enough for the present to cite only Bishop Gregory of Tours, whose truthfulness is avouched by his holy life and faith.[5] Gregory relates the following in book six of his *Histories*, chapter fourteen: 'In the seventh year of King Childebert, which was the twenty-first year of Chilperic and Guntran, in January there was frequent rain, lightning, and deep thunder. Flowers bloomed on the trees. The star that I earlier called a comet appeared, and everything around it was darkened. It shone forth in the darkness as though it had been placed in a black hole and sparkled and scattered its tail. A ray of astonishing size issued from it, which from a distance seemed to be the blaze of a great fire. This was seen in the west at the first hour of the night. On Easter Day at Soissons the sky seemed to be on fire in that two blazes appeared, the one greater, the other less. Two hours later they joined together and became one great beacon, and then they vanished. Within the city of Paris real blood rained from a cloud, fell upon the clothes of many men, and so stained them with gore that they shuddered at the sight of their own garments and tore them off. This prodigy appeared at three places within the city limits. In the area of Senlis, when one man got up in the morning, his house seemed to have been sprinkled with blood from within. In that year there was a great plague among the people. Various diseases, black spots with pustules and

---

[2] e.g. xxiv. 10; xxxiv. 45; xxxix. 46, 56; xl. 19, the last being the most suitable here. As regards how much of Livy was available at Chartres, see G. Billanovich, 'Petrarch and the Textual Tradition of Livy', *Journal of the Warburg and Courtauld Institutes*, xiv (1951), 137 ff., especially 189 n.

[3] See p. 275.

[4] *Historiae*, iv. 5 (ed. Zangemeister, *CSEL* v. 214 f.).

[5] Perhaps an allusion to the profession of orthodoxy with which Gregory begins his *Historiae Francorum* (*MGH, Scriptores rerum Merovingicarum*, i. i (2nd edn., 1951), 3 ff.).

populum affecerunt morte. Multi tamen adhibentes studium euaserunt. Audiuimus autem eo anno in Narbonensem urbem inguinarium morbum grauiter deseuisse, ita ut nullum esset spacium uitae, cum homo correptus fuisset ab eo.'[6] Hactenus Gregorius Turonensis. Liquet igitur ex hac et ex supramemoratis[p] historiis quod pluuia sanguinis publicam stragem futuram esse portendat. Quod autem nuper huiusmodi cruorem in quadam parte regni uestri pluisse audistis, et quod ille cruor ubi supra petram uel super carnem hominis ceciderat, ablui non poterat, ubi autem super lignum ceciderat, facile abluebatur, per hoc tria genera hominum significata esse uidentur: per lapidem impii, per carnem fornicarii, per lignum uero (quod neque durum est ut lapis, neque molle ut caro) illi qui neque[q] impii sunt neque fornicarii. Cum ergo uenerit super illam gentem cui portenditur gladius siue pestilencia designata per sanguinem, si antea duri et molles non fuerint mutati in melius, morientur[r] perpetualiter in sanguine suo. Medii uero per angustiam mortis uel aliter poterunt liberari, pro arbitrio secretissimi atque presentissimi iudicis. Vale, piissime rex.[s]

126

Fulbert to Archbishop Robert of Rouen: encouraging him in his adversities   *after 5/6 August 1027*

Venerabili archiepiscopo Rotomagensium R(otberto) F(ulbertus) humilis episcopus fideles oraciones.

Conpacior tibi, sancte pater, super aduersis quae indigne passus es, presertim ab eo qui et se et sua tuae fidelitati debuerat.[1] Super illo quoque doleo uehementer fratre et[a] coepiscopo nostro dum staret, in tanta nunc flagiciorum atque facinorum precipicia lapso.[2] Sed tibi, pater, haec uel magna consolacio est, quia si abstulit exteriora, interiora non potuit. Habes enim ex Dei gratia caritatem

---

---

[6] Gregory of Tours, *Historiae Francorum*, vi. 14 (edn. cit. (p. 255 n.), pp. 283 f.).

126. [1] Fulbert seems to be referring to Duke Robert I of Normandy, who succeeded his brother Richard III on his death 5/6 August 1027 (D. Douglas, *English Historical Review*, lxv (1950), 289 ff.) and then attacked his uncle

blisters killed many people, yet many took care and escaped. We have also heard that a disease of the groin raged so violently at Narbonne that year that a man died almost as soon as he was infected by it.'[6] Thus far Gregory of Tours. It is clear from this and from the histories mentioned above that when it rains blood, this portends the coming of a public disaster. As to your having heard that there has recently been a similar rain of blood in part of your kingdom and that where it fell on rock or human flesh it could not be washed off, but that where it fell on wood it was easily washed away, this seems to refer to three kinds of men: stone signifies the impious; flesh, fornicators; and wood (which is neither hard like stone nor soft like flesh), those who are neither impious nor fornicators. When the sword or plague foretold by the blood comes upon the people for whom it was portended, if the 'hard' and the 'soft' have not previously changed for the better, they will perish for ever in their own blood; but those who stand in the middle can be delivered through the straits of death or in some other way in accordance with the will of the most secret and most powerful Judge. Farewell, most pious king.

Fulbert to Archbishop Robert of Rouen
after 5/6 August 1027

To the venerable archbishop of Rouen, R(obert), from F(ulbert), a humble bishop, with his faithful prayers.

I sympathize with you, holy father, over the injuries with which you have been unjustly afflicted, especially from one who owed himself and his all to your good faith.[1] I am also deeply grieved over him who was our brother and fellow bishop as long as he stood upright, but who has now fallen into these great depths of crime and infamy.[2] But to you, father, it should be very comforting that though he has taken away your outward possessions, he could not take away those that are within; for by God's grace you have

Robert, archbishop of Rouen and count of Évreux. The latter went into exile and placed Normandy under interdict. He was later recalled and henceforth played an important role in governing Normandy. See William of Jumièges, *Gesta Normannorum Ducum*, vi. 3 (ed. J. Marx (Rouen, 1914), pp. 100 f.); D. Douglas, *William the Conqueror* (London, 1964), pp. 32 ff.

[2] Identity unknown.

qua ipsum errantem reuoces, frenum canonicae districtionis quo detrectantem coherceas, uirgam qua[b] ferias. His utere competenter, donec absolucionem promeritus dicere tibi gaudeat: 'Virga tua et baculus tuus, ipsa me consolata sunt.'[c3]

127

Fulbert to Bishop Reginardus of Liège:[1] *commending his clerk A(delman?), a student at Chartres*

late *1027–early 1028*

Venerabili episcopo Leodicensium[a] R(eginardo) F(ulbertus) Carnotensis omnia caritatis obsequia.

Cum dispersas oues sollicite ac longi itineris labore queritis,[b] leti perpendimus, pater, quod pastoris nomen necgligencia non cassatis. De illa tamen oue quae in nostris pascuis obseruatur (fratrem[c] A(delmanum) subdiaconum[2] loquor), securus estote, quia Dei gratia bene ruminat, et luporum insidias sagaciter cauet. Nec appelletis eum ultra militem fugitiuum, quoniam accurate se preparat ad debellanda coram Deo et uobis et nobis agmina uiciorum. Veniet autem ad uos quantocius[d] poterit. Sed si nostra humilitas inuenire queat gratiam in oculis uestris, suppliciter exoramus, ut nobis illum remittere ac uestris litteris commendare dignemini, ut presencia eius sit pignus uestrae caritatis erga nos ac nostrae fidelitatis erga uos inperpetuum. Valete.[e]

---

[b] quam L   [c] Vale *add.* P   Valete *add.* B

127 LDRKCPBV   [a] Leodicensium episcopo PB   [b] perquiritis LDRKC   [c] fratrem *om.* LDRKC   [d] quantocicius LDRK   [e] Vale LRC   *om.* V

the charity by which you may recall one who goes astray, the reins of ecclesiastical sanction by which you may restrain one who is headstrong, the rod with which you may strike him. Use these as you should until he deserves absolution and is glad to say to you: 'Thy rod and thy staff, they have comforted me.'[3]

Fulbert to Bishop Reginardus of Liège[1]
late 1027–early 1028

To the venerable bishop of Liège, R(eginardus), from F(ulbert) of Chartres, with all the services of charity.

When you anxiously search for your scattered sheep and send over a long and hard way for them, we rejoice to see, father, that you are not disgracing the name of pastor by negligence. But as for the sheep that is kept in our pasture (I mean Brother A(delman), the subdeacon),[2] you may rest secure, for by God's grace he is ruminating well and wisely avoiding the wiles of wolves. Please stop calling him a deserter, for he is diligently preparing himself to vanquish the armies of vice before God, you, and ourselves. He will come to you as quickly as he can. But if our lowly selves are able to find favour in your sight, we humbly beg you to send him back to us with your letter of commendation, so that his presence may be a pledge of your charity toward us and our fidelity toward you for ever. Farewell.

---

[3] Ps. 22: 4.

127. [1] After 23/4 January 1025–5 December 1037 (see H. Silvestre, 'A propos de l'épitaphe de l'évêque de Liège, Durand (†1025)', *RBPH* xli (1963), 1136 ff.; Bresslau, i. 87 ff., ii. 278).
[2] See pp. xxxv f.

128

The canons of Chartres to Archbishop Leothericus of Sens: reproaching him for consecrating Bishop Thierry

after 10 April 1028

Sacro Senonensium archipresuli L(eutherico) canonici sanctae Mariae Carnotensis in Christo salutem et adhuc fidelitatis obsequium.

Multum miramur, uenerande pater, quod bonis initiis tam malos exitus habuisti,[1] uidelicet quod nobis pastore carentibus in altero substituendo primum bene fauisti, et postremo sententiam tuam deprauasti, alium quam nos elegeramus ordinando. Ne autem dicas ignorasse te electionem nostram, mandauimus tibi per diaconos nostros Odelerium et Frotmundum elegisse nos A(lbertum) decanum[2] cum litteris nostris idipsum continentibus, qui talis nobis uidebatur, qualem episcopum ordinari debere dicit concilium Cartaginiense quartum.[3] Quod si post haec alium tibi optulerunt uel rex uel aliqui ex nostris minus sapientibus, oportuisset te causam diligenter attendere, et inter nos ipsos diiudicare quorum sanior haberetur electio, sicut in decretis Leonis papae significari optime nosti his uerbis: 'Ille omnibus preponetur quem cleri*a* plebisque consensus concorditer postularint, ita ut si in aliam forte personam parcium se uota diuiserint, metropolitani iuditio is alteri*b* preponatur, qui maioribus et studiis iuuatur et meritis.'[4] Volumus autem scire te quod ipsam electionem nostram mandauimus domino regi per suos monachos Ernaldum priorem et Restaldum prepositum sancti Dyonisii;[5] quibus etiam obitientibus nobis de Teoderico ordinando regiam uoluntatem iniunximus ut dicerent regi ne id temere fieri iuberet, uocaret autem nos antea (si sibi placeret) ad curiam suam, uel suae uoluntati consensuros, uel cur dissentiremus ostensuros. His uero dictis nostris ipse dominus rex contemptis, qualem sibi libuit personam absque nostra petitione ordinari uiolentus*c* accelerauit, inmemor fortasse

---

128 LDRCP   *a* clerici LDR   *b* alteri] saltim P   *c* uiolentiis P

128. [1] Cf. Augustine, *De civitate Dei*, xvii. 20 (*CCL* xlviii. 586), where it concerns Solomon (cf. no. 92).

[2] For Odelerius and Frotmundus see Merlet, pp. 178, 170. Albert left at this time and became a monk at Marmoutier (see nos. 65, 129).

The canons of Chartres to Archbishop Leothericus of Sens after 10 April 1028

To the holy archbishop of Sens, L(eothericus), from the canons of St. Mary's of Chartres, with their greetings in Christ and even now the service of their fidelity.

We are greatly astonished, reverend father, that your good beginnings have come to such a bad end:[1] that is, that when we were left without a pastor, you began by supporting our right to choose his successor, but ended by abandoning your good intentions and consecrating someone we had not elected. You cannot say that you did not know of our election, for we sent you word through our deacons Odelerius and Frotmundus, with letters to the same effect, that we had elected the dean, A(lbert),[2] who seemed to us to satisfy the requirements for the episcopate set down by the Fourth Council of Carthage.[3] But if afterwards the king or any of our brethren of less sound judgement presented someone else to you, you should have investigated the case carefully and decided who had been elected by the weightier part in accordance (as you know) with the following provision in the decretals of Pope Leo: 'Let preference be given to him who is chosen by the common consent of the clergy and people. If the choice is not unanimous and some favour another candidate, let preference be given to the one the metropolitan thinks is better qualified by reason of his industry and merits.'[4] We also want you to know that we sent word of our election to the king through his monks Ernaldus and Restaldus, prior and provost of Saint-Denis.[5] When they took us to task saying that the king wished to make Thierry bishop, we enjoined them to tell the king not to order it rashly, but first to summon us to his court, if he would, to consent to his wishes or to show why we dissented. But the king had no regard for what we said and without our asking it quickly forced through the consecration of the one he wanted, perhaps forgetting the

---

[3] Actually *Statuta ecclesiae antiqua*, c. 1 (Mansi, iii. 949 f.; Hinschius, p. 303) = prologue (ed. C. Munier (Strasbourg, 1960), pp. 75 ff.), usually ascribed to Carthage IV.

[4] Ep. xiv. 5 (*PL* liv. 673) = c. 4 (Hinschius, p. 619).

[5] Both witnessed a document concerning Saint-Denis, 1002–31, simply as 'priest' (L. Levillain, 'Note sur quelques abbés de Saint-Denis', *Revue Mabillon*, i (1905), 44).

illius dicti Constantini Christianissimi inperatoris de uiolentia principum contra se et contra alios principes ita se habentis: 'Quecumque', inquit, 'contra leges fuerint a principibus optenta non ualeant.'[6] Sed ut ad presens de ipso taceamus (qui[d] sane uiderit utrum omnia recte agat, ne[e] post factum peniteat)[7] ad te, pater, querimoniae nostrae flectimus articulum quem ecclesiae nostrae curam neglexisse, immo auctoritati tuae derogare uehementer dolemus, posthabito supradicto Leonis papae decreto. Quod si obseruasses, racionabiliter utique egisses, et bene nobis ut filiis pater consuluisses. At ipso uiolato, quam multa alia sanctorum patrum decreta uiolaueris, tute considera. Nos tamen pauca tibi de multis scribimus. Legitur in decretis Celestini papae: 'Nullus inuitis detur episcopus: cleri, plebis et ordinis consensus et desiderium requiratur'; et post pauca: 'Sit facultas clericis renitendi, si se uiderint pregrauari; et quos sibi ingeri ex transuerso agnouerint, non timeant refutare, qui si non debitum premium, uel liberum de eo qui eos recturus est debent habere iuditium.'[8] Item[f] ex concilio Cartaginiensi tertio: 'Et illud est statuendum, ut quando ad eligendum episcopum conuenerimus, siqua contradictio fuerit[g] oborta (quia talia facta sunt apud nos), non presumant ad purgandum eum qui ordinandus est tres iam, sed postulentur ad numerum supradictorum duo uel tres; et in eadem plebe cui ordinandus est discutiantur primo personae contradicentium, postremo illa etiam quae obitiuntur pertractentur; et cum purgatus fuerit sub conspectu[h] publico, ita demum ordinetur.'[9] Ecce quomodo patrum sententiae uiolantur. Nobis enim inuitis obtrudere uultis episcopum, nec conceditur nobis liberum de eo qui nos recturus sit habere iuditium; et cum huic[i] qui ordinandus erat contradiceretur, minime purgata sunt quae obitiebantur, nec personae uel raciones contradicentium discussae. Quae cum ita sint, cumque legem canonicam in hoc negotio multimode solueris,[10] monemus te non increpando neque diiudicando,[k]

---

[d] *corr. to* quis L   quis DR   [e] nec L   [f] Iterum LDRC
[g] uenerit L   [h] conspecta C   conspecto P   [i] his *corr. to* is L
is DR   his C   [k] iudicando LDRC

---

[6] See p. 42 n. 8.   [7] Cf. Ecclus. 32: 24.
[8] Ep. iv. 5 (*PL* 1. 434 f.; Hinschius, p. 560). As regards the meaning of *ordo* (= nobles), see F. L. Ganshof, 'Note sur l'élection des évêques dans l'empire romain', *Revue internationale des droits de l'antiquité*, iv (1950), 486 f.
[9] c. 40 (Mansi, iii. 887; Hinschius, p. 299).   [10] Cf. no. 26.

judgement as to the use of force by princes which the most Christian emperor Constantine rendered against himself and other princes as follows: 'Let whatever is done by princes contrary to law be null and void.'[6] But to say no more about him for the present (though to be sure let him see whether he is acting rightly in all that he does, so that he may not have cause to repent later),[7] it is against you, father, that we are now directing our complaint whom we deeply grieve to see neglecting to care for our church and indeed bringing your own authority into disrepute by ignoring the decretal of Pope Leo cited above. If you had followed it, you would certainly have acted in accordance with the dictates of reason and taken thought as to what was best for us as a father for his sons. But by violating it how many other decretals of the holy fathers you have violated you ought to consider for yourself; however, we are writing down just a few of them for you. One reads in the decretals of Pope Celestine: 'Let no one be given as bishop to those who do not want him, but let the consent and wishes of the clergy, people, and nobles be sought out'; and a little further on: 'Let the clergy have the right to resist if they see themselves oppressed, and let them not be afraid to reject those whom they find unexpectedly forced upon them; for even if they are owed no recompense, they should have free choice as to who is to rule them.'[8] Likewise from the Third Council of Carthage: 'Let it be decreed that when we meet to choose a bishop, if any objection should arise (for we have known it to happen), the three bishops who are already there should not take it on themselves to clear the one who is to be consecrated, but should ask for two or three more to be added to their number. In the presence of the congregation for which he is to be consecrated, first let the character of those who are making the objections be examined; then let the charges that they are bringing be investigated; and after he has been publicly cleared, let him be consecrated.'[9] Look how the decrees of the fathers are violated. You wish to thrust a bishop on us whom we do not want, nor are we allowed to have free choice of who is to rule us; and when objections were raised against the one to be consecrated, the charges were by no means disproved, and neither the character of those who objected to him nor their reasons for doing so were investigated. Since this is the case, and since in this matter you are violating canon law in many ways,[10] we enjoin you, not in rebuking or judging you,

sed affectu filiorum obsecrando, ipsi legi quam offenderis reconciliatum iri confitendo culpam et penitendo. Nec pudeat te dicere secreto[l] necessariis tuis Deum timentibus et in lege ipsius[m] bene eruditis, iam tandem te[n] animaduertisse ea quae fiunt contra statuta canonum non debere stare, sed et facientes peniteri[o] oportere. Quod si forte rex auctoritate tua deinceps corroborari uoluerit quod sine solutione canonum stare non possit, uideris, pater, ne aditias peccatum super peccatum; sed aut quantum poteris id corroborare dissimula, aut manifeste salua legum auctoritate id te exequi non ualere proclama. Postremo suppliciter oramus haec scripta nostra minime publicari, quae apud tui cari pectoris secretum promere audemus. Rescribe[p] uero nobis siquid tibi uidetur contra haec racionabiliter opponendum. Augeat tibi Deus spiritum consilii et fortitudinis, sapientiae et intellectus.[11]

129

The canons of Chartres to Bishops Garin of Beauvais and Odolricus of Orleans and Archbishop Arnulf of Tours: asking for their aid in opposing the election of Bishop Thierry after 10 April 1028

Sanctis presulibus G(uarino) Beluacensi, O(dolrico) Aurelianensi, A(rnulfo) Turonensi, clerici sanctae Mariae Carnotensis, famuli eorum et fratres, in Domino salutem.

Conquerimur aput uos, patres, de archiepiscopo nostro et rege, qui nobis inuitis episcopum donare uolunt quendam idiotam (ut scitis) et eiusmodi[a] offitio indignum et eius offitii ignarum,[b] precantes auxilium uestrum ut uigiletis sicut boni ecclesiae pastores ad portas eius, ne introeat in eam ille talis qui non quaesiuit intrare per hostium, sed aliunde ascendere, sicut fur et latro.[1] Vobis tribus portas custodientibus sciatis pro certo quartum custodem addi O(donem) comitem,[2] et nunquam recepturum illum in ciuitatem suam, nisi prius uestro iuditio examinatum utrum recipi debeat an non. Vigilate ergo attencius, et diligenter

---

[l] secreto *om.* P   [m] eius DR   [n] te *om.* DR   [o] penitere LDR
[p] Rescribi P

129 LDRCP   [a] eiusdemmodi P   [b] et eius . . . ignarum *om.* LDRC

but in beseeching you with filial affection, to make your peace
with that law you have broken by confessing your sin and doing
penance. Nor should it upset you to acknowledge privately to your
servants who fear God and are well versed in his law that at last
you have come to realize that whatever is done contrary to the
decrees of the canons should not stand and that those who are
guilty of such sins should do penance. But if the king later wants
you to confirm by your authority what cannot stand without
violating the canons, see to it, father, that you heap not sin on
sin; but do all you can to avoid confirming it, or openly declare
that you cannot do so without violating the authority of the laws.
Finally, we humbly beg you not to divulge what we have written
here and are venturing to disclose in the secrecy of your dear
breast; but write and let us know if you think anything can reasonably be done to correct what has happened. May God increase in
you the spirit of counsel and fortitude, wisdom and understanding.[11]

The canons of Chartres to Bishops Garin of Beauvais and Odolricus of Orleans and Archbishop Arnulf of Tours
after 10 April 1028

To the holy bishops G(arin) of Beauvais, O(dolricus) of Orleans,
and A(rnulf) of Tours, from the clerks of St. Mary's of Chartres,
their servants and brothers, with greetings in the Lord.

We are laying our complaint before you, fathers, as regards our
archbishop and the king, who wish to force on us a bishop who
is (as you know) illiterate and both unworthy of such an office and
unacquainted with its duties. We ask you as good shepherds of
the church to help us by standing watch at its gates and keeping
out one who has not sought to enter through the door, but who
has tried to climb in by another way like a thief and a robber.[1]
You may know for a truth that to the three of you who are keeping
the gates a fourth guard is added in Count O(do),[2] and that he will
never receive him into his city unless you first examine him and
decide whether he ought to be received or not. So keep careful

[11] Cf. Isa. 11: 2.
129. [1] Cf. John 10: 1.   [2] Of Chartres.

inquirite causam cum uestris sapientibus clericis et nobis famulis uestris si dignemini; nec propter regis reuerenciam hoc agere pigritemini, quasi hoc*c* pertineat ad infidelitatem*d* eius. Vere etenim ei fideliores eritis, siquae sunt corrigenda in regno eius*e* correxeritis, et animum eius ad eandem correctionem*f* compuleritis. Volumus autem scire uos A(lbertum) decanum[3] quem elegeramus factum esse monachum, nihilhominus tamen nos eum optare nobis fieri episcopum, cum reprobatus fuerit ille lupus quem probare potestis indignum. Quod uos inuicem caute et diligenter et*g* secrete deliberare petimus utrum fieri possit an non, et nobis seruis uestris ac*h* fratribus deliberationis uestrae finem innotescere siue litteris siue legato fideli. Haec autem uerba nostra uidete interim ne publicentur. Valete.

130

The canons of Chartres to Abbot Odilo of Cluny: asking for his aid in opposing the election of Bishop Thierry[1]

after 10 April 1028

Quem super omnes abbates diligunt sanctissimo patri O(diloni) canonici sanctae Mariae omnium uirtutum gratia prefulgere.

Obsecramus uos in nomine sanctae Trinitatis, ne faueatis contra ius et fas partibus Teoderici simulati episcopi, neque suadeatis Odoni comiti facere cum eo concordiam contra sanctorum canonum auctoritatem. Clarissimum speculum posuit uos Deus in mundo. Videte ne qualibet nigredine obscuremini qua obfuscentur*a* alii, sed semper uero lumine resplendeatis, quo et alii possint illustrari. Valete, beatissime pater, et rescribite nobis*b* quicquid melius de hac causa uobis uidetur.

---

c hoc *om.* DR   *d* fidelitatem LDR   *e* eius *om.* P   *f* correptionem L   *g* ut L   *h* et LDRC

130 LDRCP   *a* obfuscantur P   *b* uobis P

---

[3] Cf. no. 128.

130. [1] See nos. 128 f.

watch and examine the case thoroughly with your clerks of sound judgement and with us, your servants, if you deem us so worthy. Please do not hold back out of deference for the king, as if it were a question of your being unfaithful to him, for indeed you will be all the more faithful to him if you correct what needs to be corrected in his kingdom and force him to correct these matters himself. We also want you to know that our dean A(lbert),[3] whom we elected, has become a monk, but that we still want him to be our bishop after that wolf has been rejected who you can prove is unworthy. We ask you to take counsel with each other cautiously, carefully, and secretly, as to whether this can be done or not, and to let us, your servants and brothers, know what you decide by letter or a trusted messenger. Meanwhile please see to it that what we have written here is not made public. Farewell.

The canons of Chartres to Abbot Odilo of Cluny[1]
after 10 April 1028

To the abbot whom they love above all others, the most holy father O(dilo), from the canons of St. Mary's, with their prayer that he may shine forth with the grace of all virtues.

We beg you in the name of the Holy Trinity not to support, contrary to all that is just and right, the claims of that would-be bishop Thierry and not to persuade Count Odo to come to terms with him in violation of the authority of the holy canons. God has placed you in the world as his brightest mirror. See to it that you are not clouded over by any shadow by which others may be darkened, but that you always shine brightly with the true light by which they too may be illumined. Farewell, most blessed father, and please write and let us know what seems best to you in this matter.

131

Hildegar to A(scelin?):[1] *sending him writings on the Eucharist and telling him Fulbert's advice as regards evil thoughts*   *after 10 April 1028*

In Christo sibi dilecto semperque diligendo domino A(scelino) H(ildegarius) seruus eius fidelis, quae retro sunt obliuisci, et iugiter in anteriora tendere.[a2]

Causa caritatis pollicitus sum conuersari mecum Herberto nepoti tuo usque[b] fruges nouae colligantur, amice illum habiturus interim, quasi presentiae tuae[c] uicarium. Scripta quae tibi mitti poscis partim mittimus, partim minime, quia non sunt missu facilia. Quae uero mittuntur et difficilia sunt cognitu et pernecessaria, de sacramento uidelicet corporis et sanguinis Domini, quae si non fideliter ac digne percipimus, uiuere non habemus.[3] De cogitationibus autem quae se nolentibus nobis ingerunt, ita sentiebat carissimus pater noster F(ulbertus): 'Nihil eas nocere, si tandem menti minime placuerint; signo crucis abigendas esse ab animo uelud muscas ab oculis importunas; racionem ponendam esse mentis custodem, rerum utilium receptricem; quibus dum occupata fuerit, ab inutilibus impeti uel penitrari non possit.' Cui sententiae multas alias in Vitis patrum consentientes reperire potes, quae tuum animum optime releuabunt,[d] opitulante Christi gratia, sine qua nihil ualemus uel sumus. Caetera uero quae ad presens non mittuntur, quia nec adeo scriptu facilia,[e] nec satis idoneum gerulum habere modo uidentur,[f] Deo uolente spero me tibi transmissurum[g] uel delaturum, cum oportunum tempus et latorem inuenerint. Valeas, animo meo carissime:

> Mortuus huic mundo Christum tibi uiuere noris.[4]
> Virtuti uiuas; sit tibi mors uitio.[h]

Ora pro me famulo tuo, pater.

131 LDRCP   *a* extendere DR   *b* me cum Herberto nepote tuo usque dum DR   *c* tuae *om*. P   *d* reuelabunt *corr. to* releuabunt L releuabunt *post corr*. R   reuelabunt DCP   *e* uidentur *add*. DR *f* habere . . . uidentur] haberemus uidentur L   haberemus uiderentur C habemus DR   *g* trans- *om*. P *leaving a blank space*   *h* uitium DR

131. [1] Although the addressee cannot be identified with certainty, the reference to his nephew suggests that it might be Ascelin the Breton, who, with his

Hildegar to A(scelin?)[1]   *after 10 April 1028*

To his beloved in Christ and ever to be loved lord, A(scelin), from H(ildegar), his faithful servant, with his prayer that he may forget what lies behind and strive ever onward.[2]

Out of charity I have promised to let your nephew Herbert stay with me until the new first-fruits are gathered and during that time to be friends with him as though he were your other self. As for the writings that you ask to be sent to you, we are sending some, but not others, as they are not easy to send. Those that are being sent are difficult to understand, but very important, since they treat of the sacrament of the Lord's Body and Blood, which if we do not receive faithfully and worthily, we shall not have life.[3] As to evil thoughts that force themselves upon us against our very dear father F(ulbert) was of the following opinion: 'They are not harmful if the mind ultimately takes no pleasure in them. They should be driven from the mind by making the sign of the cross, just as troublesome flies are driven from the eyes. Reason should be made the guardian of the mind to admit what is beneficial. While the mind is taken up with this, it cannot be attacked or forcibly entered by harmful thoughts.' You can find many other similar sayings in the *Lives of the Fathers*, which will greatly comfort your mind by the aid of Christ's grace, without which we can do and are nothing. As for the writings which are not being sent at present since it is difficult to copy them and there is no one at hand who can conveniently take them, I hope (God willing) to bring or to send them to you when a suitable opportunity and carrier are found. Farewell, my dear friend and heart's delight.

> Die to this world, and know Christ lives in you.[4]
> Let Virtue be your life, let death take Vice.

Pray for me, your servant, father.

---

nephew Herbert, is commemorated in the cathedral necrology and said to have given a number of books to the chapter (Merlet, p. 158), and who was later involved in the Berengarian controversy (see p. xlviii).

[2] Cf. Phil. 3: 13.
[3] Cf. John 6: 54; 1 Cor. 11: 27 ff.
[4] Cf. Rom. 6: 10; Gal. 2: 20.

THE POEMS OF
FULBERT OF CHARTRES

132

[*Oratio*]

Angele consilii magni,[1] te consulo,[a] Christe,[b]
[Mi factor, mea uita, salus, fiducia sola,
Da michi consilium et uotum uiresque sequendi,]
Ambiguus[c] quid agam, quo tandem fine quiescam,
Nam[d] uereor temere suscepto pontificatu   5
Seruandis ouibus mage quam prodesse nocere,
Atque ideo puto cedendum melioribus esse.
Sed recolens quod[e] non opibus neque sanguine fretus
Conscendi cathedram pauper de sorde leuatus,
Arbitror hoc a te factum sicut tuus est mos;   10
Nec mutare locum nisi significaueris ausim,
Quamuis id[f] lesae moneat[g] mens conscia uitae.[2]
[Tu scis, sancte pater, quid sit tibi gratius horum
Vtiliusque michi. Praecor unde[h] tuam pietatem
Vt michi digneris hoc inspirare[i] labanti   15
Consilium, praesensque iuues ad perficiendum.]

133

Ad se ipsum de se ipso

Te de pauperibus natum suscepit alendum
Christus, et immeritum sic enutriuit et auxit,
Vt collata tibi miretur munera mundus.
Nam puero faciles prouidit adesse magistros,
Et iuuenem perduxit ad hoc ut episcopus esses.   5
Reges, pontifices, populi te magnificabant,
Seruum prudentem censentes atque fidelem
Esse pii Domini. Sed pro pudor ipse nefande

132 LDRCP (= f. 27ᵛ), V(= f. 110ᵛ), P¹(= f. 63ᵛ), V¹(= f. 160) There are two
versions of the poem: a shorter in LDRCPV, a longer in P¹V¹. (P has been
revised from the longer version by a later hand, but these changes are not noted
here.) The presence of both versions in P and V may point to two separate
exemplars; and the omission of the first line in P¹ and the alternative beginning
in V¹ indicate that the longer was the earlier version, that the poem originally

[A Prayer]

Angel of Great Counsel,[1] I call on you, O Christ, for I know not what to do or what will be my final rest. I fear that it was rash of me to have accepted a bishopric and that in keeping my flock I do more harm than good; hence I think I should yield it to my betters. But remembering that it was without the help of birth or riches that I rose to the episcopate, penniless and raised up from lowly origin, I believe that this was your doing in your wonted way. Nor would I dare to change my place without some sign from you, despite the promptings of a conscience which well knows my sinful life.[2]

Self-Examination

You, a child of poor parents, Christ took up to raise as his own; and undeserving as you were, he so nourished and blessed you that the world marvels at the gifts he bestowed. For he saw to it that as a boy you had understanding masters; and while you were still in your prime, he raised you to the episcopate. Kings, bishops, and people have praised you, as a wise and faithful servant of the Lord, who rightly favoured you. But alas, that you have sinned

began with lines 2 f., and that these were later dropped in favour of line 1. Preference is given here to the revised version, and the lines omitted from the earlier one have been placed in brackets. The revised version is also found in Boulogne-sur-Mer MS. 83, f. 8ʳ⁻ᵛ.   *a* consule L   *b* Angele . . . Christe *om.* P¹   AL Angele consilii magni, te consulo, Christe, ambiguus quid *written as the last lines of the preceding poem* V¹   *c* Ambiguis *corr. to* Ambiguus L   Ambiguis CV   Ambiguo P¹V¹   *d* Nunc P¹V¹ (uel Nam *supra* P¹)   *e* quia P¹V¹   *f* hoc P¹V¹   *g* moueat P¹V¹   *h* inde P¹   *i* inspirante P¹

133   P

---

132. [1] Cf. the introit of the mass for Christmas Day. In the earlier version this sentence began: 'My Maker, my Life, Salvation and sole Stay, give me your counsel and the will and strength to carry it out . . .'

[2] The following lines were added at the end of the earlier version: 'You know, holy father, which course is more pleasing to you and better for me; and so I beg you in your piety to deign to inspire my faltering self with your counsel and to be my ever-present aid in carrying it out.'

Nec prudens nec fidus eras ut res manifestat.
Nam contra memorare pudet quam nequiter ipsum   10
Laeseris et sanctos eius tua praua tuentes,
Quae uix ulla satis possunt tormenta piare.
Prestolatur adhuc Dominus tamen ille benignus,
Et te uiuere perpetitur, si forte resciscens
Segnitiem zelo perimas, meritoque reatum.   15

134

De sancta cruce[a][1]

Vexillum regis uenerabile cuncta regentis,
O crux sancta micans super omnia sidera caeli,
Mortifero lapsis gustu quae sola reportas
Antidotum uitae fructum suspensa perhennem,
Te colo, te fateor, uenerans te pronus adoro.   5
Christus, principium, finis, surrectio, uita,
Merces, lux, requies, sanctorum doxa, corona,
Pro seruis dominus redimendis hostia factus,
In te suspendens per lignum toxica ligni
Purgauit clausae reserando limina uitae.   10
Tantae pars ego sum libertatis, bone pastor,
Sed mala semper agens nunquam tibi digna rependi.
Heu mihi, iam bibulae numerum transcendit arenae
Sarcina multorum michi[b] quae creuere malorum.
Sed quia peccantis pocius bona quam mala queris,   15
Plusque tibi peccat, spem qui peccando relinquit,
Ad te confugio, tibi supplico, confiteorque.
Parce, precor, miserere mei, miserere meorum
Defuncti qui sunt et in hac qui luce parentum.
Qui bona fecerunt mihi pro te centupla redde;   20
Qui mala, conuertens peccamina cuncta remitte.
Omnes hoc signo qui te uenerantur et orant
Dirige, sustenta, custodi, protege, salua.
Da procul a nobis elatio sistat ut omnis,
Quo tibi summissi[c] placeamus pectora[d] semper.   25
Protege nos iugiter uentosae laudis ab aura,
Et nobis dignas confer tibi soluere grates.
Inuidiae maculam de mentibus ablue nostris,

---

134 LDRP   *a title om.* LDR   *b* iam . . . michi *om.* P   *c* sum-
misso DR   *d* pectore *post corr.* L, DR

by being unwise and unfaithful is plain to see. For it is shameful to remember how badly you have offended him and his saints, who have seen your wicked ways; and however harsh the penance you undertake, it is hardly enough to make amends. Yet the Lord still waits in his loving-kindness and lets you go on living, so that if you should come to your senses, you may atone for your negligence by zeal, your guilt by good works.

The Holy Cross[1]

August standard of the all-ruling King, O holy cross, outshining all heaven's stars, to those who fell through the taste of death you alone restore the remedy of life, bearing an eternal fruit. You I worship, you I confess, and prostrate on my knees I revere and adore you. Christ, the beginning, end, resurrection, and life, reward, light, rest, glory of the saints, and crown, the Lord who offered himself to redeem his servants, by hanging from you with a tree's help took away the poison that came from a tree and opened again the closed doors to life. I am one of those so gloriously freed, good Shepherd; but all that I do is evil, and never have I worthily repaid you. Wretch that I am, already the vast burden of my many sins surpasses the sum of the thirsty sands. But since you seek the good of the sinner and not his harm, and he commits a greater sin against you who in sinning loses hope, to you I flee for refuge, you I supplicate and confess. Be merciful, I beg you, and have pity on me and my kindred, both those who are dead and those yet alive. Those who have helped me for your sake, reward them a hundredfold; and those who have harmed, convert them and forgive all their sins. All who with the sign of the cross worship you and pray, direct, support, guard, protect, and save. Grant that pride may ever be far from us, that with humble heart we may always please you. Ever protect us from the windy breath of praise, and grant that we may pay you worthy thanks. Wash the stain of envy from our minds, pouring into us

---

134. [1] Though Fulbert does not seem to be using any particular model, cf. the poems on the cross by Venantius Fortunatus (*MGH AA* iv. i. 27 ff.) and Rabanus Maurus (*PL* cvii. 149 ff.).

Infundens nobis ignem caelestis amoris.
Irae compescens stimulos, fac nos pacientes,   30
Tristitiamque fugans, in damnis spem retinentes.
Crimen auaritiae nobis dona fugiamus,
Vt pietatis opus placitae[e] tibi ferre queamus.
Ingluuiem uentris nos uincere sobrietate,
Luxurieque luem casto concede pudore,   35
Vt per te mundi, per te quoque uiribus aucti,
Constanter uitam studeamus adire supernam.

135

Oratio positi in prouectu[a]

Tu qui de nichilo mundum finxisse probaris,
    Nam tibi materies nulla coeua fuit,
Et nutu facili noto tibi tempore[b] solues,
    Tam diuturne dehinc quam prius extiteras,
Quantulus hic noster modus est quo secula[c] uolui   5
    Cum uitiisque iubes strenua bella geri.
Regem militibus propriis te semper adesse[d] 1
    Ad bene certandum nos uegetando proba.

136

[*An untitled Fragment*]

Me non Argolici docuit sed uirga Latini,
Constat enim Grecum quod praecipis enucleandum.
Mecum Virgilius, nequaquam lusit Homerus.

---

[e] placide LDR

135 LDRPV The poem seems to have been revised (cf. no. 132), and preference is given here to the apparently later version.   [a] *thus*

the fire of heavenly love. Restrain the stings of anger, and make us patient; banish dejection, and in adversity keep us hopeful. Vouchsafe that we may flee the sin of avarice so as to serve you with pleasing piety. Grant us to conquer gluttony by temperance and dire lust by chaste modesty, that cleansed by you and by you strengthened we may ever strive to attain the heavenly life.

A Prayer of One who is Advancing

You who clearly fashioned the world from nothingness since matter has not existed as long as you, and who with a simple nod will destroy it at the time you appoint and then continue to exist as eternally as before, how brief is our allotted span compared with the time that has elapsed since you ordered the ages to start rolling and unremitting war to be waged against vice. That you are always there as a king to help your soldiers[1] give proof by rousing us for the good fight.

[An untitled Fragment]

The schoolmaster's rod I studied under was not a Greek's, but a Latin's, for the Greek which you enjoin on me must be explained. Virgil delighted me with his verse, but not Homer.

(Oration) V   Oratio P   *title om.* LDR   [b] facili . . . tempore] facili placito tibi tem P   facili placito (uel noto *supra*) tempore V   [c] noster . . . secula] medius modus est quo tempora PV   [d] Regem . . . adesse] Te quoque de fragili rem fingere posse ualentem PV   Regem . . . adesse *added at the end of* P *with an omission mark, but without a corresponding mark in the text* 136 P

---

135. [1] This clause originally read: 'That you can also make a fragile creature into strong . . .'

137

De timore, spe, et amore[a][1]

Trinus ab inlicitis hominum se continet ordo:
Aut penae metuens, aut prouidus emolumenti,
Aut bene conplacitae captus uirtutis amore.[b]
Qui[c] spectare licet finem uideantur ad unum,
Vt uitium uitent uelud exiciale uenenum,   5
Imparitate tamen meriti discretius absunt,
Vnde nec unitae ueniunt ad premia palmae.
Primus enim coleret genium, si posset inulte,
Sed uehementer ait: 'Zelantis abhorreo uultum
Iudicis et dirae flammis ardere gehennae.'   10
Anne secundus idem faciat[d] si premia desint?
Sed uigili ratione sagax,[e] dum gaudia pensat
Vera, uoluptatem caute postponit inertem.
Tertius ingenue bonus egregieque decorus
Te contemplatur, te diligit, aurea uirtus;   15
Malit nempe mori, quam uiuens te uiduari.[f]
Sunt igitur speties ex affectu uenientes
Se quibus effugiant, ut ab ordine discrepet ordo.
Nam quis sollicito dubitet preferre timori
Securam spei requiem? Sed et ipsa decenter   20
Vt precellenti uenerans assurgit amori.
Interea pater obtimus hec speculatus ab alto,
Cuius iuditii nichil est quod fallat acumen,
'Ille', inquit, 'meus est uernaculus, iste satelles,
Hic[g] mea conformis, mea dilectissima proles.'   25
Tunc uariis meritis distantia premia librans,
Magna quidem primo tribuit, maiora secundo,
In solo totum confert probitatis amico.

138

Idem breuius[a][1]

Tres causae faciunt homines peccata cauere:
Horror supplitii, spes mercis, amor probitatis.

---

137 LDRCPV   V may preserve readings from an earlier version (cf. nos. 132, 135). Nos. 137–42 are also found in Berlin, Deutsche Staatsbibliothek, MS. Phill. 1694, f. 77[r–v], and in British Museum, Harley 3023, ff. 65, 63 (see E.

Fear, Hope, and Love[1]

Three grades of men refrain from committing sin: those who fear punishment, those who hope for a reward, and those who are seized with love of well-pleasing virtue. Though all of them aim at the same goal, to shun vice as a deadly poison, yet they stand apart by reason of their different merits and so do not gain the same prize of victory. The first would follow his inclination could he do so without being punished, but he fervently avers: 'I am terrified of the countenance of the wrathful Judge and of burning in hell's dire flames.' And would not the second also do it if there were nothing to be gained? But wisely and with watchful Reason, in weighing true joy he prudently rejects empty pleasure. The third with innate probity and surpassing excellence has his gaze fixed on you and loves you, golden Virtue, and indeed would rather die than live without you. These are the classes into which they fall according to their internal dispositions so that one grade differs from another. For who can doubt that fearful anxiety is not as worthy as the certain hope of rest? And this out of respect duly gives way to all-surpassing love. Meanwhile the most excellent Father, watching them from on high, whose all-discerning judgement nothing can deceive, proclaims: 'The first is my servant, the second my vassal, but the third is my own likeness, my dearest child.' Then weighing their various rewards in accordance with their different merits, he gives to the first a great prize indeed, and a greater to the second, but on him who alone loves virtue's self he bestows his all.

A Shorter Version of 'Fear, Hope, and Love'[1]

There are three reasons why men refrain from sinning: fear of punishment, hope of reward, and love of virtue. Although they

Bishop, 'Unedirte Briefe zur Geschichte Berengar's v. Tours', *Historisches Jahrbuch*, i (1880), 272).   *a* title om. RC   *b* Quos licet hoc teneat simul inuiolabile pactum *add*. V   *c* Quo V   *d* faciet DR   *e* uigens V   *f* uiuens te uiduari] te uiuendo relinqui V   *g* Haec DR
138 LDRCPV   *a* De eadem re breuius P

137. [1] Cf. Cassian, *Conlationes*, xi. 6 ff. (ed. Petschenig, *CSEL* xiii. 317 ff.).
138. [1] See no. 137.

Que[b] quamuis finem uideantur tendere ad unum,
Scilicet ut uitio careant, distant tamen hoc quod
Seruulus, et miles, et regis filius. Atqui   5
Principium timidus, cupidus habet incrementum
Virtutis, totam summam sincerus amator.
At si profitiat timor in spem, spes in amorem,
De seruo miles uenit, et de milite proles.[2]

139

Idem breuissime[a][1]

Probra cauet uel flagra pauens,[b] uel premia captans,
Vel uirtutis amans, distant ut calo, satelles,
Rex: duo profitiunt, status est tibi, tertie, summus.

140

De perfectione castitatis[a][1]

Sex gradibus consummatur perfectio casta:
Primo, dum uigiles,[b] fluxum nescire petulcum;
Quem sequitur lasciua diu non uoluere corde;
Tum, ne uel leuiter speciem cernendo cupiscas;
Quartus erit nec simpliciter genitale moueri;   5
Quintus, ob auditum ueneris nil mente uagari;
Vltimus, in somnis nullo fantasmate ludi.[c]
Hoc[d] sibi nemo rapit, sed Christi gratia prestat.
Est tamen obseruanda diurna medela dietae:
Libra cibi solidi, simplex emina falerni,[2]   10
Preterea labor, excubiae, rogatio[e] crebra,
Ne caro languentem necet incrassata pudorem.

---

[b] Qui CP

139 LDRCPV   [a] Item breuius (*misplaced*) C   Item de eodem [*sic*] re
breuius P   *title om.* LDR   [b] timens V

aim at the same goal, namely to avoid sin, they are as different as a servant, a knight, and a king's son. Yet he who fears punishment has the beginning of virtue, he who hopes for a reward has still more, and he who truly loves it has it all. But if fear should develop into hope, and hope into love, the servant will be transformed into a knight, and the knight into a king's son.[2]

A Very Short Version of 'Fear, Hope, and Love'[1]

Those who avoid sin from fear of punishment, hope of reward, or love of virtue, are as different as a groom, a vassal, and a king. The first two are doing well, but the third is doing best.

Perfect Chastity[1]

There are six stages in attaining perfect chastity: first, when you are awake, not to experience carnal pleasure; next, not to entertain lustful desires; then, when you see someone who is pretty, not to feel any craving; fourth, not to be physically aroused in any way; fifth, not to let the sound of love-making distract you; finally, when asleep not to dream of anything provocative. No one acquires this by his own effort: it is the gift of Christ's grace. Yet it is helpful to watch your daily diet: a pound of solid food, a single measure of wine,[2] besides work, vigils, and frequent prayer, so that a glutted body will not weaken and destroy your sense of shame.

140 LDRCPV It is also found in Saint-Omer MS. 115.   [a] Versus de castitate P *title om.* LDRC   [b] uigilas DR   [c] ledi V   [d] Hos DR [e] rogitatio PV

---

[2] Cf. Berengar of Tours, *De sacra coena:* '. . . Fulbertus episcopus, qui scripsit de provectu fidelium: "de seruo miles fiet et de milite proles" . . .' (ed. W. H. Beekenkamp (The Hague, 1941), p. 45).

139. [1] See nos. 137 f.

140. [1] Cf. Cassian, *Conlationes,* xii. 7 (ed. Petschenig, *CSEL* xiii. 345 ff.).

[2] Cf. St. Benedict, *Regula,* cc. xxxix–xl; no. 142.

141

Idem breuius[a]1

Castus agit quem nulla libido mouet uigilantem,
Nec uiolare potest sopitum illusio feda.

142

De dieta[a]1

Prandia lauta modum turbant plerumque dietae.
Indulges stomacho, mentem male crapula uexat.
Si parcas epulis, sequitur detractio uel laus.
Vt medium teneas, labor est, et ualde cauendum,
Ne tibi tristitiam pariat sicut suus est mos.   5
Si possis igitur prorsus haec prandia uita.
At si non liceat, hilaris cautusque recumbe, et
Liba cuncta parum tua quae tibi regula dictat,
Ne[b] summam nimiam coniectent[c] multa minuta.

143

De sobrietate

Cura sit haec tibi nec plus quam tria fercula[1] gustes,
Et post singula fercla semel bibe, sobrius ut sis.
Ter gula mande uorax, bibe ter—melius semel esset:
Extincta pecus omne siti nichil amplius haurit.

---

141 LDRCPV   [a] De eadem re breuius P   *title om.* LDR
142 LDRCP   [a] uel discrecione *add.* P   *title om.* LDR   [b] Nec
LDRP   [c] coniectant L
143 P

A Shorter Version of 'Perfect Chastity'[1]

The chaste man is he who is not aroused by lustful desires when awake and who cannot be polluted by shameful dreams when asleep.

A Rule for Eating[1]

Lavish dinners usually play havoc with a well-ordered diet. If you give in to your stomach, over-indulgence clouds your mind. If you eat but little, it results in your being disparaged or praised. To keep in between is hard, and you must especially watch that it does not result in the depression that commonly follows. So if you can, avoid such meals altogether. But if you cannot, take your place cheerfully and be on your guard. Taste a little of everything that your way of life allows, but don't let a lot of nibbling add up to your eating too much.

Temperance

Be careful not to taste more than three dishes;[1] and after each, drink but once, so that you will be sober. Eat thrice, greedy glutton, drink thrice—only once would be better: when its thirst is quenched, not even an animal keeps on drinking.

---

141. [1] See no. 140; Cassian, *Conlationes*, xii. 16 (ed. Petschenig, *CSEL* xiii. 359).

142. [1] The title in P and the apparent source for nos. 137 ff. suggest that this may be based on Cassian, *Conlationes*, ii. 16 ff. (ed. Petschenig, *CSEL* xiii. 59 ff.), though their contents are not altogether identical.

143. [1] Cf. St. Benedict, *Regula*, c. xxxix, who allows his monks to have as many as three dishes; Suetonius, *Aug.* lxxvii, and following him Einhard, *Vita Karoli*, c. xxiv (ed. L. Halphen (3rd edn., Paris, 1947), p. 72), who report that Augustus and Charlemagne usually drank only three times during a meal.

144

De duplicitate[a]

Duplex est qui dulcia uult et hic et inante;
Duplex est laudem cupiens de religione;
Duplex est diffidens impetrare quod orat.
Ve duplici, certum quia non habet emolumentum.

145

Diffinitio uirtutis

Virtus est Domino parendi firma uoluntas;
Virtus est medium retinendi accepta potestas.

146

De libra et partibus[a] *eius*[1]

Libra uel as ex unciolis constat duodenis.
Vncia[b] de libra linquit subtracta deuncem;
Et sextans (hoc est eadem geminata) decuncem;[c]
Hinc quadrans (haec scilicet ipsa ter acta) dodrantem;
Inde triens (ipsius quadruplicacio) bissem;[d]   5
Quincunx septuncem,[e] que sat sua pondera produnt;
Semis semissem, medium[f] dum diuidit assem;
Nec uacat unciolae mediam sescuncia iungens.

---

144 LDRCP In P it is placed with similar verses in the miscellaneous material
following the Hildegar collection, and the lines are arranged as here. In LDRC
it forms part of a florilegium on penance, and the first and third lines have
been exchanged.   [a] *title om.* LDRC

145 P

146 LDRP(= f. 38ᵛ), P¹(= f. 63) In LPP¹ the conventional signs for some of the
terms are placed between the lines or in the margins. The poem is also found
in Paris, Bibliothèque Nationale, latin 8069, 18081 (B. Hauréau, *Notices et*

Hypocrisy

The hypocrite wants his pleasure both now and hereafter The hypocrite wants to be praised for his piety. The hypocrite has no confidence that he will get what he prays for. Woe to the hypocrite, for indeed he gains nothing.

Virtue Defined

Virtue consists in the firm resolve to obey the Lord and in the gift of the ability to hold to the golden mean.

The Pound and its Parts[1]

The pound or *as* is composed of twelve ounces. If one ounce is subtracted from it, it leaves a *deunx*; and if a sixth (that is, two ounces) is subtracted, it leaves a *decunx*. If a quarter (that is, three ounces) is taken away, it leaves a *dodrans*; and if a third (four ounces), it leaves a *bis*. A *quincunx* leaves a *septunx*—their very names tell what they weigh. A half leaves a *semis*, for it divides the *as* in two. There is also a *sescuncia*, which adds half again to the tiny ounce.

---

extraits de quelques manuscrits latins de la Bibliothèque Nationale, vi (Paris, 1893), 9 f.); Avranches MS. 235, f. 52; Klagenfurt, Bischöfliche Bibliothek, MS. XXIX. d. 3, f. 35^v (L. Thorndike and P. Kibre, *A Catalogue of Incipits of Mediaeval Scientific Writings in Latin* (2nd edn., Cambridge, Mass., 1963), col. 824); British Museum, Additional MS. 17808, f. 73, where it lacks the titles, but has a full set of signs (printed in F. A. Yeldham, 'Notation of Fractions in the earlier Middle Ages', *Archeion*, viii (1927), 314, omitting the signs, but giving a convenient table of them on p. 319).   [a] patribus L *also in the following two titles*   [b] est *add.* L   [c] deuncem LPP1, *ante corr.* D   [d] bisse LP   [e] Quncus (Quintus P) septus est semis LP Quincus septus sē P1   [f] mediam DR

---

146. [1] See Pfister, *Fulbert*, pp. 35 f.; F. Hultsch, *Metrologicorum scriptorum reliquiae*, ii (Leipzig, 1866), 31 f.

De untia et partibus eius

Vncia uiginti scripulos et quattuor ambit;
Dimidium stater ac semuncia dicitur eius;   10
Terna due sescle pars est eademque duella;
Quarta, siclus[g] uel sicilicus uel denique sicel;
Sextula sexta modo solet et[h] modo sescla uocari;
Octauam appellant dragmam uel rarius olcem;
Et duodenariam mediam[i] sesclam uocitarunt;   15
Vigenam quartam scripulus seu gramma retentant.

De scripulo et partibus eius

Vnus item scripulus calcis componitur octo;
Dimidium scripuli est obolus, pars quarta cerates;[k]
Hic sextam fingi[l] placuit siliquamque uocari;
Vltimus est calcus ciceris duo granula pensans.   20

147

De signis et mensibus et diebus et horis
compendium computi[a] [1]

Annum sol duodena means per signa rotundat.
Singula ter denis percurrit signa diebus
Atque decem horis et dimidia,[b] faciuntque
Partes hae duodenario, si multiplicentur,
Tercentum sexagenos et quinque dies et   5
Sex horas, quas quadrantem liquet esse diei.
Hoc igitur numero proprium sol perficit annum.
Sed quia planius est toto quam parte diei
Annum metiri, uoluit chorus astrologorum
Tercentum sexagenis et quinque diebus   10
Claudi tres annos, quarto superaddier unum
Qui de quatuor annorum quadrantibus exit.
Hunc bissextilem dixerunt propter hoc annum,

---

[g] sidus LP   [h] et *om.* DR   [i] media LP   [k] ceratos LP
[l] figi DR

147 LDRP(= f. 65), P[1] (= B, f. 27; the preceding leaf, which presumably contained the title and the first six lines, is lost). The numerals used in the manuscripts have been converted into words, and the paragraphing has been slightly

The Ounce and its Parts

The ounce contains twenty-four scruples. A half-ounce is called a *stater* or *semuncia*. A third is equal to two *sesclae* and is called a *duella*. A fourth is called a shekel, *sicilicus*, or *sicel*. A sixth is known now as a *sextula*, now as a *sescla*. They call an eighth a drachma and occasionally an *olce*, and a twelfth they named a *media sescla*. A twenty-fourth is what a scruple or gram weighs.

The Scruple and its Parts

The scruple is made up of eight *calci*. A half-scruple is an *obolus*, and a fourth is a *cerates*. Then it seemed suitable to invent a sixth and to call it a *siliqua*. Last comes the *calcus*, which weighs two little chickpeas.

The Signs, Months, Days, and Hours
Essentials of the Calendar[1]

The sun goes through twelve signs in the course of a year. To go through each sign takes it thirty days and ten and a half hours; and if this is multiplied by twelve, it makes 365 days and six hours, which to be sure are one-fourth of a day. This is how long it takes the sun to complete its year. But since it is easier to measure the year by whole days rather than fractions, the astrologers' association decided to allot 365 days to three years and to add to the fourth year the extra day that results from combining the quarter days of the four years. They named this the bissextile year because two days are numbered as the sixth day before the

altered. The manuscripts vary as to the position of the accompanying tables, and the first is lacking in P. The poem is also found in Bibliothèque Nationale, latin 12117, f. 127[v] (L. Thorndike and P. Kibre, *A Catalogue of Incipits of Mediaeval Scientific Writings in Latin* (2nd edn., Cambridge, Mass., 1963), col. 105).   [a] compoti P   *title om.* LDR   [b] dimidio L

147. [1] Although the fundamentals of calculation as given here were widely known in the early middle ages, and there was a tradition of such mnemonic verses (cf. Ausonius, *Ecl.*, xii ff.), Fulbert's source was probably Bede's *De temporum ratione*, of which the chapter library seems to have possessed at least two copies (Chartres MSS. 19, 75). For other computistic writings from Chartres at this time, again showing Bede's influence, see Merlet, pp. 1 ff. In general, see Bede, *Opera de temporibus*, ed. C. W. Jones (Cambridge, Mass., 1943).

Bis quoniam sextum[c] Martis notat ante calendas,
Annos preteritos supplens, redimensque futuros.   15

Per menses anni soles ita distribuerunt:[2]
Ianus et Augustus iaculoque December acutus
Fert quarto nonas, nono decimoque kalendas
Post idus:[d] soles triginta scilicet unum;
Mars, Maius, Iulius, libripens October et aequus   20
Sexto nonas, septeno decimoque kalendas
Post idus: soles triginta rursus et unum;
Iunius, Aprilis,[e] post Septembremque Nouember
Quarto nonas, octauo decimoque kalendas
Post idus: soles triginta; Februus autem   25
Fert quarto nonas, sexto decimoque kalendas
Post idus: soles uiginti pauper et octo,
Sed per bissextum gaudet sibi crescere nonum.
Adnumerat proprias mensis sibi quisque kalendas,
Nullus et octauo mensis non computat[f] idus.   30

Mensis habet numerum normalem quisque notatum,
Annus habet concurrentem,[g] qui conuenientes
Donant scire dies, qui menses rite kalendant.[3]
Hi sunt normales numeri qui mensibus   34
  herent:

Quinque placent Marti, nec displicet unus Aprili,	Martius v	Aprilis i
Maius habet ternos, duplicat sibi Iunius ipsos,	Maius iii	Iunius vi
Vnus item Iuli,[h] tibi sunt Auguste quaterni,	Iulius i	Augustus iiii
September septem, binis[i] October agit rem,	September vii	October ii
Quinque Nouember abhinc repetens, septemque December,	Nouember v	December vii
Nec cupiunt Iano tres, nec sex tollere Febro.	Ianus iii	Februus vi

[c] sexto DR   [d] idem L *also in lines 22, 25, 27*   [e] Apriles (-s *sup. ras.*) L
Aprilem PP[1]   [f] computet LDR   [g] concurrentes DR   [h] Iulii L
Iulio DR   [i] bis *corr. to* bini L

[2] The contents of the present paragraph are perhaps more easily grasped from
the jingle:

> In March, July, October, May,
> The Ides are on the fifteenth day,
> The Nones the seventh; but all besides
> Have two days less for Nones and Ides.

calends of March. This supplies what was wanting in preceding years and gives future ones their true beginning.

The days are distributed among the months of the year as follows.[2] January, August, and December of Sagittarius' keen bow have four days of nones and nineteen of calends after the ides, and thus thirty-one days. March, May, July, and October of well-balanced Libra have six days of nones and seventeen of calends after the ides, again thirty-one days. June, April, September, and then November have four days of nones and eighteen of calends after the ides, and so thirty days. February has four of nones and sixteen of calends after the ides, thus a meagre twenty-eight days; but in leap year it rejoices to grow to twenty-nine. Each month also has its own calends, and all reckon eight days of ides.

Each month has a 'regular' and each year a 'concurrent' number assigned to it, and the combination of the two gives the day of the week on which each month begins.[3] These are the regular numbers attached to the months: five pleases March, and April is satisfied with one; May has three, and June has twice three; one belongs to July, and August's is four; September's is seven, October's two; November reverts to five, and December to seven; three is happy with January, and six with February.

(B. L. Gildersleeve and G. Lodge, *Latin Grammar* (3rd edn., London, 1895), p. 491.) The days were otherwise reckoned backwards as being so many days before the nones or ides of the present month or the calends of the following, the day before each being counted as the second rather than the first.

[3] The rest of the poem is concerned with the so-called 'regular' and 'concurrent' numbers, here treated in reverse order. The concurrent or 'solar epact' is assigned to the year and tells how many days it is after the last Sunday of the preceding year before the new one begins: e.g. a concurrent of '1' indicates that the present year begins on Tuesday, of '6' on Sunday. As the common solar year consists of fifty-two weeks and one day and so begins and ends on the same day of the week, the following year begins and ends on the next day of the week, and the year after that on yet the next. Hence if every year had 365 days, they would fall into a cycle in which the year would begin on the same day of the week every seventh year. However, this cycle is broken by leap year, and the added day every fourth year so changes it that it is only after seven such days (= twenty-eight years) that the cycle can begin again. This period of twenty-eight years is known as the solar cycle. The second table here gives the concurrent numbers for the years of the solar cycle (B = leap year). Thus in the first line, the first year is a leap year with a concurrent 'one'; the next three are common solar years with concurrents of 'two', 'three', and 'four'.

The regular number indicates the day of the week with which each month of the year begins (cf. the first table). This is determined by adding it to the concurrent number of the year, and if the total is more than seven, by sub-tracting seven from it. The resultant number is that of the day of the week

Huic[k] alter numerus[l] concurrit ad inueniendum   41
Quam sibi quisque diem[m] mensis uelit esse kalendas;
Septem lineolis ipsum tibi cerne notatum.
Harum septem lineolarum quaelibet una
Spectatur summas numeri gestare quaternas;   45
Et sic uiginti summae numerantur et octo,
Diuisae totidem certa racione per annos.
Hae quoque summae solares uocitantur epactae.
Hi[n] concurrentes numeri uersantur in annis:

Vnus bissexti,[o] duo non neque tres neque quadri;	B	i	ii	iii	iiii
Sex sunt bissexti, non uos septem, une, gemelli;	B	vi	vii	i	ii
Quadri ad bissextum, quini, sex, septem aliorsum;	B	iiii	v	vi	vii
Bini ad bissextum, tres, quadri, quinque seorsum;	B	ii	iii	iiii	v
Septem bissextant, unus, duo, tresque recusant;	B	vii	i	ii	iii
Quini bissextant, sex, septem, unusque reiectant;	B	v	vi	vii	i
Tres bissexte, quadris, quinis, nec iungito senis.	B	iii	iiii	v	vi

148

[On the Astrolabe][1]

Abdebaran tauro, geminis menkeque rigelque,
Frons et calbalazet prestant insigne leoni;
Scorpie galbalagrab, tua sit capricornie deneb,
Tu, batanalhaut, piscibus es satis una duobus.

---

[k] Nun (uel huic *supra*) P   Nunc P[1]   [l] numero L   numerus *corr. to* numero
(-os?) P   [m] Qua . . . die DR   [n] Hii PP[1]   [o] bissexto DR   *also in
line 51*

148 LDRP(= f. 39), P[1](= f. 65), P[2](= B, f. 27[v])

---

reckoned as beginning with Sunday: e.g. in 1022, which had a concurrent of 7, June
began on 7+6 = 13, −7 = 6, or Friday. The numbering of the regulars from March
rather than January was traditional throughout the middle ages and does not indicate
(as has been argued) that Fulbert regarded the year as beginning in March (see
R. L. Poole, *Studies in Chronology and History* (Oxford, 1934), pp. 4 ff.). In general see
A. Giry, *Manuel de diplomatique* (Paris, 1894), pp. 134 ff.

148. [1] See pp. xxvii f.

A second number combines with it to give the day on which
each month begins, and it is laid out for you in these seven little
lines. Each of them contains four numbers, and the total twenty-
eight are distributed over the same number of years according to
a fixed pattern. These numbers are also called the solar epacts.
These are the concurrent numbers for the years: the leap year's
number is one, the next years' are two, three, and four; the leap
year's is six, and the next's are seven, one, and two; to the leap
year belongs four, while five, six, and seven belong to the following; to the leap year goes two, while three, four, and five have
their own years; when the leap year is seven, the next years are
one, two, and three; when it is five, they are six, seven, and one;
a leap year of three is followed by four, five, and six.

[*On the Astrolabe*][1]

Aldebaran stands out in Taurus, Menke and Rigel in Gemini,
and Frons and bright Calbalazet in Leo. Scorpio, you have
Galbalagrab; and you, Capricorn, Deneb. You, Batanalhaut, are
alone enough for Pisces.

149

Pre gaudio pacis[a]1

Sanctum simpliciter patrem cole, pauperum caterua,
  Quantumque nosti laudibus honora,
Ad normam redigit qui subdita secla prauitati,
  Potens nouandi sicut et creandi,
Et graue dampnatae[b] longi tibi subuenit laboris,   5
  Opem ferendo pacis et quietis.
Iam proceres legum[c] racionibus ante desueti
  Quae recta[d] discunt strenue capessunt.
Predo manum cohibet furcae memor, et latrone coram
  Inermis alte precinit uiator.[2]   10
Dente saturnali restringitur euagata uitis,[3]
  Cultuque tellus senta mansuescit.
Gaudet lancea falx, gaudet spata deuenire uomis,[e]4
  Pax ditat imos, pauperat superbos.
Salue, summe[f] pater, fer et omnibus integram salutem,   15
  Quicumque pacis diligunt quietem;
Et qui bella uolunt, hos contere dextera potenti,
  Tradens gehennae filios maligni.

150

Rithmus de Fide, Spe, et Caritate[a]

Incorporeae personae gratia colloquii
  Conuenerunt in cubile cuiusdam notarii,
Nomina qui singularum simul cum sententiis
  Ratus digna memoratu sic excepit[b] litteris.
Fides ait: 'Ter beatum facit Dei uisio,   5
  Sed nequit uideri nisi sano mentis oculo.'
Spes subiecit: 'Est ut ais; potest tamen morbidus
  Quamuis cum labore quodam expurgari oculus.'
Addit Caritas: 'Iocundam michi prestat requiem
  Labor tolerari iussus ob beatitudinem.'   10

---

149 LDRP(= B, f. 25)V   [a] Versus de pace V   *title om.* LDR   [b] dam-
pnati LDR (-i *sup. ras.* L)   [c] legum proceres V   [d] recte DR
[e] uomer DR   [f] sancte V

The Joy of Peace[1]

Worship the holy Father in your simple way, O host of the poor. Honour him with all the praises that you can. For he restores a world which depravity held in bondage, having the power to renew no less than to create, and comes to aid you who are heavily oppressed by long toil, bringing the help of peace and quiet. Now the nobles, who in the past knew not the ways of law, are learning what is right and striving to enforce it. The robber remembers the gallows and holds his hand, and before the highwayman's very eyes the unarmed traveller sings aloud.[2] The rambling vine is held in check with Saturn's pruning-shears,[3] and the overgrown land is tended and grows tame. The spear rejoices to become a scythe, the sword to become a ploughshare.[4] Peace brings riches to the lowly and despoils the mighty. Hail highest Father! Grant perfect salvation to all who love quiet peace; and those who want war, crush them with your powerful right arm, handing the sons of darkness over to the power of hell.

Faith, Hope, and Charity

Some incorporeal persons held a meeting in the chamber of a clerk, who thought it worth recounting their names and what they said, and so he took it down. Faith stated: 'To see God makes one triply blessed, but he can only be seen by the mind's eye when it is unclouded.' Hope followed: 'What you say is true; yet a sickly eye can be cured, though not without an effort.' Charity added: 'The effort that must be endured to attain blessedness is

150 P(= B, f. 25ᵛ)V   *a* Eiusdem de uirtutibus V   *b* excaepit V
excipit P

149. [1] See Hoffmann, pp. 66 ff.   [2] Cf. Juvenal, x. 22.
     [3] Cf. Virgil, *Geor.* ii. 406 f.   [4] Cf. Isa. 2: 4.

Ratio argumentosa his acceptis[c] intulit:
  'Quia sic est, lippae Menti medicina competit,
Sed de multis illa tantum facile curabitur,
  Cui labor per amorem iocundus efficitur.'
Postquam est huic assensum Rationis clausulae,   15
  Lippa Mens adepta locum ita cepit dicere:
'Quis det michi miserandae hunc amorem bibere,
  Qui lenire possit michi crucem paenitentiae?'

151

Rithmus de sententiis philosophorum de summo bono[a]1

Inter illa quae profani bona putant maxime
  Solent amare quietem iunctam opulentiae;
Sed philosophi uidentes hoc commune beluis
  Aliud sanxerunt esse priuum[b] bonum hominis.
Indignum enim duxerunt ut humana ratio   5
  Pigro uentri famuletur et inerti ocio,
Quae magis aeternum nomen sibi debet parere,
  Sicut ipsa immortalis probatur existere.
Sensus perit corporalis capax pereuntium;
  Sensus perstat rationis capax permanentium.   10
Nec resolui potest simplex mens et incorporea,
  Que de nullis fuit ante partibus composita;
Et quia sine defectu semper habet uiuere,
  Bonum suum in caducis nunquam debet querere.
Destinarunt ergo sibi[c] stabilem materiam,   15
  Scilicet rationalem, physicam, et ethicam.
Tunc sagaci arbitratu secludentes uitium,
  In uirtute statuerunt hominis officium,
Hoc diffinientes tandem esse bene uiuere,
  Quod est bene scire semper atque bene facere.   20
Tradiderunt ergo uitae praecepta utilia,
  Quae non seruauerunt tamen pressi mole carnea.
Fuit illis et de Deo tandem magna quaestio,
  Et sententiarum quidem non parua dissensio.
Nullum hic et ille plures esse deos[d] autumat,   25
  Sed utroque Plato maior unum tantum approbat.

[c] accepistis V

151 P(=B, f. 26)V   [a] Sententiae antiquorum (philosophorum *supra*)
de summo bono V   [b] primum P   [c] sibi *om.* V   [d] deos esse P

to me but a pleasant rest.' Reason, ever logical, listened to them and then deduced: 'What this means is that while there is a medicine for bleary-eyed Mind, of the many the only one who can easily be cured is she whose labour is lightened by love.' After they assented to what Reason had concluded, bleary-eyed Mind took the floor and said: 'Who will give my pitiful self to drink of this love which can make it easier for me to bear the cross of penance?'

The Teachings of the Philosophers concerning the Highest Good[1]

Of all that common men regard as life's greatest blessings they normally prize peace and plenty. But the philosophers, seeing that this is shared with brute beasts, put forth something else as the proper good of man; for they did not think it fitting for human reason to cater to a full belly and idle leisure, since it ought to be striving for eternal fame just as it itself is evidently immortal. The body's ability to perceive what is temporal perishes, the intellect's to perceive what is eternal remains. Nor can the mind, which is simple and incorporeal, be dissolved, for it was never composed of parts. Since it will not pass away, but live for ever, it should never look for its true good in what is transitory. So the philosophers devoted themselves to the study of immutable truth: to wit, rational, physical, and ethical. Then wisely excluding vice, they declared that man must strive for virtue; and this they finally defined as the upright life, which consists in right knowledge and action. So they handed down useful instructions on how to live, though they themselves did not follow them as they were weighed down by the burden of the flesh. There was also among them a great discussion concerning God and no little difference of opinion. One thought that there was no god, and another that there were several; but Plato knew better than both and proved there was only one.

---

151. [1] Cf. Sallust, *Cat.* i f.; and, though it may not be a direct source, Augustine, *De civitate Dei*, viii, especially 8 ff. (*CCL* xlvii. 224 ff.).

152

Rithmus de distantia dialectice et rethoricae[1]

Multi rethores uocantur atque dialectici
Propter libros Ciceronis, propter Aristotilis,
Quos sese uidisse iactant ac legisse praedicant.
Vani qui si consulantur de communi genere
Duarum professionum et diuersa specie,   5
Quo iungantur aut quo distent, non habent quid hiscere.
His qui cupis impar esse cauta diligentia
Perscrutari ne graueris quid haec ludant rithmica.
Species sunt facultatis,[2] hoc iunguntur capite;
Distant autem usu, fine, necnon et materie.   10
Thesis dialecticorum, rethorum ypothesis
Est materia uocata, sic diuisae propriis,
Quaestio quia thesis est circumstantiis carens,
Quaestio et ypothesis est circumstantias habens.
Vsu quoque supradictae facultates logicae   15
Distant, quod rogatione breui dialectica
Agit rem, oratione ductili rethorica,
Vel quod illa sillogismis coangustat integris,
Haec contenta est diminuta clausula entimematis.
Fine differunt, quod ista persuadere arbitrio,[a]   20
Illa tendit extorquere quod uult aduersario.

153

Rithmus de abbate Iohanne breuis staturae[a][1]

In gestis patrum ueterum	quiddam legi ridiculum,
Exemplo tamen habile,	quod uobis dico rithmice.
Iohannes abba paruulus	statura non uirtutibus
Ita maiori socio	quicum erat in heremo:
'Volo', dicebat, 'uiuere	secure sicut angelus,
Nec ueste nec cibo frui	qui laboretur manibus.'

5

152 P(= B, f. 26) It is also found in Hereford Cathedral, MS. P. i. 4, f. 46, and Oxford, Bodleian Library, d'Orville MS. 158, f. 122. See p. xxxi.   [a] So *Hereford and d'Orville MSS.*   arbitror P

153 LDRCP(= B, f. 26ᵛ)   For other manuscripts see *Die Cambridger Lieder*, ed. K. Strecker (*MGH, Scriptores rerum Germanicarum*, xl), pp. 97 f.   [a] *title om.* LDRC

How Dialectic and Rhetoric Differ[1]

Many are called rhetoricians and dialecticians because they boast they have seen and proclaim they have read the works of Cicero and Aristotle. But if these braggarts are questioned about the common genus of their two subjects and their specific difference, what unites and what distinguishes them, they cannot tell you. If you do not want to be like them, you had better take a careful look at what these playful verses have to say.

Both are species of the 'faculty',[2] and this is what unites them; but they differ as to their method, end, and matter. The dialecticians' matter is known as the thesis, the rhetoricians' as the hypothesis, their difference being that the thesis is a proposition that lacks individuating notes, while the hypothesis is one that has them. These two faculties of logic also differ in their method, for dialectic proceeds by short questions and answers and rhetoric by continuous speech, and the one reduces the argument to perfect syllogisms, while the other is satisfied with less rigorously formulated enthymemes. As to the difference in their end, the one tries to persuade its opponent to change his mind, while the other strives to force him to concede.

Abbot John the Small[1]

In the lives of the ancient fathers I read an amusing little tale, but with a moral to it, which I shall tell to you in verse. Abbot John, small in stature, but not in virtue, said to his older companion in the wilderness: 'I wish to live like an angel and not be troubled by having to work for food and clothing.' His older friend replied: 'I advise you not to try it hastily, brother, for later you may wish

---

152. [1] As regards the source (namely Boethius, *De differentiis topicis*, iv), see pp. xxvi, xxx–xxxii.

[2] As to Boethius' use of the term 'faculty', see R. McKeon, *Speculum*, xvii (1942), 11.

153. [1] Cf. *Vitae patrum*, v. 10. 27 (*PL* lxxiii. 916 f.). There is a translation in verse in Helen Waddell, *The Wandering Scholars* (7th edn., London, 1949), pp. 98 f.

Respondit[b] maior: 'Moneo   ne sis incepti properus,
Frater, quod tibi postmodum   sit[c] non caepisse sacius.'
At minor: 'Qui non dimicat,   non cadit neque superat'
Ait, et nudus heremum   interiorem penetrat.[d]   10
Septem dies gramineo   uix ubi[e] durat pabulo;
Octauo fames imperat   ut ad sodalem redeat.
Qui sero clausa ianua   tutus sedet in cellula,
Cum minor uoce debili   'Frater', appellat, 'aperi.
Iohannes opis indigus   notis assistit foribus;   15
Ne spernat tua pietas   quem redigit necessitas.'
Respondet ille deintus: 'Iohannes factus[f] angelus
Miratur caeli cardines,   ultra non curat homines.'
Foris Iohannes excubat,   malamque noctem tolerat,
Et preter uoluntariam   hanc agit penitentiam.   20
Facto mane recipitur,   satisque uerbis uritur;
Sed intentus ad crustula   fert pacienter omnia.[g]
Refocilatus domino   grates agit ac socio;
Dehinc rastellum brachiis   temptat mouere languidis.
Castigatus angustia   de leuitate nimia,   25
Cum angelus non potuit,   uir bonus esse didicit.

154

[*Saint Martin of Tours*][1]

Inter patres monastici[a]   uel clericalis ordinis
Virtutis excellencia   Martinus est[b] notabilis.[c]
Non quilibet de pluribus,   sed ille solitarius
Primo, dehinc Turonicae   presul paterque patriae,
Directa[d] quem prudencia   fortisque temperancia,   5
Quin uniuersa sanctitas   ornauit, hoc est caritas.
Is pauperi quam diuidit   se ueste Christus induit,
Dans signa tantae gratiae   nondum renato cernere.
Mox fonte celi roscidus   sancti repletur Spiritus,[e]
Diuoque fretus numine   it ut potens apostolus.   10

---

[b] Respondet P   [c] si *corr. to* sit L   si DC   [d] penitrat LP   Quis
explicare ualeat illa mus . . . genera *add.* P *as the last line on the page, the*
following leaf being lost   [e] ibi C   [f] est *add.* DR   [g] crustulam . . .
omniam (?) LC

you had not.' The younger answered: 'He who does not fight neither falls nor conquers'; and so he left all and withdrew deep into the wilderness. He lasted hardly seven days with fodder his only food; and on the eighth hunger forced him to return to his companion. The latter was seated in his cell late at night with the door barred, when the younger feebly called out: 'Brother, open up! John needs your aid and is standing at these well-known doors. In your piety do not spurn one who has been forced back by necessity.' The other replied from inside: 'John has become an angel. He gazes in ecstasy on the heavens and is no longer concerned with human cares.' John slept outside and passed an unbearable night, thus doing more penance than he wished. In the morning he was let inside, and his ears burned at what he heard; but absorbed with his piece of crust, he said not a word. Refreshed he thanked the Lord and his friend and weakly tried to hoe. Chastised for his exceeding rashness, since he could not be an angel, he strove to be a virtuous man.

[*Saint Martin of Tours*][1]

Among the fathers who were monks or clerks Martin is distinguished by his pre-eminent virtue. He was not just anyone; but first as a hermit and then as bishop of Tours and father of his country he was adorned with honest prudence, steadfast temperance, and the height of holiness, namely charity. The cloak that he shared with a beggar Christ himself put on and granted that one who was not yet reborn might see tokens of his great favour. Then wet from the heavenly font he was filled with the Holy Spirit; and relying on God's aid, he went forth as a mighty

154   LDRCP(= B, f. 28ᵛ) The poem seems to have been revised (cf. nos. 132, 135, 137), and preference is given here to the apparently later version. It is also found in Rouen MS. 243 (Y. Delaporte, *Études grégoriennes*, ii (1957), 68) and several later manuscripts (cf. *Analecta hymnica*, l (Leipzig, 1907), 287). [a] monachi L   monachilis DR   [b] est *om.* DR   [c] Virtutis... notabilis] Martinus est uirtutibus insignis et miraculis P   [d] Direpta L Diserta DR   [e] sancto . . . spiritu P

154. [1] Cf. Sulpicius Severus, *Vita sancti Martini*, especially cc. 3, 6, 17 f., 7 f., 14, 13, 16, 19 (ed. Halm, *CSEL* i. 113, 116 f., 126 f., 117 f., 123, 122 f., 125 f., 128).

Confutat ortas hereses,
Leprae medetur osculo
Quid igne rapto caelitus
Grauesque moles per fidem
Dedisse cecis sidera,
Mutisque precinentibus
Quot gesserit huiusmodi
Fugit ligari calculo

iussu repellit demones,
et mortuis precario.
cremasse fana funditus,
hunc transtulisse predicem,
sentire surdis organa,   15
aptasse claudos saltibus?
miraculorum milia
uelud saburra pontica.

155

Rithmus de trinitate[a1]

Verbum Dei Spiritumque legifer in Genesi,
Rex Dauid secundo psalmo post trigenum cecinit,
Sic uterque trinitatem unitatis prodidit.[2]
Sapiens cum genitore suo sancto[b] Salomon
Plano uerbo declarauit esse Deo filium,   5
Verbum scilicet eternum corde eius genitum.[3]
Moysi et Isaie testis est psalmographus
Quia filius cum patre Deus est et dominus,
Nihil enim[c] patre Deo gignitur nisi Deus.[4]
Deum hominem futurum esse sicut extitit   10
Post psalmistam Isaias liquido predocuit:[d5]
Dispensacio salutem illa nobis edidit.
Quodque Deus nasciturus esset matre uirgine
Idem ante Gabrihelem iussus est predicere:[6]
Talis porro decet ortus auctorem munditiae.   15
Legislator Danihelque notauerunt terminum
Quando rex uenturus esset expectatus gentium:[7]
Is neglectus male perdit[e] populum Iudaicum.
Summum regem affuturum pauperem et humilem
Sion ostendit propheta quasi iam uisibilem,   20
Corruit superbus hostis ante cuius faciem.[8]

---

155 LDRCP(= B, f. 25ᵛ)V The title and first three lines are missing in V, apparently owing to the loss of the preceding leaf. The poem is also found in Vatican, latin 466, f. 13, and British Museum, Royal 5. A. xiii, f. 187.
[a] Rithmus eiusdem LDRC   [b] sancto suo P   sancto *om.* V   [c] enim *om.* LC   [d] perdocuit DR   [e] perdit male P   male *om.* V

155. [1] This poem seems to be based on a systematic collection of Biblical excerpts found in V and manuscripts of the L-family and printed as sermon vii in *PL* cxli. 331 ff. (cf. pp. xxii n., xxvii f.). I have indicated what appear to be the appropriate passages and their respective headings.

apostle. He repressed heresies that had arisen and drove out
devils by his command. He healed a leper by his kiss and raised
the dead by his prayers. Why should I tell of how he totally
destroyed temples by fire called down from heaven, of how by
faith he turned back a huge tree that was falling, of how he made
the blind to see the stars, the deaf to hear music, the dumb to
sing out, and the lame to leap up? How many thousands of such
miracles he performed can no more be reckoned than the sea's
sands.

The Trinity[1]

Of God's Word and Spirit sang the Lawgiver in Genesis and
King David in psalm thirty-two and so made known that there
were Three in One.[2] Wise Solomon and his holy father plainly
declared that God had a Son, the eternal Word begotten in his
heart.[3] The psalmist bears witness with Moses and Isaiah that the
Son as well as the Father is God and Lord, for nothing is begotten of God the Father that is not God.[4] Isaiah, following the
psalmist, clearly foretold that God would become man, just as he
did.[5] It was this dispensation that brought us salvation. Gabriel
was sent to announce that God would be born of a virgin mother,[6]
for it was a fitting birth for the author of purity. The Lawgiver
and Daniel foretold when the king would come who was the desired
of the nations,[7] and refusal to acknowledge him destroyed the
Jewish people. That the highest king would come poor and lowly
the prophet showed to Sion as clearly as if he were already there
before whose face the proud enemy fell prostrate.[8]

[2] Cf. Gen. 1: 2 f.; Ps. 32: 6, under the heading 'Quod Deus unus est in
trinitate'.

[3] Cf. Ps. 2: 7; Prov. 30: 4, under the heading 'Quod Christus a Deo sit genitus'.

[4] The passages under the heading 'Quod [Christus] cum patre Deus et dominus
est' are Gen. 1: 27 and Ps. 44: 7; but cf. Ps. 109: 1, 3. The reference to Isaiah
is possibly to the passage under the heading cited in note 3, namely Isa. 66:
9, or perhaps those cited in note 5.

[5] There is no separate heading for this; but in addition to the other texts
cited here, see Isa. 35: 4; 40: 9 f.

[6] Cf. Luke 1: 26 ff., which is not found in the excerpts, nor is there a suitable
heading. Cf. Isa. 7: 14.

[7] Cf. Gen. 49: 10; Dan. 9: 21 ff., under the heading 'De termino aduentus
eius'.

[8] Cf. Isa. 62: 11, actually quoted indirectly from Matt. 21: 5, under the
heading 'Quod in humilitate uenturus esset'. Cf. Zech. 9: 9.

APPENDIX A

Fulbert's Obituary and Epitaph

Hac die migrauit ad Dominum pater noster bonae memoriae Fulbertus, suae tempestatis pontificum decus, praeclara lux[a] mundo a Deo data, pauperum sustentator, desolatorum consolator, praedonum et latronum refrenator, uir eloquentissimus[b] tam in diuinis quam in omnium liberalium artium libris, qui ad restaurationem huius sancti templi,[c] quod ipse post incendium a fundamento reedificare ceperat, bonam partem auri sui et argenti reliquit, et discipline ac sapientiae radiis hunc[d] locum illuminauit, et clericis suis multa bona fecit.

Tumulus (Merlet, photo-reproduction following p. 46 (see above, pp. xliii f.)), cathedral necrology (ibid., p. 159), P   [a] Hac . . . lux] Obiit dilectus Deo et hominibus pater noster bone memorie Fulbertus, hujus sancte sedis episcopus, lux preclara *necrology*   Annum ab incarnatione Domini mxxviii, iiii idus Aprilis, obiit dilectus Deo et hominibus pater noster uenerandae memoriae Fulbertus, suae tempestatis pontificum decus, lux praeclara P   [b] et sapientissimus *add. necrology* P   [c] huius . . . templi] sancti templi suae diocesis P   [d] illum P

Incipit epitaphium

> Quem tibi, Carnotis, concessit Fons bonitatis,
>   Doctrinae fluuium duplicis egregium,
> Pontificum sidus, Fulbertus, fulgidus actu,
>   Vestis pauperibus uictus et assiduus,
> En clausus iacet hic, factus de puluere puluis,   5
>   Et prestolatur surgere cum reliquis.
> Virtutum cultor, uiciorum mortificator
>   Auxiliante Deo perstitit a puero.
> Bis denos annos atque unum dimidiumque,
>   Virgo Maria, tuae praefuit ecclesiae.   10
> Ingressurus erat Phebus post lumina septem
>   Taurum, cum mestum deseruit populum.

Explicit

P   It is also found in Paris, Bibliothèque Nationale, latin 17177, f. 69ᵛ (see p. xliii n.).

APPENDIX B

Interpolations in the Collection

Nos. 1–3 are found only in L-class manuscripts. No. 1 is a notice of the election of Abbot Bernard of Montier-la-Celle, which seems to have taken place shortly after the death of Count Odo of Chartres (15 November 1037).[1] It apparently served as the model for the announcements of the elections of Abbot Thierry of Saint-Aubin d'Angers (14 January 1056) and Abbess Richildis of Le Ronceray (23/4 June 1073).[2] Nos. 2 f. concern the rain of blood that is the subject of no. 125. They are also found in *Vita Gauzlini*, pp. 136 ff., where the quotations in no. 3 have been omitted; hence it is used here only for no. 2. No. 4 is found only in V, f. 125 (see p. lxxxii).

1

Notice of the election of Abbot Bernard of Montier-la-Celle
c. late 1037–8

Certum est omnibus qui fundamenta catholicae puritatis nouerunt totius aecclesiae soliditatem in pace consistere, et signum Christi discipulatus in dilectione. Nam sicut in euuangelio Dominum dixisse legimus: 'Pacem relinquo uobis, pacem meam do uobis', et iterum: 'In hoc cognoscent omnes quia mei estis discipuli, si dilectionem habueritis ad inuicem',[1] liquet ergo neminem fore Christi discipulum, nisi signo dilectionis ac pacis fuerit insignitus. Hoc uero signaculum non adipiscitur, nisi ab his in quibus fuerit unitas uoluntatum. Vnitas autem uoluntatum inueniri non potest, nisi in his qui suum uelle nolleue in unius prepositi iuditio constituunt.[a2] Vnde et auctor pacis nullum ordinem in ecclesia sine prelati regimine relinquens, pro certo insinuat nulla alia racione fragilitatem humanae labilitatis ad

---

[1] It also mentions Odo's wife Hermengardis, who was still alive in 1042, and his son Stephen, who died *c.* 1048 (Lex, pp. 237 ff.).

[2] *Cartulaire de l'abbaye de Saint-Aubin d'Angers*, ed. B. de Brousillon, i (Paris, 1903), 48 f., no. 28; *Cartularium Monasterii Beatae Mariae Caritatis Andegavensis*, ed. P. Marchegay (Archives d'Anjou, iii (1854)), pp. 17 f., no. 16. See Guillot, i. 156 ff., 181 ff.

unitatem spiritus posse redigi siue in pace conseruari. Quare nos pauci fratres in cenobio cui Cella Boboni nomen est Deo pro posse famulantes, quia uinculum pacis et signaculum Christianae disciplinae dilectionem per unitatem cordis uel animae possidere cupimus, post obitum domni Warini abbatis, uiri religiosi, elegimus fratrem quendam morum probitate ornatum nomine[b] Bernardum, quem nobis uice patris preesse uolumus, et in diffinicione eius sententiarum nostrarum uniri diuersitatem, ne diuersa sencientes a Christi doctrina inueniamur extranei. Facta est autem electio ista consilio atque auctoritate domni abbatis Maioris Monasterii[3] post excessum gloriosi principis Odonis, a quo huius rei curam susceperat. Qui hoc in conuentu monachorum ritu celebri peracto optulit etiam fratrem praedictum nobilissimae H(ermengardi) comitissae, sub cuius dicione locus ipse consistit, et Stephano comiti eius filio, a quibus donum rerum temporalium ad idem pertinentium cenobium suscepit. Dehinc uero statuit eum uenerabili Mainardo Trecassinorum presuli,[4] cuius ecclesiastica auctoritate electionem huiusmodi corroborari oportuit, atque ab ipso animarum curam suscipi, necnon abbatis benedictionem[c] secundum institutionem patrum celebrari. Quod ipse benignissime annuit, et omnia prout mos expostulat ecclesiasticus utpote uir prudentissimus atque erudicione clarus compleuit.

LDRC *a* consistunt C *b* nomine *om.* DR *c* necnon . . . benedictionem] non abbatis benedictio L

[1] John 14: 27, 13: 35. [2] See p. 87 n. 4.
[3] Abbot Albert of Marmoutier (see p. 111 n. 2).
[4] Bishop Frotmundus of Troyes' (see p. 49 n. 5) successor, who in 1049 was translated to Sens, which he ruled until his death in 1062 (*GC* xii. 37 f., 495).

2

Epistola transmissa Gauzlino abbati a piissimo rege Rotberto de quodam portento[a]   c. *late June 1027*

Rotbertus nutu Dei Francorum rex Gauzlino presuli Bituricensium salutem.

Volo uos scire mei animi motum[b] qualiter se habet, ut forte accidere solet, cum mens humana mouetur[c] siquid mirabile preter solitum insperate auditur. Dum ergo die sabbati iam exacto[d] sederem ad cenam, allata fuit mihi quaedam epistola a Willelmo comite[e] de quodam portento mirabile[f] auditu: scilicet tribus diebus ante solempnitatem sancti Iohannis Baptistae[1] in quibusdam partibus mei regni (uidelicet in partibus Aquitaniae iuxta plagam maritimam) pluisse de caelo talis naturae sanguinem,[g] ut cum fortuitu[h] cadebat super carnem hominis aut super uestimentum aut super petram, non poterat[i] auferri lauando; si uero cadebat super lignum, tunc bene lauabatur. Siquidem per eamdem epistolam petiit a me idem Willelmus comes, ut ego requirerem a mei regni sapientioribus[k] quid significaret[l] hoc portentum. Ego uero eo[m] uolo et precor, ut perquiratis in quibusdam historiis si umquam accidisset huius simile, et quod factum sequeretur huius rei portentum, michique hoc eodem legato rescribite quomodo acciderit, et in qua historia inueniri possit. Attamen deprecor ne differatis ad rescribendum michi, quia tamdiu legatum huius portenti tenebo, donec michi respondeatis. Valete.

LDRC *Vita Gauzlini* (see p. 273)   [a] *title om.* R *Vita Gauzlini*   [b] totum LC   [c] morietur LC   [d] exaucto *corr. to* exhausto L   [e] missa *add.* DR   [f] mirabili DRC   [g] sanguinem *om.* LC   [h] confortuitu LC *Vita Gauzlini* (*textual note d*)   [i] posset DR   [k] sapientibus DR   [l] significaret *om.* L hoc portentum significaret DR   [m] eo *om.* DR

---

[1] 24 June.

3

Rescriptum Gauzlini abbatis[a]   c. *late June 1027*

Domino regi Francorum excellentissimo Rotberto humilis Gauzlinus aeterni regis consortium.

Quod placuit uobis interrogari[b] de prodigio quod accidit, hoc nobis ex historiis aperte patet quod sanguis semper[c] gladium, aut ciuile bellum, aut gentem super gentem exurgere portendit. Valerius Rufus in Libro memorabilium, capitulo quarto de prodigiis, hoc[d] refert: 'Gaio Volunnio, Seruilio Sulpicio consulibus in urbe Roma [inter] initia[e] motusque bellorum ciuilium hoc prodigium accidit. Carnis in modum nimbi dissipatae partes ceciderunt; quarum maiorem numerum prepetes diripuerunt aues, reliquum humi per aliquot dies neque odore tetro neque deformi aspectu mutatum iacuit. In Sicilia scuta duo sanguinem sudasse, etiam metentibus cruentas spicas in corbem cecidisse, oppido Cerites aquas sanguine mixtas fluxisse.'[1] Cronica Eusebii de prodigiis hoc refert: 'Valentiniano imperante, post solis occasum ab aquilone caelum[f] quasi ignis aut sanguis effectum est. Gentis Hunorum pace rupta inruptio in Galliis[g] subsecuta est.' Item 'anno Leonis imperatoris vii, medio Tolosae ciuitatis sanguis erupit de terra, et tota die fluxit, significans dominationem Gothorum sublatam.'[2]

Item Historia Longobardorum, libro iii, capitulo vi: 'Tempore Teodeberti regis Francorum signum sanguineum in caelum[h] apparuit et quasi hastae sanguineae. Eo tempore ipse Theodebertus cum Lothario auunculo suo bellum gerens eius exercitum uehementer afflixit.'[3] Item in eadem historia: 'Temporibus Iustiniani in prouintia precipue Liguriae maxima pestilentia exorta est. Subito enim apparebant quedam signacula per domos, hostia, uasa uel uestimenta; quae siquis uoluisset abluere, magis magisque apparebant. Post annum uero expletum, ceperunt nasci in inguinibus hominum uel in aliis delicatioribus[i] locis glandulae in modum nucis seu dactili, quas mox subsequebatur febrium intolerabilis estus, ita ut in triduo homo extingueretur. Sin uero aliquis triduum transegisset, habebat spem uiuendi. Erat autem ubique pauor, ubique luctus, ubique lacrimae. Nam, ut uulgi rumor[k] habebat, fugientes[l] cladem uitare,[m] relinquebantur domus desertae habitatoribus, solis catulis domus[n] seruantibus. Peculia sola remanebant in pascuis nullo astante pastore. Cerneres[o] pridem uillas seu castra repleta agminibus hominum, postera die uniuersis fugientibus cuncta esse in summo silentio. Fugiebant filii, cadauera insepulta parentum relinquentes. Parentes obliti pietatis uiscera natos relinquebant estuantes. Siquem forte antiqua pietas perstringebat[p] ut uellet sepelire proximum, restabat ipse insepultus; et dum obsequebatur, perimebatur; dum funeri obsequium prebebat, ipsius funus sine obsequio manebat. Videres seculum in antiquum redactum silentium. Nulla uox in rure, nullus sibilus, nullae insidiae bestiarum in pecudibus, nulla dampna in domesticis uolucribus. Sata transgressa metendi tempus intacta expectabant messorem. Vinea amissis foliis, radiantibus uuis, inlesa manebat hieme propinquante. Nocturnis seu diurnis horis personabat turba[q] bellantium, audiebatur a pluribus quasi murmur exercitus. Nulla erant uestigia commeantium;[r] nullus cernebatur percussor;[s] et tamen uisum oculorum superabant cadauera mortuorum. Pastoralia loca uersa fuerant in sepulturam hominum, et habitacula humana facta fuerant confugia bestiarum.'[4] Haec de historiis pauca prenotauimus. Quod uero cecidit supra petram et ablui non poterat uidetur significare aecclesiam sanctam quae supra petram (id est Christum) fundata tribulationem passura sit. Quod uero super carnem hominis et uestimentum eius cecidit et[t] ablui poterat, non incongrue accipitur per carnem populus, per uestimentum substantia, quae ad adiutorium huius uitae nobis[u] conceditur. Ligno etiam datur intelligi uitale lignum sanctae crucis et baptismum quo sumus regenerati ad uitam. Lignum enim ad humorem aquae uirescit; et quando Iudaicus populus in heremo sitiuit, et pre amaritudine aquas bibere non potuit, iubente Domino misit Moyses lignum in aquam,[x] et conuersa est amaritudo in dulcedinem, et refocilatus est populus.[5] Archa etiam Noae de lignis fabricata quid significet, non ignoratis.[6] In quibus omnibus per lignum non nisi misericordiam suam Dominus operatus est. Quia igitur de ligno sanguis lauabatur, creditur quia per penitentiam et elemosinam et caeteros fructus misericordiae qui intra sinum matris ecclesiae exercentur seueritas et indignatio iusti iudicis Dei, quae peccatoribus merito debetur, ad misericordiam possit reflecti. Misericors est enim Dominus adeo, sicut psalmista loquitur, ut non solum homines sed etiam iumenta saluet.[7] Omnipotens Deus dilatet imperium uestrum, et dextera sua uos semper protegat, et ad pacem sanctae ecclesiae uitam uobis longeuam tribuat, et sua uos benedictione in omnibus exornet.

LDRC   [a] *title om.* LDR   [b] interrogare DR   [c] super DR
[d] hoc *om.* DR   [e] initii DR   initio C   [f] de caelo L   [g] Gallias C
[h] caelo DR   [i] *thus Historia Langobardorum*   delitationibus L
debilitatioribus DR   delectatioribus C   [k] rumorum L   [l] fugientis
DR   [m] *thus Historia Langobardorum*   uitae LDRC   [n] domum C
[o] Cernentes L   [p] prestringebat L   [q] tuba C   [r] commeantum
LD   [s] percursor L   [t] et *supra* L   *om.* DR   [u] nobis *om.* DR
[x] aqua LD

[1] Valerius Maximus, i. 6. 5 (ed. Halm (1865), pp. 26 f.).
[2] Hydatius' continuation of Jerome's translation of Eusebius (*MGH AA* xi. 26 (nos. 149 f.), 34 f. (no. 244)).
[3] Paul the Deacon, *Historia Langobardorum*, iv. 15 (*MGH, Scriptores rerum Langobardicarum*, p. 121).
[4] Ibid. ii. 4 (p. 74).   [5] Cf. Exod. 15: 22 ff.
[6] Probably *sancta ecclesia*. Cf. Gregory I, *Regula pastoralis*, ii. 11 (*PL* lxxvii. 49); Ivo of Chartres, ep. 234 (*PL* clxii. 236 f.).
[7] Ps. 35: 7.

4

A scholasticus of Chartres to Archdeacon R.: asking him to send the gift that he promised[1]

Caro suo R. merito probitatis et industriae facto archidiacono haec[a] aecclesiae Carnotensis humilis scolasticus rem bene agere et orationum suffragia.

Quamdiu apud nos studuisti, siquid tui commodi causa laborauerim, siquid michi pollicitus sis, tute nosti. Officium quidem meum exiguum fuisse censeo; remuneratio uero tua cuius momenti sit, dum uenire cunctatur ignoro. Plurimum tamen saluere te in te nec diffidere ad obsequium tuum me paratum esse iubeo. Vale memor meritatis et gratiae.

V   [a] *sic*   *Perhaps misread from H.* = *Hildegarius?*

[1] Cf. nos. 67 f.

APPENDIX C

Charters issued, confirmed, or witnessed by Fulbert

The present list does not include charters known to be spurious.

1. 17 May 1008, Chelles, witness to a royal charter granted to Saint-Denis (Newman, no. 31). Cf. J.-F. Lemarignier, 'Autour d'un diplôme de Robert le Pieux pour Saint-Denis (1008)', *Comptes rendus de l'Académie des Inscriptions et Belles-Lettres*, 1971, pp. 329 ff.
2. 1006–13, Chartres?, granting an exchange of property ultimately to revert to Saint-Père (*Cart. S.-Père*, i. 99 f.).
3. 1006–28, Chartres?, grant to Marmoutier (*Cartulaire de Marmoutier pour le Vendômois*, ed. C. A. de Trémault (Paris, 1893), no. 1).
4. 1016?, petition to Rome asking for a reduction in the number of canons serving the church of Saint-Maurice (Zimmermann, no. 1163).
5. 1017?, witness to the foundation charter of Fruttuaria (Newman, no. 56). Fulbert's name was perhaps added on the same occasion as no. 6. See H. Kaminsky, 'Zur Gründung von Fruttuaria durch den Abt Wilhelm von Dijon', *Zeitschrift für Kirchengeschichte*, lxxvii (1966), 238 ff., especially 252 ff.
6. 9 June 1017, Compiègne, witness to a royal charter granted on the occasion of King Hugh's coronation (Newman, no. 46 = Fauroux, no. 22).
7. 12 May 1018, Paris/Chartres?, witness to a grant to Saint-Maur-des-Fossés (cited in Depoin, p. 235).
8. 1021–5, Orleans, witness to a charter of Bishop Odolricus of Orleans (Newman, no. 62).
9. 1023–4?, Poitiers?, witness to a grant to Saint-Hilaire (Rédet, xiv, no. 76).
10. 1025?, Chartres?, confirmation of a grant to Saint-Père (*Cart. S.-Père*, ii. 400 f.), also witnessed by 'Ebrardus gramaticus' (cf. no. 106).
11. 1025–8, Châtenai?, party to a judgement rendered and confirmed by Bishop Odolricus of Orleans (*Cart. S.-Père*, i. 105 f.). Cf. A. J. Macdonald, *Berengar and the Reform of Sacramental Doctrine* (London, 1930), p. 24 n.
12. 1028, Paris, witness to a royal charter granted to Coulombs (Newman, no. 72).

INDEX OF MANUSCRIPTS

This index is to descriptions and analyses of manuscripts and does not include references to the individual letters and poems where they are used to establish the text.[1] References are to pages.

---

[1] After this book was already in proof, I learned that Chartres MS. 111 contained not only no. 153 (see Strecker's edition cited there), but also nos. 142 and 149. The manuscript itself was destroyed in 1944, but there is a single frame of microfilm of the page (f. 92ʳ) containing the last two in the L. C. MacKinney Collection in the Wilson Library of the University of North Carolina at Chapel Hill, and I hope to publish it. No. 144 is also found in Vatican, latin 466, f. 17ᵛ. The excerpt on the name Yahweh in V, f. 160ᵛ, is from Pseudo-Alcuin, *De divinis officiis*, c. xxxix (*PL* ci. 1243–4), and that in British Museum, Additional MS. 19835, f. 25ᵛ, is the standard passage on the use of Greek letters in *epistolae formatae* (see M. Thiel, *Grundlagen und Gestalt der Hebräischkenntnisse des frühen Mittelalters* (Spoleto, 1973), 80 f.; C. Fabricius, 'Die Litterae Formatae im Frühmittelalter', *Archiv für Urkundenforschung*, ix (1926), 39 ff., 168 ff.).

As regards the problem of *Fulbertus exiguus*, now see my article 'Berengar of Tours, Fulbert of Chartres, and "Fulbertus Exiguus" ', *RB* lxxxv (1975), 333 ff.

INDEX OF QUOTATIONS AND ALLUSIONS

See the General Index for works mentioned only by author or title in the letters and for sources used to reconstruct the historical background or cited merely by way of illustration.

A. BIBLICAL

(Vulgate)

B. CLASSICAL, PATRISTIC, AND MEDIEVAL

GENERAL INDEX

Names are indexed under the form used in the translation with the following abbreviations: abb. = abbess, abbey, abbot; abp. = archbishop; archd. = archdeacon; bp. = bishop; c. = count, countess; can. = canon; cath. = cathedral; clk. = clerk; d. = duke; k. = king; m. = monk; pr. = provost; sch. = scholasticus; v. = vicomte. References are to pages.